AND SAVE JUDY GARLAND

A gay Christian's journey

Randy Eddy-McCain

Copyright © 2014 Randy Eddy-McCain
All rights reserved.

PRESCIENT BOOKS

books@neal.tv

Handwritten inscription:

To Patrick, Gretta & Master Benjamin, I am excited about your future! Patrick, you have the heart of Jesus. I am very proud of you.

Dreams do come true!

Love, Randy Eddy-McCain

Glad we are now friends!

About the Author

"The people who know God well—mystics, hermits, prayerful people, those who risk everything to find God—always meet a lover, not a dictator."

Richard Rohr

Randy Eddy-McCain serves as founding pastor of Open Door Community Church in Sherwood, Arkansas. He lives with his husband Gary and their son Bobby in North Little Rock, Arkansas. Randy has been in ministry most of his life. He has served as youth and music minister, associate pastor, and as senior pastor. He has also traveled extensively performing concerts and original one-man biblical plays. Randy is also co-host of The Nexus, a radio show about the intersection of faith and doubt.

Visit us online for extra content:

Email Randy at savejudy@gmail.com.

Website: SaveJudy.com

Facebook: Facebook.com/AndGodSaveJudyGarland

Twitter: Twitter.com/savejudy

The Nexus: machine.fm/nexus

AUTHOR'S NOTE

This memoir is a true story based on my best recollections of various events in my life. Some names and identifying characteristics of people mentioned in the book have been changed in order to protect their privacy. For the sake of the narrative, I compressed some events and time periods, and I recreated dialogue to match my best recollection of those conversations.

This book is dedicated to my beloved husband Gary, who makes the phrase, "There's no place like home" a living reality to me.

AND GOD SAVE JUDY GARLAND: *A gay Christian's journey.*

CREDITS

Cover Design and Internal Layout: @NealCampbell
Content Editors: Peggy Campolo, Sheryl Myers, and Harold Ivan Smith
Copy Editor: Jessica Northrop Fritsche

FIRST EDITION

Library of Congress Cataloging-in-Publication Data

Eddy-McCain, Randy.

    And God Save Judy Garland : a gay Christian's journey / Randy Eddy-McCain.—1st. ed.

        p. cm.
   ISBN 978-0-9904731-0-7 (pbk.)
   ISBN 978-0-9904731-1-4 (Kindle)
   ISBN 978-0-9904731-2-1 (Audio)
    1. Eddy-McCain, Randy. 2. LGBTQ. 3. Gay. 4. Christian. 5. Campolo, Peggy.
6. McLaren, Brian. 7. Campolo, Tony. 8. Clergy—United States—Biography

SaveJudy.com

Contents

Foreword by Brian McLaren

There's a kind of unique club in the world called "friends of Tony and Peggy Campolo." I'm a grateful member of that group. It began when Tony was the first "big name author" to read my first manuscript and send me some encouraging words. While some established authors might see "up and comers" as a threat, Tony saw me as an ally and colleague and his encouragement and support have meant the world to me.

One of the nicest things Tony ever did for me was introduce me to his charming and brilliant wife. Once, when I was still a pastor with some standing in the Evangelical world, Peggy called me. There was an LGBT-friendly church pastored by a gay man in Little Rock, Arkansas, she explained. They wanted to invite me to speak at a conference they were hosting, but didn't want to put me in an awkward situation by doing so.

They knew that I was clearly sympathetic to the LGBT cause and critical of the typical conservative Evangelical attitude to LGBT people. But they also knew that if I accepted their invitation, I would be labeled as a "friend of sinners" and association with a "gay church" could cost me whatever fragile credibility I had left in the Evangelical community. Peggy wanted to test the waters with me so she could let them know whether or not to make the invitation.

I prayed about it and said yes, which led to my meeting Randy Eddy-McCain and the beautiful church he served.

What neither Randy, Peggy, nor I knew was that about four months later, one of my sons would be coming out. When he did, I kept thinking, "Thank God my son didn't have to worry that his coming out would in any way hurt my work and reputation. Thank God Randy and Peggy invited me and I had the chance to 'come out' as a publicly gay-affirming ally ... before the issue of sexual orientation became a personal reality in my own family."

With that backstory in mind, you can see why Randy and Open Door Community Church would mean so much to me. And you can see why I'm so thrilled that he is telling his story in this book. But it's not just that connection that makes me want to be an advocate for this book. It's also that Randy tells a story that needs to be told, and he tells it honestly, compassionately, courageously, and beautifully.

Sadly, the people who most need to read a book like this too seldom do. And when they do, they often do so (pardon the nerdy Star Trek references) on red alert with their deflector shields up and their photon torpedoes fully armed. If you're one of those readers who feels nervous even listening to the words of an outspoken "gay Christian," first, let me congratulate you for your courage in getting this far. And second, let me remind you that Jesus' message similarly made people nervous. He dared question old certitudes about who was clean and unclean, who was acceptable and unacceptable, who was in and out. That's why he so often had to say, "Whoever has ears to hear, let them hear!"

You may be a Christian who is questioning your own sexual orientation and you're opening this book feeling a different kind of uncertainty mixed with hope. You're wondering how "coming out" will affect your family relationships, your church relationships, and most important, your relationship with God. All I can say is that I can think of no better pastoral care for you at this moment than what you'll receive in these pages from Randy.

You may already be part of the choir, people who are sympathetic to Randy and the good work he is doing. "Preaching to the choir," I've learned, isn't a bad thing. If the choir learns to sing better, more and more people will hear the music.

If that happens, "somewhere over the rainbow" may, like the Kingdom of God, appear a little more among us, here and now, "on earth as it is in heaven."

**Brian McLaren with Randy Eddy-McCain at
Open Door Community Church**

Part One

It's good to be a seeker, but sooner or later you have to be a finder. And then it is well to give what you have found, a gift into the world for whoever will accept it.

Jonathan Livingston Seagull

Randy and Grandpa McCain after a walk

Chapter 1
Jesus and Judy Garland

Now I lay me down to sleep
I pray the Lord my soul to keep
If I should die before I wake
I pray the Lord my soul to take
If I should live another day
I pray the Lord to guide my way
God save Grandpa Rhodes
God heal Grandpa McCain
And God save Judy Garland, Amen!

As an eight-year-old kneeling by my bed in prayer, hands folded in reverence, other names came and went, but Grandpa Rhodes, Grandpa McCain, and Judy Garland were permanent staples of my nightly bedtime ritual.

Grandpa Rhodes had never prayed the sinner's prayer, much to the pain and regret of my grandma and mother. Mom would talk about how sad it was that Grandpa wouldn't go to heaven when he died because he didn't know Jesus as his personal savior. Then she would give a terrifying account of hell, the place of punishment that awaited all those who didn't take advantage of God's offer of salvation. I would cringe at the thought of my beloved grandpa agonizing in the eternal flames, begging God to let one of us dip a finger in water and hold it to his parched lips. Every night I prayed that Grandpa Rhodes would see his need of salvation before it was too late.

Then there was Grandpa McCain, who had Parkinson's disease and was slowly losing his grasp on reality. He was a slight man who, for most of his life, had earned his living in a paper mill. He no longer could work and sometimes forgot who my grandma was. I walked with him in the neighborhood, and sometimes he would get us lost in the sleepy little town of Warren, Arkansas. But somehow, we always made it back home. Although Grandpa McCain was not able to remember me, I made sure I never forgot him. I prayed every night that God would remove the confusion from my grandpa's mind so that we could be friends, and he would remember!

Then there was Judy. Ah, Judy! Growing up in an Assemblies of God home, my older sisters, Pam and Linda, and I were not allowed to go to the movies. But thanks to Dad we had a television, and one of my all-time favorite movies was *The Wizard of Oz.* I remember how excited I would get, sitting in front of our black-and-white set as the opening music burst into the sweet strains of "Somewhere Over the Rainbow." I felt goose bumps as I excitedly waited for Judy to make her appearance. Oh, how I loved Judy! I told Mom that one day I was going to marry her.

"Oh honey," she chuckled, "Judy Garland isn't a little girl anymore. That movie was made a long time ago. Judy Garland is an older woman now. But you do need to pray for her, because she's a very troubled woman and needs God in her life."

So that night, and every night that followed, I prayed for Judy to find Jesus.

I learned later in life that Judy Garland is a gay icon. Gay men relate instinctively to certain celebrities who have overcome major handicaps in life on their way to stardom. One example is the fascination gay men have with little Dorothy from Kansas in *The Wizard of Oz.* From the movie came a phrase gay men coined to identify each other in a time when homosexuality was still *"the love that dared not speak its name."* When two gay men saw another man who they suspected was also a homosexual, they might say, "I think that guy over there is a 'friend of Dorothy's'!" Looking back on my childhood, I was always a 'friend of Dorothy's'. I listened to Judy's records and I saved every picture of her I could find. I was Judy's biggest fan.

It was a miracle that I even got to watch *The Wizard of Oz.* The movie house was sinful! I couldn't really figure out why. Sometimes I said, "Mom, my friends get to go to the movies."

"Yes," she answered, "but their families don't know any better. They go to the Baptist church. They believe that once you are saved, you can't lose your salvation. There are going to be a lot of surprised Baptists on judgment day. They'll be sorry *then* that they watched those worldly movies in the sinful movie houses."

"But Momma, *we* watch movies at home on TV."

"Yes, we do son, because your daddy just put his foot down and demanded that we get a television! Sometimes I feel so ashamed when people from the church walk in our home and they see that ungodly idol sitting there. But I'm told in the word of God that I am to be submissive to your father, so the sin's on his head, not mine."

Mamma talked a good game, but I think she was secretly thankful that she married a less religious guy. She loved *Peyton Place, The Twilight Zone, I Love Lucy,* and *The Big Valley,* not to mention her favorite soaps every afternoon. Linda and Pam often battled with me over who got to watch their favorite show. Back then, there wasn't that much to choose from.

Although the church preached against owning a television, church folk had a suspicious habit of stopping by just about the time *their* favorite show would air. Our Pastor, Brother Rorex, was partial to *Gunsmoke*. (In the Assemblies of God church we called every adult *brother* and *sister*, because we believed that we were all brothers and sisters in the family of God.)

Brother Rorex was fascinated by this devilish contraption. He'd sit there and watch as Matt Dillon chased the robbers. When Matt was about to be jumped from behind, Brother Rorex would yell, "Watch out, Doc!" *Doc* was the name Brother Rorex used to refer to all men.

We got a real kick out of watching Brother Rorex watching *our* TV. Many times he was more entertaining than the show. It was curious to me how church folk would willingly partake of the pleasure of television at our home, and yet preach so passionately against it at church. One church close by had a traveling evangelist who preached against owning a television. On the next to last night of the two-week revival, he challenged the people to bring their TVs to the last service. He said he would load them up in the back of his pickup and, on his way out of town, dump them in the Arkansas River. The faithful filled his pickup to overflowing. Word got around that he made his way later to a pawn shop and left town a richer man than when he arrived.

One evening, a gospel trio from our church was featured on a local television show. Brother and Sister Rorex's daughter, Janice, was one of the singers. My sister Linda played the piano for them. This was quite an event. Daddy invited the Rorexes over to watch their daughter's television debut. To his surprise, they accepted!

Sister Rorex was very uncomfortable. She remained true to her convictions, turning her chair so that she was facing away from the television set; she could hear the singing, but didn't have to lay eyes on that satanic contraption. I was amazed at her saintliness and her power to resist temptation.

My world totally revolved around the church. We weren't allowed to take part in athletics at school. We couldn't read comic books. We couldn't play cards because that was associated with gambling, although we did own a Monopoly game my family enjoyed, and it contained a pair of dice.

Thank God for my daddy, Randall Allen McCain, Sr. Although he'd been raised in an Assemblies of God home, his mom wasn't as strict with him as Mother was with us. He got to go to dances and movies. He joined the army in 1941 and had some really wild times which he liked to reminisce about. Dad confided in me once that he married Mom because he knew she would settle him down and he'd be able to stop partying and graduate from college. Well he picked the right woman to settle him down!

The first thing Mom did was insist that he stop his drinking. Once us kids came along, Mom got serious about her faith. Dad went along with my mom's desire for our family to attend church on Sunday morning, Sunday night, Wednesday night, and sometimes every night during those long three- or four-week revivals. But his approach to faith was not as emotional as Mom's. That was a real heartbreak to her. Daddy even joined a bowling league, which bowled on the night our church had mid-week service! My mom would tell us to pray for Daddy so that he would be cleansed of his desires to live so much in sin.

One night when I was six, Daddy decided that Mom was imparting too much religion into me and that he needed to include me a little more in his world. He told my mom one Wednesday night that he was taking me with him to the bowling alley. You would've thought someone had died. My mother knew she had to be submissive, but she let Daddy know she was *not happy*.

Momma helped me get dressed and whispered in my ear, "Momma will be praying at church for you tonight, Honey. Now, I can't stop your daddy from taking you down there to that Devil's Den! But I can pray that God will send his angels to watch over you and protect you from the evil that's in that place."

I was scared to death! I cried and cried, but Daddy insisted that I was going with him. He pulled me from Momma's arms and carried me to the car. Once we were at the bowling alley, Daddy came around and opened my door but I wouldn't get out. He said, "Come on son! We're going to have a real good time. I'll teach you how to bowl."

"No!" I protested. "I am not going in there. Momma says that the devil lives in there."

"Your momma doesn't know because she's never been in a bowling alley. Now come on son. Get out of the car."

"No! I'm not going! I want to go to church with Momma!"

"All right, if you won't get out, fine! Just stay here in the car!"

He shut the door and walked toward the front door of the bowling alley.

I couldn't believe that Daddy was going to leave me alone in the car, but he did. I remember sobbing and praying, "Jesus, please let my daddy come back and take me home. Don't let the ol' Devil get him in there!" After what seemed like an eternity to me, I saw my dad walking toward the car.

"Son, come on now. The gang from the office is here and they want to see you. Let's go in, and I'll buy you a hamburger!"

Oh dear, the greatest temptation of all, a hamburger! Boy, when Satan tempts you, he *don't* play around. You have to understand that was a really big step for my dad, who had this conviction that it was a sin to eat out when you had groceries in the house. Every Sunday night after church, we'd go to the Polar Freeze Drive-In. My sisters and I would smell those hamburgers cooking and our mouths would water!

Sunday night services in the Pentecostal church we attended could last a long time. The service culminated in a time of prayer around the altar that could last for hours. The dear old saints referred to this as "praying through." This passionate praying gave you the munchies something awful! But we kids knew that when we made our Sunday night trek to the Polar Freeze, Daddy would only allow us to have a ten-cent drink and a *salty*, which consisted of Fritos, potato chips, or those little packages of peanut butter and crackers.

Now, back then, you could buy five hamburgers for a dollar, but my dad would have none of that nonsense. We had food at home! Why, that'd just be a waste of hard-earned dollars. So for Daddy to tempt me now with a hamburger was pretty low! And not just a hamburger, not just one of those puny little Polar Freeze hamburgers. He was offering a *Bowling Alley Hamburger*! I had heard tell that those things were as big as a hub cap!

I thought about it for a moment and I saw my momma's sad face. I thought about how disappointed she would be in me, not to mention how disappointed God would be. And there was the threat of being met by the devil as I entered the door. But a *Bowling Alley Hamburger*!

The decision was made almost from the moment the bait was offered. I thought, "I'll wrestle even the devil himself for a bowling alley hamburger!" and jumped out of the car into my dad's arms. As he carried me into the big building, I heard the sound of pins falling and balls rolling. I could smell the hamburgers cooking. I had proven to be easy prey! Dad introduced me to his buddies, and they really spoiled me by letting me roll the ball down the alley and cheering for me. I was the center of attention.

What a night! I was giddy as we said good night to Daddy's friends. As we pulled out of the parking lot, the "guilties" hit me something awful. I followed Daddy into the house, and Momma was not happy. She came over and hugged me and took me right to my bedroom, fussing at Daddy for keeping me out so late. Of course, if it had been a revival and we had been to one of those "Holy Ghost run away" services that lasted for three to four hours, I don't think she would have complained.

Once inside the bedroom she hugged me and said, "Momma was praying for you the whole time tonight." With hamburger breath, I belched out a lie about how awful it'd been and how I tried to resist, but Daddy made me go into that awful, sinful place! We said our nightly prayers and my mom said an extra special prayer over me that none of the devil's evil spirits could follow me into our home. I lay awake trembling and begging God to forgive me for my transgression!

Worship services at a Pentecostal church were never boring. The singing was lively with hand-clapping, foot-stomping hymns and choruses such as "Victory in

Jesus," "Power in the Blood," and "Give Me That Old Time Religion." There was an outbreak of shouting and aerobic-style worship at almost every service, consisting of dancing and jumping, running all around the church sanctuary, and yelling loudly, mostly in tongues. (Speaking in tongues is a phenomenon Pentecostals believe to be an outward sign that the person has been totally taken over and filled inwardly by the Holy Spirit.)

Charlie Harris was a handsome young man, just entering puberty, who would've been a great athlete in a perfect world. But since school sports were off-limits for us holy rollers, his athletic skills manifested themselves in his shouting style. He would get happy and start jumping up and down. He would jump so high that, had he been playing basketball, he could easily have dunked the basket. Then he would take off running up and down the aisles of the church as fast as he could. This was a miracle because he would do it with his eyes closed and never bump into a single pew. Sometimes, when he was really "in the Spirit," he would hurdle the pews or run along the tops of the pews like a tight rope walker.

Then there was Sister Mattie Faye. When this blessed sister felt the Spirit, she gave out three short whoops. Those familiar with her routine knew that those three whoops, each a little louder than the one before, was the Holy Spirit's way of warning anyone sitting next to this joyful saint to get out of the way. On that third whoop she would explode, hands raised to face level, flailing back and forth while she yelled out a war cry and burst out speaking in tongues. The young people sitting in the back of the church loved it when a visitor had the misfortune of sitting next to Sister Mattie Faye. Unless someone had tipped them off, they didn't know to move on the third whoop and got a stinging slap to the side of their face.

The very sweet and stately old preacher, Brother Thompson, was what some called a "bootleg preacher." This type of preacher would minister wherever he got an invitation, but also had a secular job. When Brother Thompson wasn't preaching somewhere else, he attended *our* church. Brother Rorex loved to call on him to dismiss the service in prayer. Brother Thompson prayed the dismissal prayer so often that we young folks had his prayer memorized and would mouth the words along with him, "Lord, bind us together with a love that the enemy cannot tear down or break through." Actually, it was a beautiful petition I have often incorporated into my own prayers.

Once in a while, Brother Rorex would ask Brother Thompson to preach. On one such occasion, Brother T was really getting with it, moving up and down the aisle, swinging his hands and pointing his bony finger at us, as he brought home one of his more powerful statements. On this night he must not have used enough Poli-Grip, because, right in midstream, his false teeth flew out of his mouth, landing on the carpet in front of him. The crowd chuckled nervously. Everyone was frozen, wondering how Brother T would get out of this. Well, not to worry. He was a true believer that not only must the show go on, so must the sermon! He bent over, picked up his teeth, wiped them off with his tie, and stuck them back in his mouth.

We young folks could not help laughing out loud. Brother T pointed that scary, bony finger at us and said, "Don't you laugh. I've seen falser things than *that* around the church!" An enthusiastic round of, "Amen, Brother! Preach it!" broke out around the sanctuary, and Brother T jumped right back to his sermon, not missing a beat!

There were times when it was really hard being a Pentecostal kid. When I was in the third grade, I had to take a note to school that said, "Please excuse Randy from square-dancing because it is against his religion." I remember sitting there and watching the kids do-si-do with their partners, wondering what it would be like to dance in public and not feel guilty. The other kids seemed to be having so much fun. It was then that the Pentecostal kids would slip into our martyr roles and think to ourselves, "I am standing up for Jesus by not partaking in such worldly pleasures. I am not ashamed of my Lord. I will *not* compromise with the sinful world." The other kids would mock us, saying things like, "Hey, if you are penny costal, does that mean it costs a penny to go to your church?" or, "There go the Holy Rollers. They roll down the aisles at their church and swing from the chandeliers."

All of us at Midway Assembly of God Church loved it when the evangelists would come and preach on the "Second Coming of Jesus." It was sort of like watching *The Twilight Zone*. The evangelists displayed a chronological map of events surrounding the return of Jesus to the earth across the front wall of the church, behind the pulpit. The graphic pictures were drawn in cartoon style.

First there was the angel Gabriel sounding the trumpet; then, the depiction of the dead who had received Jesus as their Savior, bursting out of their graves to meet Jesus in the air. Next was the tribulation period, when all the wicked of the world who did not believe in Jesus would suffer their punishment for not obeying God's commandments. The devil's number, 666, would be tattooed on their foreheads or hands. Anyone who refused the devil's mark would not be allowed to buy food. If they continued to refuse, they were beheaded. These pictures of heads being separated from bodies gave me more than one nightmare. The chart showed different dragons that would be released on the sinful people left behind. War, famine, and plagues followed.

The evangelist, after explaining all the pictures on the poster in graphic detail, would say, "Just think, boys and girls. If you have sin in your life, when the trumpet blows you will be left behind! Your mom and dad, if believers in Christ, will be taken, and you will be left behind to face the terrible wrath of an angry God! Then you will be thrown into a devil's hell and burn for all eternity!"

Then the evangelist gave a tearful call for us to come to the altar and ask Jesus to wash away our sins. I usually led the race for the altar. We didn't know when that trumpet would sound. It was going to happen quickly, in the twinkling of an eye. Jesus might come back before I made it to the front of the church!

I fell at the altar and cried, "Please Jesus, forgive me of my sins. I want you to wash me white as snow! I want to go with you when you return." The little old ladies of the church would surround me, patting me on the back, laying hands on my forehead, and praying over me, saying, "Little Randy, let God have His way in your life. Don't hold anything back. Make sure you have repented of every sin. Make love to Jesus. Tell Him how much you love Him."

So I did. I'd cry out, "O Jesus, I love you!" at the top of my lungs, tears streaming down my cheeks, hands raised as high as I could reach, toward heaven. I stayed at the altar for hours some nights, praying, crying, singing, and speaking in tongues. One night I stood up from a kneeling position at the altar and kicked off my shoes. Later, when asked why, I told them that the Lord had told me to because I was on Holy Ground. I went dancing across the front of the church. This was not a strange occurrence. There were many doing the same thing while the musicians played and sang songs with a fast, happy beat. I left the altar feeling safe, but once we got home, the doubts would start.

"What if I haven't thought of every sin and Jesus comes back tonight while I am sleeping? What if He has *already* come and I have been left behind to face the anti-Christ and the mark of the beast?" I broke out in a cold sweat as I lay quiet and still, listening to see if I could hear my daddy snoring. If I did, I knew I was safe and that the trumpet had not yet been blown. Thank God Daddy was a loud snorer.

One afternoon after I walked home from school, I yelled, "Mom, I'm home." Mom didn't answer me. I walked through the whole house, but Mom was nowhere to be found. I entered the kitchen and a pot of beans was boiling away on the stove. I remembered the evangelist's story about the mother cooking at the stove when the trumpet sounds and suddenly she disappears, the food left to burn on the stove. Goose bumps of fear started rising up my spine. I searched more earnestly, running to the screened-in back porch to survey the back yard. Mom was nowhere to be found. I just knew I'd been left behind!

I ran to the phone and started dialing numbers of folks in the church, but no one was home. Finally I dialed the pastor's home number. Sister Rorex answered, and I quickly hung up the phone. If Sister Rorex was still around, I was safe. If anyone went to Heaven in the rapture, it would be her!

It turned out that Mom had gone next door to borrow some sugar from our neighbor. Just as I hung up the phone, she walked in. I ran and threw my arms around her and held on for a long time. Mom and I had a prayer meeting right then and there so I could be sure all my sins were confessed.

Unlike the Baptists, who believed that you needed to be saved just once, we Pentecostals were taught that salvation could be lost at the drop of a hat. I was always unsure of my status as a Christian. You could be saved and love Jesus, but if you hit your finger with a hammer, said a dirty word, and died before you asked the Lord to forgive you, you would go to hell. I always wondered what was so amazing about God's grace. I even had prayer drills as a boy to practice my sinner's prayer. "Jesus-forgivemeofmysins,amen!" I timed myself to see how fast I could spit out the words so that if I was in a car and saw that we were about to have a head-on collision, I could get my prayer in under the wire.

I look back on my time in the Pentecostal church with mixed emotions. Some of you may be thinking that my childhood was very bizarre and surreal. Others relate to the stories of my Pentecostal upbringing. I must admit that the religious education I received was strange to say the least. My sister Pam says she remembers being jealous of kids who were allowed to be "normal," who went to movies and dances and dressed in the latest fashions. There are, however, aspects of my childhood for which I am thankful. One of the things the Assemblies of God did well was teach children to be sensitive to the moving of God's Spirit. They presented spiritual pursuit as something exciting and filled with awe and wonder.

I've seen many people try to take the miraculous away from the story of Christ. I call that intention "taking the magic out of Christianity." I thank God for my childish pursuit of the miracle who is Jesus. Even though there was a lot of fear in the theology of my adolescent years, there were also great moments of joy and tangible encounters with the Savior. The Jesus I met as a child has brought me through the most painful years of my life.

My desire has always been to serve God, but the God people told me about in my youth was a jealous God, susceptible to fits of anger during which his mighty power was unleashed on those who angered Him. During childhood, our minds are like wet cement. Concepts that we learn at an early age get stuck in our imaginations and harden to the point that we remain influenced by them, even into adulthood. I was taught a theology that was heavy on guilt. The God I came to know was a lot like Santa Claus: "He's making a list, checking it twice. Gonna find out who's naughty and nice...He sees you when you're sleeping; He knows when you're awake. He knows if you've been bad or good so be good for goodness sake!"

My mom and Sunday school teachers told me, "You better be good, because God is watching, and God will punish bad boys and girls. He loves you when you are good, but He won't love you if you disobey Him." While these dear saints were well intentioned, they were wrong. Not until I was a grown man would I allow the Holy Spirit to take a jackhammer to that hard, error-filled theology and to make room for a new way of experiencing God's love as unconditional and full of grace.

I now believe that God's grace *is* amazing! As a gay man, there was no place for me in the theology I had been taught. I had to seek God for myself. Feeling estranged from God was the true *Twilight Zone* for me, and it brought me to the end of my rope. I could no longer hold on and I fell into what seemed like a frightening black hole. All my life I had believed that I had God figured out. The awareness that I was a gay man forced me out of my spiritual comfort zone and compelled me to face life without any answers. I questioned the existence of God. The pain I felt was so terrible that I still lack words to describe it. But those who have been to that spiritual black hole can relate to my experience.

It's taken half a lifetime for the new, loving, grace-filled image of God to take shape. Once again I know the Jesus I loved as a child. This is the story of a boy who loved Jesus and wanted with all his heart to please God, of a Christian young man who struggled with his sexual orientation without any help from his family, his society, his school, or his church...and survived.

If the story of my journey brings hope to one fearful questioner, my prayers for this book will be answered.

Chapter 2

What is Normal?

As a child, I was uncommonly curious. One way that I gleaned information was by feigning sleep while grown-ups talked. I was first introduced to the subject of homosexuality during one of these "naps" in 1964. My dad and Brother Rorex were in my dad's car, discussing a scandalous situation involving a certain minister in town who had been caught by the police doing something with another man in a public restroom. Dad was in the driver's seat, Brother Rorex was on the passenger side, and I was stretched out on the back seat. The men would never have dreamed of discussing this while I was in earshot, but they were convinced that I was asleep. I sensed that they had started talking in code and my interest was piqued. Being a good little actor, I started to audibly breathe through my mouth and positioned my body so that my right ear was close enough to the front seat to hear their hushed conversation.

"So Brother Rorex, what actually happened?" my dad asked.

"Well, they say he went to Memphis on church business. He stopped at a park and went into the restroom. There was another man inside. When the police walked in, they were having sex." Brother Rorex's words were slow and uncertain. He was clearly uncomfortable.

Dad let out a sigh of disgust. "Well I'll be doggoned!" This was one of Dad's old stand-by phrases when he was at a loss for words.

"Does his wife know?"

"Yes, and she's very upset. I imagine the kids will hear about it sooner or later, because people are talking about it all over town. It is a real scandal."

After a pause my dad said, "So Brother Rorex, does this mean Pastor Holland is a homosexual?"

"I don't know."

"What would make a man want to have sex with another man? It's just not natural. It really makes me sick at my stomach to think about such a thing."

"I know what you mean, Brother McCain. I surely don't understand it."

After a few silent moments, Dad spoke again. "Well, I guess the man is to be pitied. You know, they say there are men like that. But can you imagine what kind of miserable life they live?"

"No Brother McCain, I can't. It must be terrible."

As I lay there listening, I tried to piece all this together. I didn't quite know what sex was. I knew that it was something that people did when they were naked. We lived in a very modest home. If my dad or I came out of the bedroom without a shirt on, my mom would yell out, "Get back in there and put some clothes on. You're half naked!"

Just the thought of doing something with someone else while you were both naked boggled my little eight-year-old mind. But these two men were naked in a public restroom, doing something that usually is done between a man and a woman. What were they doing? I didn't know, but one thing I picked up on was that sex between two men was very evil and very wrong!

When I turned twelve, I entered puberty unexpectedly. I had my first sexual experience by myself in the bathtub, completely by accident. The experience scared me. I had no point of reference for the powerful explosion of energy and excitement that took my breath away. I immediately went to my father.

"Daddy, I think I have cancer." I was in tears. My dad looked up from the newspaper.

"You think you have what?"

"I think I have cancer. I think I'm going to die."

Dad put down the paper. "Now Randy, what makes you think you have cancer?"

To this day I don't know why I associated cancer with my first sexual release, but knowing the religion I was brought up in, anything that felt good had to be bad and sinful. I knew that "the wages of sin is death." Cancer was a death sentence back then, and hardly spoken of. Therefore, my thinking probably went something like:

I did something that felt good. If it felt good, it must be a sin. The wages of sin is death. I must have cancer! That would explain the white stuff in the bath water!

Dad asked me to explain what had happened. I told him, and he grinned real big and said, "Well son, I think you're going to live. But you and I need to have a little talk."

The talk took place soon after. It was obvious that Dad had been anticipating this talk because it was well thought out. He explained to me all about the birds and the bees. He told me that masturbation was not necessarily a bad thing, as long as it didn't become a habit that kept me from doing the things I needed to do in my everyday life. He told me how boys and girls were different, and what the boy had was to go into what the girl had.

I had one concern. "Dad, what if the boy pees inside the girl?"

He quickly assured me that this would not happen. Something came out of the boy, but it wasn't pee.

Dad mentioned that there were men that I needed to watch out for. These men were sick and they were attracted sexually to other men. Then he explained about a run-in he had with such a man in England during World War Two. While on furlough in London, he and a buddy got dates for the night. During the course of the evening, Dad excused himself and stepped into a public men's room. While standing at a urinal, a man came up and started peeing next to him. Dad was drunk at the time, swaying side to side.

The man spoke to Dad. "You sure have a big one."

"Yeah," Dad responded with pride.

"I bet there are a lot of women that would like to get hold of that."

"Yeah there are, and some of them have!" Dad bragged.

"I bet there are a lot of men that would like to get hold of that, too." With that, the man reached over and grabbed my dad's penis. Dad turned and punched the guy in the face. The man fell to the floor. Dad zipped up and kicked the guy for good measure as he exited the restroom. That story reinforced for me that men who like other men are sick and dangerous.

The next time I remember hearing about men loving men was when a rumor made the rounds about a wedding between Jim Nabors and Rock Hudson, two well-known actors. The rumor, though untrue, is believed to have started as a party joke. In California, a certain middle-aged gay couple's annual theme party was a big social event. They sent engraved invitations to friends inviting them to the coronation of Queen Elizabeth or other fake events, always including some famous names. In 1971, they decided to invite their friends to a wedding reception for these two actors. An invitation got into the hands of a reporter and the story went all over the world. We even heard about it in Walnut Ridge, Arkansas.

I was 13 at the time and remember laughing with a friend at the idea of two men getting married. Little did I know that one day I would walk down the aisle of a church and promise another man to be faithful "'til death do us part."

Although I laughed with my friends at this rumor, I had already started sexual exploration with my guy friends. While the young people had been given specific warnings about the dangers of boys and girls getting too physical, nothing had been said about sexual "horsing around" between boys. So the guys would talk about our sexual feelings when we were together for sleepovers or on camping trips. We began to share what we had discovered about masturbation. At first it seemed like a game, but then we began to have guilty feelings about it. Of course there was no one to go to for advice. I started to worry that perhaps I was well on my way to becoming one of those men my daddy warned about. My parents gave me a book when I turned 13 called *Love, and the Facts Of Life* by Evelyn Millis Duvall, written for teenagers entering puberty. In one chapter, titled *What about those sex problems?*, it discussed homosexuality. I thought, "Finally I will be able to get some information without anyone knowing I am interested in the subject!"

Duvall wrote, "Possibly no word in the English language is as misunderstood as is homosexuality. In our society we are so afraid of it and we know so little about it that we are apt to become anxious whenever we hear a whisper of homosexual behavior."

I remembered hearing Brother Rorex and my dad's conversation about the unfortunate minister in Memphis. The author was right. People's very speech patterns seemed to change when discussing homosexuality. It was whispered disgust.

Duvall noted that most people at some point in their lives have experienced some kind of homosexual "tie." I was not sure about the word "tie," but was relieved to know I was not alone in my feelings. There was, according to the author, little evidence to support the claim that people are born with predetermined tendencies toward homosexuality. Rather, we learn to love as we grow up with other people in our lives. She implied that sometimes we are influenced by situations and circumstances in life to have "twisted feelings" for other people, such as homosexual attractions. Although the author was not as homophobic in her approach to the subject as others in my world, she reinforced the belief that this was *not* something I should see as positive or normal. She added that many boys and girls go through a period when they have "crushes" on members of their own sex. This was not something to get upset about, but was part of growing up. Maybe I was normal after all!

"Normal" was a word that did not accurately describe much of my world. My sister Linda was away at college. My sister Pam was in high school and dating a boy who was an agnostic. This was not acceptable to my parents. Not only was this boy agnostic, but he also liked living life on the edge. I am sure this character trait attracted my sister to him. Like me, Pam had been raised in a world where the church dictated how you should live. Dating Ronnie was Pam's way of trying to break free from the restraints that stifled her. Ronnie, who was attractive, lean and dark, with unruly hair and clothes, had a James Dean quality to him. He threw caution to the wind and loved to live his life in a way that shocked "the establishment." Pam fell for him.

Ronnie was a free thinker and gave Pam books to read that spoke of life in terms foreign to those in our church. My mom found a book in Pam's room one night, while my sister was out on a date with Ronnie, entitled *Summerhill School, A New View of Childhood*, by Alexander S. Neill and Albert Lamb. It was about a radical boarding school in England where children were given lots of freedom to accept or reject ideas and concepts about life. These children were given the freedom to explore their sexuality and to go naked in public. By giving children freedom to explore life outside the box, the authors argued, they would grow up to be more intelligent and happier. Obviously this went against everything our mother believed about child rearing. Mom saw the book as subversive and "of the devil." She was not about to have such a book in her home! When Pam came in from her date with Ronnie, Mom and Dad were waiting. I was in the den watching television when I heard the screaming.

"Where have you been? How can you date a boy who doesn't know Jesus? There is no telling what the two of you have been doing this evening! I found this book in your room. It has Ronnie's name in it. Do you think this perverted school is a place you would want *your* children to attend someday?"

Pam screamed at mother to stay out of her personal things. "You have no right!"

"I most certainly _do_ have the right as long as you are under my roof," Mother responded. "Pam, I am heartbroken for you. You have gone back on your commitment to God. If you were to die tonight, where would you spend eternity? Hell is real young lady!"

Pam ran to her room and slammed the door. Dad yelled at her to show more respect. I wrapped up in a blanket and turned up the television volume. I began to pray for Pam. I did not want her to go to hell. I cried and asked Jesus to please speak to her heart. The next day I walked home from school with Pam. She was still angry at Mom and Dad. I asked her what was wrong.

"Wrong?" she yelled. "I'll tell you what's wrong. We live in a crazy family! We are all crazy. I'm crazy, Mom's crazy, Dad's crazy, Linda's crazy, you're crazy, we're all crazy!"

Stunned, I walked the rest of the way in a daze. I went straight to my bedroom and fell on my bed. I kept hearing Pam's words over and over. "We're crazy!" I thought. "Oh no! I am crazy. My family is crazy. What is to happen to us?"

Pam was the first to try and break free of the religious abuse in which we were raised. She received the first of the wounds that are inflicted on any who try to escape. But Pam proved to be a trailblazer for her little brother. She married Ronnie against her own better judgment. I believe my parents' constant rejection of Ronnie drew Pam to him. He seemed to be her ticket to freedom. In the end, it was not Ronnie's agnostic beliefs that were the real problem, but that he was drawn to drugs and had a tendency to drop out of everything that was constructive in his life. Their marriage ended in divorce after the arrival of their beautiful daughter, Leandra. Pam could no longer put up with Ronnie's drunken lifestyle, or the other down-and-out drug addicts who crashed at their home. She could not allow her daughter to be brought up in that kind of environment.

Pam taught school and raised their daughter as a single mom. Ronnie's life ended tragically. One night Pam got word from the state police that he had ended up a drunken vagrant. Along with several other homeless people, Ronnie built a fire in an abandoned house for warmth before falling asleep. They never woke up. The fire destroyed the house and took their lives. I liked Ronnie and mourned his passing. I remember him as a handsome, bright young man with much potential.

More and more I was becoming aware that my life was not normal. I kept hoping that I would grow out of my attraction to men. It was confusing to me. Although I was being raised in a heterosexual home by heterosexual parents, attended a church that taught heterosexual marriage, and lived in a society where all love songs were about heterosexual couples, I found myself identifying more with a girl's feelings about boys than with a boy's feelings about girls.

Though we were not allowed to go to movies, we could buy movie soundtracks. I memorized every song from *The Sound of Music* and *Funny Girl.* I had a record of Judy Garland's movie songs and one of my favorites was "The Boy Next Door."

Of course, when singing it for other people, I always substituted "girl next door" for "boy next door." But when alone, I sang it with the masculine pronoun, the way Judy sang it.

Pam and Randy

Randy with Mom, Dad, and Sister

Randy, Pam, and Linda in 1957

Chapter 3

A Horse Ride into Puberty

Growing up in Walnut Ridge, I had a lot of things going against my being accepted by the "in" crowd around the neighborhood or at school. I did not want to play sports, but instead liked to cook and loved singing show tunes. And I was determined to stay close to God and learn as much about Jesus as I could. That set me apart from the other boys in my neighborhood until my uncle gave me two Shetland ponies. All the guys wanted to ride my ponies. I loved playing cowboys with Paul, who was two years older and a hunk even in the sixth grade. I knew him from church. One day I said, "Paul, why don't we pretend that I am your partner back in the days of the wild, wild west, I get ambushed by a band of robbers, and you come along and find me? You give me a drink from your canteen. When you see that my arm is broken, you take your shirt off and make a sling for my arm. Then you pick me up and put me on your horse and take me into town to the doctor's office."

As you can see, I really had an active imagination.

Paul thought for a moment. "OK, but don't tell anybody about this."

I will never forget the butterflies in my stomach when he took off his shirt and made a makeshift sling for me. When he picked me up in his already muscular arms and carried me to the horse, I was in heaven! Then, riding with him behind me, his arm reaching around to steady me on our ride through the fields behind my house, I experienced feelings that felt so ordinary and right to my fourth-grade mind. I now understand that those feelings I had for Paul were a natural and healthy part of the maturing process of a young gay boy. I understand, too, that if our society was educated and honest about sexual orientations, gay and lesbian kids would not have to go through the kind of hell that I did when I began to understand my own natural attractions.

When a little heterosexual boy starts noticing little girls, his mom and dad say to each other, "Isn't that sweet! Joey has a crush on Gretchen. Pretty soon he will be old enough to date." The parents are proud of their red-blooded American boy. They see it as a rite of passage. Joey also has many programs on television and tales in books to assure him that this is a normal part of growing up. But when a young gay boy starts feeling attraction to other boys, he has had no teaching to prepare him for this experience. He could not name a song about boys liking boys or girls liking girls. No gay love stories on television or fairy tales explained this as a natural progression for him. Even if he never says anything about these feelings, he still internalizes the homophobia that surrounds him, especially when he hears other boys use words like faggot, queer, and sick to describe this kind of attraction. The gay adolescent, in his most private moments, laying awake in bed, all alone in the dark, dares to ask himself, "Are they talking about me? Am I like those men they make fun of and joke about?"

The emotional pain is almost unbearable, and for many gay teens it becomes too great a burden. That is why gay teen suicides are so prevalent. According to the Center for Disease Control and Prevention, LGBT youth are more than twice as likely to attempt suicide as their heterosexual peers.

I wonder what life would have been like if I had been born into a world that was knowledgeable on issues of sexual orientation and was able to see my attractions as healthy and normal. What if I had had gay role models to show me how to deal responsibly with my sexuality? What if Christian authors had written books to teach me the importance of respecting other boys to whom I was attracted and give me pointers on how to ask a boy out on a date? I hope and pray that one day this world will be that kind of place.

As I reflect on that innocent horseback ride with Paul, I see it now as a time when my natural God-given sexuality was beginning to take shape. I cherish the memory of that time with my young friend. Unfortunately I was robbed of the joy of being able to celebrate my coming of age. I kept my promise to Paul, and I never told of our afternoon role-playing. That is until now. But to be faithful to my promise, I have changed his name to protect our innocence.

Randy with his horses, Ringo and Redfeather

Chapter 4

The Monster Inside

Living in Walnut Ridge, Arkansas, with a population a little over 4000, was not easy for a boy who was different.

I loved Jesus, Broadway music, Judy Garland, Barbra Streisand, and the Beatles. That made me different from most of my friends. The other boys wanted to go hunting with their fathers. I liked the idea of getting out in the woods with my dad, but I hated the guns and the shooting of those cute little animals. But the real difference was my attraction to boys. I clung to the idea that boys experimenting and having crushes on other boys was a normal part of growing up. But I felt guilty after we had mutual-masturbation sessions or told dirty jokes. The more I promised God I wouldn't do "it" again, the more I found myself trying to figure out a way to make it happen.

In 1971, my dad received a job promotion and was transferred to Little Rock. This meant that I would move for the first time in my life. I had never needed to make all new friends before, nor had I lived in a big city or attended a large church. Although initially excited, I started getting scared. At 15, I would be going to a new school for the first time and would be the "new kid" on the block. The hometown I had always known would be almost two hours away.

As I lay on my bed, pondering all of this, a thought crossed my mind. "Randy, perhaps this is God's way of giving you a fresh start. You can make a vow to never play around with boys again and you can start dating girls. You can be normal!"

This thought gave me hope. But when I moved to North Little Rock, the same desires were still within me. It wasn't long until I made new male friends who liked to experiment, and so the struggle continued.

Our new home was located in Sherwood, a very conservative suburb of North Little Rock, Arkansas. The church we decided to attend, First Assembly of God, had over 500 members, compared to the church of 150 in Walnut Ridge. The first time we walked into this "citified" church, I was really uncomfortable. I had heard how these "city churches" had stopped preaching the uncompromising Word of God, and fallen into Satan's clever trap called "worldliness."

But I discovered that larger churches had more to offer their young people. I soon loved the youth group, which was a great place to make friends who were "on fire" for Jesus. After the music director found out that I had sung solos in church, he put me on the list to sing in an upcoming service. I joined the youth choir and was given a solo part right away. My singing gave me a certain amount of "star" quality with peers. I was also asked to prepare devotionals for the youth meetings and, from time to time, to close in prayer. It wasn't long before I was considered a leader by the other teens.

Although I loved church, school was a different story! Most of the guys viewed me suspiciously, but I always had lots of friends among the girls. I carried my Bible to school every day and became known as a "Jesus freak," but I was still dealing with my strong sexual drive.

In the Assemblies of God, in the 60s and 70s, a minister named David Wilkerson was considered radical for his approach to ministry. He advocated reaching out and loving drug addicts and street gang members. Wilkerson founded a drug rehabilitation program called Teen Challenge and wrote a bestseller, *The Cross and the Switchblade*, describing his work with gangs and drug addicts on the streets of New York. (The book was later made into a very bad movie starring Pat Boone and Eric Estrada.)

I idolized David. He seemed to care about young people the church had given up on. I looked to him as someone who might be more understanding and less judgmental about my secret struggles with sexuality. In 1971, Dave put out a real "hip" paperback book for young people called *The Jesus Person Maturity Manual*. Each teen in our church youth group was given a copy. The back cover text read that Dave "discusses the Jesus person's problems such as True Love, Petting, Easy Sex, Homosexuality, Masturbation, V.D, and Witchcraft...."

All I saw were the words *homosexuality* and *masturbation*. I couldn't wait until I got home, behind the privacy of my bedroom door, to see what this compassionate Christian minister had to say about homosexuality.

The chapter was entitled "The Jesus Person and Homosexuality and Lesbianism." After an explanation of what *homosexual* meant, I read this statement: "Those who are hooked by homosexuality are ordinary people who are tangled in a strange web."

For the first time I began to see myself as "hooked" on a specific kind of addiction. Although Wilkerson compared homosexuality to other dangerous addictions, like drugs or alcohol, he seemed to take a compassionate approach to this addiction. He wrote:

"It is absolutely un-Christian to call them names and heap scorn and ridicule on young people who are fighting the loneliest battle known to mankind. It is tragic to see parents

disown sons and daughters who have become homosexuals. ...The attitude of the religious world has been unmerciful, too. Too quickly the church has written off these people as queers and hopeless addicts who deserve only the wrath of God."

Then came the pronouncement that would form the basis for twenty years of blaming myself and my environment for the gay feelings with which I struggled:

"Homosexuals are not born that way. ...There are many factors that contribute to the development of these tendencies supporting the idea that homosexuals are made, not born. It is often related to a disturbed relationship between parent and child. A possessive mother, a cruel and uncaring father, an unsatisfying sexual experience in early years, wrong indoctrination about sex, enforced isolation from the opposite sex, all are factors blamed for causing homosexuality."

Wilkerson declared, "Homosexuality is not incurable. Homosexuals can and do change."

Wow, there was hope! Homosexuality was not a life sentence! I continued reading:

"The cure is most likely for those under 25 years who have not developed a strong attachment to one person."

Hey, I qualified! I was under 25, and I did not see myself as being strongly attached to one person.

"A few grow out of the habit, but those who are confirmed homosexuals stand very little chance of being cured unless they become totally desperate to change."

For years these words would ring in my head. I was never to say the words "I am gay" or "I am a homosexual," because if I did, then there was very little chance for me to recover my "God-given heterosexuality." I tried to ignore my attraction to men, and kept telling myself that it was a phase that I would grow out of. Then, Wilkerson added this caustic statement:

"I have never met a truly happy homosexual. The majority are sad, lonely, full of fear, shame, guilt, anxiety and torment. Loneliness describes their condition most accurately. They are always looking for the perfect love that keeps eluding them. ...Homosexuality is a life of self-torture, of unfulfilled desires, of inner conflicts, of feelings of inferiority and helplessness."

I have met many heterosexuals in the church to whom those words would apply, but it would be wrong to blame heterosexuality for that person's misery. I would like to say to David that it has taken me many years to overcome false information such as what I read in his book, but today I can truthfully say that I *am* a happy homosexual.

My relationship with God is beyond wonderful, and I am experiencing the joys of a Christ-centered, loving, monogamous relationship with an incredible man who also loves Jesus with all his heart. My days of self-torture have come to an end, because the truth has set me free!

Unfortunately, as a young gay man, Wilkerson's words were like a death sentence. Although I believe that he sincerely felt he was helping gay people, he was wrong—wrong in his theology, and wrong in his teaching about homosexuality.

I tried everything his book told me to do so that I could become "normal" in my desires for women. If I was ever to become a minister in the Assemblies of God, I would be expected to marry a Christian girl, preferably one who could sing and play the piano.

I dated a few girls in the church because I was in love with "love." I adored romantic movies. I wanted to be an actor. I practiced love scenes from the classic movies in my bedroom. The girls I dated were good friends, nothing more. I loved talking to them about my favorite books, movies, and about my faith. I even tried "making out" with them, because I liked to imagine myself as a romantic male lead in the movies. I saw myself as a young Rock Hudson. I would later find out I had more in common with Rock than I knew.

I went "parking" for the first time with a girl from the church youth group. I took Mary to the top of Baptist Memorial Hill, where you could park your car and look out over the lights of Little Rock. I had heard others talk about how romantic the place was, so on Mary's 16th birthday, we were, I hoped, going to have a mountain-top experience. After we talked for a while, I took her hand. We talked, then talked some more. Finally, I got up the nerve and made my move. She was more than ready. Our lips met. We connected with each other and we stayed that way for quite a while. Finally, I pulled away. My lips were sore, as the pressure from puckering that long had taken its toll.

I thought, "So that's what kissing is all about? It's a little overrated, in my book." (I still had no idea about the twist the French had added to this pastime.) We sat in silence holding hands, looking out at the lights of the city. Then I took her home. I could check off one rite of passage: I had taken a girl parking!

Julie was another girl from church that I dated. We would go out to eat, then return to her parents' house and sit in the living room, listening to Karen Carpenter records. One night, I decided I would try out my kissing skills on Julie. The lights were low, and the music was romantic, just like in a Doris Day/ Rock Hudson movie. I moved into position and started the slow motion toward her mouth, puckered and ready for contact.

But to my surprise, Julie was not puckering. I panicked. She had no lips! At least that's what it felt like. I opened my tightly shut eyes and peeked down. I was shocked to see that Julie had her mouth wide open.

"What was that all about?" I wondered. Try as I might, I could not decide how my puckered lips and her open mouth were suppose to connect. The situation felt awkward, so I made some excuse and left as soon as possible.

Later, while visiting my Grandma McCain, I had a date with a "take charge" kind of girl from her church. As I was leaving her house, she walked me to my car to say good night. She grabbed hold of me and, using what felt like superhuman force, zeroed in on her target. In my state of open-mouthed shock, she drove her tongue deep into my mouth, causing me to let out a surprised little whimper. Driving back to my grandma's, I thought, "So that is why Julie had no lips." Lips were not really required in this modern form of kissing. Lips just sort of got in the way.

Wow, Julie must have sensed how inexperienced I was! I could not wait to go back to her parents' living room, put the record on, dim the lights, and get down to business. Later, when Julie asked me if I had gone out with anyone while visiting my grandma's, I wondered to myself, "How did she know?"

Although this exploration was interesting, I did not feel the burning need that the other guys seemed to have to see how far they could go with a girl. I was simply an actor, caught up in the fantasy of playing a role. I was never curious about a woman's body, her breasts, or her other unmentionables. I thought breasts were pretty in a blouse or a dress and gave shape to the outfit, but when I would see a picture of a naked woman, the breasts were not pretty to me. They looked like large pockets of body fat. I much preferred a man's muscular pecs. Back when I lived in Walnut Ridge, the boy who lived next door had a storm cellar we turned into a club house for guys. We hid some porn pictures of men and women having sex. I was always drawn to the men's physiques, rather than the shapes of the women. When one of the guys would say, "Check out them knockers on that girl," I would go along with him, but inside I just didn't get it. When I masturbated, I always found myself picturing one of the guys from the porn magazine. In my most private thoughts, I would sometimes wonder, "What if I am homosexual and I am doomed to be this way all my life?"

But I would remember the book my parents had given me, which said that all boys are curious about other boys' physiques and genitals. It quoted studies revealing that most boys wanted to look at other boys in the showers or at the urinals at school to compare the size of other guys with their own equipment. So, I reassured myself that one day I would wake up and find the naked breasts of women stunningly attractive.

I prayed, begging God to take away these unwanted desires. The desires never diminished. The more I denounced the desires, the stronger my homosexual feelings became. I concluded this was Satan attempting to defeat me and to destroy any possibility of God using me in the ministry.

With most young boys, the sexual awakening is strong. I thought I must be a sexual maniac because I fantasized about sex so often. Only much later in life would I learn that this was normal. It happened as an "aha" moment.

Driving around town with my gay friends, I heard one whistle and say, "Look at that hot guy! Check out those abs!"

"So that is what my straight friends were so excited about," I thought. For them, a girl's body was as exciting as a guys' physique was to me. But as a very young man, feeling different just confused the heck out of me.

Chapter 5

Jesus Called, Randy Answered

Entering my second year of high school in Sherwood, I had many friends, but still I struggled with my sexual desires. I worried. In two years I would graduate from high school and have to decide where to attend college. Even more importantly, it was time to put up or shut up about going into the ministry. I dreamed of being a full-time minister. That is all I ever really wanted to do with my life.

When I was about ten or eleven, I loved Andy Williams and his music. I had all of his albums. I came home after school, went immediately to my room, and played Andy's records. One of my favorite albums was a live recording of *The Andy Williams Show*, which came out in 1970. At age 13, alone in my bedroom, I played that album and pantomimed the song "What Are You Doing the Rest of Your Life" as Andy sang. I had so closely watched him on television that I knew every facial expression. I would meld into Andy and lose myself in his identity.

As Andy and I finished the song, the applause on the live recording was deafening. They loved me! They really, really loved me! At that moment, it was as if I heard a voice saying, "Randy, you can have all this applause if you will just put to rest these desires of becoming a minister. If you will sing secular music instead of gospel, you really could have a future in show biz."

For a moment the thought was intoxicating, but the words of the song came back to me. The lyrics spoke of being devoted to one love for a lifetime. Always before, I sang the lyrics as if I were directing them to my dream lover. But this day, I turned it into a love song to Jesus.

What would life be like without knowing that I was spending my life serving Him? I wanted the ministry more than fame. Did I have the talent to achieve notoriety? I will never know. I do know that at that moment I made a conscious decision that *if* God called me, I would say yes. But how would I know for sure that He was calling me?

I assumed all my life that I would be in full-time ministry someday. When I was still in my mother's womb, she had dedicated me to the Lord. When I was five years old, my mother took me to the altar and asked me to kneel beside her. Mama prayed,

"God, make Little Randy your servant."

In my childish mind, I could see myself holding a great big silver tray filled with scrumptious pastries and luscious fruit. I stood in front of a huge ornamental door that went from the ceiling to the floor. After the doors magically opened, I walked in and saw an ornate throne. Sitting on that throne was my childish image of God, who resembled Santa Claus quite a bit. I approached the throne and offered my tray up to Him. That was my concept of being God's servant.

I believe God heard my mom's prayer, because all my life I have had a strong desire to draw as close to God as I could. When the other boys wanted to play outside, I wanted to be in with the grown-ups having a Bible study. I loved Sunday school and children's church, held for us while the adults were in their worship service. In the summers, I lived for Vacation Bible School. I began singing solos in church at the age of six. During my preteen years, I often got up before the congregation and gave a testimony of my love for Jesus.

Every evangelist who held a revival service at our church would tell my mom and dad, "This boy has a special calling on his life. He is going to be used of God in a very mighty way." Those words thrilled me every time I heard them.

When someone asked me what I wanted to be when I grew up, I squared my skinny little shoulders, stood on my tiptoes and proclaimed, "Someday, I am going to be a minister of the gospel!"

In the back of my mind, however, I wondered how a person knew they were really called by God. Many times I have thought that I could help God with His communication skills. (He has never taken me up on my offer.) At one point as a young boy, I thought, "Why doesn't God just use the telephone?"

I could envision the phone ringing, my mother answering the phone and calling out, "Randy, it's for you." I would take the phone from her and say hello. Then, I would hear this deep voice on the other end say, "Is this Randall Allen McCain, Jr.?"

"Yes."

"This is Gabriel. I have an important message for you from God. He would like to know if you would be willing to be one of His ministers."

Wouldn't that be easier than trying to hear an inaudible voice? That phone call never came. Now I was in the eleventh grade, still unsure of what I was going to do with my life. Admittedly, I felt I had been called into the ministry by my pastor, my mother, and every evangelist that had ever held revivals at my church, but still I was not 100 percent sure that I had been called by *God*. Grandma McCain, my spiritual teacher in so many ways, assured me that God would let me know.

"Randy, when He does, you will not be able to doubt it."

Well, Grandma was so right! Every year the youth group at First Assembly of

God in North Little Rock, which had become the center of my universe, took the young people on a spiritual retreat to a remote campground. We arrived on a Friday evening and stayed until Sunday afternoon. During a weekend filled with fun activities and lots of church, the youth were encouraged to seek God. At this retreat I received God's call to the ministry.

This terminology may sound foreign to many readers. In the Pentecostal churches, "God's call" is well understood. Pentecostal churches encourage young people to surrender their lives to the Lord to determine if God is calling them to a life of occupational ministry as an evangelist, missionary, or pastor. My call came on Saturday night, October 27, 1973.

After the teens had spent a fun day playing ball, we gathered for the Saturday night worship service. John Gifford, the evangelist for the retreat, preached on the woman in the Bible who washed Jesus' feet with expensive perfume and dried His feet with her hair. Two questions in that sermon were, "What do you have that is of value *and* are you willing to give it all to Jesus, your Savior and Lord?"

At the end of the sermon, Rev. Gifford asked us all to kneel at our seats and surrender our very life and future, which was our most prized possession, to Jesus. As I knelt, I cried out to Jesus that I wanted to totally surrender my life to Him, and at that moment I felt I was caught up in a dream. In my mind, I saw a garden and I saw a man kneeling in prayer in front of a large boulder. He wept as though His heart was breaking. I realized I was in the Garden of Gethsemane and I saw Jesus praying to God.

I heard Him pray, "Father, if there be any way, let this cup of suffering pass from me, but if not, Thy will be done." At that moment, He rose slowly and walked over to His trusted disciples whom He had asked to watch and pray with him. They were asleep. I heard His voice, filled with loneliness and disappointment. "Could you not watch with me one hour?" He said.

The disciples did not wake. I felt His need for a friend and, in my dreamlike state, stepped out of the shadows and said, "Jesus, *I* will watch with you. *I* will be your friend." His beautiful eyes found me and He seemed relieved that someone would watch and pray with Him. But then Jesus looked troubled.

"Randy," He asked, "When are you going to stop saying no to my call on your life? When are you going to stop doubting my will for you?"

I was hurt. "Lord, surely you know my heart and can see that I want to be your servant more than anything in this world. I always have. But I need to know for sure that you are calling me. I don't want to embarrass my family, my pastor, myself, and most of all you by saying I am called if I'm not. How do I know for sure that you are calling me?"

His answer was clear.

"Randy, the knowing will come in the accepting."

WOW! What a revelation! I raised my hands heavenward and cried, "Lord, I accept your call upon my life. I will go where you want me to go, say what you want me to say. I am *yours,* Lord Jesus. I give my all to you."

The tears were like water spouts. I envisioned an Old Testament prophet with a long white beard, holding a flask of anointing oil over my head. As He tipped it, oil ran down my head onto my face. The tears running down my cheeks felt like the oil, signifying the presence of the Holy Spirit. What a joyful experience! The others in the room had melted away. It was just Jesus and me.

I walked outside, breathing the crisp October air. The service was over and the teens were headed to the bonfire. I could see the sparks and orange light glowing in the distance. As I moved in that direction, I was actually running, jumping, and laughing. It felt like Jesus was running and jumping beside me. Then I just fell down on the ground and looked up into the starlit night. Jesus and I lay there for a moment, catching our breaths. A line from the play Romeo and Juliet came to me and I spoke it aloud in my generic English accent.

"O blessed, blessed night. I am a-feared, being in night, this is but a dream, too flatteringly sweet to be substantial."

Then I burst into laughter, or I should say, *we* burst into laughter. I felt so close to Jesus that I could sense His emotions. All of a sudden, I felt His expression change from joy to concern. In my dream-like state I heard Him say, "Randy, look out there in front of you. What do you see?"

I really got excited. I had heard of people seeing visions from God, so I looked hard into the dark night, but no vision appeared. Finally, disappointed, I answered,

"All I see is darkness."

"That is the world for so many, Randy. Take them the light."

At that moment a feeling of awe settled over me and I began to feel the awesome responsibility to which I had been called. I stood up and walked toward the fire. I knew the routine. The fire represented the place into which you throw those things that weigh you down in your Christian walk. There were sticks to represent those things we were giving up as a sacrifice to God. I picked one up and threw it into the fire. I said to the other teens, "Tonight I have said 'YES' to God's call on my life in the ministry. This stick represents all other hopes, dreams, or aspirations I might have had. I am giving myself completely to the work God has for me to do."

The other youth applauded and joined in a round of "Praise the Lord!" "Halle-lujah!" and "Thank you, Jesus."

That weekend was a turning point in my life. I could not wait to tell my folks, who were very pleased. But the person I wanted most to tell was Grandma McCain, so I asked Daddy to take me to see her in the sleepy little town of Warren, Arkansas.

When I told her about my Call, Grandma smiled and hugged me. "Randy, your ministry will be unique because you are different from most ministers," she said. "You have been given unique gifts in drama and music. There will be times in your life when you will doubt that you are really *called*, when others will tell you that you are not called. But son, remember this experience you had with God. It is your touchstone. God knew you would need to remember your calling, so He gave you a very dramatic calling that you will never be able to forget. Keep those moments fresh in your heart. God has His hand on you, Randy. I have always known it. Stay true to the Lord. I am proud of you, my grandson."

Grandma was prophetic. There have been times I doubted my calling and times when the church told me I was not suited for ministry. But I have never been able to forget that night when God gave me a very special gift. He called me in a way I could hear. I answered Him, "Speak, Lord, your servant is listening." I am still listening, Lord.

Randy's Senior Picture

Chapter 6

What Now?

My dream had come true. I had been called into the ministry and I knew it! But now came the hard part. I was a junior in high school, and college was approaching with lightning speed. Today, parents and schools do a good job preparing teens for college, but in the early 70s, this was not a priority. Even though it was a given that I would attend college, and my parents were prepared to provide for that, I was starting my senior year without a clue as to what type of education to pursue.

My sister Linda attended Evangel College in Springfield Missouri, graduating with a degree in music. Since I admired Linda, and I knew I wanted to go to a Christian college, I started telling everyone that I planned to attend Evangel. Word circulated through the Assemblies of God that I had received "the Call" and I began receiving invitations to hold youth revivals around the state. I already had some name recognition because I won a statewide youth vocal contest sponsored by the Assemblies of God and sang at youth camps each year. I was sure and confidant as a singer, so my youth and my music carried me even though my sermons were not that great.

The senior class of '74 at Sylvan Hills High School was allowed to choose a member of the graduating class to give the baccalaureate address. Always before, that honor had been given to a local minister, but this year the school administration decided they wanted the speaker to be a graduating senior who was a person of faith. I was overjoyed when I was chosen to preach to my class.

For my graduation gifts, my parents helped me get the word out to my relatives and friends that I would appreciate financial donations to go toward a sound system. I needed this so I could travel to small churches in Arkansas and hold youth revivals during the summer following my graduation. Enough money came in to purchase an amplifier, two speakers, and a reel-to-reel tape player. I got several invitations to preach and sing that summer. I was flying high. I had a great time, and then all too soon it was time to leave for Evangel College.

My parents set me up in my dorm room and said their goodbyes, leaving me alone in the world for the very first time. I realized right away that most of the students were from northern states. They all talked funny, but most of them thought *I* had the weird accent. They were always asking me to "say something, anything. We just like to hear you talk." This got on my nerves after a while.

I was also very homesick. I missed my family, my friends, and my church. I declared my major to be Biblical Studies, but made the mistake of declaring a minor in music. No one had warned me that a minor in music was like having two majors. I was not very studious anyway, so right off the bat, I was overwhelmed!

As the semester was drawing to a close, I was in a deep depression. Clancy, a friend I had made from Maine, listened to my troubles. Clancy didn't offer much advice, but he had an empathetic roommate from South Dakota named Gary Eddy. Sometimes, when I dropped by Clancy's room to visit, he was not there. So I talked to Gary, who was a good listener. I often poured out my heart to him. Gary always seemed to be a safe place. As an art major, he asked me to sit as a model for his assignments, drawing my face. I did not feel as homesick when I spent time with Gary. With the semester coming to a close, I told Gary I was thinking about not coming back after Christmas break.

"Well Randy," he said. "If you are this unhappy, just stand up to your parents when you go home for Christmas and tell them you want to do something different with your life."

Never before had I thought this was a real possibility, but Gary convinced me that it was. He asked me to stay in touch, and I promised I would.

During Christmas vacation, I broke the news to my parents that I was not going to continue my education at Evangel. Reluctantly, they accepted my decision. I decided to resume my evangelistic ministry. This was somewhat successful, but I was living at home, which was not much fun. I certainly was not getting rich or breaking even with the "love offerings" I received at the little rural churches where I preached. But I took comfort in the fact that I was trying to stay true to my calling.

I stayed in touch with Gary. One day, I opened a letter from him, expecting the usual dribble about his life at college. I got a real shock.

Randy, I must confess to you that I have strong feelings for you. I don't know if you have the same feelings for me or not. When you would come into my room and sit on my bed, I would experience feelings inside that were sensual and exciting. When you left, I would not be able to sleep. I would go on long walks and while I walked I pictured in my mind a beautiful fantasy. You and I were shipwrecked on a deserted island. We were the only inhabitants. We had no need for clothes and would run naked, hand in hand, through the waves and collapse on the sand as we made love to the sound of waves crashing on the shore. I am taking a real risk in telling you this, but I cannot get you out of my mind. I think I love you, Randy. When I think of you, I feel a rush of sexual emotions as well as tender loving thoughts. If I have offended you please forgive me. But please let me know how you feel about my revelation to you.

I was shocked by Gary's admission! I had enjoyed the attention Gary gave me while I was at Evangel. Subconsciously, I too had enjoyed the closeness as we sat on his bed. But I had been in denial about my attraction to men while attending Evangel and was *still* in denial. In all my moments of sexual exploration and experimentation, I never had had any guy actually put words to the emotions I felt. I had experienced the sensuality in silence. Now, with the arrival of Gary's letter, the spell of denial had been compromised.

Nothing had happened between the two of us, but as I reread his letter, fear gripped me. How had he known I had these tendencies? Were they obvious? I thought I had covered them well, but he must have picked up on something, some mannerisms. What were they? I panicked. There were competing emotions of fear, anger, and disgust, mixed with a touch of breathtaking excitement. As I read his vivid fantasy, I felt sexual energy building. I quickly repressed it and zeroed in on an appropriate response. I replied with a scathing letter, castigating him for making me a part of this lurid, sexual fantasy.

It is wrong, Gary. That is an abomination! You cannot think of me that way. God hates that sin! It is wrong, wrong, wrong! I am sorry if I somehow led you to believe that we were anything more than friends. I am not that way! Do not ever think of me that way. God destroyed Sodom because of this grievous wrong. Gary, I want to be your friend, but you must never speak to me of this sort of thing again.

I did not hear from Gary for two or three weeks. During that time, I found myself pulling his letter out from under my bed where I had hidden it. I reread the part about the two of us running naked through the waves and making love on the beach. I allowed the sensual waves to take me away to that place of total release. Afterwards, I repented to the God who had destroyed Sodom and Gomorrah for their sin of homosexuality. Guilt hung around as an unwanted companion as I drifted off to sleep. I woke with a new commitment to put my sensual self behind me.

Finally, Gary responded to my letter. He wrote that, at first, he was angry at me for my judgmental letter and waited for a few weeks to respond. Then he thought about my words, and realized that I was only saying what I had been taught in church. He had been raised with the same theology, so even though my rejection had been disappointing, it was not surprising. He still wanted us to be friends.

I have never been good at keeping in touch by letter, so I did not write to him for a while. This upset him, because he needed some response from me that all was forgiven. After a few of his letters received no reply, he did not write for some time. Then, out of the blue, I received a letter.

As I take pen in hand I am uncertain as to how this letter will be received by you because I don't know if we are still friends. I have not written because I never received any answers to my last letters. I hope it is because you are very busy, but even so, that is too bad, for it is sad to be too busy for people. One day you may wake up to find yourself very much alone, but I want still to be here as your friend. Please let me. I don't know what is wrong. Perhaps you have changed and hence also your attitude toward me and what I've written in past letters. I hope this is not so, because it will hurt me to lose a friend. If you wish to discontinue our relationship please write and say so. I'm mature enough to grant your desires and I will get over my own pain eventually. Time and business tend to erase much of even the tender feelings. This also is sad…I hope the attitude this letter presents is not cruel or angry. I am disappointed though. I still love you, Randy, and wish you to be my friend (in the purest way, please believe that). You may not even be alive for all I know, and it's awful to think that I might be writing to a corpse. That is how it feels. But I won't hound you if I don't receive an answer to this. I will never write again and I will accept the fact that you have a good reason, albeit a reason unbeknownst to me, which you are unable to voice.

If you do choose to write, do tell me about yourself, any loves you have. Tell me how you are and what you are doing. But know that, even if you don't write again, I appreciate your past friendship. Do not feel guilty or pressured. You have your life to live; live it to the best of your abilities which are great, Randy. You have marvelous potential; use it for God's glory. Do not worry about me. I am fine! Take care and God richly bless you,

> *I love you still,*
>
> *Gary*
>
> *P.S. Forgive my melodramatics.*

As I read the letter, I felt badly for not keeping in touch. I immediately wrote Gary a newsy letter about my everyday life. I also told him that I was getting ready to take a trip to Springfield and perhaps I could stop by Evangel and say hi while I was in town. He was elated.

When I did visit Evangel, it was nice seeing Gary again, even though it felt weird being back on campus. The next week I received a letter from Gary.

Randy, I am so happy that you still love me. I should not have doubted it. Please forgive me for writing that bad letter. I'm really sorry. But putting all sorrow behind, I am happy to be writing to you again. I missed you and your letters, but your absence soon led to a dulling of my affection for you (on a conscious level anyway). When I first saw you in chapel a few days ago, I didn't feel much. However, as I kept looking at you and remembering last year and this past summer, my love for you was rekindled, and when I would look into your soft brown eyes I felt good. You look good Randy. I like your calm disposition and the way you are growing up. You've matured a lot. The difference is very noticeable and most encouraging. I'm super happy you came for a visit and that we were able to set our relationship right and clear the air of the misunderstanding between us. It hurts me to know that I hurt you by my letter, and I'm sorry. I love you very much, Randy. You're a beautiful guy. Thanks for loving me. Take care of yourself. God bless you.

With all my love, your buddy, friend, and pal,

Gary.

We both had good intentions of corresponding but, as long distance friendships go, before long we again lost touch. Little did I know that Gary would play such a starring role in my life's story. We both had a lot of bridges to cross before we would find each other again.

Randy reading in his dorm room

Gary Drawing a Portrait of Randy

Evangel College in Springfield, Missouri

Chapter 7

An Encounter in the Park

The summer of 1975 was another turning point. The event that changed my way of looking at my sexuality took place in our city park.

I had gone there to enjoy nature. Being raised in the country, I missed the trees and the sounds of the forest, so I took a book and headed to the park. Eventually, I needed to use the restroom. When I went inside, there was another man standing at the urinal next to me. He made it clear that he wanted a sexual encounter. Frightened, yet intrigued, I started to leave. Then I stopped, turned around, and reassumed my position at the urinal, thinking to myself, "Well, now he knows that you are interested. Why else would you walk away and then return to the urinal?"

I was shaking inside. This would be the first time that I would allow myself to touch and be touched sexually by a total stranger. Instinctively, I knew that I had crossed a line. Always before, I had convinced myself that I was "just horsing around" with my buddies. This was different. This was a man I did not know. There was no way I could consider this experience as just normal experimentation between young friends.

The stranger was very polite. He suggested that we take a walk out back in the woods where we would be in less danger of getting caught. He gave me every chance to change my mind. He did not force me in any way. It was quite apparent by my actions and my quick shallow breathing and my shaking hands that I was afraid and inexperienced, but willing. I was of age and knew that I was ready to find out more about sex from someone older and more experienced.

When it was over, I walked to my car alone, afraid, guilt-ridden, and remorseful. Yet the experience had been very sensually exciting and exhilarating. I was hooked. I started hanging out at the parks regularly. My youthful good looks seemed to be a plus in my pursuit of more pleasurable experiences. The excitement of newfound pleasures produced a heavy amount of guilt.

I would try to go to sleep at night remembering that I had been called by God into the ministry, and I had said yes. Yet here I was, trampling on all my values. I was becoming someone I did not even recognize. As a pastor today, this is what I tell young gay and lesbian kids, who are just becoming aware of their sexual orientation:

> *"When you come out of the closet, bring your values with you. Your sexual orientation, whether it is heterosexual or homosexual, is not a choice, but a gift from God. At the same time, God asks us to deal with our sexuality in a responsible way."*

I wish there had been someone to offer some guidance, but there was no one. I saw myself as being split down the middle. Either I had to say no to my desires for another man and be a Christian, or accept the fact that I was a homosexual and leave my love for Jesus behind. So, for many years, my life was a pattern of abstaining from my sexual desires and then giving in to the strong urges.

I was never taught that Jesus could take my sexuality and make something beautiful out of it. "Gay Christian" was an oxymoron to me. The church I knew was totally silent when I needed it the most. I felt like the psalmist who said, "No one cares for my soul!" (Psalm 142:4)

Chapter 8

A Death too Close to Home

In the summer of 1976, my dad got a call from Grandma McCain. He was on the phone for quite a while. When he walked into the den, his face was troubled. Mom asked him what was wrong.

"That was Mother. She called to tell me that Brother's son, Floyd, killed himself."

"Oh no, surely not!" Mom responded.

I was in shock. I had not seen my second cousin in a while, but remembered playing with him as a child. Floyd was my Grandma's brother's son. His dad went by the name Brother because he was a twin, and the twins were the babies in a family of ten children. So, they called the girl Sister and the boy Brother. Floyd's dad and my dad were about the same age, even though they were uncle and nephew. After they came back from World War Two, they hung out together. From the stories my dad had told me, they had some pretty wild times! They were close and had a lot of love and admiration for each other.

Floyd, Brother's son, was five years older than me. When I stayed in Warren with Grandma for the summer, Floyd would come by and we would hang out together. He was very effeminate and sometimes I, or another cousin, would tease him. This came back to me with painful regret as I heard Dad speak of his death at his own hands. Mom asked what had happened.

"Well, he had gone to a friend's house. His friend was not home. When the friend returned, he found Floyd dead of a self-inflicted bullet wound."

"What would have caused him to do such a thing?"

"Well, Mother told me that Floyd told Brother that he was a homosexual."

"Oh no," Momma sighed.

I turned away and walked to my bedroom, shocked and terrified. I shut the door and fell on my bed. I could not move. I started to sweat. Was this going to happen to me? Was being gay so horrible that a person would take a gun and end his life? I was lost in these macabre thoughts when I heard knocking on my door.

"Son, I need to ask you something."

I panicked! Did Dad know about me? Was he going to ask me the question I had always feared?

"Son, open the door. I need to talk to you."

I jumped up off the bed and unlocked my door.

"Son, I'm going to Warren tomorrow for the funeral. Do you want to go with me? Your Grandma is pretty upset. I know it would mean a lot to her, and also to Brother, if we were there for the funeral."

"Sure Dad, I'll go."

He closed the door, but not before I saw the pain in his eyes. My dad was tender-hearted. His heart was aching for his friend and uncle, and for the loss of his cousin.

The two hour drive to Warren seemed like an eternity. We arrived about six in the evening. Grandma had a meal fixed for us and the others from Dad's family who had come for the funeral the next morning. Later, after most of the family had gone to bed, Dad and his mother sat up and talked. I joined them.

"Mother, did you know that Floyd was a homosexual?" Dad asked.

"Yes. One day Brother came over and he was very upset and said he needed to talk. He asked if I had a good cup of coffee, and I told him I could make one real quick. So I started the coffee and he commenced to unburdening his heart to me.

"He said, 'Floyd was in the army, as you know. Well, when he came back home he started hanging out with some guys that his mom and I did not know. He never brought them to the house. So, one night when he came in, we asked him why he didn't bring his friends in to meet us. He said, 'Dad, you and Mom wouldn't want to know these guys.' I asked him why, and he started crying. I said, 'Son, what is wrong. Talk to us.' He said, 'Mom, Dad, I am a homosexual. I found out while I was in the army. I couldn't believe it. I said, 'Floyd, son, I would rather have had someone come in here and tell me you were killed in a car wreck than to have heard you say this to us.'"

Grandma's voice broke as she continued. "When Brother told me what he had said to Floyd, I stopped him and said, Brother, you can't treat him like he was scum from the pits of hell.

"But that is the way I have always thought of people like that," he said.

"Yes, but Brother, this is your son. He needs you right now like he has never needed you before. You have to show him that you love him.

"But I tried! I tried to get him to go fishing or to play sports but he was never interested in things other boys liked to do. He always preferred staying home with his mom."

Grandma was crying now. "It just breaks my heart that he would take his own life!" she told Dad and me. "Floyd was such a good boy."

She told us that the day before he died, he rode his bike to the nursing home to spend time with some elderly women there who he visited on a regular basis, just because he knew they were lonely.

"Floyd loved old people and always was doing things for them, yet he had so much pain inside," she said. "I just feel like there should have been something we could have done for him, but now it's too late. Brother is beside himself with grief."

I could not listen any longer. I went into the bathroom and closed the door. I cried for Floyd, but I also cried for myself. What was to become of me? If Grandma and Daddy knew that I was a homosexual like Floyd, what would they say? I vowed that they would never find out. I had to get a hold of this monster and defeat it.

Dave Wilkerson, in *The Jesus People Manual*, insisted that many had overcome homosexuality with the help of the Lord. I had to get serious about this. I did not want to end up like Floyd. I wanted so badly to be normal, to have a wife and children and to make my parents and my grandma proud of me. That night, I fell asleep with a prayer for deliverance on my lips. There was a part of me that wanted to judge Uncle Brother for reacting the way he did when Floyd announced to him that he was gay. But I also knew what a shock Floyd's words must have been to his simple, God-fearing, southern preacher Daddy.

I made it through the funeral, but not without looking at the casket and seeing myself in it. Floyd's death by his own hand affected me profoundly, and did much to strengthen my resolve to continue the fight against what I believed to be a trap of Satan—homosexuality.

Randy with His Uncle Brother (Rev. R.V. White)
July 2008

Chapter 9

A Casualty of Hypocrisy

That summer, a traveling drama and music group from Southwestern Assemblies of God Bible College in Waxahachie, Texas ministered at our church. I was mesmerized by their performance. I decided that I would ask my parents if I could attend that college in the fall. They agreed, wanting me to continue my education, and I attended Southwestern for three semesters. I liked the college because it was located in the south and had a more southern feel than Evangel. To my great joy, I was accepted into the traveling music ministry ensemble. We sang worship music in churches across the southern states.

Steve was a member of the group. He was tall, with dark brown hair and eyes, and he was very self-assured. I thought he was quite stuck on himself. I was strongly attracted to Steve. He played the trumpet and directed the instrumentalists who traveled with our group. Steve's love for God impressed me, and I vowed that somehow I would become Steve's friend. Whenever our group went on an extended weekend trip by bus to several different churches, I tried to sit close to Steve. He did not seem interested in getting to know me. On tours, we stayed in the homes of church members. On the second night of one of our trips, I got the assignment I had been waiting for. Steve and I were to spend the night together.

Our hosts took us to their home after the concert and showed us to our bedroom. There was one regular size bed. This thrilled and scared me at the same time. I started getting ready for bed, feeling awkward because Steve had not said much. There was a half-bath in our bedroom. Steve went in and shut the door. I quickly got into my pajamas and under the covers just as Steve came out of the bathroom. To my surprise, all he had on was a pair of red bikini underwear. His lean, long body looked practically naked as he pulled back the covers on his side of the bed and crawled in.

I started praying: "God give me strength to resist temptation!" We talked way into the night. Steve seemed pleased to discover that we had a lot in common spiritually. That night we became fast friends. However, I got very little sleep because I was afraid of what I might do in my unconscious state lying so close to this handsome hunk.

Back on campus, Steve and I became inseparable. When we caught up at the end of every day, often Steve would say something like, "Randy, today at three o'clock I got this real strong urge to pray for you. Were you going through a difficult time around then?"

I would think, and usually realized that I had been in a situation that was troubling me just about the time Steve had been urged by the Holy Spirit to pray for me. That is how close we became. We even double dated together. I look back at those pictures of us with our dates and remember how often I wished that we could ditch the girls and date each other. But when I had those thoughts, I immediately felt guilty and tried to push them aside.

Steve and I always tried to sit together on the tour bus and talk about Jesus and the Bible, but we were not always assigned to stay overnight in the same house. One morning after we had stayed in different homes, Steve signaled to me with his beautiful, troubled eyes that he needed to talk. It seemed something had happened that bothered him greatly. We found a seat at the back of the bus and as soon as it began moving I asked him what was wrong.

"Randy, I am just sick—sick to my stomach!"

"Do you have a stomach virus?"

"No!" Steve replied emphatically. "I stayed with Jeff last night."

Jeff, a senior in the group, was very effeminate. He kept to himself most of the time. He spoke with a lisp, and some people joked that he *walked* with a lisp. Jeff was one of those gays who could never be in a closet because he was so easy to spot. In the dorm, Jeff never showered if anyone else was in the shower room. He waited until the rest of us had gone to bed and showered at one or two in the morning. When he traveled with our group, Jeff would never get changed in the guy's dressing room. He went into the men's room, locked the door, and put on his suit for the service. We all figured Jeff was gay.

As I sat with Steve, I started putting two and two together. Jeff had shared a bed with Steve. Steve had probably worn those sexy red bikini briefs. Steve shared his lurid nocturnal experience of waking up and realizing that someone was touching his "privates." Jeff had not been able to resist the hunk with whom he had been assigned to spend the night.

Immediately, I felt jealousy rearing its ugly head. I hated Jeff at that moment. How dare he attempt what I had longed to do that night when Steve and I had shared a bed! I harnessed my jealous rage to appear disgusted. "Oh Steve, he's sick! Yuck!"

I should have won an Academy Award for my performance that day.

"Randy, I don't know what to do about this. But I feel I have to report it to the dean of students. Don't you agree?"

"Yes, absolutely," I replied, practically wrapping my pharisaic robes around me.

"Randy, if I decide to tell the dean on Monday, will you go with me for moral support?"

Steve needed me! He was asking me to be there with him. There was no way I was going to turn him down. Besides, the school needed to know about this. Jeff was about to graduate from a Bible college. The administration should be alerted to the kind of person he was before they awarded him their seal of approval!

I tried to envision what had happened between Jeff and Steve. I had wondered if Steve struggled with homosexual feelings. Had he ever fantasized about acting on those feelings with me? How could I find out if male/male sexual play was a turn-on to him? If I knew Steve's initial reaction to Jeff's attempts to arouse him, it would give me a clue.

"Steve, you know if you go to the dean of students with this accusation, there will be questions asked of you. Are you prepared for that?"

"I have thought about that and I still feel that it is my Christian duty to report it, so whatever I have to face, I will do it for Christ."

We rode along in silence for a few minutes while I thought of a clever way to ask the next question.

"Steve, Jeff might try to say…that this was a mutual incident…that you participated in this."

"But I didn't, Randy. You know I wouldn't do that."

"I know you wouldn't, Steve. I am just trying to think this through so there are no surprises when you go to the dean."

"I know you are, Randy. Sorry, go ahead. Ask me anything that you think the dean will ask."

"When you first woke up and you became conscious of your surroundings, were you…aroused?"

Steve's face reddened. I had my answer.

"Well, when your penis is stimulated, it becomes erect. I was asleep. I didn't know who was doing the stimulating. But the moment I *did* know, I lost the erection."

The thought of Steve in his bikini underwear, elicited a physical response in me that I quickly readjusted my seating to hide.

"Sure, Steve, I understand. No one could hold that against you."

"I was sexually attacked, Randy."

"What did you do when you realized it was Jeff?"

"I immediately lost it. I pushed him off me and off the bed. I told him he was sick, and that he had better ask God to forgive him. And I let him know that he had sure better never try anything like that with me again, or I would make him wish he hadn't."

We did go to the dean's office, where Steve told his sordid tale. When he finished, the dean said that he understood Steve's anger and assured us that he would handle it. Steve asked what he would do.

"We will tell Jeff he has to step down from the singing group."

"Is that all?" asked Steve.

"What else would you have us do?" asked the dean.

"I think he should be expelled from the school," said Steve, very assured in his judgment. "Don't you, Randy?"

I sat trembling inside. If the dean only knew the thoughts I had for Steve, or if Steve himself knew about my feelings for him! How could I sit in judgment of Jeff when I was just as guilty in my heart? But I had promised Steve to back him, so I opened my mouth and started talking.

"How will it look if Jeff graduates from an Assemblies of God college, is given a position in a church based on his diploma from this school, and then later tries something like he tried with Steve with one of the kids in the church youth group? Then, if that church comes to you and asks if you know he had this problem, what will you say?"

Steve nodded his head in agreement. This gave me a great feeling, because I could tell that he was impressed by my logic.

The dean of students, however, offered more grace that day than most other ministers would have, and certainly more than Steve or me. "Traveling with the group means a great deal to Jeff," he said. "And to have that taken away from him would be punishment enough."

Steve became enraged. "I can't believe that you would wink at sin!" Steve said. "You know he is a homosexual, and yet you are going to allow him to graduate with a degree in ministry?"

"Steve, listen. I understand that you feel animosity toward Jeff. What he did was wrong. But Jeff has worked very hard for almost four years now. His grades have been excellent. I think it would be wrong to take all that away without providing an opportunity for him to deal with his problem. Having to leave the group will be humiliating to Jeff. I appreciate you for sharing what happened with me. Steve and Randy, you need to pray for Jeff. God is able to give him victory over this sin. Have a good day, guys."

The meeting was over.

Many times I have regretted my role in that conversation. When I was later the target of homophobic attacks, I could not look at my accusers as "them against me." I *was* them. I do not know what happened to Jeff after graduation, but I hope that he was able to come to terms with his sexuality and live a fulfilling life as a gay Christian man. I have asked God to forgive me for the hypocritical stance I took in that exposure of his life story. But back then, I could show no mercy or grace to myself, and I certainly could not show it to others like me.

I tried to get enthused about getting my degree, but I was always painfully aware that there was a part of me that would not let me get on with my life. I was scared to death that I was a homosexual. How could I ever be in ministry and fight against this sin? If only there had been someone to talk to, someone who could have helped me understand my inward struggle. But at that moment in time, very little was known about sexual orientation. I was on my own. After three more semesters, I dropped out to take another stab at traveling as an evangelist.

Randy McCain, youth evangelist

Chapter 10

A Terroristic Stranger

Being home made me want to take another trip to the park. One afternoon I met Tommy Joe, a lonely, impotent 38-year-old man who lived with his mother and worked at a local hospital. I developed a crush on him and he seemed to adore me. I thought I was falling in love. Tommy Joe was a smoker and drinker, both of which were foreign to me, but somehow made him seem more exciting and desirable.

I lived at home with my parents and he lived with his elderly mother, so all our alone time was spent in his Lincoln. Tommy Joe felt badly about his impotency, but I told him it did not matter. I enjoyed his company, and reveled in the attention from this strangely different, quiet, deep-voiced, tall, and lanky stranger.

After we had dated for a while, a local pastor asked me to work for his church as the youth and music minister. This was the job I had dreamed of! I would be able to move into an apartment and start living my own life doing what I loved. But I knew that if I committed to this position in an Assembly of God church, I would have to renounce my gay associations, specifically Tommy Joe. I called him and broke the news.

"Tommy Joe," I started out. "I cannot see you anymore."

He panicked. "Randy, please don't tell me this. I love you. I need you."

"I love you too, Tommy Joe, but you know how much I have always wanted to be in ministry. I now have that chance. But to accept it, I have to repent of my homosexuality and make things right with God."

He persuaded me to meet him in the park so we could talk face-to-face. He cried and asked if his impotency was causing me to break up with him. I assured him that was not the case.

"I just cannot live a double life, Tommy Joe. Please try and understand." He was in tears.

"Randy, I hear what you are saying and I can't fight God. I know you are right in doing this, but it hurts so badly. Will you pray for me? I need to ask forgiveness too. Please pray for me."

So I prayed with Tommy Joe, and when we had finished our prayer, he assured me that he felt better. He held me tight. There was an awkward moment when I tried to pull away and he kept holding on.

"Tommy Joe, we are doing the right thing. God will help us. I have to go now."

He released me. I got in my car, and as I drove away I looked back in the rear view mirror at Tommy Joe's car and thought to myself, "This is the last time I will see him. I am free from all that is in my past. I am a new creation. Old things are passed away and all things are new." Little did I know that what we assign to the past does not always stay there.

I met with the pastor and we agreed on a salary, my hours, and duties. I really liked this pastor. He had a great sense of humor, loved people, and loved ministry. We hit it off from the beginning. He liked the fact that I had directed plays in churches and told me he hoped I would incorporate drama into worship at the church. Almost immediately I began to fall in love with the congregation. The feeling was mutual.

I found an apartment and began making plans to move. One day, while I was still living with Mom and Dad, the phone rang. I answered it, and a strange male voice that I did not recognize asked for me by name. I responded, "This is Randy."

The man propositioned me sexually. I froze! "How did you get my name and number?" I asked, my voice shaking.

"It's on every men's room wall in town," he answered sarcastically.

I slammed down the receiver. I felt I knew who was responsible for this. I was sure it was Tommy Joe. The next night my dad answered the phone. After saying hello, I watched as a disgusted look came over his face. He, too, had been propositioned. As Dad forcefully hung up the receiver, for the first time I felt murderous hatred for someone, namely Tommy Joe.

Surprisingly, my parents never suspected me. Mom, Dad, and I were driving to dinner one night when Mom asked, "I wonder how they got your name and phone number?" I pleaded ignorance.

"Well, some sick man obviously got your name and phone number from a check you wrote somewhere," Mom said.

I breathed a sigh of relief. They didn't suspect me! But as the days went by, I became more and more apprehensive each time the phone would ring. I was carrying so much inside, and there was no one to confide in. Who could I talk to about something so horrible?

Gay young people, especially those in conservative families and in rural communities, have few resources to turn to when they begin to fear or discover that they are different. I was not about to check any of the few books on the subject out of the library, fearing my interest might give me away. Paranoia is part of everyday existence when you are trying to hide your true identity. As a gay youth, you catch yourself, even in the warmest times of friendship or family gatherings, thinking, "Sure you love me and accept me now, but what if I told you who I really am? How would you feel then? Would you reject me and not want to have anything else to do with me?"

For any young person to try to find their place in life is hard enough. To be gay, especially to be gay *and* Christian, is lonely and frightening. The gay or lesbian teen has the added burden of being threatened and told they are a menace to society, a criminal, psychotic and, worst of all, an abomination to God. Is it any wonder that the number of teenage suicides is higher for gay and lesbian teens?

My world was about to crumble. Tommy Joe could destroy my reputation, my ministry and my future.

As I tried to compile a list of significant people in my life who would be prospective confessors, not one minister came to mind. The one person that kept making her way to the top of that short list was my sister. Pam would understand because she had been through so much in her marriage and divorce. She had left Ronnie because of his drinking and drug use, and was raising her two-year-old daughter alone. I had accompanied my sister the day she appeared before a judge to finalize her divorce. We had a strong bond. Maybe Pam would be sympathetic. So I called and asked if she would come by while Mom and Dad were gone for the day. Pam could tell by the quiver in my voice that something was terribly wrong and wasted no time getting there. We sat down and immediately I spilled my guts.

"Pam, I think I am…I think I…" I couldn't get the word out. I could not admit to my sister what I was so afraid of believing about myself. I had never actually spoken the words "homosexual" and "I am" in the same sentence.

"Randy, what is it?" Pam asked, a worried look clouding her face.

"Pam, I don't know if I can tell you this."

"Randy, you can tell me anything. You've been there for me. I want to be here for you."

"I…I think I'm a homosexual."

There it was. As soon as I said it, I wanted to take back the words. I was too naked, too vulnerable for rejection. As long as I didn't speak it, I could live in a sort of denial because no one else was there to confirm it. Now I had said it and there was no taking the confession back. Pam was shocked. "What?" she asked.

"I don't know. I think I might be a homosexual, Pam."

"Randy, what makes you think that?"

"I don't know. Well, I do know. I am attracted to men. Pam, I don't like girls in that way I like guys. I know it sounds horrible. I have been carrying this secret inside for so long and I had to tell someone. I trust you, Pam. You are the only one I felt wouldn't reject me."

Pam had a frightened look on her face. "Have you had any sexual experiences with men?"

"Yes, I have." I began to cry. "I feel dirty. I am ashamed to tell you this Pam. I have fought and fought these feelings, but they won't go away. I have prayed and begged God to heal me. I hate what I am. I don't want to be like this. And now there is this older man who I was seeing before I got the job at the church. He knows Mom and Dad's phone number and has been writing it on the walls in men's restrooms around town. He is angry because I broke up with him."

"Oh no!" she gasped. "Randy, I don't believe you are really a homosexual. I think it's just the repressive church we were raised in. You haven't given girls a chance. You just need to date more. Don't give into this. I love you and want you to be happy, and you *can* be. It will be all right. We will get through this. I'm here for you."

At this we both began to cry. The next day she drove me to restrooms around town that I knew were meeting places for gays. I found my name and my parent's phone number on the dingy walls. I took a magic marker and crossed out the information. The phone calls stopped. I thought I was in the clear.

Then one night at two a.m., I awoke to someone knocking on my bedroom door. It was my mom.

"Randy, there is a strange man on the phone who says he wants to speak to you."

I jumped out of bed, instantly in a panic, and threw on my robe. On my way, I made a calculated decision to go to the phone beside my parent's bed. Had I gone to the one in the other part of the house, I knew my mother would have listened in on the conversation. I had a good idea who was calling. My sweaty hand took the phone from Mother. She looked troubled. I slowly raised the phone to my ear.

"Hello?"

"Faggot!" the drunken voice of my stalker shouted, and then the line went dead. I felt faint. I almost dropped the phone.

"Who was it?" Mom asked.

"I don't know. There was no one there."

I walked back to my room in a zombie state. I crawled into bed and covered myself as I lay in a fetal position, tears streaming down my face. I had finally found my calling. I was working in a church I loved, for a pastor I loved, was soon to get my first apartment, and yet my secret life was about to cancel out all the good that had come to me. I prayed: "Jesus, if you will protect me and not let anyone find out about this, I promise I will never do it again. Please God, make Tommy Joe stop tormenting me. Oh God, please help me! Change me. Make me normal. Jesus, you opened blinded eyes and made the lame to walk, even raised the dead. Surely you can take away my attraction to men. I want so badly to please you. I want to be your servant. Please protect me from my past."

God's Spirit gave me rest that night. I drifted back to sleep. The next morning the call seemed like a bad dream. Mom and Dad talked about getting a new phone number. I hated that my actions were causing them this inconvenience.

Several weeks later, I moved into a studio apartment and felt like I was finally on my own. I brought home a paycheck that allowed me to pay my bills and have a little left over. Work was going well, too. The church had land behind the building, so I came up with the idea of producing an outdoor passion play about the life, death, and resurrection of Christ. After I wrote the script, the men in the church built the necessary structures along a natural rise on the hillside directly behind the church. They worked after they got off their jobs until sundown. The women cooked meals for us and started sewing costumes for the actors. Everyone got more and more excited as our project began to take shape.

The media found out about what we were doing, and we started getting lots of free advertising. I was interviewed on the local morning television news programs, and both hometown papers sent reporters to take pictures and write stories about the play. We sent letters to every Assemblies of God church in Arkansas.

Unbelievable crowds came the two nights we performed the play. Bus loads of church people came to see our production. The folks at the church were overjoyed at the success of the event. I felt that God had heard my prayer.

One Sunday the pastor was out of town, so I was to preach and perform his duties. As I was delivering the sermon, I noticed a middle-aged woman at the back of the sanctuary whom I had never seen before. She seemed to smile at me every time we made eye contact.

At the end of the service, I asked those who needed special prayer to come forward. Several responded, including the visitor. When I came to her, I quietly asked what her need was. She looked up at me, and when her eyes met mine she whispered, "Tommy Joe really misses you. Please call him."

Bam! Did she ever drop a bombshell! This woman knew.

Tommy Joe was telling others. I choked out a generic prayer of blessing and she stood and walked back to her seat. I followed her with my eyes and, in that moment, I was totally unaware of my surroundings. I was lost in my own terrible, tormenting thoughts.

The next Sunday the stranger was back, and the next, and the next. Each Sunday, she stared a hole right through me as I sat on the platform. I continued to pray for God's protection. One day, the church secretary told me I had a call. When I answered it, I heard that familiar deep raspy voice of my tormentor.

"Randy, this is Tommy Joe."

"Yes, I know." I responded curtly.

"Randy, please I need to see you so badly. "

"Tommy Joe, you have some nerve calling me at church after the hell you have put me through. You think I would want to see you after you wrote my parents' phone number on bathroom walls and called my parents' house at two in the morning?" Although it was quiet, my whisper had a lot of force behind it.

"I am sorry Randy, I am truly sorry. I was out of my mind with missing you. Life has become unbearable for me. I miss sharing time with you." He was crying.

"Tommy Joe, I am so sorry. I care for you, but you know the reasons I had to break it off. Now, if you really do love me, you will stop calling me. And please, tell your lady friend not to come to church and torment me anymore. The one thing I have always wanted the most in my life has happened. I have a place to minister. Don't destroy this for me, please. Don't keep hurting me this way. I beg you. Just leave me alone."

There was a long pause. I heard sniffling. "All right Randy, I do love you enough to let you go. I won't cause you any more embarrassment. You will never hear from me again."

"Thank you Tommy Joe. I…I'm sorry. I'm sorry I hurt you."

CLICK!

Tommy Joe kept his word. Although I saw his car from time to time, which caused my heart to race with fear, he never called me again.

Chapter 11

Stepping Out of the Closet

I worked for the church for one year and abstained from any pursuit of male sexual contact. But the fantasies were still haunting me. As I approached my first year anniversary of working for the church, the pastor resigned. I was devastated. During the two months it took to find a replacement, I performed the duties of pastor as well as youth and music minister. My plate was full! I was glad when the church filled the position. Unfortunately, the man they elected was different than the former pastor. We tried to work together, but it became clear that we had different approaches to ministry. When I offered my resignation, he accepted it.

Unsure of what to do next, I headed for Warren and Grandma McCain's house. She always had a way of helping me believe in the calling God had placed on my life. I always arrived at Grandma's weary and discouraged, but I left feeling that, with her prayers behind me, I could fight the largest giant and win.

I stayed about two weeks at Grandma's house and got my spiritual batteries recharged, then headed back to Little Rock. Eventually, I took a position as publicity coordinator for Teen Challenge, a Christian drug rehabilitation program. I found the ministry part of the position appealing, yet my duties were more a desk job than hands-on ministry. Moreover, I was wrestling with my need to know more about my sexual orientation. The conflict between who I was spiritually and sexually was all consuming, and apparently affected my ability to concentrate on my new position. A few months later the director said that I needed to make plans to leave the ministry.

I was unemployed again. Nothing seemed to work out for me. I started feeling anger and resentment toward the church because I could not find help within its walls. I became disillusioned with ministry. Why would I want to give my life to preaching a message of good news when it did not apply to me personally? Although I prayed and prayed, I still had the same sexual desires for men and did not believe this was likely to change.

My disillusionment drove me to seek out people who were like me. At least they would not judge me. The only place I had met any other gay person was the park, so I headed back to see if this time I could meet and talk with others who were struggling with their sexuality and see how they were coping.

On one outing I met Donnie. I was sitting on a picnic table reading a book and a young man roared up on his motorcycle. He stopped, took off his helmet, and said, "Hey there, what're you reading?"

"Just a book of plays."

"Are you an actor?"

"Well, I would like to be. I have done some plays in my home church, but I really love the theatre."

"You live around here?" Recalling my situation with Tommy Joe, I realized that I had better not give out any personal information.

"No," I lied, "I am from Florida."

"Florida? So why do you have Arkansas tags on your car?"

Busted! I had to think quickly. "Well, I'm here visiting my aunt and uncle and this is their car."

"Oh, okay." He still sounded a little suspicious. "My name is Donnie, what's yours?"

Once again, I panicked. I was afraid to give out too much information, so again I lied. "My name is George."

"George?" Donnie asked, "You don't look like a George. I had a monkey named George."

"Well, that's my name."

"Okay, George, you want to come over to my place for a while and hang out?"

I was pretty sure that Donnie was gay. I didn't have a name for it then, but I was beginning to discover my inner "gay-dar," or that innate ability some gay people have to recognize each other. Donnie was inviting me to his house. I would see how gay people actually live. I told him yes and we left the park.

I followed him in my "uncle's" car until arriving at his apartment. We walked in, and Donnie asked if I wanted something to drink. I asked him what he had. He said he had beer, or mixed drinks or Coke.

"Coke will be fine. I don't drink alcohol."

"Coke it is."

While he was in the kitchen getting my soda, I looked around. Although the apartment was colorfully decorated, Donnie was not one of those interior designer gays. The furnishings were sparse, and the pictures on the wall appeared to be Las Vegas show girls. "What's that about?" I wondered.

Donnie returned with my Coke. We sat on the couch and he started the conversation. "So, I don't remember ever seeing you at the bar."

"Oh, I've never been to a bar."

"You're gay?"

"I think so."

"And you've *never* been to a gay bar?"

"I haven't been to any kind of bar. I've never had an alcoholic drink."

"Well, you could still go to the bar to dance."

"I don't do that either. The church I was raised in doesn't think it's right to drink or dance."

"So what are you, a preacher?" Donnie jested.

"Actually, I…I *used* to be."

"Really?! I was just kidding about that. So why aren't you a preacher now?"

"I don't know what to tell you. I guess because …well because…"

Donnie could see I was having a hard time explaining. "Because you're gay, right?"

"I…I don't know for sure…but I, well I *think* I might be gay."

"Are you into guys or are you into girls?"

"I have dated girls."

"Oh, well, we've all done that. That's not what I asked you. Are you into guys, attracted to them, turned on by a guy?"

"I…I think I am."

"Well let me ask you this. Are you turned on by *me*?"

I didn't answer. Donnie moved closer to me on the couch and took my hand in his.

"Does this feel right to you?"

My palms were sweating. I was shaking. My heart beat so fast I was afraid I was going to pass out. Then Donnie leaned in closer and his lips moved toward mine. I wanted him to kiss me. Of course I was gay. Yes, I was turned on by men. At this moment, I was really turned on by Donnie's gentleness. He was not pawing at me like the other strangers I had been with. He acted like he cared about me. I kissed back. For the first time I was feeling things I had always wanted to feel for a girl. There was romance in the air and in my jeans. We kissed and kissed. Donnie loved to cuddle and kiss. I was in heaven!

We started seeing each other as often as we could. I tried to find a job not associated with ministry. I took a position at a department store, but still had not told Donnie that I lied to him about where I was from and my name. We frequently met at a certain spot in North Little Rock, going to a secluded spot in his van and making out. On one date, I started feeling guilty for lying to Donnie. As we held each other, I confessed.

"Donnie, I need to tell you something. I haven't been totally honest with you."

"Okay, fess up, George. What have you lied to me about?"

"I am not really from Florida. I live here."

"OK, is that all you've lied about?"

"No, I…I lied about my name."

"So you aren't George? I knew you didn't look like a George! Tell me, what is your real name?"

The flashbacks of Tommy Joe struck fear in my heart. There was a voice inside me that was screaming not to tell him my name.

"I need to tell you why I haven't been honest with you. There was this guy who I met at the park. I told him my name and…"

I told him the whole Tommy Joe saga. "So that is why I can't tell you my real name. I still don't know you very well, and I have a real hard time trusting anyone."

Donnie looked hurt. "Look, we haven't known each other that long, but give me a break. I would never do that to you. That is not the kind of person I am. Can't you tell that about me?"

"Donnie, you seem like a really nice guy. You just have to understand that I am really gun-shy. I am scared to death and very unsure."

Donnie reached out and grabbed me. "I promise you. I *promise* you I will never purposely hurt you. I really like you and I want us to get to know each other better, but how can we, if you won't even tell me your real name?"

"Okay. I'll tell you. My name is Randy."

"Randy? I like that name. You look more like a Randy than a George."

I laughed and the tension broke. We kissed. Donnie whispered in my ear, "Randy WHAT?"

"What?" I asked.

"What is your last name?"

"Isn't it enough that I have told you my first name? Please, don't ask me for my last name. I *will* tell you, but not tonight."

Donnie was quiet for a moment, and then he pulled away from me. We straightened our clothing and buttoned up our clothes, riding back in silence. When we got to my car, I got in and started to pull out of the parking lot. As I did, Donnie spun around his van and suddenly blocked my exit. He stopped in front of me, jumped out of the van, and came to my window.

"Look Randy, if you don't tell me your last name, I will go and look up your license plate number to see what name the car is registered under. I am a dispatcher at the police department and I can do that, you know, so you might as well tell me. I will find out one way or the other."

I parked the car, got out and walked over to him. "My name is Randy McCain."

"Randy, don't lie to me again!"

Then I realized we were standing in the parking lot of the local mall—*McCain Mall*. I could see how it must look to Donnie.

"No, honestly, it really is my last name."

"Sure it is, Randy McCain Mall! Come on Randy, stop playing games."

When I pulled out my driver's license he finally believed me. We later laughed about the whole last name incident.

We continued dating. The times we had together were precious. I was in love and wanted to shout it to the world. Yet I had to keep it all pent up inside. I had never written a love song before, but one day I sat down at the piano and wrote one for Donnie:

Time moves so swiftly when we are together.
We have so little time to make believe together.
Hours that pass so slowly when we are apart
Speed past us quickly,
Leaving only seconds to say goodbye.
Time moves so slowly when we are far apart.
Each day's an eternity that lasts forever in my heart.
Still I'm glad for what we have.
These times we spend together
Make all my forevers a little easier to bear.
Where has the time gone?
Where has it been?
Where is it going?
Is she our friend?

Chapter 12

Drag Queens and Gay Bars

One day I asked Donnie about the show girls' pictures on the wall of his living room.

"Those are drag queens, Randy."

"What are drag queens?" I asked.

"They are guys that dress up as women and perform at the bar."

"You mean those two beautiful women are really men?"

"Yes they are…willies and all!"

"You have got to be kidding me!"

"No, Randy," Donnie laughed. "They are men dressed like women. I swear."

"Even that one right there?" I pointed to a blond bombshell.

"That is Bobby Holiday. Beautiful, isn't she? But you ought to see her out of drag! She makes a much prettier woman than a man. Would you like to meet her? She lives in this apartment complex."

"I don't know if I am ready for this just yet, Donnie."

"I'll call her. I think she's home today."

He picked up the phone. In just a few minutes there was a knock at the door, and the guy that walked in looked nothing like the woman in the picture. He had oily, unkempt long hair, a two-day growth of beard, and what appeared to be breasts under his dirty sweatshirt.

"Randy, meet Miss Bobby Holiday. Girl, you are a wreck! You look like you've been rode hard and put up wet!"

"I've been working on my car." It was then that Bobby noticed me.

"And who is this cutie? Hi there!"

"Hello," I answered awkwardly. I stood there looking at this rough looking character and then at the picture hanging on the wall, trying to imagine how this creature standing in front of me could look like that!

"So Bobby," Donnie asked, "why don't you stop by tonight before you leave for the bar and let Randy see your transformation? He's never met a real live drag queen before."

"Really?" Bobby cooed, looking at me in a seductive way. "Okay, I'll be back later."

The doorbell rang about two hours later. Donnie said, "Randy, would you get the door?" I opened it and there stood the beautiful woman in the picture.

"Well, aren't you going to invite me in?"

The gruff voice gave him away. It was the same guy I had met earlier that afternoon. I was in awe. There were women who would kill for those legs. Bobby asked if I was coming to the show that night.

"No, we have other plans tonight, Bobby."

Bobby started for the door. "It was nice meeting you Randy. Don't be a stranger!"

Donnie went to let him out, and Bobby leaned into him, whispering loud enough for me to hear, "Honey, he's hot!" Bobby disappeared into the night.

"That is amazing! The transformation is incredible. I think he could fool a lot of guys."

"Oh believe me, he has," Donnie assured me.

I was getting an education. Donnie was a good teacher. The whole gay slang thing was another language to me. Terms like *read your beads* meant, "I am about to give you a piece of my mind!" *Trick* meant a one-night stand. *Old Troll* meant an old guy out looking for younger men. *Cruising* meant guys looking for a guy to hook up with for the night. Donnie actually worked an extra job at the bar as a waiter, so he had seen it all. He enjoyed helping with my transition into the gay world. I had lived such a sheltered life, and this new world was both strange and exciting. Even though Donnie tried his best to get me to go to the bar with him, I always said no.

"Why won't you go, Randy? I'll stay by your side and you'll be safe with me."

"If I go to a gay bar and see someone I know from church, I would just die!" I protested.

"But Randy, if they are there too, how could they say anything against you?"

"I just can't take that risk. I can't let my parents or anyone from the church find out."

"Okay. I understand."

Donnie did not pressure me anymore. Eventually, we saw less and less of each other because of my desire to stay in the closet. Donnie was as out as anyone could be. Even though he was good to me, and patient, Donnie needed someone who could share his life more openly. We parted friends.

When I started going back to the park, I noticed many young gay guys there were just hanging out together. One day, I forced myself to walk over to where they were congregated. I introduced myself to a couple of them and they introduced me to the others. They became my friends. We were not involved sexually, but just enjoyed joking around and talking about which guys we found attractive and which movie actors we thought were sexy.

Being with those guys was a liberating experience for me. For the first time, I could use the right pronoun when talking about someone I found attractive. Liking guys felt so natural. Eventually, the gang asked me to accompany them to a gay bar. At first I protested, but then I threw caution to the wind and said, "Okay, let's do it!"

We arrived at the bar early and hardly anyone was there. I was to find out later that things did not really get started until around eleven at night. As we walked in, I was immediately aware of the unusually musty, damp scent, the heavy fog of cigarette smoke, and low and intimate lighting. Disco music blared so loudly that we had to lean forward and yell into each other's ear to talk. We walked to the bar and sat down. As my eyes tried to adjust to the dim lighting, I heard a familiar voice.

"Well, look who's here. It's *the preacher*!" I turned to see Donnie, waiting tables, tray in hand.

"Hey there, Donnie. So, you really do work at the bar."

"Yes I do, but I didn't think I would ever see *you* in here. What changed your mind?"

"I guess my curiosity finally got the best of me."

"Seen anyone you know from church?"

"Not yet," I answered. "But we haven't been here long."

Donnie was proud of me taking another step on my journey. All night long, he would come up behind and warn me about certain men.

"Stay away from *that* one. He is bad news."

As the bar filled up with patrons, I was amazed at how many gay people there were in Little Rock. I was also astonished at how many different personality types I saw. Many of the men did not look gay. Then there were the real effeminate gays, and the older men with big bellies, some of whom had really bad hair pieces. All ages were represented. Some guys were dressed in business suits, and some in cowboy outfits with the hat and leather chaps. The most popular attire was tight Calvin Klein jeans with a pastel Izod shirt and cowboy boots. When the bartender came over and asked what we were drinking, I was at a loss for words. I didn't know beer from wine or margaritas from screwdrivers. One of my buddies said, "Order a beer, Randy." So I ordered a beer.

"Bottle or draft?" the bartender asked. I was stumped. How could a beer be drafted? One of my friends realized my dilemma.

"He'll have a bottle of Miller."

When the beer arrived, I took a small swig. It tasted awful! I suppose I thought beer would taste like soda pop, but was I ever surprised. I made a face.

The guys saw it, and one of them said, "It always tastes bad the first time. Just keep forcing the first one down. By the time you drink the second beer, it will taste better, I promise."

I followed his advice and the second beer did taste better. As the night went on, the place got more crowded. Donnie told me I needed to mingle. So, I fell into the constantly moving parade that walked around the bar. As I passed one group, some-one pinched my butt. I didn't dare look around to see who, not until I was a safe distance away. When I did turn around to sneak a peek, my heart jumped up into my throat. My worst nightmare had come true. I knew the pincher! The guy was from my church! His name screamed in my head louder than the pulsating beat of the dance music: Joey Santos! I immediately bolted for the door, ran to my car and tore out of the parking lot.

As I sped away, I began running scenarios through my head of Joey telling all the guys at church about seeing me at the gay bar. I hated myself for letting those guys talk me into going with them. I should have listened to that inner voice that had warned me that this would happen! As I drove, I began to calm down and stopped gulping for air. If Joey was there, Joey was gay. I had heard that Joey and his wife were getting a divorce. No one seemed to know why. Now it started to make sense. Joey was gay! Suddenly, I wanted to talk with him. Finally there was someone like me in so many ways, someone I could identify with. Joey had been raised in the Assemblies of God and must have struggled the same way I had. I turned the car around and headed back, rushing back into the bar. Joey was standing right where he had been when I left. I walked over to him and he greeted me.

"Randy, where did you get off to? It's so good to see you. So you're gay, too?"

"Yes I am, Joey." I screamed over the music. "I just didn't know about you."

"I never suspected you either. Hey, you want to get out of here and go for coffee?"

I was glad to get away from the loud music so I could actually hear myself think. We went to a nearby Denny's restaurant and talked for hours, sharing horror sto-ries of the guilt and struggle we had gone through. Joey and I had never been close before, but now we were sharing experiences. The friendship that started that night continued for many years. We were never sexually intimate. Regardless of what many think, gay people are *not* always having sex with one another. Joey and I became like brothers. I was there for him and he was there for me, many times.

A few years after our meeting, Joey discovered that he was HIV-positive. As his health deteriorated, he ended up a resident of a depressing nursing home. I visited him and grieved for my dear friend. He died and became another AIDS statistic, but to me, he was so much more. Joey was one of many friends that I would lose to that horrible disease. But that night in 1980, sitting in the coffee shop, I was glad that finally I had found someone who understood. I miss Joey. I know he is at peace, but I weep for the sadness he endured here on earth.

Randy, the Entertainer

Chapter 13

My Life as an Actor

I met a young guy named Ricky at the bar and we became friends. He, too, had an Assemblies of God background. We had not attended the same church, but we both had received the same spiritual teaching about the sinfulness of being gay.

Ricky was shy but a good piano player. One night, while I was visiting him at his home, he sat down at the piano and asked me to sing. He played and I sang until late into the night.

"You know, Randy, you should go try out for the shows at the local dinner theatre. They are holding auditions Monday night for the musical *Oklahoma*. I'll go along and play for you, if you want."

Here was my first chance to do professional theatre! I had been enchanted with the stage from the time I was a boy and Daddy took me to a high school production of Lloyd C. Douglas' *The Robe*, a story about the soldier who crucified Christ and then became a follower of Jesus. I had always loved acting.

I jumped at the chance to live out my fantasy of being a professional actor. The audition went so well I received a call informing me that I had been chosen to be in the chorus. The commitment was for two weeks of rehearsal during the day and the show would run every night (except Monday) and twice on Sundays for six weeks. The pay was $50 per week for the two rehearsal weeks, and $100 per week for the run of the show. It was not a lot, but I would be getting paid to do something I loved! Plus, being in the shows at the dinner theatre gave me a little bit of star status at the gay bars, which sure didn't hurt my chance of getting dates.

The rehearsal time was fun, as I learned a lot about the behind-the-scenes activity that makes a play successful. I also found that there were other gay actors in the show who made no secret about their sexuality. The theatre is a safe place to be gay. There are no disapproving looks if a guy mentions his boyfriend. I fell in love with the theatre community. Admittedly, being in the chorus was a minor role, but, as they say in the theatre, "There are no small roles, only small actors." I worked hard, learning my vocal parts, words to the songs, and dance moves. I couldn't wait for each practice to begin!

We opened *Oklahoma* and the crowds loved us. That first opening night there was a certain excitement about standing backstage, smelling the fresh paint of the set, seeing the lights through the curtain, and hearing the audience as they quieted down and awaited the opening scene. Then the overture began and it was show time! I never tired of that intoxicating moment.

And speaking of intoxication, it was during the run of the play that I got drunk for the very first time at a cast party at the home of one of the actors. After we danced and sang our hearts out on stage, I was tired and thirsty. I headed straight for the food table after I arrived at the party. It was loaded with lots of salty snacks and a big bowl of punch in the middle of the table, surrounded by big red plastic party cups. I filled my cup to the brim. It tasted like Hawaiian Punch, which I loved. I was so thirsty that, when I took my first swig, I could not stop drinking until I had emptied my cup. I quickly filled it up again.

By the time I was on my third, I suddenly started feeling this strange sensation. The room was spinning and I became aware of how hot and stuffy the air was. I thanked my host for inviting me and made an excuse to leave. I wanted to get home, but I had trouble driving. My friend Jerry lived close by, so I headed for his place. When he saw me, he noticed right away that I didn't look well.

"What is wrong with you Randy?"

"I don't know. Everything seems to be spinning."

"What did you drink at the cast party?"

"Just some Hawaiian Punch."

"Randy that *punch* was spiked. You're drunk!"

I later found out that I had been drinking PGA punch. The PGA stands for "pure grain alcohol." When it is added to a sweet drink it has no flavor of its own, but it will make you forget your own name. Jerry quickly put me to bed. He was kind the next morning when I woke up with the worst headache of my life.

Chapter 14

Mom Opens the Closet Door

With the play at the dinner theatre, and the attention I was receiving at the local bar, my life was exciting and pleasurable, for the most part. Only one major storm cloud on the horizon—my parents. They had become concerned by my absence from church and my new friends. I had a feeling they might be putting two and two together. I went to see my sister Pam and told her that I suspected that Mom and Dad were getting ready to ask the big question.

"What makes you think so, Randy?"

"I don't know. I just have this feeling. It really scares me to think how they will react."

"What are you going to tell them?"

"I am not going to lie to them about it, Pam. I have decided that I will not voluntarily come out to them, but if they ask, I will tell them the truth."

Pam was concerned. If anyone else in the world could empathize with me in this situation, it was Pam. She knew how outraged Mom and Dad would be. Pam, a single mother with a four-year-old daughter, assured me that I could always come and stay with her for a while if I needed to.

"They probably will kick me out of the house. I need to get a place of my own. I'll start looking right away." (I had moved back in with Mom and Dad when I could no longer pay my rent.)

A week later, on a Sunday night when my parents should have been leaving for church, I was in the bathroom styling my hair and preparing for a night at the bar. Dad knocked on the door.

"Son, your mom and I want to talk with you out in the den."

A chill went through my body. "Here it comes," I thought.

I walked into the den and my mother was sitting there, holding a piece of paper. I sat down in an atmosphere heavy with doom and gloom.

"Mom, Dad said you wanted to talk to me."

"Where are you going tonight?" she asked.

"Just over to a friend's house."

"Why have you stopped attending church?"

"I don't know. I am just going through a really confusing time in my life."

She stood, walked over to me, and handed me the piece of paper she had been holding. It was a bulletin from a church I had attended with friends. It was obvious from the bulletin that it was a gay-friendly church.

"What does this mean? I found it in your bedroom."

"I went to visit the church with a friend."

"Randy, that church is for homosexuals. Why did *you* go there?"

At this point I still wanted to give my parents a chance to back out of this really serious confrontation. So I hedged. "I have friends who are gay."

Then Mom, never one to beat around the bush, got right to the point. "That's not what I'm asking. Randy. I want to know." Her voice was quivering with emotion. "Have you had homosexual experiences?" There it was. She really wanted to go there.

"Yes. I have."

I have no words to explain how vulnerable I felt at that moment in front of my parents. Even though I was trying to "come out" as a gay man, I had a lot of unresolved issues and internalized homophobia. My parents represented God to me in many ways. At that moment, I saw myself through their eyes and I hated what they were seeing. I also felt that they were mirroring God's emotions, God's disappointment. At the same time, I was angry that they had asked me such an intimate question.

Mother started repeating over and over, "No! No! No! No! No!"

My dad put his head in his hands and moaned loudly. I wanted to run, to get as far away from them as I could. Then Mom resumed her interrogation.

"No Randy, tell me this isn't true. You are just making this up."

"Mother, why in the world would I do that?"

"I don't know…to hurt us I guess."

"Mother, I don't want to hurt you and Daddy, honest. I am just telling you the truth."

She kept saying over and over, "Why, why God, Why? I gave you this boy when he was born…I tried to raise him right…why, why, why? What did we do wrong?" Then she got personal.

"Randy, how could you have chosen this? You looked around and found the worst sin in the world, and you chose *this* to show your open rebellion to us and to God."

Her words really angered me. I didn't know why I was gay, but knew I had not chosen these feelings. Up until this point I felt sorry for her, but now I was angry. How could she make this all about her, with no thought of what I had been going through for years?

"Yes, Mother, you are right. I looked at all the sins in the world and I chose the worst one. I considered murder for a moment, but then, I went right for the top!"

I stopped in the middle of my tirade, and desperately tried to explain myself. "First of all, I did not *choose* this. This is who I am. Secondly, I am not so sure this is a sin."

"Oh Randy, how could you believe such a lie? I don't believe for one minute that you could see this as anything but a sin. You are not stupid, and you have the Holy Spirit in your life. You know what sin is, and this is one of the worst. God destroyed whole cities because of it. If you can't see that, then Satan has seared your conscience and blinded you to the truth of God's word!"

Dad was quiet up until this moment. "Son", he said, we want to get you help."

"Help? What kind of help?"

"Help in getting out of this terrible lifestyle."

At that moment I felt as though they were seeing me like some diseased animal. All the anger at life, at myself, at all those who judged me, erupted.

"I don't want your help! I tried to be what *you* consider normal. It didn't work! And now, for the first time in my life, I have friends that don't judge me for being who I am. They accept me just for me. I am gay, Mom and Dad, gay! You wanted the truth. Well, that is the truth. Your son is gay!"

Mom began quoting scripture about how God gave them over to vile affections where the men started lusting after each other. She quoted the Old Testament passage about not lying with a man as with a woman.

"Oh God, my own son! How could this happen? It was that dinner theatre, wasn't it? That's what turned you this way."

I had to laugh at this. Mom was trying to receive vindication for all the years she had tried to keep us from that theatre.

"Son, you need help," Dad pleaded, "Let us help you."

I jumped up. "No, I don't want your help! I am finally to the place where I am making some sense of my life. Dad, if you and Mom can't accept that I am gay, then just forget that you even have a son!"

With that, I headed for my room to get my jacket. Mother followed me to the bedroom door.

"Randy, son, don't leave. Please don't leave."

"Mom, I have to. I am not going to stay here and have you and Daddy judge and condemn me!"

"Randy, please, don't go to your homosexual friends," she cried. "Your dad says that they are very bad people."

"Is my father gay?"

Mother was stunned by this question. "No, of course not!"

"Does he even know any gay people?"

"No."

"Then how would he know what gay people are like?"

I hurried past both of them and stormed out to the car. I peeled my tires out of the driveway, leaving behind two very distraught parents to sort through what had just happened. Where could I go? I headed for Pam's house. When she opened the door, I did not have to tell her; she instinctively knew. I could no longer hold back the tears. She put her arm around me and led me into the living room. We talked until I was so tired I could not put sentences together, and she let me spend the night. I pulled the covers around me for comfort and thanked God that at least I had one family member who was there for me.

The following days were dark for the McCain family. I thought my mom was going to have a nervous breakdown. I felt relieved when she told me that she was going to see a therapist. I hoped that he could help her see that my sexual orientation did not have to be such a devastating revelation. Then she asked if I would talk to her therapist.

"But Mother, I don't feel that I need a therapist. I think it is good that you are going, but I…"

"Just do it for me, Randy. Please."

I gave in to her request. Perhaps something I could tell him would help with my mother's treatment. What I didn't know was that she was telling me half-truths. When I sat down, the therapist greeted me, opened a folder, then looked up and took off his glasses.

"So, you are Randy McCain."

"Yes, sir."

"Randy, you seem to be closed off to me. You are sitting there with your arms tightly crossed. Usually that is a sign that you feel you have something to hide. Let me assure you that you can be totally open here with me. This is a safe place."

I had taken counseling classes before and knew all about the "body language" theories. This guy was talking psychobabble.

"No, I have nothing to hide. It's just cold in here."   He immediately jumped up and adjusted the thermostat, then sat back down, somewhat flustered.

"So Randy, what seems to be the trouble at home?"

"Well, I'm sure my mother has told you that I am gay and she doesn't approve, and now she is about to have a nervous breakdown." The therapist looked surprised.

"I haven't even met your mother. She has told me nothing."

"What?" I had been set up! Later, I found out that mother had gone to a family counseling center and asked specifically for a "born again" Christian counselor. The counseling was not for her.

"Look sir, I do not believe it is possible for me to change who I am, and I know I did not choose to be gay. I just happen to be gay, the same way I just *happen* to have brown eyes and *happen* to be right-handed. I am not the one who needs therapy. You should be talking to my mother."

The counselor shifted in his seat. "There are reparative therapy techniques to change a person's sexual orientation, but the person must desire to change."

"I've heard a little about those therapies, sir—electric shock treatments, where you wire my genitals for electrical shocks administered when showing me pictures of naked men."

"Well, that is only one form of therapy. There are other, less dramatic treatments."

"Forget it. If you want to help me learn to be a happy, well-adjusted gay man, then we can talk. Otherwise, there is no reason for me to see you. But now my mom, *she* is the one who desperately needs help."

The counselor asked questions about my life. I was still angry at being coerced into being there under false pretenses.

"Wait a minute. If you are going to ask me questions, then can I ask you a few?"

"Sure, what do you want to know?"

"Are you from Arkansas?"

"Yes, I am."

"Are you married?"

"Yes."

"Any kids?"

"Yes, I have a boy who is eight from my first marriage, and a four-year-old girl by my present wife. Now, Randy, let's talk about you."

"Well, I am from Arkansas, and I am not married and I have no kids. I am a Christian and I have been in ministry. I have also worked as an actor."

"So you say you are a Christian, and yet you tell me that you are gay? How is that possible? Are you aware that being gay is a sin?"

Now I was really angry.

"Well sir, obviously you are *not* a professional therapist. If you were, you would not be sitting there in judgment of me. How dare you judge me! I didn't come here today to hear a sermon!"

Then I had one of those inspired moments when just the right words come at just the right time.

"Sir, didn't you tell me that you have been married before?"

He looked puzzled. "Yes."

"So did your first wife die of cancer, or was she killed in a car accident?"

"She didn't die, we divorced."

"And then you married your present wife?"

"Yes. We've been married for five years."

"So let me ask you this. Are you a Christian, sir?"

"Yes, I am."

"You are telling me that you are a Christian and a divorcee who has remarried?"

"Yes, I am."

"Are you aware that there are many churches that would tell you that you are living in a perpetual state of sin because you are divorced and remarried? There are many ministers who would tell you that you are committing adultery every time you have sex with your present wife, because, in the eyes of God, you are still married to your first wife."

The counselor was visibly shaken.

"Well, as a matter of fact, my wife and I recently had to change churches because of the divorce issue."

"And you have the audacity to sit there and point a finger of judgment at me, and tell me that I am going to hell for being gay? Physician, heal thyself!"

He did not know what to say next. He opened his folder again and shuffled some more of his papers.

"Well, I see we have gotten off on the wrong foot here. Let's try again. If you don't want to change your orientation, then what do you want me to help you with? What is your greatest obstacle right now in life?"

"I don't know what I really want to do occupationally. All I have ever wanted to do is be in ministry. I have worked in churches and I have traveled as an evangelist and singer. I love the theatre, but it is hard to make a living there. I am working right now at a clothing store, trying to save enough money to move out of my parent's house."

"Well, maybe we should look into ways in which you can start taking charge of your life."

"That would be a good thing, sir."

The session was over. There would only be two more. At the end of our third session, the counselor looked me in the eye and said,

"You know, Randy, I think we are just wasting your mom's money. She wants me to wave a magic wand and change you. You don't want to change. I have come to see that your main problem is one of finding where you fit into life as a gay man, a gay *Christian* man. I think you are truly the first gay Christian I have ever met. I am going to tell your mother that I have done all that I can do for you. Best wishes in the future, young man."

I went home and told Mom what the counselor had said. She was livid and wanted her money back! It was another month before I was able to locate a place to live. During that time, Mother asked me some bizarre questions. One day she informed me that she had been "reading up" on homosexual men.

"I read a book that says that there are two ways homosexual men have sex. Which one do you do?"

I was shocked! My mother never talked about sex. I wanted to ask her what out-of-date book she had been reading, but good sense prevailed.

"Mother, I have never asked you what you and Daddy do in the bedroom and I expect the same respect from you."

"That's the problem with you and me, Randy. We don't respect one another. We need to find some way to understand each other. I am so worried about you."

"Mother, don't worry about me. I am fine. You need to worry about yourself."

"A mother always worries about her children. I am worried about your eternal soul, Randy."

"Mother, let's not go there," I said, walking out of the room.

On another occasion, right after we had finished eating Sunday lunch, Mother asked me where I was headed.

"Over to a friend's apartment. Then we're going to go out and throw a Frisbee at the park."

I was stopped dead in my tracks by her next statement.

"Randy, your dad and I have been going through your pants pockets and we found a matchbook with the name of a bar in town. Also, there were lots of nickels, quarters, dimes, and pennies. We have decided that you are stripping at the bar and men are throwing coins at you for tips."

I was shocked that they would think I could ever get up and strip in a gay club.

First, I was much too self-conscious of my body. Second, I was insulted that she thought men would throw *coins* at me. Strippers *did* get tips in the form of *bills*—like ones, fives, or tens—but nickels, dimes and quarters?! Please! I just stared into space as I grabbed my keys and headed out the door.

I was working desperately to find a place that I could afford. I lived in an efficiency apartment before, with one room, a kitchen, and a bath, but those were all taken. One thing was certain—I had to get out as soon as possible. The clincher came one day when I walked in from work and Mom snapped at me.

"Randy, I want you out of this house by the end of the month. I can't stand it any longer. I can't stand to watch this happening to you. You are not even the same child I gave birth to, loved and nourished and brought up in the fear and admonition of God. I cannot live in this kind of atmosphere. I mean it! I want you *out*! If your daddy says that you can stay, I will divorce him! I am about to lose my mind!"

"Mom, how can you say these things to me? Don't you love me anymore?"

Then came the most painful blow of all, and I was really not expecting it.

"Randy," she said coldly, "I think my love for you has just about run out."

I was frozen for a moment in time. I forced myself to turn away and walked out to my car in a daze. I started the engine and backed out of the driveway. Then the tears burst through, and I could hardly see to drive. It was about eleven o'clock at night, and somehow I made my way to a friend's apartment. He came to the door in his robe. I told him what had happened. He put his arms around me and assured me that my mom did still love me, that she was just confused and hurt.

"Give her time, Randy. Just think, you have had to deal with this revelation for many years. She is just finding out. Think how long it took you to get to the place where you could say, 'I am gay.' Well, it is going to take your mom a long process to say, 'My son is gay.' Be patient. In the meantime, you need to get out of there and get on with your life. You have been trying too hard to bring your parents along with you on this journey. They may never join you. If they don't, then that's their decision. But you have got to stop demanding their approval and start taking responsibility for your own life! Someday your mom and dad may accept you."

"Oh no, that day will *never* come. Believe me, not with their Assembly of God beliefs. They could never accept me as gay."

"Well, Randy, you may be right, but I have a rule in life: Never say never!"

I slept on my friend's couch that night and thought about what he had said. It made a lot of sense. There *was* hope. I could not see the future. For that, God is merciful. God did not let me see the many twists and turns that awaited my family and me. Looking back from my present perspective, I see how God has worked throughout my life. It has been rough at times, but well worth the journey. And in the words of an old Happy Goodman Family southern gospel hit song, "I wouldn't take nothin' for my journey now!"

Chapter 15

Out of Control

By the early 80s, I had walked away from the church in order to embrace my sexual orientation. I was a gay man in a world that was very different from all I had known before. I looked for love without success. I seemed to attract men who would tell me what I wanted to hear, but mentally abused me. Deep inside, I felt I deserved to be punished and was not worthy of someone who would treat me with respect. I had a long series of scenarios in which I fell for a guy, moved in with him, then split up.

Pam was there for me through all of these painful episodes. One day, when I called her to pour out my heart about my latest heartbreak, she said, "Randy, I really worry about you making such a strong commitment to being gay."

"What do you mean by that, Pam?"

"If there is any way you can stop being gay, I wish you would. This life is just too painful for you. You always give your heart to a guy who eventually breaks it. This keeps happening over and over again, and I just don't know how many of these sad episodes your psyche can take!"

Part of me agreed with Pam, but I did not see any way I could be ex-gay. Then, one day I met a man who seemed to be the one I was looking for. I met Robert at the park. When he found out that I had been in ministry, Robert confided that he had been, too. He had played the piano for a traveling gospel quartet. We talked at length about our struggles as gay men and as Christians. We started seeing each other every day until one night he told me, "Randy, I want you to give up your apartment and move in with me. I really feel God has sent you to me."

I said yes.

Several friends at the bar warned that Robert was bad news, but I didn't want to hear it. They just didn't understand him the way I did. Robert had struggled in the past because he really didn't have peace with God in his heart. Now that we had found each other, he had renewed his faith. We started having devotions and even praying together. Wow! This was a dream come true for me.

The first two months we lived together were wonderful. I told my parents that I had found the man with whom I wanted to spend the rest of my life. Mother laughed in my face and told me it was a total farce.

One weekend, I got a call from my dad that Grandma McCain was visiting from out of town. He asked if I would drop by to see her. I did, and invited her and my parents over for dinner with Robert and me. My dad immediately said no. When I got home, I received a call from Dad informing me that Grandma had decided she wanted to come for dinner, but that he and Mom would not be with her. I told Dad that I would pick Grandma up. I was overjoyed!

I found out later that Grandma had told my parents that she did not approve of me living with this man, but that I was her grandson and she loved me, and she was not going to just throw me away. She did not want me to end up like Cousin Floyd.

I couldn't wait to pick Grandma up. She seemed a little uncomfortable on her arrival. Our apartment was in an old Victorian home in downtown Little Rock. As I showed Grandma through the apartment, it was obvious that we slept together, because there was only one bedroom. It must have been hard for her not to show me her disapproval. Rather, she showed me the great extent to which she would go to keep me in her life. Having Grandma at our table in our home made our relationship seem real. I was finally experiencing what it was like to have a family and a home with someone who loved me and who loved God.

After a time, Jimmy, one of Robert's childhood gay friends, who had attended church with him when they were kids, became jealous of our relationship and began sowing the seeds of destruction.

One night, as Robert and I prepared to begin our devotions, he said, "I don't think I can do this any longer, Randy. Jimmy says that it is not possible for two men to be in a relationship together and serve God at the same time. He says that what we are trying to do is blasphemous."

"But you and I love each other."

"I know," he replied.

"And we both love God. You even told me that you felt God brought me into your life."

"I know, Randy, but what Jimmy said got me thinking. I feel like a hypocrite praying with you after we have been sexual."

Though I tried to dissuade him, my arguments were not too convincing. The devotions stopped, and we tried to go on with our relationship without God being a part of it.

Things quickly went from bad to worse after Robert confessed that he had been into S&M (sadomasochism, a word that describes people who receive pleasure, especially sexual gratification, from inflicting or submitting to physical or emotional pain and abuse). This was definitely not something I found appealing. Why would anyone want to be sexually humiliated, or want to sexually humiliate anyone? That had always seemed creepy to me. Now this man, whom I thought I knew and loved, was telling me that he was into this unhealthy form of sexual expression.

I didn't know how to handle Robert's revelation. He assured me that it was okay if I was not turned on by S&M. He said he would abstain. Shortly after this revelation, I became suspicious about Robert's many nights working late, but then I would feel guilty for thinking bad things about him. I fought the urge to drive by his office to see if his car was there, until one night when I could not resist.

I was shaking as I pulled up to the empty parking spot where Robert's car *should* have been. I went back home and waited. When he arrived an hour later, I told Robert what I had done. He was enraged. How dare I question his loyalty to me! Somehow he turned the blame around and made everything *my* fault. Robert denied that he had ever been unfaithful. He added that he was so angry at me for accusing him falsely, that he didn't know whether to continue our relationship or not.

Somehow, the *cheater* convinced me that *I* was the bad guy! He made me feel so guilty that I pleaded for another chance. The next day Robert seemed totally normal. He kissed me goodbye as we went our separate ways for the day.

I had answered a newspaper ad for a job doing singing telegrams. With this job, along with my work at the dinner theatre, I started to make a modest living. I loved dressing up in a white tuxedo and going to businesses and restaurants to surprise and embarrass unsuspecting people on their birthdays or anniversaries. I seemed to be made for this type of entertainment. I even proposed in song to a few women on behalf of their boyfriends. When men had birthdays, I sometimes took along a female belly dancer to liven up the party! As time went by my boss informed me that if I would allow her to teach me Middle Eastern Dance, I could double my deliveries. She had women belly dancers for her male clients but no male belly dancers for her female customers. So I became Arkansas' first male belly dancer. My stage name was Ibrahim.

One day Robert seemed in a really bad mood. We had gone to the river that Saturday afternoon, swimming and picnicking with friends. He made it clear all day that he did not want to be seen with me. When we arrived back home, I questioned him about his behavior.

"Is it my imagination, or have you been trying to avoid me all afternoon?" There was a long pause, and then he looked at me.

"Randy, I can't do this anymore. I want to date other people."

He said the words I dreaded to hear. I wasn't enough for him. I had felt it in my gut, but I didn't want to believe it. I summoned all my courage and asked, "*Have* you been seeing other people?"

"Yes."

At that moment, my whole world caved in. I had pinned all my hopes and dreams on this relationship that was now disintegrating before my eyes and heart. I was so lost. I felt like such a fool.

Robert was tall, lean, and had a deep, sexy voice. He was well known in the gay community for his wild sexual exploits and his hot sensual body. While these things had attracted me to Robert, I wanted to love the man inside. Robert told me that he missed the accolades he had gotten from his many sexual partners. My adulation was not enough for him. He longed for the days when he had men clamoring for him. He missed the orgies and the wild S&M scenes. I felt like a fool for thinking I could have ever made him happy. He came into the bedroom and tried to say he was sorry.

"I don't want to hear that!" I screamed at him. "I was warned by everyone not to move in with you. 'He'll break your heart Randy! He's no good!' But I didn't listen to them. I believed in you. Well, I should have listened to them after all. I am such a fool!"

Suddenly, Robert was devastated—not by my pain, but by his own selfish hurt at having been talked about negatively. This wounded me even more.

I got up and went to shower off the sand from the beach and to be alone with my pain. I stood under the shower and let cool water fall on my sunburned skin. My tears blended into the river of water now cascading over me. I reminded myself that we had not even been together one year. In all my attempts at making it work with a man, I had still not been able to keep a guy for a whole year. What would it be like, I thought, not to worry about whether the two of us would be together at Christmas? What would it be like to plan a future together, to be able to count on the person I loved being there forever?

About that time I heard the door open and Robert, crying, pulled back the shower curtain.

"I'm sorry, Randy, I'm sick. I really am. I just can't say no to other guys. I really do love you, but I don't deserve someone like you. I am a curse to anyone who really loves me. I'm so sorry I hurt you."

As angry as I was, I could not resist reaching out to him. We held each other and cried. Later that night, Robert told me he wanted us to stay together.

"But can you tell me that I will be the only one in your life? Will you be faithful to me?"

"Randy, all I can say is that I will try really hard. I have never had anyone who loved me like you. You are truly what I asked God for. I respect you, Randy. You are such a wonderful man. I don't deserve you, but I want to really try. I don't want to lose you."

So we stayed together. The first few weeks were pretty good. One night as we were lying in bed holding one another, Robert said, "I'm afraid I'm going to lose you."

"Why would you be afraid of that, Robert? I'm yours for life! I love you so much."

"I know, Randy, but I'm afraid of losing you to God. What if He calls you back into the ministry? I could fight for you against another man, but how could I fight against God?"

I didn't like to talk about ministry. I had put that all behind me because being gay had killed that dream. Robert's words made me uncomfortable, and I was more than a little puzzled.

"Well, you don't have to worry about God. He wouldn't take me away from you. He knows how much you mean to me."

Nothing more was said that night but now a shadow hung over both of us. So much was against us making it as a couple. Society refused to recognize our union, the church denounced our relationship, our families refused to validate us, and we didn't feel we could pray for God's help because we felt condemned by God.

About two months after we had vowed to try again, I walked into our bathroom during a Labor Day party we were hosting and found Robert in a compromising position with another guy. I moved out the next day, my heart in pieces.

Now I can see the signs of the codependency in our relationship, but at the time I wanted the pain to stop. One dark night, when pain got the best of me, I found myself back at "our" house begging Robert to let me stay the night and sleep with him one last time.

"Robert, I know this is really dumb, but I can't go to sleep. I need so badly to be close to you right now. I know we are no longer together, and you seem to be dealing with that a lot better than I am. I'm not doing so well. Please, just let me lay next to you. I promise I won't try anything physical. I just want to be near you. Please?"

Robert, at the door half asleep, motioned me in. We went to the bedroom and he crawled back in bed. I slipped off my clothes and took my old place on my side of the bed. Immediately, I knew I was making a big mistake. I had thought that if I reminded Robert of what we use to have, he would not be able to resist me. He went back to sleep. Sad and angry, I started crying but he did not respond. Totally humiliated, I got up, dressed, and headed for the door. He never stirred.

I lost touch with Robert, but friends told me sometime later that he had developed AIDS and died. I look back at him with sadness. I remember those first few weeks we spent together, how we prayed together and how I could see Robert's love for Jesus reawakening. He was beginning to believe that God could love him as a gay man. I remember hearing the recordings Robert made when he had played for the gospel quartet years before I met him. He was so gifted and really loved ministry. I never got him to play a piano after his friend Jimmy told him that God hated all gay people. I wish Robert could have known for himself the peace I have in my heart today. He was an attractive but conflicted and troubled man. When I remember him, my only consolation is that he is now with the One who loves him unconditionally, the One who will spend eternity loving him. Robert, may you rest in peace.

My ego had taken quite a beating through the break-up. I looked for ways to reassure myself that I was still desirable. I found myself at the bar almost every night and forced myself to develop a taste for beer. I gave up finding the right man to settle down with and started viewing sex as recreational. I totally abandoned my values, ignored red flags, and, though I was not conscious of it, I was hell-bent on a self-destructive track. Admittedly, there were moments of great excitement when men at the bar found me desirable and showed me attention. I gave up seeking God and bought into the lie that God hated me. If I was going to hell, I might as well do whatever felt good while I had the chance. It is a miracle that I am still alive.

The bar and the theatre were two places where I did not feel condemned, so I spent as much time as I could in these judgment-free zones. I auditioned for *Fiddler on the Roof* and was given the role of Motel the Tailor. This was a starring role and I was thrilled. I even had a solo! At the gay bar, I began to sing live during the drag shows. I also became one of the male leads. This meant that I dressed as a guy and did duet numbers with the guys who dressed as girls.

Dan, the director of the shows, became a close friend. Brandy Lane, Dan's stage name, had taken 12 years of dance and we worked hard on our opening numbers for the shows. Brandy had a lot of class as a female impersonator, and had worked in many straight bars in Las Vegas as a professional entertainer. She usually wore a slinky dress and boa and knew how to work the audience. I became her constant companion during the week, even accompanying her to New Orleans to assist in finding dresses and accessories for her to wear on stage.

One of Brandy's signature musical numbers was Carol Channing's version of "Diamonds are a Girl's Best Friend." For that number, she wore a bright blue bugle-beaded gown with trails of rhinestones woven through it. On her head sat a wild feather and rhinestone headpiece. Brandy would make her entrance on the shoulders of two young men in white tuxedos. I was one of them. We would sit her down and then do dance steps along with her during the song, taking turns adorning her with rhinestone necklaces, bracelets, and rings as she pantomimed the famous song. Being one of the male leads in the show made me somewhat of a celebrity at the bar. Everyone seemed to know me. But inside, I felt empty because I had lost my spiritual moorings. I was adrift in a sea of sensual pleasures. I soared on waves of sexual exploits. My real self was dying.

I was very self-conscious on the dance floor. Having grown up in a church that frowned on dancing, I felt awkward and clumsy trying to move to the beat of the music. I had rhythm and I could learn choreography, but freely moving on the dance floor seemed impossible. Then a friend told me about speed.

I started taking a form of this drug my friends called "pink hearts." This sped up my heart rate and caused my hair to tingle. The burst of energy I felt was out of this world. With the help of pink hearts, I found myself joining my friends on the dance floor and losing myself in the flow of music and bodies. Speed gave me added energy and kept me awake for two days straight. When I came down, I slammed rock bottom. Depression overtook me. I longed to hide from the world.

After going through a couple of the depressions associated with speed, I decided not to take it anymore. I tried marijuana a few times, but this gave me a bad case of the munchies. Every time I smoked it, I craved food and lots of it. Since I had always been weight-conscious, I did not want to develop this habit!

Alcohol was enjoyable. I liked feeling tipsy. I discovered sweet drinks, like tequila sunrise and screwdrivers, that tasted good and made me feel great. The thing that saved me from abusing alcohol was that, before I got too drunk, I got sick to my stomach. After a few times of overindulging in alcohol and paying the consequences, kneeling in front of a toilet, I learned to drink just enough to get a buzz, then stop. Alcohol made it easier for me to ignore my conscience. Under the influence I made some bad choices that I regret to this day.

Thank God I never got hooked on drugs or alcohol. I was so afraid of being out of control that I was very cautious about what I took and how much. However, my concern for "being in control" did not translate to another addiction. Needing intimacy, in the absence of spiritual direction in my life, was what led to my addiction to sex.

Sexual addiction robbed me of my creativity and my personality. It controlled most of the hours of my day, continually driving me to seek a satisfactory sexual encounter. But each time I had one, the experience left me empty and needing another fix. Many nights I would be tired and in need of sleep, yet unable to go home until I had found someone to hook up with. I longed for some sort of normalcy, but at that time my life was out of control. I was finding out that sexual expression was not designed to be used recreationally. It is too powerfully linked, not only to our emotions, but also to the deepest part of who we are. I had many different types of experiences that left me over-the-top excited one moment, then humiliated and depressed the next. Worst of all, I was trampling on all the values that I once held dear. When I think back on those times, I become aware of the many factors that set me up for disaster.

Now that I have studied and learned much about sexual orientation and behavior, I clearly see that my attraction to men was as healthy as my dad's sexual attraction to women. For years, heterosexuals, especially Christians, have been made aware that a person needs to keep certain boundaries on sexual expression. They are warned that if the powerful human sexual drive gets "out of control," the results can be catastrophic. Society, families, and the church have sought to help young heterosexual people learn to sort through these emotions and to make rational decisions as to how to live as sexual beings.

Young gay kids, however, are given no teaching, no suggestions, other than "Just say no!" Consequently, the young gay or lesbian person faces a world in which there is no reliable information available on how to respond responsibly with their gift of sexuality. If you are a heterosexual reading this book, ask yourself:

How would your story read had you not been given any positive explanations for your sexual feelings?

What if you had no answers as to why you felt attracted to the opposite sex?

What if there had been no societal structures in which you could celebrate the feelings you had for that person to whom you were first attracted?

What if there was no dating, no holding hands in public, no walking arm-in-arm, no romantic greeting cards with pictures of guys and girls together, no movies with heterosexual love stories, no heterosexual love songs, no heterosexual poetry, no heterosexual role models, no classes or books to teach you about heterosexual relationships?

What if you went to church and heard, in sermons, that anyone who felt heterosexual attraction had deliberately chosen to feel that way and responding to that evil choice put you in danger of hell—yet, every time you saw a member of the opposite sex, you found yourself more and more attracted to them?

Imagine trying to pinpoint that moment in your childhood and young adulthood when you first made the decision to be attracted to the opposite sex.

Imagine separating your heterosexuality from the rest of all that makes you who you are.

Imagine the people you love most, telling you that, even though they love you very much, they hate your heterosexual sinfulness.

Try to grasp what it would feel like to sit in church and hear the preacher speak in disgust and disapproval of "those wicked heterosexuals who choose to live in their filthy sin."

Imagine growing up knowing that heterosexuals could not marry.

What if your church distributed bumper stickers saying that marriage equals two men or two women?

What if your pastor said over and over again in sermons, "Heterosexual Christian is an oxymoron."

If you had grown up in a world like that, how might <u>your</u> life story read?

Randy, the Belly Dancer

Chapter 16

Boy Meets Girl

One night, I met a girl at the bar named Katie. She was my friend Joey's sister-in-law, the wife of his brother, Wayne. Joey brought Katie to the dinner theatre to see *Fiddler*, and after the show I went with them to the gay club, where I asked Katie to dance.

Blond and pretty, dressed in her party clothes, she looked like a young Angie Dickenson. The two of us had a great time on the disco floor. After we finished dancing, Katie and I talked for hours. I was delighted when she suggested that we hang out together.

The two of us became fast friends. Like me, Katie had been raised in a very conservative Assembly of God church. Now, separated from her husband and a single mother to a four-year-old daughter, Katie was discovering the forbidden pleasures of life. Like so many Pentecostals who are sheltered all their lives, she was ready to sow some wild oats. Katie loved country music and her favorite song at the time was Tammy Wynette's, "Good Girl's Gonna Go Bad." The title seemed to be an editorial of our lives. We became known as "Randy and Katie." My dad even got his hopes up that perhaps I had seen the light.

"Son, that Katie is a pretty girl."

"Yes, she is Dad, but we're just friends. Don't jump to any conclusions."

"Well son, why not try dating her? She is obviously crazy about you."

"Dad, would you stop? I'm gay. I am not into dating girls."

"I just don't understand, son. Why, if I had had a pretty girl like Katie showing me lots of attention back when I was young and single, I would have done anything I could to win her. I would have written her poetry, bought her candy, and flowers…"

"But Dad, you weren't gay. Being gay isn't something you just turn off and on. I like Katie as a friend, nothing more."

"Son, if you would just try. Your mom and I have talked this over. If you will just try to change, we will buy you a new car and pay for you to finish college."

"Dad, I am not going to change. I can't change. And the sooner you get that through your heads, the better off you and Mother will be."

I was sure that Katie viewed our friendship the way I did until one day, out of the blue, she asked, "Randy, have you ever been with a girl?"

"By 'being with,' do you mean have I had sex with a girl?"

"Yes."

"No Katie, I'm gay."

"But how do you know you are gay if you have never tried it with a woman?"

"Katie, I just know. Believe me."

"But you like *me*, don't you?"

"Yes, I do. You are one of my best friends. "

"Well, I just want you to know that if you ever decide that you want to…"

"Katie, don't go there. I don't think of you that way."

"I know, but if you do decide to try it, we could, you know. And there would be no strings attached."

"Well thanks, but no thanks."

I began to worry that Katie wanted more from our relationship than I was able to give. Maybe it was wrong for me to hang out with her so much if she was starting to develop feelings for me that went beyond friendship. I didn't want to hurt her.

One night we were watching television at Katie's house because neither of us had any money to go out. Her daughter was staying with friends. Katie was mixing screwdrivers that were so strong you could see through them. I started feeling happy. We drank, laughed, and were having the best time, when suddenly I realized I had drunk too much. Feeling quite nauseous, I rushed for the bathroom, barely making it in time. When I had finished heaving, I fell back onto the floor in front of the toilet.

Katie was right there with a wet rag and pillow for my head. I told her I needed to go home, but she insisted that I stay the night. I tried to resist, but felt so woozy and weak, that eventually I gave in to her suggestion.

She helped me undress and get in bed. It felt good to lie back on the pillows. I closed my eyes to stop the room from spinning. I must have dozed off, and I was awakened by Katie pulling the covers back to get into bed with me. As she started to kiss me, it was clear that she wanted us to "do it." In my drunken stupor, I went along, thinking,

"Randy, you have always wondered if it would be possible for you to have sex with a woman. Here's your chance to find out."

To my amazement, I was able to accomplish "the mission." In fact we "did it" twice in a row. I was elated and thought to myself, "Randy, you are a *real* man! You just made love to a woman! Wow!" I laid there wondering what this meant. Was I bisexual? Had God finally answered my prayers to make me straight? We drifted off to sleep.

The next morning I had a terrible headache. Katie called my boss and told him I was unable to make it to work. I got up and left after we ate breakfast, badly in need of some time alone to process what had happened. As I thought about it, I realized that I responded to Katie because I was so turned on by the fact that she was so turned on by me. For me, it was like we were kids playing doctor. It was exciting to try something different. But it did not take long for me to realize that I had no emotional tie to that sexual experience with Katie. If I had been intimate with a man, I would have wondered if he would call me the next day or if I would see him again. With Katie, there was no intimate connection. Sex with Katie had been interesting, not romantic. The act had been an isolated event. My lack of emotion reminded me of the young heterosexual guys with whom I had experimented in our puberty days. For them, the exploration between us was simply that. They had no romantic feelings for me as I did for them.

Many people marvel that some gay men marry, father children, and have sexual relations with their wives for years before they come out. There is so much pressure put on young men to get married and have children that too often gay men, especially those who have been raised with Christian values, believe they have no choice. Many men have told me that they had to fantasize being with a man to have sex with their wives. Some gay men have sex with women, but the emotional and inner connection is not there. Being gay is more than the sexual act. It is the way a gay man relates to another man in terms of attraction, romance, and bonding. The deep feelings and attractions that a gay man experiences for another gay man are not only so much more powerful, but as different as night and day to the response they have for women. My sexual experience with Katie was nothing more than exploration for me.

We tried intimacy a few more times. Again, I reminded her that I was gay. While she said she understood, I am not sure it was possible for her to really *understand*. I knew it was unfair to continue the sexual aspect of our friendship because it seemed to mean so much more to her than it did to me. I loved Katie and I did not want to lose her friendship, so we stopped our sexual exploration altogether.

My life continued spiraling downward and took a frightening turn. I had been warned about getting certain sexual diseases and what symptoms I should look for. One morning, I went to the bathroom and realized I had some troubling signs. I called a friend who knew a lot about sexual diseases and he confirmed that I had gonorrhea. He told me that I could get treatment at the free health clinic downtown, and soon I found myself in the waiting room along with some interesting people. One of them sitting next to me was a prostitute, accompanied by a guy I assumed to be her pimp. I thought, "This is it Randy. *This* is as low as you can go."

When I saw the nurse, after my condition was confirmed, she told me to pull down my pants for a shot in both cheeks. The needle was enormous, and the shots hurt terribly. Then I had to swallow six huge tablets. After that, I was ushered into another room where a doctor showed me graphic pictures of people who had contracted sexually transmitted diseases. The doctor warned me to be careful and offered me condoms. At that time, AIDS had not shown up in Arkansas. No warnings were given to the gay community about sexually transmitted diseases and how to prevent them. "Why would I need condoms?" I thought. "I'm gay. It's not like I'm going to get a girl pregnant."

A few weeks later, I was diagnosed with Hepatitis B, which I had picked up being promiscuous. The illness was devastating. I lost a lot of weight and felt sicker than I had ever felt before. I seemed to be out to destroy myself, left to drift without any awareness of God, without the church, or any spiritual guidance. I remember going to a restaurant to eat with friends and thinking that the waiter looked familiar. Then it hit me—he was one of my many anonymous sexual partners, and I didn't even know his name. Values? I had buried them so deeply that I didn't even recognize myself any longer. I was lost and there was no one to show me the way home. In Isaiah 59:16, God is speaking through the prophet, and the word of the Lord is, "I saw no one was helping you and I wondered that no one intervened. Therefore, I, myself, stepped in to save you through my mighty power and justice."

I believe that this next event was a divine intervention.

One Sunday morning, I lay in bed remembering the Sundays I had spent at home with my family. Sundays had always been days of celebration. Mama would have the television tuned to the southern gospel program, *Gospel Jubilee*. We would listen to songs sung by The Happy Goodman Family, The Rambos, and many other groups. My parents, my sisters, and I would go to church with friends who worshiped Jesus like we did. It always gave me a feeling of joy to know I was in the house of God.

Now, Sunday mornings were a time to nurse a hangover from being out late partying. My depression was so deep that a terrible sense of dread enveloped me.

I got up to go to the bathroom. My spiritual pain was unbearable. I leaned against the wall for support as the tears came. All I could do was moan, "Oh God! What have I become?"

Suddenly I was aware of a presence in that tiny bathroom. I did not see Him, I did not audibly hear Him, but Jesus was there. I sensed Him calling my name. I cried out loud, "Jesus, what are you doing here?"

It was as though I could hear Him saying, "I am here because I love you, Randy. You feel so alone and I want you to know that I am here for you."

I screamed, "You don't love me! Don't tease me with empty words. I am an abomination to you. You could not *possibly* love me."

"Who told you that, Randy?"

"A lot of people, a lot of *preachers* have told me. They say that the Bible says it. It's obvious what you think of me. All I have to do is look at what you did to Sodom. I'm going to burn in hell for eternity! I didn't choose to have these feelings, yet somehow I'm condemned by you for something I didn't even sign up for."

"Randy, those preachers, those people, they do not speak for me. Listen to me, son. I love you more than you could ever possibly know. Don't let anyone ever tell you differently."

From a leaning position, I suddenly went limp and slid down the wall, collapsing in the cleansing tears that come from knowing you are in the presence of unconditional love. It was as if Jesus was holding me, rocking me back and forth, and breathing sweet words of comfort into my troubled soul.

Jesus came to me that day, when I felt that no one cared for my soul, when I wanted to die. I wish I could say that I left that bathroom that day, assured of God's love for me and spiritually whole. But the healing I needed was a slow process, and there were many more miles to go before I found my secure place in his arms of grace. However, from that day on, there was something inside me that never failed to tell me that I knew better when anyone said that God hated me. I had it on good authority that I was loved by my creator.

Chapter 17

Dreams Turn to Nightmares

I saw my friend Jim one night while at the gay bar. He was a married man who would show up when his wife was out of town. Jim had a friend with him, Jerry, who I had never met. Immediately I was attracted to his rugged good looks. I found out later that Jerry was also married. His wife and kids had gone to visit his wife's parents over the Labor Day weekend. When Jerry asked me to dance, I accepted. All night long he courted me, buying me drinks and asking me personal questions. I was heady from all the attention. I learned that Jerry and his family lived in a rural town about an hour's drive away. When he asked me if I wanted to get together for the night, I accepted his offer.

We spent the whole weekend together, and Jerry swept me off my feet. When Monday night rolled around, he told me he did not want to leave me because he was falling in love. He said he wanted me to be his one and only.

"How can you ask me to be your one and only, when you have a wife and kids?" I asked.

"Well, you know I'm gay. My wife could never give me what I get from you. I will come and see you as often as I can. Randy, I have been looking for someone like you all my life. I can't let you go now that I've finally found you."

"Jerry, I have really strong convictions about marriage. I cannot be with you if you remain in a marriage that is basically a lie. You owe it to your wife to be honest. The only way we will ever be together is if you leave your wife and come out as a gay man. I am not going to be your lover on the side."

He told me that he needed some time to think. We parted on Tuesday morning after three days together. I told myself I probably would never hear from him again. Jerry had been in the Air Force for 17 years. He told me that he had left the military early so he could get a degree, and that someday he wanted to work for NASA. He said that he totally respected me for my love of God and my desire to be in a committed relationship. Jerry seemed almost too good to be true. I should have remembered my father's life rule: "If something seems too good to be true, it usually is."

Later that same evening, I received a phone call from Jerry. He told me to meet him at one of the local gay bars because he had something to tell me. I was in shock. I raced downtown to the club and found him sitting at the bar, nursing a beer.

"What is it? What did you want to tell me?"

"Randy, I met my wife after she got off work today. I told her that I was gay and that I had met a man I was in love with. I told her I wanted a divorce. I'm all yours."

I felt numb, sort of like the dog that chases a car, catches it, and then does not know what to do with it. Everything was happening too quickly. My head was spinning. There had been no dating, no getting to know each other. We just moved in together. Suddenly, I was in a committed relationship with a man I did not even know.

For the first few months, I was blissfully happy and became very domestic. I loved showing Jerry off to my friends. I met Jerry's children. Initially they seemed standoffish, but before long, I had won their approval. Their mother was awarded custody and Jerry got visitation rights. We decided that we wanted to go to church, so we checked out the one whose bulletin had outed me to my folks. I had attended that church one time before and had not been impressed, but I told Jerry that I missed church and, since this one seemed our only option as a gay couple, maybe we should give it another try.

Before long we joined the church, and I told Jerry that now perhaps I could resume my ministry since we had found a place that would accept us as a couple. He agreed with me. I couldn't wait to tell my mother. I called her and broke the news that I was back in church. She was happy at first, until she heard where I was attending.

"Son, I would have felt better if you had told me you had joined the Jehovah's Witnesses!" That was the worst insult mother could have given our church. She had always taught my sisters and me to guard ourselves against the Jehovah's Witness, who she called a cult. So, to say the least, she was not thrilled with my news.

My sexual addiction was now under control since I was in a committed relationship. If anything good came out of my relationship with Jerry, it was the fact that, during our three and a half years together, I was faithful to one person sexually. I had finally found a man who wanted to be in relationship with me for the long haul. We spent Christmases together. We attended church together and even hosted my family for dinner at our apartment. I was still delivering singing telegrams, and my boss had also gotten me a gig singing and playing the piano at a local bar. Jerry was enrolled in college classes and performed maintenance jobs for a friend of ours who owned rental properties. Our relationship seemed to be doing well, but then I started noticing signs of trouble.

The first one came when I realized that Jerry was constantly changing colleges. I did a little investigating and found out that, as a veteran, Jerry was getting checks from the government for his education. However, instead of using the checks to pay his school bills, he was pocketing the money. When the school sent a final warning about payment, Jerry dropped out and found another college or trade school to attend. Now I knew that all his talk about working for NASA was a lie. I remembered wondering how Jerry got the money to buy our friends drinks at the bar. I also found out that Jerry was keeping the money I gave him out of my paycheck each month to pay the rent. Now I knew why we had to move every few months. He always had a seemingly logical explanation, but after the second move, I got suspicious and found he was not paying the rent.

These devastating discoveries were complicated by the fact that I was learning that Jerry could be very controlling and had quite a temper. I found myself walking on eggshells around him to keep him from blowing up at me. My friends did not like the way he always put me down in front of them. I was losing my friends, and worse, I realized that Jerry *wanted* it that way. He resented anyone who was significant to me. Jerry wanted me to rely on only him for companionship. He was constantly setting up scenarios in which he would test me to see if I passed his loyalty standards.

For example, one day my friend Mike stopped by to see if we wanted to go play tennis. I loved tennis, but Jerry was not very athletic.

"Well, I'm not much of a tennis player", Jerry responded. "But Randy is. Randy, honey, why don't you go on and play tennis with Mike."

"Are you sure you don't mind if I go?"

"No", he said with a grin. "I don't mind. You guys go have fun."

I went into our bedroom to change into my tennis shorts and Jerry followed me. He shut the door behind him. I went over and gave him a big hug.

"Thanks, honey, for being so understanding."

I suddenly noticed that Jerry's demeanor had changed drastically from the happy-go-lucky attitude he had displayed just a few minutes ago in front of Mike. He pushed me away.

"What's wrong, Jerry?"

"I can't believe you chose him over me."

"Jerry, I *asked* if it was okay with you for me to go, and you said…"

"Well, I was just testing you to see who means more to you. Obviously I got my answer!"

There were many such incidents. Another time we were sitting together on the couch watching television and Jerry asked me out of the blue, "Randy, if our house was on fire, would you risk your own life to save mine?"

That struck me as a strange thing to ask, but by now, I knew Jerry well enough to recognize this as another test.

"Jerry, I hope I would, but who knows. I have heard reports of people panicking and running out of burning houses without stopping to save their own kids."

Jerry looked a little hurt. Then he spoke with all the sanctimonious piety he could muster. "Randy, there is no doubt in my mind that I would give my life to save you, because you mean the world to me. I wouldn't want to live in a world without you in it. You are my world. Sometimes I wonder about you, though. You seem to need a lot of friends in your life in addition to me."

"Jerry, I love you. Surely you know that. But I do need friends. No *one* person can provide someone with everything they need. But just because I need my friends doesn't mean that I don't love you and that I am not committed to you."

"Well, Randy, I guess that is where we're different. I don't need anyone else. I would be totally happy if it were always just you and me in our own little world."

Jerry's mask was coming off and I was frightened. By this time, I was so deeply embedded in our codependent relationship that I could see no way out. Jerry was good at manipulating me to feel that everything was my fault. Sometimes I would think that I had all my arguments together about the real reason we did not have enough money to pay the rent, or why it was wrong for him to test me with his mind games. When I tried to confront him, he somehow always convinced me that I was the guilty party.

The church we attended had a kind pastor. He knew of my desire to minister again and had asked me to assist him in ministerial duties. I was to preach once a month and also help in the music ministry. Although this was exciting to me, it angered Jerry. He always found a way to pick a fight with me right before I left the house to preach. I constantly had to choose between God and Jerry.

During this time, Jerry handled our finances. I was expected to make quarterly payments to the IRS. I learned three years later that Jerry had not been paying quarterly and that my taxes and penalties were adding up at an alarming rate. It also became obvious to me that Jerry and I were on two different wavelengths when it came to our world views. He was one of those people who thought that men had never really walked on the moon. According to him, that whole television event was filmed in Hollywood and was a big government cover-up.

Worse was the fact that Jerry always tried to look smart by doing his best to make me look dumb. It became more and more demeaning to constantly be put down by a man who I was growing to detest. Yet I know now that I was as unhealthy as Jerry for putting up with this kind of treatment. It takes two to form a codependent relationship, and both people need intervention and healing.

During the first year of our relationship, I came across the address for my old friend Gary Eddy from Evangel. It was actually his parents' address in South Dakota. When I saw his name, I began to feel guilty for writing that judgmental letter to him several years before. Gary and I had kept in touch for a while after the letter in which he confessed his crush on me. Because of the distance and the instability of my life, we had not been in contact for several years. I decided that I wanted, somehow, to get word to Gary that I had finally come out as a gay man. I also wanted to apologize for the letter I wrote, chastising him for his sexual interest in me. I knew that I was taking the chance that his mother might open his mail by writing to her address. So, I crafted a letter in such a way that if his mother opened and read it she would not have a clue, but if Gary read it, he would understand "the code."

"Gary," I wrote, "something <u>very interesting</u> has happened in my life that I think you would be <u>very interested</u> in knowing about."

I sent the letter but didn't receive a reply. I mailed that same letter several times over the next year or two, but never received an answer. Then, in 1985, I came across the address again. Things had gone from bad to worse with Jerry. I really needed to talk to a friend, and Gary had been such a good listener and advisor. So, I decided that I would write one more time. If I did not hear back, I would not try again. Perhaps his mom and dad had moved or died.

To my surprise and joy, a letter arrived from Rapid City. Gary wrote that he had become convinced that it was wrong to be gay and had decided that he would try to change. He married a girl and they attempted for five years to make the marriage work before Gary came to the realization that he was still gay and could not change. When they divorced, Gary moved home with his widowed mom. His wife stayed in the house in which they had lived together. The very day Gary moved in with his mom, my letter arrived! He said he was anxious to hear what my big news was all about, even though he thought he knew.

I immediately wrote Gary that I had come out as a gay man in 1980 and wanted to tell him how sorry I was for the judgmental way I had answered his letter years ago. I wrote that I realized he had taken a risk confiding in me and how it must have stung when I responded so piously.

I explained that I was in a relationship with a man. As I wrote, I almost found myself regretting that I was not free to pursue a relationship with Gary, but I put that out of my mind. I was a firm believer in being faithful to one person in a committed relationship. However, I imagined what it would be like not to have Jerry constantly controlling me and making my life hell.

Gary wrote back immediately and told me that he was happy to hear about my self-realization. He asked how I had reconciled my Christianity and my sexuality. We wrote regularly. Finally I had someone I trusted, to whom I could pour out my heart. The frequent letters troubled Jerry. He demanded that I let him read them. I wrote to Gary and warned him not to put anything in his letters that might make Jerry jealous.

One day Gary wrote that he was taking me up on my invitation to visit Arkansas. For years I had wondered what it would have been like had I been receptive to Gary's interest in me. I was curious to see what he looked like now. I could hardly wait for his arrival. Jerry seemed somewhat apprehensive. One day when we were walking, he questioned me about my feelings for Gary.

"So, are you looking forward to Gary's visit?"

"Yes I am. It will be fun to see him after all these years."

"Do you think there will be an attraction there between the two of you? I mean, he had such a big crush on you back in college."

"Jerry, please don't go making something out of this. I am committed to you. Even if there turns out to be some interest on his part, Gary respects our relationship and you know that I do. I've always been faithful to you. Lighten up. I bet you'll really like Gary."

"Well, I am just wondering about that thing called unrequited love."

"Jerry, I'm telling you for the last time, you don't have anything to worry about. Gary and I are just friends and I need friends in my life. Please don't spoil this for me."

"All right, I'll try to enjoy the time while Gary is here. It will be fun meeting someone from your past."

When Gary arrived, I was immediately impressed with how well-proportioned he was for his size. He stood 5 foot 6 and was slim. His arms had a nice muscular shape to them and his Midwestern accent was charming. I remembered how safe and peaceful I felt around him, with his way of making me believe that everything was going to be all right. Jerry quizzed Gary about his recent coming out. He took it upon himself to make sure that Gary got the gay education he needed, which included a trip to the gay bar and Gary's first drag show.

We had a really good time. It was Beer Bust that night, which meant you paid three dollars and you could drink all the beer you wanted until a certain hour. The three of us certainly got our money's worth. The downside to the evening was the way Jerry constantly put me down. He always needed to make me look stupid in front of my friends, and I had put up with it for so long that I was almost oblivious to it. Yet, I am sure my ego felt the blows. Gary picked up immediately on Jerry's abuse tactics. When we were alone for a few moments while Jerry was pumping gas, Gary asked me, "Randy, does Jerry always put you down like that?"

"Oh, that is just his way. He doesn't really mean it."

"But Randy, I don't like it. I can't imagine living with someone who constantly berated me. You are a good man, Randy. You don't deserve to be treated this way. You deserve better."

Gary's words hit home. I began to realize that he was right and that I was being abused. If any of my friends was being treated the way Jerry treated me, I would be upset. Gary showed me so much respect and made me feel attractive and intelligent, like a man who deserved to be loved. My self-esteem was so low from having lived with Jerry for three years that I was unaware how wounded I was. I constantly defended Jerry to friends who tried to talk me into leaving him. Actually, most of them had stopped coming around because they could not stand Jerry. I always told myself they were being disloyal to me by rejecting the person I loved. Gary began to point out the many times he had seen Jerry mistreat me. For the first time, I did not come to my partner's defense. It was like a curtain had opened and I could see my relationship for what it was—spousal abuse.

Gary stayed with us for a week. I began dreading his departure because now I had thoughts of actually leaving Jerry. I knew that, without Gary there, I would not be strong enough to act on my desire to be free of my partner's abuse. Right before he was to leave, he and I were alone at the house while Jerry ran an errand, one of our few "alone" times.

"Randy, you know how I felt about you in college. Then when your letter arrived a few months ago, I could not wait to hear back from you. I knew what you were going to tell me. My only disappointment was that you were not free. This week, seeing you again, being close to you, looking once again into those warm brown eyes, I find myself falling in love with you all over again."

There was a part of me that felt guilty for letting Gary say these things. But at the same time, these words flowed like a healing ointment on open wounds.

"Randy, you are so loving and kind and compassionate. You are being used by Jerry, and it hurts me to see him treat you this way. I would never hurt you the way Jerry does. I would appreciate you for all that you are."

"Gary, I…"

"Randy, just let me finish before you say anything. You told me the other night that you feel ugly and undesirable. Jerry has made you believe that. But to me, you are a beautiful man, inside and out. The love you have in your heart shines through your eyes. I wish I could take care of you and shield you from the pain you're experiencing. It may be wrong for me to say this, but I hope you will leave Jerry. Randy, he is not good for you."

"But Jerry has had such a sad life. His father was an alcoholic and abused him sexually as a child. His mother became an alcoholic because of his dad's drinking. Everyone he has ever cared about has abandoned him. If I were to leave him, he might give up completely."

"Randy, you cannot be Jerry's savior. Do you want to sacrifice your whole life for this man who treats you like dirt? I know you are a good man. It is your compassion that has kept you in this relationship for so long. But has Jerry gotten any better?"

"No! He seems to be getting worse."

"Then obviously you cannot help him. Jerry needs help, but he will never ask for it if you continue to allow him to get by with this kind of behavior. All I know is that I love you Randy. Take that however you will. But I am someone who sees you for the wonderful man that you are. I want to be with you. I want to make you happy. You *deserve* happiness after all you've been through."

I couldn't help myself and I reached for him. He put his arms around me and held me so close I could feel his heart. We kissed. It was the most powerfully emotional kiss I had ever given or received.

At that moment, I made my decision. I had to get away from Jerry. Later, when we said goodbye to Gary, Jerry hugged him, but it was not a generous hug. He had seen how much I cared for Gary, and that troubled him. When I hugged Gary, I wanted to hold onto him, but I knew he had to leave. What I had to do must be done on my own. I had to find the strength and courage to take back my life. Gary could not do it for me. No one could.

I was so blessed to have a friend like Gary. I knew I could count on him. He had assured me that if I needed him, he would be there. I could phone him collect or I could come to live with him. Or, if I wanted, he would move to Arkansas to be with me. Just knowing that Gary believed in me that much helped me gather enough self-respect to say the words I needed to say.

A few days later, I found the courage.

"Jerry, I'm leaving. I want out of our relationship. I'm so unhappy and I'm not willing to put up with your abuse any longer."

Jerry was shocked. Naturally he blamed Gary, but I assured him that this was *my* decision.

My boss at the singing telegram business and her husband, Dave, helped me find a place to live, a little one bedroom house tucked behind another larger home. The rent was cheap and I so looked forward to living on my own. Dave went with me to pick up my things. Jerry was there.

Jerry was still trying to talk me out of leaving. I knew I had to keep his abuse first and foremost in my mind to be able to leave. Jerry was so good at manipulating me. I felt myself weakening, until he provided me the impetus to follow through with my plan. I had purchased a sound system for playing at the piano bar. We agreed that I would take the system because Jerry had no use for it. But when I started carrying the speakers out the door, Jerry stepped in front of me, jerking them out of my hand.

"I don't want you to take these, Randy. I will sell them and we will split the money."

This angered me. He knew how much that sound system meant to me. It was his way of punishing me. I have never felt so much rage. Three years of anger started boiling to the surface.

"Give those speakers back. They are mine! I use them in my work."

"No," he responded. "They belong to both of us."

Dave was a very quiet man. He was standing out in the backyard, watching us through the open doorway. Although he felt uncomfortable that we were making a scene, the *real* scene was just beginning. When I look back on what happened next, I am amazed at my actions. I grabbed the speakers. Jerry tried to wrestle with me as I was turning to leave. I stopped, put down the speakers, turned around, picked Jerry up off his feet, and threw him across the room, where he slammed against the wall. His glasses broke and his nose began to bleed.

I picked up the speakers and walked out the door to the truck. As Dave and I drove away, I looked in the mirror and saw Jerry standing at the door holding a paper towel to his nose. We drove in stunned silence. Finally, Dave looked at me.

"Wow, Randy, I didn't know you had *that* in you."

"That makes two of us, Dave. I've never gotten violent before. I really don't like being that way. I feel so drained right now and it's not a good feeling. I'm sorry you had to see that."

"Hey, I would have bought a ticket to see that fight!"

The next few days were filled with arranging things, unpacking, and trying to make sense of my new life. Just as I expected, I started hearing from Jerry. He came to see me at work. He visited my mother to talk her into helping him get me back, telling her that I was promiscuous before we got together and, now that I was single again, I was at risk of getting the new "gay cancer" everyone was talking about. Of all the things he had ever done, this was the most absurd. I could not hold back the cynical laughter.

"You didn't honestly think that my mom was going to help you, did you?"

"Well, she told me she was very happy that we had broken up. It was what she had been praying for."

"Jerry, talking to her was really stupid on your part."

"I know Randy, but I want you back so bad. Look, I will do anything! Please. I know I haven't been the person I should be. I've really been hard on you."

"That's an understatement."

"I know. I accept blame for everything. Just come back to me, Randy. My life is so empty without you."

I quickly reminded myself of the reasons I left Jerry. I felt myself getting weak. He was pushing all my buttons. I had gone through the pain of being left by someone I loved, and now the pain of being the one to leave. Leaving requires so much strength. When you love the person you are leaving, but know you must leave to survive emotionally, you are constantly bombarded with guilt and misgivings. I could see that Jerry was suffering, and it seemed the easiest thing to do would be to take him back. But I stayed strong.

I called Gary many times during this period. He asked if he could move to Arkansas to be with me. At first I told him yes. He shared this news with his sister, and she sent a card welcoming me to the Eddy family. But the more I thought about Gary moving here, the more I questioned the wisdom of such a decision. I knew I was still so unhealthy. I didn't know, from one day to the next, if I could stay committed to my decision to leave Jerry. What if I told Gary yes, and he gave up his job, family, and friends, to move to a strange city and state? What if, when he got here, I could not commit to a relationship with him? I didn't think it was fair to ask him to take such a risk.

So I wrote to Gary and told him of my decision not to be in a relationship at that time. He was obviously hurt. He told me later that he felt he had been rejected by me twice over a ten-year period. But deep inside, I was afraid that I could never get away from Jerry's hold on me.

One Sunday, I went to church and there was Jerry sitting with another man. I was not prepared for this. He was holding hands with the guy! Of course, many in the congregation sensed my uneasiness. It was painful for me to see that Jerry could replace me so quickly. It hurt even more to look at the person with him. The guy was nothing like me. In fact, I was embarrassed for Jerry even to be seen with him. I would never have thought Jerry would have such poor taste in men. And what did that say about me? I tried to play it off with friends, but inwardly, Jerry's agenda to get me back was working.

I woke up early on Tuesday morning, January 28, 1986. I had the television in the living room on just for background noise. The station I was watching was broadcasting the Challenger space shuttle launching. I stopped what I was doing to watch the countdown. The launch was successful, so I walked into the bedroom. When I came back out, the newscasters were talking about an accident. The shuttle had exploded just a few moments after takeoff. I sat down in the floor in front of the television and cried as they replayed the explosion, over and over. That afternoon, I felt so alone in the house by myself. I started thinking about Jerry. I longed then to be held, so I got up and left, walking four miles to where Jerry lived. When I knocked on the door, he answered, a look of surprise spreading across his face. I started to cry as I reached out and grabbed him. He pulled me into the house and we went to the bedroom. We spent hours just holding each other and renewing our intimacy. I had fallen off the wagon.

Jerry wanted to move in with me right away, but I knew I would face criticism from my friends and my boss if I said yes. I told him that we could date. He promised he would reform and even told me I could take over the finances. I tried to hold my ground, but it was not long before he was staying at my house full time.

For a while things were good between us, but soon the trouble signs started. Jerry had taken a job as an assistant manager of a barbecue restaurant and hired me. Being together almost all the time led to tensions.

My thirtieth birthday was just around the corner, and for the first time in my life, I started thinking about aging. When I was a teenager there was a saying: "Never trust anyone over thirty." I never had thought seriously about my own mortality, but now, facing this defining birthday, I began thinking about the brevity of life.

I found myself missing family. The whole gay issue had certainly put up a wall between me and the rest of my kin. Grandma McCain was still very loving to me when I was around her, but there was a strain in our relationship. This is the pain that most gays and lesbians experience when they come out, which is why it is so hard to say "I'm gay" to your family, colleagues, and friends. Every time you tell someone you love that you are gay, you risk losing their approval and their love.

Now, as I approached my thirtieth birthday, I had panic attacks at night in bed. I taunted myself, "Randy, you are about to be 30. You have no goals, no dreams. You are in a gay relationship that is going nowhere. You have alienated yourself from your family. You are drifting farther from God because you are not sure of how God views the whole gay issue. You are stuck in a dead-end job and there are no prospects for any changes whatsoever in your future. What a sad, pathetic life you have."

On my birthday I received a card from my mom with a letter inside that added to my uncertainty and self-doubt.

Dear Son,

Today, you become 30 years old and many things flood my thoughts as I let the years of your life parade before my memory. I go back to the time I carried your precious life within me. You were being given to us by God and we could hardly wait to receive you into our arms, our hearts and our family…and then the years of loving you, of nourishing you, seeing that you were provided with the things you needed in life and more. So many memories. I remember the many times in your oh, so very young days, you were at the altar crying your heart out to God; getting God's blessings and then getting up and loving everybody…God's grace and anointing filling your life, with His love spreading out to everyone around you! How reassuring this was to me, your mother. I saw God's hand upon your life…I tried the best way I knew how to watch over you, love you, take you to Sunday school and church, live the life before you, and teach you right from wrong, and I trusted God to do the rest. Randy, all I know is God put a call to the full-time ministry on your life. You know that. I know that.

Your whole family knows that. A lot of the whole state and beyond knows that…

Are you happy with your life as it is? Do you somehow believe you are reaching as many people for God as He intended for you to? What has happened to your ministry? Did God change His mind? Do our (your dad's and mine) hearts ache day and night and our burden

how long??? All I know is that God is faithful…God restores…and even though I might not live to see the day (Oh I hope so) someday—God will deliver you and make you whole! I love you my son, Mother.

The letter added to my angst over my current situation. I started pondering ways that I could, once and for all, free myself from Jerry's control.

I stayed in touch with Gary by phone and letters. While he had been so upset with me for going back to Jerry, to his credit, Gary stayed connected to me. He was never judgmental. He let me blow off steam, even though I suspect he wanted to say "I told you so" many times.

One afternoon, I could not stand it any longer. I called Gary and told him that I wanted out. He said that I could come live with him in South Dakota. He would even send me the money to get there. It felt so comforting to hear Gary say, "Randy, you are doing the right thing by leaving Jerry. I know my advice could be suspect because of my feelings for you. But Randy, you have got to do something before you lose your mind."

"I know you are right," I said. "But if I am a Christian, how can I turn my back on him? Jesus laid down His life for me. Shouldn't I be willing to lay down mine for Jerry?"

"Randy, first of all, you're not Jesus. Jerry is on a self-destructive road, and he is taking you down with him. You have to let go of him to save yourself. You are right back where you were a year ago, when he said he would change. Has he? No! He's not going to change. You can pray for Jerry but you can't save him. Randy, you have tried and tried to make this work. If it hasn't worked by now…"

"I know it never will. I have to do it, Gary."

That night I prayed and asked God if it was right for me to leave Jerry. The answer that came to me was, "Son, I love Jerry more than you do and I will help him if he will reach out to me. But you are not his answer; I am."

I felt I had my green light. I began to wonder what I would do with my life after Jerry. The one thing I missed, more than anything, was ministry. I tried to make peace with God through the church we were attending, but I still had not convinced myself that it was okay to be gay and Christian. I listened to the explanations by others in my church, but I was not confident of God's love for me. Also, I was disappointed in the fact that the church I attended would not give gay and lesbian people any Christian guidelines as to how to live their lives. I pled with them to at least admit that there were certain sexual practices that were unhealthy.

"Like sadomasochism. Can't we teach that this form of sexual expression is unhealthy?"

"No, Randy, we can't say that, because, for some people, S&M can be a very meaningful sexual experience."

"Well, can we encourage couples to be monogamous? Isn't that a Christian principle?"

"No, we can't tell a couple how they should set up their relationships. There are some who are incapable of monogamy. What we can do is encourage them to lay out ground rules for their extracurricular sexual affairs before they make the decision to move in with each other. As long as the two of them agree to these terms, then extramarital affairs can be beneficial to them as a couple."

This seemed like hogwash to me and went against my core beliefs. Marriage was to be a commitment to fidelity. Many of my gay friends said that we should not pattern gay relationships after heterosexual marriage, but I knew what I wanted in my life. I wanted to be someone's one and only. Also, I was growing uncomfortable with so much "gayness" in the worship service. I missed going to church with all kinds of people. I did not want to live and worship in a gay ghetto. A church that was exclusively gay and did not encourage what I believed to be a Christian lifestyle was not the answer to my personal, spiritual questions. I missed the fellowship I once had with fellow believers. I missed the Bible studies. I missed the praise and worship music. I missed God.

On Easter Sunday 1986, Jerry and I attended a local charismatic church to view a dramatic production of the death and resurrection of Jesus. The music minister, who was a friend of mine, was a deeply tormented person who did not believe you could be both gay and Christian. He struggled with his concepts of God and sexuality, a struggle I knew well. I sat remembering the church plays that I had directed. I longed to do it again. But that seemed impossible.

Again, I began to have second thoughts about being gay, since this aspect of my life had brought me nothing but heartache and loss. If it were possible to change, I no longer wanted to be gay. This desire now became my motivation to leave Jerry. I called Grandma McCain and asked if I could live with her for a while. She was more than happy to give me a place of refuge. Her health was failing, and it would be a comfort to have someone living with her. I knew that if I were going to leave Jerry and break his manipulating hold, I would have to take drastic measures. If I lived too close to Jerry, I would be in danger of giving in to my codependency and running back. When I broke the news to Jerry, he was devastated. He t̶̶ ̶ ̶ ̶ did not want to live without me.

"Randy, God brought you into my life, so God woul̶ Although he was not a very spiritual person, Jerry certai̶ make me feel guilty.

"Jerry, I am not happy. I miss ministry. I believe̶ cannot see any way that I am ever going to be able ̶ ready to do whatever it takes to please God."

"Now you are telling me that you think it is wrong̶ ̶ ̶ ̶

"I don't know, Jerry. I am going to stay at my grandma's house ̶ to study my Bible and spend time in prayer. I am asking God to show me the t̶ ̶

"Randy, please, you are killing me! Don't leave me again. Please don't leave me again."

"Jerry, I just need some time away from you to think about my life and what I need to do to regain my sanity."

Jerry immediately went into crisis mode, which meant maximum manipulation. He asked his kids to talk to me. They begged me not to leave their dad. This was painful, because I loved his kids.

Next, he called one of my friends from church. Roger had been a Methodist minister. He was married, had two sons, had left the Methodist church, came out to his wife, and was now well on his way to accepting himself as the gay man God created him to be. I was his friend as he went through this process. We had both been raised in Assembly of God churches. He looked to me for answers to many of his questions. When Jerry told him my plans, Roger agreed to talk to me.

"Randy, surely you are not saying that they got to you, those Bible-beating fundamentalists! Have you lost your mind?"

"Roger, I don't know right now. I need some time to think. I am so unhappy."

"Well Randy, just because you are not happy with Jerry doesn't mean that it's wrong to be gay."

"But Roger, before Jerry, there were so many other men. I have not found happiness in any of my gay relationships."

"Randy, perhaps that is because you have made poor choices. Look, I am not saying that it is a bad thing for you to go to your grandma's house for meditation and study. But if you do go, don't take along books by "ex-gay" theologians who want to sway you to believe that being gay is wrong. Randy, they can really push your buttons and play on your fear of God to make you see things the way they want you to. Just take your Bible and ask God to show you the answers."

"You're right. I will take just my Bible. But Roger, I know you are talking to me because Jerry asked you to. He's trying so hard to keep me from leaving him."

"Yes, I did come because Jerry asked me to, but Randy, that's not the only reason. I also came because you are my friend. You are the one who helped me when I was suicidal. You helped me see God as my friend and not my enemy. You were there for me. You helped me make sense of the mess that was my life."

I could see I was confusing Roger. I understood why he was frustrated, because I was unsure myself. I promised him that I would keep an open mind. We hugged and he left.

The next day, I called my mother and told her that I was thinking about leaving Jerry for good. She was *so* happy. Later I met her at the local mall. We were sitting in a restaurant when I told her that I was having doubts about being gay. I thought she was going to have a Pentecostal camp meeting right there in the middle of the mall! She told me that if I decided to leave Jerry, all I had to do was call my dad and he would be there with his truck to move my things.

That night, Jerry started talking about things that convinced me I better leave while I could.

"Randy, I believe that God put us together. If you go to your grandma's house and don't come back to me…if you are doing this so you can leave me for someone else, male or female, I will know it! I have psychic powers. I will put a curse on you, so that everyone in your family will suffer serious illnesses and die, while you live to watch their tragic fate."

His words chilled me to my bones. Would Jerry become violent?

The next morning I didn't let on that anything was up, but as soon as Jerry left for work, I called my dad. He brought the truck and we were packed and ready to pull out when Jerry returned home for lunch. He tried to stop me, but I told Dad to drive away. I know this sounds heartless, but I was fighting for my life against my addiction to this troubled man. I was also afraid of what Jerry might do to me once he became convinced that I was leaving for good.

I decided to write a letter to *Love in Action*, a ministry based in San Rafael, California, dedicated to bringing healing and hope to homosexuals. They believed they could change sexual orientation from homosexual, to heterosexual. Many referred to it as an "ex-gay" ministry. In my letter, I told of my decision to leave the gay lifestyle, and that I had moved away from my gay friends and had repented of being homosexual. I asked them to send study materials to help me keep myself free from the sin of homosexuality. One of the men from the ministry sent me back a hand-written response:

Dear Randy, Greetings in the name of Jesus! Praise God for the work that He is doing in your life. Like you, I also went to an Assembly of God church before entering the gay life-style. After being deceived and lied to by Satan for five years, I was brought back to the Lord and have surrendered my life totally to him. You have made the right choice by getting away from your gay friends. I am sending you materials that I feel will be helpful to you along with my testimony. May God show special favor and mercy upon you.

I did exactly what I had promised my friend Roger I would not do. I was seeking books and material that would show why homosexuality was a sin. But at this point, I wanted so badly to fit in to the evangelical church world. I needed affirmation and I missed my spiritual connection with the Christian community. If it was possible for me to change and become *normal*, I was going to give it my best shot and trust God to do the rest. The material I received gave me hope that I could change. There were testimonies of men and women, once caught in Satan's trap of homosexuality, now freed by the power of Jesus Christ. If this was a true cure, I wanted to learn as much as I could.

Randy in the roll of Jesus in a Passion Play

Chapter 18

AIDS Arrives in Arkansas

Deciding to move to Grandma's pleased my parents, because they were concerned about her health. They asked me to observe how she was getting along living by herself.

Before I moved, I wanted to visit a friend in the hospital. Jimmy had AIDS. He had been a good friend since I met him in the park when he was 19. He was too young to go to the bars then, so we would just hang out together. I had a crush on him at one time, but he only saw me as a friend.

At the hospital, I took a deep breath and hesitated before opening the door to Jimmy's room. I almost panicked. In what condition would I find my friend? I had heard the horror stories about AIDS, a strange, rare cancer that seemed to be sweeping through the gay community like wildfire. Up until this time in Arkansas, we hadn't thought much about it. AIDS was seen mostly among gays in major cities like New York, San Francisco, Los Angeles, and Houston. Recently, rumor had it that AIDS was spreading to smaller communities.

At the bar one night, I overheard someone whispering Jimmy's name…

"You know he's got <u>it</u>."

I was shocked! In 1986, there were no miracle drugs for people with AIDS. Once someone discovered they had the disease, they usually had only six months to a year to live. My friend Jimmy was at the state medical hospital that would, over the years, care for hundreds of persons with AIDS. At this time, Jimmy was only their fifth patient with AIDS. The nurses and doctors were learning as they went along, trying desperately to treat this strange killer, running rampant through the gay community. At that time there were many theories as to how a person contracted AIDS, some of which proved false, some *ridiculously* false.

In agony, I realized that I had done all the things then suspected of spreading the virus. Outside Jimmy's room, preparing myself for whatever I would see, fear overwhelmed me. Could I be infected? Would I be looking into my future when I entered that room? I forced myself to push the door open and walked in. Jimmy was sleeping soundly. He looked so weak and pale. There was a man at the foot of the bed, massaging Jimmy's feet. I introduced myself.

"Hi, I'm Randy McCain."

"Hi, I'm Robert. I'm a friend of Jimmy's."

"How is he?

"Well, he's having a pretty rough time of it right now. He seems to be losing his eyesight because of the swelling on his brain." (I learned later that an opportunistic disease called Cryptococcus meningitis had caused Jimmy's brain to swell.) "He's been asleep for quite a while. He should be waking up soon. His mother just stepped out to get a bite to eat."

I took a seat and conversed with Robert for a while. As we were talking, Jimmy awoke.

"Hi Jimmy, this is Randy...Randy McCain."

"Oh, hi Randy," Jimmy answered sleepily.

"How are you making it?"

What a dumb question to ask. Yet the answer was one I would hear from my brave friend again and again over the next few weeks.

"I'm fine. But I can't really see you too well." Jimmy said, squinting. "You look like a shadow to me."

When I took his hand, he squeezed tightly.

"What are you doing these days, Randy?"

"Well, you know how I used to be in church ministry?"

"Yes."

"I have decided that I want to do that again."

"That's great, Randy."

"I wanted to come by and see you. I wanted to let you know I'm praying for you. I'll leave my telephone number, so if you need anything, have someone call me."

"Thanks Randy, I will."

"Jimmy, would it be all right if I said a prayer with you before I leave?"

"Please do," he replied. I prayed for protection, healing and rest. When I finished, I reached down and kissed the back of Jimmy's hand that was firmly holding mine.

"I'll be back soon. I love you, Jimmy."

"Thanks for coming to see me."

I moved from the bed, spoke briefly with Robert, and stepped into the hallway, wiping the sweat from my forehead. I had felt death in that room. I got to my car and began driving toward Grandma's house. During the drive, I kept seeing Jimmy's swollen head and his beautiful eyes. He was twenty-six years old and terminally ill! It seemed so unfair.

Grandma was glad to see me. We talked into the night about my decision to leave Jerry and my commitment to try and change my sexual orientation. I met with Grandma's pastor the next day. When he found out that I had been in ministry, he wanted to know more. I told him that I had left the ministry for a few years and had "backslidden." (Backslidden was a term we used in Pentecostal circles to describe someone who had once been a committed Christian, but had lost the zeal she or he previously possessed.) Pastor Jerry assured me that if I had been called to ministry, the gifts I needed to live out that call were still within me.

My grandma lived three houses from her Assembly of God church and Pastor Jerry's house, where he lived with his wife Linda and their four daughters. Sister Linda, a cancer survivor, was a gentle woman who always had a smile and a kind word for everyone. Although Brother Jerry and I hit it off, I stuck to my decision not to disclose my past. He was a country guy, and I was afraid the subject of homosexuality would freak him out. I loved being in church and pursuing my relationship with God once again.

After about a month at Grandma's house, I felt a need to see what I could do to help Jimmy. When I told Grandma, she said she was proud of me for wanting to help my friend. Jimmy had a very supportive family. His mom and dad were both deaf. It became apparent that they needed help talking with the doctors and nurses about Jimmy's illness. I began studying sign language to help them understand the doctor's instructions.

Jimmy's condition had deteriorated since I had last seen him. He was totally blind and not as alert. He started hallucinating and needed someone to sit with him constantly. I spent many hours at his bedside, holding his hand. I learned to bathe him, changed his diapers, and wiped his forehead with a cool washcloth when his fever spiked to 105. As I rubbed his back and legs and massaged his feet, I began to understand Jesus' instructions to his disciples: "Now that I, your Lord and Teacher, have washed your feet, you also should wash one another's feet. I have set you an example that you should do as I have done for you." John 13:14-15 NIV

My mother, concerned that I was taking care of an AIDS patient, questioned me closely about it one day.

"You know, Randy, they don't know yet all the ways you can catch that disease. What if you get it yourself, by taking care of Jimmy?"

"Mother, I know what it is to run from the call of God on my life. I did that for over five years. Now that I've decided to recommit myself to the ministry, most churches would not let me behind their pulpits. I don't get many offers to preach or sing in churches. No pastors want to hire me as their assistant. But when I walk into a hospital room where someone is dying of AIDS, I am not asked to show my ordination papers. Those to whom I minister do not ask about my past. They just want a hand they can hold, someone who will sit with them and bathe them and pray with them. I know I am doing what God wants me to do, and I refuse to run any longer from the call that God has placed on my life."

To Mom's credit, she did not question me further.

During the next several months, I divided my time between Grandma's house and Little Rock, staying with my folks so I could help look after Jimmy. On one of my stays with Grandma, I visited with Pastor Jerry. I told him I had decided to be baptized.

"But haven't you been baptized before, Randy?"

"Yes, Brother Jerry, but I feel like I am making a brand new start, and I want to do this as an act of rededicating my life to Jesus."

He had no problem with that. He even asked me if I would preach the following Wednesday night. This surprised me. I could not believe that Pastor Jerry would take a chance on me like that. I felt I needed to confess.

"Brother Jerry, there are some things you need to know about me…about my past."

"Randy, have you talked to God about your past?"

"Yes, I have."

"Then Randy, it is none of my business. What is in the past is past. Now, if you feel you need to talk about it, I will listen. But I sense the presence of God in your life. That's all I need to know. Don't let your past keep you from getting in that pulpit next Wednesday night. We're all sinners, saved by grace."

The following Sunday, I was baptized. It was so different from my first baptism at Midway Assembly of God in 1964, when I was eight. Back then, it was winter, and the baptistery was not heated. Brother Rorex dipped me under that cold water and I came up, my teeth chattering uncontrollably. The congregation thought I was speaking in tongues. In reality, I was speaking the language of cold!

This time, the baptistery was not only heated, but had water jets that massaged your legs! When I came up out of the water, I felt so clean, forgiven, and close to God. What a special night for me. Grandma was there cheering me on. I preached the next Wednesday night, and it felt good to be back in the pulpit.

As Christmas approached in 1986, I was more involved in Jimmy's care. I asked the nurses what precautions I should take to protect myself. They told me there was much that they didn't know. They did tell me to be sure I always wore disposable gloves when caring for Jimmy, and I should avoid contact with his bodily fluids. I wore gloves, but refused to wear the mask that they recommended. I was spending hours at a time with Jimmy. The mask was not comfortable or practical. Moreover, I did not want him to feel like he was some monster from which I had to protect myself. I had not been tested for AIDS at that time, so there was the possibility that I already had the disease. But if I did not have AIDS, I wanted to avoid exposure.

One day, I was feeding Jimmy his oatmeal. He had just taken a mouthful when he sneezed unexpectedly. Without warning, food from Jimmy's mouth was all over my face. Inside, I was screaming, "You're infected Randy, you've got AIDS now!" Because I needed to stay calm for Jimmy's sake, I slowly put down the oatmeal bowl, rose from my seat, and walked to the sink. I washed my face and finished feeding him. From then on, I made sure that I sat to his side, rather than facing him when I fed him. I was not at risk that day, but due to the misinformation at the time, I was afraid I had been infected.

A few days later, the doctor told us that Jimmy was doing so much better that she thought he could spend Christmas at home with his family. We were overjoyed. I arrived early at the hospital on December 20, 1986 with a spring in my step. Christmas has always been my favorite time of the year. I smelled the cold, crisp December air as I got off the city bus and headed for the hospital. Jimmy would be at home for Christmas! Walking into his room, I was immediately aware of a change. He was very restless. He was rolling from one side of the bed to the other, his hands nervously pulling at his sheets until they were balled up in a wad. He then threw them over the side of his bed. Although he was completely blind, Jimmy's eyes were wide open, darting wildly. I tried to calm him down by talking to him, but it did not help. I left the room and found his doctor in the hallway. She was worried.

"Randy, I'm afraid Jimmy's meningitis is returning. His disorientation and fidgeting are definite symptoms."

I was amazed at this doctor's compassion as tears streamed down her cheeks. "How will you treat it?" I asked.

"That's just it. If this is a return of meningitis, we won't be able to treat it. The medication that we gave him last time made him deathly ill. We can't give him any more of it. I had so hoped that Jimmy could go home for Christmas, that he and his family could have a happy holiday together, and now this!"

As we stood outside his room, suddenly the door flew open and his mother ran out, motioning us into the room. The doctor and I hurried in. Jimmy was on his side, his body rigid, his breathing quick and shallow. The doctor forced open his eyelid and his eyeball had rolled to the back of his head.

"He's seizing!" she said nervously. "Keep him on his side and I'll go get another doctor to help me."

I began to pray, "Dear Jesus, help Jimmy. Please, help Jimmy!" I whispered to him as my hands held him so he would not turn over, "Jimmy, Jimmy, it's going to be all right. We're here for you." I kept saying the name of Jesus over and over under my breath.

Suddenly Jimmy relaxed. I spoke to him and he responded. When the doctors returned, Jimmy was resting peacefully.

That horrific morning was the beginning of several frightening experiences with Jimmy in the next few days, as his condition worsened. By December 24th, it became clear that he would not see the new year. I told his mom and dad that I would stay with him so they could have Christmas Eve with the rest of their family, at home. They promised to come and relieve me after their dinner and gift exchange.

I had never been in a hospital on Christmas Eve. I had never thought about the fact that there were people in hospitals during the holidays. When the nurses came in to see Jimmy, and I stepped out to stretch, I saw the sad faces of the people visiting a son, a daughter, a spouse, a mother or father, or a grandparent. To be in a hospital on Christmas Eve, as a loved one is dying, is a pain beyond words. Most of the evening, I stood by Jimmy's bed because of his restless fidgeting. If I sat down, he might fall out of bed. I had to change his bedclothes repeatedly that evening because his sweat drenched them. I must confess feeling relieved when Jimmy's dad walked in after midnight. I reported what I knew about his son's condition, and then I hugged Jimmy.

"Jimmy, I'm going home for a while. Your dad is here with you. Merry Christmas. I love you." I kissed him on the forehead, but he stared out into space and continued swaying. When I got into my car, I felt like collapsing. It was all I could do to drive to my parents' house.

The next morning I woke up to the smell of turkey baking in the oven. Mom had started preparing her traditional Christmas feast. Dad was puttering around in his robe, pouring cereal into a bowl. I called the nurse's station at the hospital and learned that Jimmy's condition was about the same. I asked if I was needed, but the nurses told me to stay home and enjoy Christmas with my family. They would call if anything changed.

That Christmas was a special day. It felt good to be at home during the holidays. I had missed being part of the family Christmas meal and gift exchange. Mom gave me a journal. Inside she wrote, "To Randy, from Mom. A daily journal for you to keep during the year of 1987. Merry Christmas, 1986!!! I love you and have faith to believe that by the end of 1987, you, with God's help, will have your life in order and will be doing God's work. I know He has a wonderful ministry for you! Mother."

I wrote in big letters on the first page, "MAY EVERY DAY COUNT FOR JESUS IN 87."

As we were opening presents after our Christmas meal, the phone rang. A nurse from the hospital told me that Jimmy had taken a turn for the worse. His mom asked them to call. I rushed to the hospital and hurried to Jimmy's room. All his family surrounded his bed—his mom, dad, sisters, aunts, and uncles. No words were spoken, because most of them were deaf. This was a silent vigil.

I looked at Jimmy. He was so still. At first, I was relieved that he was finally resting, but looking more closely, I realized my friend was not breathing. Jimmy had died just moments before. I took his hand in mine and I bent over and hugged his poor, emaciated body one last time. I had learned so much through taking care of him. Jimmy was my teacher, and he taught me how to be a servant. Knowing that Jimmy was with the Lord, I went to his mother and signed, "Jimmy went home for Christmas." She hugged me and we cried together. Then Jimmy's sister came over to me and asked if I would call Jimmy's partner, Donnie, who also had AIDS. He had gone home to his parents, who lived about three hours away, so they could help take care of him. Imagine how difficult that phone call was for me.

"Donnie, this is Randy. Listen, I'm calling to tell you that Jimmy just passed away. I'm here at the hospital with his family. They asked me to call you."

Donnie started to cry. He thanked me. I told him that we would let him know what the funeral plans were. Then I went with Jimmy's family back to their house to help them with the arrangements.

Jimmy's funeral was sad, but deeply meaningful to me. Donnie didn't sit with the family. He sat in the back with friends. He'd lost a lot of weight since I had last seen him, and he had just found out that he had Kaposi's Sarcoma, a rare skin disease, diagnosed primarily in elderly Italian and Jewish men. Among this population, the lesions developed slowly, but in AIDS patients it often developed aggressively and could affect the skin, lungs, gastrointestinal tract, and other organs. Donnie also had a dry, hacking cough that he tried to control with cough drops. I watched him as he suffered through the whole funeral process. This must have seemed to him somewhat like a dress rehearsal for his own funeral.

Thankfully, I had no idea the sadness and tragedy I would see in the next few years because of this horrible disease. I certainly would not have predicted its disastrous effect on Arkansas, or my own life. I had only seen the tip of the iceberg.

Chapter 19

Cancer

Sunday, January 11, 1987, my parents and I attended church together. Afterward, we went out to eat and then came home to spend a lazy afternoon…until Mother answered the phone. She talked a while, and I could tell by her voice that she was troubled. When she finished, Mom came to my room with a worried look on her face.

"That was your sister, Linda. She found a lump in her breast. She has already seen the doctor, and they are going to operate a week from tomorrow."

"Is it cancer?"

"They won't know until they remove it. If it *is* cancerous, they will remove her breast."

Linda, my oldest sister, was seven when I entered the world. She took piano lessons for years and majored in piano in college. She taught me to love music and enjoy singing. We spent hours at the piano, Linda playing and teaching me to belt out those gospel songs we heard on the *Gospel Jubilee* and on the southern gospel records we loved to play. I adored my big sister. I can remember during her college years when she would come home for the weekend, she would wake me on Saturday morning with a kiss on the forehead.

"Wake up, Randy. I fixed your favorite breakfast."

I would open my eyes and jump out of bed. We were having French toast! Mom didn't make it often, but Linda knew it was my favorite.

Linda was the "perfect child" in the McCain family. As the oldest, she strove for excellence. Her life seemed to follow a perfect plan. She attended Evangel College and received her bachelor's degree in music on a Thursday evening, came home for her wedding rehearsal on Friday evening, got married on Saturday, drove to Branson, Missouri on Sunday, and started a summer job on Monday, working at a quaint little tourist lodge with her new husband Mike. Not a moment was wasted.

Linda married her childhood sweetheart whom she had met at church. Mike was handsome, personable, yet quiet and reserved. I wanted to like Mike, but he saw me as a spoiled kid who had not been taught the importance of work. Almost immediately, he seemed to influence Linda to see me that way, too. Immediately after their wedding rehearsal, I felt the sting of Linda's words.

"Linda," I said, "I guess now that you'll be married to Mike, I'll be the second man in your life."

She looked at me with a sort of smirk and said, "No, Daddy will be second. You'll be number three."

Three years later, Linda gave birth to a beautiful baby girl named Jana. I was at the hospital when they brought her out of the delivery room. Jana became the love of my life. When she was still very little, I started taking her on dates. I bought her a corsage when she was five years old and told her that Uncle Dandy, as she called me, was taking her out to eat, *anywhere* she wanted to go. She chose Long John Silver's, where we ate chicken and fish. Then we stopped by Farrell's Ice Cream Parlor for sundaes. To top off the evening, I bought her a great big multicolored lollipop that was bigger than her head.

Two years later, both my sisters found themselves expecting babies at the same time. Leandra and Diana, their baby girls, were born two weeks apart, and I was there for the births. Waiting outside the delivery room made me think about being a daddy someday. I felt sure I would be the best father in the world! I loved children. But for the time being, I had nieces to love and cherish. Two years later, Linda had a baby boy named Ben. Ben weighed 12 pounds and was the biggest baby in the nursery window. Someone in the family jokingly called him "Big Ben." I asked Linda how many babies she and Mike were going to have.

"Oh, a dozen at least. I love having babies!"

Linda would have only one more. Baby Jessica was born with a rare chromosome disease and the doctors told us that she probably would not live long. Linda would not accept this prognosis. She took Jessica home and gave that precious little angel all kinds of love. Jessica did not grow at all for a year and a half, nor did she interact with us. Yet we all loved and cherished her. Then one day, she started to fill out and grow. This unfortunately proved too much for her little heart, and two-year-old Jessica went to heaven.

Linda was the perfect daughter. She graduated college, married a Christian man, had grandchildren for Mom and Dad, stayed married, and worked in her church. My sister Pam married an atheist and divorced after having a child. I turned out gay. Linda was Mom and Dad's shining star, the one who made them very proud.

When I came out as a gay man, Linda was upset with me. She considered my being gay as rebellion toward God, our family, and our church. She could not, *would* not, deal with it. When we saw each other, she would give me her condescending, judgmental look and say, "I am praying for you to get your life right with God, Randy."

Linda never called or wrote to me. It was as if she did not have a brother any more. This hurt me deeply. Then, as my nieces and nephew got older, I could tell that she and Mike were influencing the way they looked at me.

One of the hardest things about accepting my sexual orientation was realizing that I would never have children. I grieved that the offspring I had dreamed of would never exist because I was gay. Today there are options available for gay couples to have children, but then it was almost unheard of. Thus, my nieces and nephew had become very precious to me. Although Pam allowed my niece Leandra to stay in touch with me on a regular basis, I began to realize that Linda did not want her kids to get close to Uncle Randy. In her eyes, I was a bad role model for them.

After I came back to the church and renounced my homosexuality in 1986, I was allowed to be a part of family gatherings again. Linda was a little more pleasant towards me, but not much. We were never as close as we had been before. Linda was suspicious of my ministry to gay men dying with AIDS. She made a point of telling me once that she was glad certain restaurants were firing gay employees because she sure "didn't want someone infected with AIDS serving *her* food."

Linda also seemed to have a problem with the fact that I wanted to minister again so soon after returning to the fold. In her mind, I was not sorry enough for my past. When I came back to the church, so many people told me, "Your sister, Linda, loved you so much. She was constantly praying for your salvation." I never felt that love from her, only condemnation. Then, when I came back and tried to live my life her way, abstaining from gay behavior, she resented me and gave only tepid support. This hurt me deeply, but never stopped me from loving Linda, or from praying that we could somehow find a way to be close again.

When I heard mother's news about Linda's cancer, my heart seemed to stop beating. When we hear the word "cancer," we think of death. I could not imagine living without Linda. A week later, my parents and I drove to Jonesboro, Arkansas for Linda's surgery. Upon arriving, we learned that she had already been taken into the operating room. Soon, we found out that her tumor was malignant and the doctors removed Linda's breast.

When we walked into her hospital room, she looked up at us and smiled. Daddy walked over to Linda, hugged her, and started to cry. My mom, however, was characteristically stoic. She has always said that it is a mystery to her how people cry. Crying was never a natural response for Mom.

"Did the doctor tell you they removed your breast?" Mom asked her.

"Yes," Linda replied with a smile. "They took one look at it and said, 'It's so small she'll never miss it.'"

We all laughed uncomfortably. Later, Mom stayed with Linda when Dad and I drove back to Little Rock. Cancer would be a menacing intruder in our family for years to come.

Linda did not have chemotherapy. Soon my other sister decided to have a mammogram. When Pam learned that she had a lump in *her* breast, her doctors performed a lumpectomy and recommended radiation treatments. I was in a state of shock. I could not imagine losing both my sisters.

I decided to go back to Grandma's house because I needed time to recharge my spiritual and emotional batteries. When I arrived, I found out that Sister Linda, the wife of my grandma's pastor, was very ill. Her breast cancer had returned. I was honored when Pastor Jerry asked if I would preach for him from time to time. A few weeks later, Sister Linda lost her battle with cancer. Sickness and death were all around me.

Gary and I stayed in touch with frequent letters and phone calls. Gary knew that I had left Jerry for the second time, and that I had recommitted myself to the ministry. He knew I was praying that Jesus would change my sexual orientation. He was glad that I had left Jerry, but not so sure about my decision to go straight. The more we talked, the more convinced he became that he, too, would fight his urges and try to overcome his homosexuality. Gary joined a Wesleyan church and, during an appointment with his pastor, disclosed his struggle. The pastor suggested meeting with Gary on a weekly basis to watch a video designed to help individuals overcome homosexuality.

Gary got involved with church and signed up to go on a church mission trip to Haiti to help build a school. I began teaching an adult singles' Bible study at church and directed two Easter dramas. I could not believe God's goodness to me. The year before, at Easter, I sat in church thinking I would never do Christian drama again. One year later, I was actively using my ministry gifts, and I loved it.

Randy and his sister, Linda

Chapter 20

Temptation in Washington D.C.

A couple of weeks after his wife's death, Brother Jerry came by my grandma's and asked if I would like to take a trip with his family. Convinced his girls needed a vacation to get their minds off their mom's death, he borrowed a friend's RV to drive to Washington D.C., inviting his mom to go along.

"Is the RV big enough for all of us?"

"Wait until you see it, Randy. It's huge."

"And you can drive something that big?"

"You bet!"

I decided to go, since he promised it would not cost me anything. Brother Jerry said he would appreciate my company. Grateful for all he had done for me, how could I not go?

Since Brother Jerry was a big kid at heart, the trip was loads of fun. We stopped for the night in state parks on lakes in Tennessee, where we swam and boated. I was having a blast!

When we got to Arlington, just outside Washington D.C., we parked the RV at an Assembly of God church where Brother Jerry knew the pastor. This would be home base. We could walk to the subway that took us to downtown Washington. I loved history, and could not wait to see all the monuments and museums.

The first day, I could tell that if I stayed with Brother Jerry and his girls, I was not going to see very much. They were not history buffs, so I asked Brother Jerry if he minded me taking off on my own. I was in heaven walking through the Smithsonian museums. Finally, exhausted, I sat down on a park bench between the Capitol and the Lincoln Monument. It was a beautiful day, but hot and muggy. I noticed a young man sitting on the next bench who kept looking at me. I had always been attracted to Hispanic men, and he was *beautiful*.

"Now, Randy," I thought. "Stop thinking those thoughts. You are not gay any-more, remember?" I made myself look the other way. Suddenly, I heard the young man speaking to me.

"Excuse me." He had a heavy accent…another turn-on! "Excuse me, are you visiting here?"

"Yes, I am."

"I thought so."

I wondered what gave me away. (Could it have been the red shorts with red suspenders and the flowery yellow shirt I was wearing that made me look like Pinocchio?)

"Are you enjoying your visit?"

"Yes, I am, thank you." I looked into his eyes when I answered. They sparkled with excitement for life.

"My name is Carlos," he offered. "I come from Venezuela. I am here in the USA visiting my sister. I have been here several months, so I could serve as a tour guide for you, show you around if you would like."

If I would like? Here was the man of my dreams, and I was having the misfortune to meet him *after* I had sworn off men! I reminded myself to be careful, but what harm could come from spending a little time sightseeing with him? He was probably straight anyway. I told him I would enjoy the company.

We walked toward the Capitol, talking as we made our way from one monument to the next. I found out that he was an architect in Venezuela. I could not help but notice his bulging arms, displayed nicely thanks to his tank top, and his muscular brown legs. I was surprised at how attracted I was to Carlos, because I thought God had delivered me from homosexuality. Yet it felt nice to walk with this exquisite looking man from a foreign country, taking in the sights of Washington, D.C. It was like a romantic dream!

Carlos asked me what I did, and I told him I was a minister. He asked what kind of ministry I was involved in. I told him about my work with AIDS patients, and he wanted to hear about my experiences. As I told him about Jimmy and others, I noticed tears in his eyes.

"That is what Jesus would do if He were here today. He would love all people. You are a very compassionate man, I can see it in your eyes."

"Thank you, Carlos." I was eating up this attention. I asked him a few personal questions.

"So, are you married?"

"Well, I am divorced. I have a son. His mother has custody, but I visit him often."

I thought, "Good, he's straight after all." I was so relieved.

When we walked through the Vietnam Memorial, I was not prepared for the emotions I felt. Like all children who grew up in the sixties, I watched footage of the wounded men being carried through the jungles to waiting helicopters night after night on the six o'clock news. Now, as I saw row after row of the names of so many young lives, snuffed out in war, I could not hold back the tears. Carlos walked over to me and took my hand in his, pulling me close and hugging me with the other. It felt good to be comforted. Then the thought ran through my head, "What must the other people think?"

It was not unusual to see guys comforting other guys at this monument. As we walked away, Carlos said, "I hope you didn't mind me taking your hand. You see, in my country, it is not unusual for men to show affection to one another in public."

"Well, in this country, it is not considered normal."

"That is sad, Randy, very sad."

We had to run the last part of the way to the Lincoln Memorial because of a sudden thunderstorm. Actually, the rain felt good as relief from the sun. We reached the top of the steps and ran under the shelter of the roof just in time. We watched the rain approaching like a sheet of water coming straight up the mall toward us. Again, I thought how perfect the day had been.

Carlos and I walked along the Potomac River toward the Jefferson Memorial. The rain shower had been brief, and now we enjoyed a beautiful sunset as we walked close together on the path leading to the temple-like memorial. We took pictures, then sat and talked about our countries and our lives. I was enthralled with Carlos' accent and enjoyed his stories.

It was getting dark, so I told Carlos I had better start walking toward the subway to return to Arlington. He said he would join me. As we headed for the subway, Carlos started asking more questions about my spiritual beliefs and about the church I attended.

"How do they view drinking alcohol?"

"Oh, they're against it. They think it is a sin."

"What about a man dating another man?"

I was shocked by this question.

"Oh they definitely don't like that…at all!"

"I think that it is a good thing. I have dated men before."

There, he had said it! He was gay! My heart seemed to stop in mid-beat. I was afraid and visibly agitated.

"Randy, have I upset you? Please forgive me, my friend."

I didn't say anything at first. We kept walking and my pace got faster. I was ahead of him when I suddenly stopped, turned around and faced him.

"You are scaring me! You are really messing with my head."

"No, Randy, please. I am sorry."

"Look, I used to be gay, but I asked God to take those desires away from me. I was doing pretty well until today—until I met you! Now I can't seem to turn off the feelings and the thoughts I've been having ever since you first spoke to me. You are so beautiful. It's like someone could read my mind and see a perfect description of my dream man, and then created *you*. This is just too much! I am so angry at myself. I thought I had this under control but now the feelings are back! Maybe they never left…I don't know! Oh, God help me!"

The subway pulled up. We got on and sat down next to each other. Carlos had a very sad look in his eyes.

"Randy, I have hurt you. I feel so bad."

"It's not your fault. You can't help the way you look, or the way I am feeling toward you. You have been very nice to me today. I am just very confused right now. I am sure you think I'm crazy! Maybe I am."

Carlos reached over and gently took my hand, but I pulled it away. We came to our stop. As we got off the subway, we walked a few yards and found ourselves in front of a coffee house.

"Randy, let me buy you something to eat."

At this point, I had run out of willpower and followed Carlos into the restaurant. We sat in a booth and I ordered my favorite sandwich, a patty melt and fries, which I did not eat.

"Randy, please, may I tell you what I am feeling for you?"

I nodded yes.

"You are a very beautiful man."

"No, I'm not!"

"Yes you are, Randy. I wish you could see what I see when I look at you. My heart is beating so fast just being near you. When you told me of your love and care for those men who were dying, and of your faith in Jesus, I was drawn to you. You made me want to know Jesus because I could see Him in you and hear Him through your words."

"No, no, I am *nothing* like Jesus. I am a very sinful person."

"Randy, you are a good man. I wish I could love you, hold you, and protect you."

I thought, "Okay Lord, if this is a test, you have gone too far! This is not fair!"

We left the restaurant and walked to the church. A short distance down the road there was a little strip mall, which was closed for the night. We found a pay phone, and Carlos called a taxi to take him to his sister's house in the suburb of Falls Church. Since the dispatcher said it would be about a thirty minute wait, we found a small city park with many trees and a few park benches. Carlos took my hand, and I let him lead me into the center of the darkened forest.

Once we were out of the glow of the street light, he stopped and turned to face me. He was so close I could feel his breath on my face. I knew what was about to happen, and I did not resist. It had been over a year since I had kissed a man. Suddenly, his lips were on mine and I almost lost consciousness. It felt so right. My breath was fast and audible as he whispered in my ear.

"Randy, your heart is beating so fast I can feel it."

He blew softly on my face. We kissed again, and this time I let all my inhibitions go and kissed him back. It was magical! I could not fool myself any longer. I was still very much attracted to men, at least this one. I finally pulled away. I told him that the taxi should be getting there any minute and we had better go.

As we started back, Carlos asked if he could see me the next day. I told him that I would be in church in the morning. He told me that he would try to get his sister's car and pick me up around two o' clock in the afternoon.

"I want to take you to Georgetown and show you around."

The next afternoon, we had a wonderful time exploring the little shops in Georgetown. It felt like a date. That night, I sang in church and Carlos attended. He told me afterward that I was very talented. We went out after church and ended the night with about thirty minutes of making out in the car. It felt nice, but I was confused. I had made a promise to God and to myself that I would never again think of men in a romantic or sexual way. But how do you turn off feelings that are so much a part of who you are?

My encounter with Carlos was a painful reminder that I had not received the miracle I had prayed for. I was not yet heterosexual. Carlos and I exchanged addresses, and the next morning Brother Jerry's family and I headed back to Arkansas. When we stopped for the night at a rest area, I called Gary from a pay phone. I told him all about my encounter with Carlos.

"Gary, I feel so rotten inside. I am such a failure."

"Randy, you are not a failure; you are human. My God, how could you have resisted under those circumstances? It was like being in a romantic movie and you were the star. I don't think I would have done any differently than you. I probably would have done more. Don't beat yourself up about this."

"But God must be so angry at me right now," I said despondently.

"Randy, God understands that you are human. Please don't let this make you lose hope. You're still a good person. Carlos recognized that in you, and so do I."

Gary always made me feel better. He never panicked when I came to him with my problems. He was level-headed, and he was always there to love me and help me believe in myself.

That fall, Gary decided to come to Arkansas for another visit. We talked about it on the phone one night.

"Randy, do you think we can promise that we will not be a temptation to each other?"

"Well, we will just make a vow to respect one another and not allow our passions to get out of hand. You know Gary, we have to trust God that our heterosexuality is in the process of making itself known to us. The literature I received from the ex-gay ministry says that we must not doubt God's ability to make us new creations."

Gary arrived, and from the moment I saw him, I fought the physical attraction I felt for him. He seemed cuter than the last time I saw him. However, one major deterrent to any physical contact between us was the fact that I was living at home with my parents. Mother was so afraid that I would slip back into my old ways that she kept watch like a prison guard, always on duty. She knew that Gary struggled with the same desires, so she made sure that our bedrooms were far removed from each other. When we went for rides, I could not resist taking his hand. It felt so natural, so right.

One afternoon, we drove to a state park about an hour away. As the sun was going down, we sat at a picnic table and we could no longer resist the strong desire for physical contact that both of us felt. Before I knew what hit me, we were in each other's arms, kissing passionately.

When Gary got home to South Dakota, he called and apologized for his behavior. "I guess I feel like a real hypocrite. I promised you that I would not allow things to get out of control. If I really loved you Randy, I would have been stronger."

"Gary, I am to blame just as much as you. We're going to have to be more careful in the future. When we're together, we need to make sure we don't get into any situations where we can be tempted that way."

Gary's visit had been another reality check. Once again, I was reminded that the cure for my homosexuality had not yet been achieved.

Randy at the White House in Washington D.C.

Chapter 21

Patrick Forbush

Determined more than ever to help people with AIDS, I joined a weekly AIDS support group comprised of AIDS victims, their caregivers, friends, and family members. At the support group, I met a young man named Patrick Forbush. He was tall, blond, and skinny. Pat could be very witty with his caustic humor. One evening he brought his mom, Dolly, to our group session…or, I should say, Dolly brought Pat. Pat was in the hospital on an IV when he told his mom he wanted to come to our group. Although the doctors would not release him, Dolly decided that if her son wanted to be at group, no doctor was going to tell him he couldn't. She helped him into a wheelchair, disconnected the IV, and brought him to group. All of us were amazed at Dolly's chutzpa.

Dolly was an attractive woman in her late 40s with an interesting and gruff voice. I would learn later that she was raised in the country by her Pentecostal preacher mother without much input from her dad. Her birth name was Delilah. How odd that a Pentecostal preacher would name her daughter after one of the most notorious women in the Old Testament. Dolly was married to Wally, a quiet, unassuming, retired military man. They had another son, Michael. Little did I know that night that I would become closely involved with this amazing family. Dolly could be very blunt at times, which was initially intimidating. The first time I saw her at group she was quiet and seemed to be a little ill at ease, so I thought I would try to make her feel welcome and more comfortable.

"Hi there, my name is Randy." She didn't respond at first, so I added, "And your name is…?"

"Dolly."

"Helllooo Dolly!" I replied, barely resisting the urge to break into the famous song. Dolly's hat looked like a cold weather beret. "That's quite an interesting hat you have on," I ventured.

"I can wear a hat if I want to." she responded defensively, seeming to be somewhat miffed at me.

"Yes you can, and you wear it well."

Had I said something wrong? Had I insulted her? I would learn later that Dolly was screaming at the whole world out of the anger she felt toward the disease that had overtaken her son. Moreover, because she did not have a formal education, Dolly felt inferior at social gatherings and public forums. But I learned that beneath her gruff exterior beat a heart of gold.

During our group session, Pat volunteered that he was upset because his "half-assed" brother had moved in with the family. Michael had recently gone through a divorce, and he and his three children now lived with Pat and his parents. Pat was angry because, as he put it, "Dad had to cut the toilet in two."

"Why did he do that?" someone asked.

"Weren't you listening?" Pat snapped sarcastically, "*Because* my half-assed brother moved in."

In a setting where people are discussing terminal illnesses, laughter is welcomed. I wondered if Dolly would be embarrassed by Pat's humor. Obviously, she enjoyed it. Although her body posture was guarded, you could not miss the sly smile on her face. Clearly, Dolly loved and admired her son's off-beat wit. No wonder, since he got it from her. Pat, too, was to be a most interesting character.

After the meeting ended, I introduced myself to Pat. I asked if he would like me to visit him in the hospital and he nodded yes. He was not demonstrative, but something in his manner alerted me to his desperate need for a friend. I told him I would visit.

The next day, when I walked into Pat's hospital room, his mom was not there. I breathed a sigh of relief. I felt uncomfortable around Dolly. I wasn't sure she liked me. After greeting him, I asked Pat where his mother was.

"She got mad at me and told me to 'eat shit and die!' I told her to leave me alone, so she did."

I was appalled that a mother would talk to her son in this way. I asked Pat if I could do anything for him. He said I could get him a Coke, so I went down to the canteen to get the drink. When I walked back into his room, Dolly was sitting in the chair beside the bed.

"Oh no," I thought. "She's back!"

I gave Pat the Coke and took the chair on the other side of the bed. Dolly looked me over.

"I know I met you at group, but I don't remember your name."

"Randy," I replied. "I asked Pat last night if he could use some company, and he said he could."

"He better behave himself," Dolly said. "He better watch his smart mouth."

120

Pat just looked at her, gave her a fake smile, and then looked away.

"So Pat, what do you like to do to pass the time?"

Pat did not answer at first. The silence was deafening. I shuffled nervously in my chair, hoping for some kind of response. Finally, he said that he liked to play cards.

"I'll play with you if you teach me how. We weren't allowed to play cards in my family. We're Pentecostal."

This got Dolly's attention. Her head jerked up from the magazine she was reading.

"You're Pentecostal and you're a gay boy!?"

I had not said that I was gay. Why did she assume that? Maybe because I was volunteering with the AIDS group and had come to visit her gay son. Maybe she had "gaydar."

"Well, I am Pentecostal, but I'm not gay."

Pat jerked his head around and looked at me with a shocked expression on his face. Dolly simply raised her eyebrows in a way that signaled that she was not too convinced of my answer.

It was springtime in 1988 when Pat was released from the hospital and I started visiting him at his parents' home. He was a hairstylist before he got sick.

One day Pat said to me, in his sarcastic tone, "Girl, your hair looks pitiful. You need a good cut!"

"Well Pat, I can't afford to go to the barber shop right now."

"Barber shop? You go to a barber shop to get your hair cut? No wonder you look like you do."

"Where should I go?"

"I'll cut it for you." This frightened me a little. Pat was weak and his hands shook most of the time. With his wacky sense of humor, who knew what kind of cut he would give me! But I realized this could be a bonding time to help Pat trust me more as a friend, so I acquiesced. We went out to the back porch so we wouldn't get his mom's dining room floor messy. Dolly came out to see what we were up to.

"You're going to let Pat cut your hair? You're a brave man."

She walked away laughing. This did not help allay my fears. But Pat had been a very good hairstylist, and he had not lost his touch. When he finished, my hair had never looked better. I was relieved when I saw myself in the mirror.

Then Pat told me he thought I was gay. I told him that I used to be gay, but was now changing my sexual orientation. This did not seem to make any sense to him, but he said, "Whatever."

Pat loved to go to restaurants, but he could not drive anymore. One day he called me. "I'm hungry. If you'll take me out to eat lunch, I'll buy yours."

That was the first of many lunches for Pat and me. He had expensive tastes and looked forward to our outings, even though when I came to pick him up he tried to act like he could not care less.

Then one day Dolly said to me, "Pat may act like he doesn't like you, but he gets so anxious for your arrival. It's all he talks about."

One of his friends told me Pat was disappointed that I didn't want to be gay anymore, because he would have liked for me to be his boyfriend. Yet Pat was not a man who liked to be patted or hugged. One day he told me, "I'm a touch-me-not."

This seemed strange to me, because all my life I have been a hugger. I have also always made it a practice to say "I love you" to my friends. One day, as I was saying goodbye after lunch, I made the mistake of telling Pat I loved him.

He gave me a hard look and said, "Don't say you love me."

"Why not?"

"'Cause you're not my boyfriend."

"Well then, what can I say to you?"

Pat thought for a minute and then, looking away from me, he replied, "You can say you like me a lot, but you can't say you love me."

"Okay then, Patrick Forbush, I sure do like you a lot."

He just looked at me and said, "Hmm, oh well."

Patrick Forbush and his mom, Dolly in 1982

Chapter 22

Saint Dolly

I saw God's grace and unconditional love through the life of Dolly Forbush. Although she was not your typical "Christian example," I experienced more of God's love through her than in all my years of searching for God in organized religion. These words, of the late Christian writer Mike Yaconelli, remind me of Dolly:

The truly holy people I've met in my life are really interesting people. They're a mix of the most incredible godliness, and at the same time, the most unbelievable earthiness. I know a woman who curses like a sailor, but she's the most holy woman I know. She is! I'm not kidding. We've created this image of what holiness looks like that's just nonsense. Good holy people probably drink too much some times, and have colorful language, and there's plenty of room in the Bible to see people like that. We have to see life for what it is, entirely more complicated than simple. Spirituality is not simple; it's complicated. It gets messy sometimes.

The more I got to know Dolly, the more she impressed me. She had a gift for knowing when I was spiritually down. Sometimes, when I visited Pat, she had wise words for me. Then there were times when she would call me on the phone and say something like, "You're bugging me! What's wrong with you?"

Many times Dolly would do this just when I would be struggling within myself. She seemed to have the gift of discernment where I was concerned. There were times when I would be thinking of doing something foolish, and her call would snap me back into reality. Dolly always had a truth that she wanted me to live by: "Don't ever do anything that you would be ashamed of."

She talked with me about my decision to change my sexual orientation. She never told me I shouldn't, but she always said, "Just remember, if you find out you are *still* a gay boy, Dolly still loves you."

It took a while to see Dolly as a spiritual giant. When I first met her, I considered her "a lost heathen" God had sent me to save. The truth is, she was the one doing the saving.

My friendship with Pat grew close in those early days of summer 1988. Pat seemed to be getting more of the HIV-related opportunistic illnesses. He developed neuropathy, a disease of the nerves which caused him to lose sensation in his feet. At times, his feet would swell and throb with pain; naturally, he was unsteady when he walked. Pat's movements were slow and his footing unsure, yet he was proud and did not want anyone to hold onto him. This caused many frightening moments as we walked in and out of restaurants and stores. If I took Pat's arm, he would pull away from me. I learned to walk as close to him as I possibly could without making him feel uncomfortable. Pat did not want to be seen as an invalid.

One day, he took a turn for the worse. Dolly and I went out for a walk to get some fresh air and a little exercise. She spoke about her frustrations with church people and certain preachers.

"They all preach hellfire and damnation. That's why I don't go to church anymore. Everything's a sin. You can't have any fun! Everybody's sitting around judging you."

"I've heard my share of hellfire sermons, Dolly, but Jesus isn't like that. He went to parties and He hung out with the outcasts of his day."

I knew there was something more on Dolly's mind. Finally, it came out.

"I ran into this woman from the Pentecostal church who knows me and my family. She's close to my mama. She told me that Patrick got AIDS because God was mad at me for leaving the church."

I glanced over at Dolly as we walked and saw the pain and sadness in her eyes. Righteous indignation rose up in me. I wanted to give that Pentecostal woman a piece of my mind! She didn't know Dolly—I *did*. I was there every day, watching Dolly take care of her son. Patrick had started having problems with diarrhea and Dolly was wearing herself out, changing his bed and cleaning up her grown son. I begged her to take Pat back to the hospital.

"No! Pat don't want to go to no hospital. He don't like it. If Pat don't want to go back, he's not going back! I'll take care of him myself."

"But Dolly, I'm worried about *you*. You may be a super mom but you are not Superwoman, you know. You're going to get sick yourself."

"No, I won't. I'll make it fine. Besides, I've got you."

I watched Dolly in action during the preceding week. She had her care for Patrick down to a fine art. This mother changed Pat's sheets four times in one day. She bathed him, fed him, and saw that his every need was met. I hugged her and I said, "Dolly, I was wrong. Not only are you a super mom, you *are* Superwoman!"

My heart broke for Dolly as we walked along and I saw her so hurt by another's callous, judgmental words. She looked at me and asked, "Do you think God gave Pat AIDS because I stopped going to church?"

Dolly's question brought back a memory. After my little niece, Jessica, died, our family was greeting the people who attended the funeral. A pastor's wife came up to me and said, "Randy, perhaps God took little Jessica to heaven to get your attention, so that you would make things right with him."

I remembered how angry her words made me. I wanted to slap her for her unbelievably insensitive remark. There I was, painfully grieving the death of our little angel, and that woman tried to take advantage of my vulnerable state to manipulate me into living my life according to her standards. I had experienced the pain Dolly was feeling, and now I was angry. I was just beginning to see God as a God of love myself, and this woman, who supposedly knew and loved God, misrepresented Him to Dolly in such an unloving way.

"Dolly," I said, finally giving voice to my deepest hope, "God would *never* do such an unloving thing to you or Pat. God sees you when you are washing out those dirty sheets. He sees you taking such good care of your son, and in those quiet moments when you let the pain rise to the surface, God weeps when you weep. Remember Dolly, God knows what it feels like to watch a beloved son suffer and die."

As we arrived back in front of Dolly's house, her bottom lip began to tremble. Dolly didn't like for anyone to see her cry. She sped up her pace, cutting across the yard to reach the front porch before me. I heard her gasping air as the tears began to pour before she made it back to the house.

Pat spent more and more time in his room. He only got out of bed to take a shower or come to the table to eat with his family. When he hobbled slowly down the hallway, every step seemed painful. Pat never complained. He had told me once that his grandmother taught him that not only does complaining not help, but it actually makes the pain worse.

One night, we helped Pat get dressed so he could join us in the dining room for dinner. He seemed more feeble than usual. As I walked closely behind him, he crumpled down to his knees. The neuropathy had gotten worse. Dolly and I got on both sides of Pat and lifted him back up to a standing position, but it was obvious that he could not stand on his own.

Yet he kept trying. It was like he was having an argument with his limbs. He spoke out loud to them, "Work, work, *dammit!*" But his body did not obey. We got the wheelchair and sat him in it. Pat never walked on his own again.

We were having special services at First Assembly of God Church in North Little Rock, where I was directing a dramatic production. I invited Dolly and Pat. They showed up, Dolly pushing her son's wheelchair, along with a few other guys from our AIDS support group. I sat with them at the very front of the sanctuary. Johanna, the pastor's wife, walked across in front of us, sporting one of her many stylish outfits, and Pat, who was quiet most of the time, surprised us all as he spoke out loudly.

"Girl, I love your purple pumps."

Johanna was gracious, although shocked, by this unexpected salutation. "Well, thank you," she said, smiling at Pat.

Some days when I sat with Pat, and I could tell that he was in a lot of pain, I would ask if I could pray for him. He would always roll his head around to look right at me and give me a sarcastic scowl before saying, "Not out loud."

So I prayed for him silently. Pat's dad, Wally, was on a spiritual search of his own. He was studying the Catholic faith, which he would eventually embrace. We had some great theological discussions at the dining room table. Although Wally had the look of a tough, insensitive Southern man, I saw underneath his outer persona a sensitive, loving father. He would become a dear friend to me. One day, when Dolly and I were on one of our stress-relieving walks, she assured me of Wally's positive feelings toward me.

"You know, Randy, you are the first preacher Wally Forbush has allowed in our house. I can tell he really likes you. And it's not just because you work your butt off over here helping take care of Pat. He really does like you."

I was amazed as I watched this quiet man cook meals for Pat, bathe and dress him, make his bed, and bring home his favorite jelly-filled donuts. I saw the pain in Wally's eyes as he became angrier at this debilitating illness claiming his son. One day when I arrived for a visit, Pat was sulking.

"What's wrong, Pat?"

"My dad's been manhandling me."

While giving him a bath, Pat thought his father had been impatient and a little rough. The truth was that Wally was a "let's get this done" guy who didn't waste a lot of time. Even though Pat sometimes complained about his dad's bath skills, and liked to give his mom a hard time, it was quite evident to me he was aware of the love he was receiving from these amazing parents, Team Dolly and Wally. I watched Pat's little Pentecostal grandmother sit with him and do all she could to help Pat feel loved and cared for. Although she was not pleased that Pat was gay, she overcame her fears, and any disapproving thoughts she may have had, to simply love her grandson. Pat had a real respect for his grandmother's faith.

Michael, Pat's brother, was a really macho guy. It was not okay with him that his brother was gay. I could tell he was uneasy around Pat's friends. Even so, I noticed how he fought his own prejudices to do many things to help with Pat's care. Those two brothers did not know how to show each other affection, but it was evident that they really loved each other.

Michael was a single dad with three kids. To my surprise, he wanted to hang out with me. We would go to the mall, and he got me interested in lifting weights. I fought my tendency to feel uncomfortable around really macho guys to form a friendship with Michael. The more I got to know him, the more I saw how much like Dolly he was. He might think I was a little "fruity," but if anyone tried to hurt me, he would defend me to the end. I was proud to be considered part of the Forbush family, and I still am.

Dolly became the hit of the AIDS support group. The gay guys absolutely adored her because she accepted them without judgment. They also enjoyed her irreverent, quirky ways. As the days went by, the number attending our AIDS support group grew at a staggering rate. It became clear to Dolly and me that there were not enough volunteers for people with AIDS and their families. We concluded that more sharing of information was needed for those in the hospital who were just starting to deal with their infections, and more support was needed for their families. Dolly and I had more than we could handle caring for Patrick. Yet, I would see Dolly get a phone call from a guy who needed a mom, and off she would go to see him. I sometimes stayed with Pat while she attended the funeral for a guy from our group. Dolly was a strong woman. I marveled at how she kept going.

Pat had gotten so weak that he and I had not gone on a luncheon date in a long time. One day Dolly called.

"Pat woke up this morning and said he wants to go out to eat."

I told her I had an engagement for lunch, but if he would like to go somewhere for dinner I would be glad to take him. "Dolly, is he able to go out?" I asked.

"Well, he says he wants to go, and if you're crazy enough to take him out in public, then it's all right with me."

I arrived at the Forbush home about three o'clock, and Dolly and I started the difficult task of bathing and dressing Pat. Pat was 6'1". In the past few days, he had developed a problem because of the stiffening of his body, and it was hard for him to bend at the waist. Dolly and I had to try several approaches to eventually maneuver his arms and legs into his clothes. Plus, Pat was difficult to lift. We always felt it was quite an accomplishment to have him bathed, shaved, and dressed. Dolly asked if he wanted to wear an apparatus that would make it possible for him to urinate without going to the restroom. Dolly called it his "Texas Rig." But Pat's pride kicked into high gear, and he shook his head, NO!

"So Pat, what if you have to pee while we are there at the restaurant?" I asked.

He did not offer any suggestions, but was not about to give in to wearing any "Texas Rig!" Dolly took a urinal bottle, wrapped it in a towel, and placed it in Pat's lap after we got him into the wheelchair. We rolled him out to my car and I opened the passenger door. Dolly and I looked at each other and wondered how we were ever going to get Pat's tall, rigid body into the front seat. I picked him up, Dolly pulled the wheelchair away, and I shuffled him over to the car. When Dolly tried to help bend his legs, it did not go well. I held on to Pat, afraid he was going to fall. When I felt us losing our balance, I aimed my butt at the car seat. Somehow, in the process of falling, I ended up in the front seat with Pat in my lap, his long legs hanging out the door.

Pat's face told his emotions. He was totally appalled at our lack of ingenuity. The whole scene suddenly seemed funny to me. Instinctively, I asked, "And what do you want for Christmas, little boy?" Dolly started laughing and fell down on the driveway, doubled up in hilarity.

Pat thought both of us had lost our minds. He could speak only in a whisper, but we heard him say, "It's not funny."

Dolly came over to the car door and pulled Pat up, so I could get out. "Pat, we have to laugh to keep from crying!" she said firmly.

We finally got Pat in my car and I drove away. I asked Pat where he wanted to eat.

"Red Lobster." Pat confidently replied.

Since I lived in North Little Rock, I was glad we would be going to the Red Lobster on *his* side of town. Pat loved to embarrass me in public. At least I would be less likely to run into someone I knew.

Then I heard Pat say, "Let's go to the Red Lobster in *North* Little Rock." It was as if he could read my mind and determined to "get" me one last time.

When we arrived at the restaurant, I lifted Pat's wheelchair out of the trunk. Luckily, I had an easier time getting him out of my car than we had getting him into it. When I went to retrieve the portable urinal, wrapped in the towel, Pat looked at me crossly.

"What did I do wrong now?" I asked.

He answered with his eyes. Pat did not want to take the urinal into the restaurant.

"Pat, no one will know what it is. It will be wrapped in a towel."

"I don't want it."

"But Pat, what if you need to pee in the middle of dinner? What will we do? It would be much easier to use the portable urinal in the restroom than for me to try and stand you up to pee, or transfer you to the toilet seat."

Nothing I could say would convince him to give in to what seemed a reasonable idea to me. I reluctantly left the urinal in the car and prayed that God would strengthen Pat's bladder.

When we approached the front desk, the hostess instructed us to follow our waitress to a wheelchair accessible table. I quickly looked around to spot the restrooms, in case Pat needed one quickly. Although the restrooms were located at the front of the restaurant, our waitress proceeded to take us to the very back of the dining room. We could not have been seated farther from the men's room. I tried to put my worries out of my head, as we got settled at our table and began looking at the menu. I was trying to be sensitive to Pat's desire to do as much for himself as possible. It was hard to know when to offer help. While he was looking at his menu, Pat sneezed. Encephalitis, which contributed to his stiffness, caused Pat's movements to be slow and deliberate. Even though his sneeze had been messy, my friend made no move to wipe his face with his napkin. I tried to pretend there was no one else in the room, but I could feel the staring eyes around us. I struggled to stay calm.

"Pat, would you like a napkin to wipe your nose?" He slowly nodded, yes, as the snot made its way down onto the table like a waterfall. I gave him a napkin and he slowly cleaned his face.

I chose popcorn shrimp, but Pat's taste was more high-brow. He wanted lobster tail and steak. I wanted to help feed him his salad, but Pat would have none of that. He struggled with getting salad to his mouth, but spilled it all over his side of the table.

When the entrees arrived, I could not imagine how he was going to handle lobster tail and steak, but I did not question him. After a few futile attempts to eat, Pat put his fork down, very deliberately, and said, "Girl, I got to pee."

Pat called me "girl" all the time. I asked once why he did this, and he informed me that he called all his gay friends "girl."

"But I'm not gay, Pat," I objected. "And the last time I checked down there, I was a boy."

Pat had just looked at me with that famous Patrick Allen Forbush smirk and said, "Oh well!"

Now he needed to pee. My nightmare had come to pass. Pat, was in this nice restaurant, in his wheelchair, and we were seated what seemed light years from the restroom.

"Of *course* you have to pee!" I said, the frustration clearly evident in my voice. "So, now what are we going to do? You wouldn't let me bring in the urinal, *would* you? Nooooooo!"

"Girl, you had better hurry and get me to the restroom."

I jumped up and wheeled Pat out from the table. The race was on! We dodged wait staff and tables as we rushed to the front of the restaurant. Once inside the restroom, I pushed Pat into a stall, all the time wondering how we were going to accomplish the feat of emptying his bladder. Perturbed, I looked at him and said,

"Okay, *now what?*"

Pat didn't say a word, but again, his eyes did the talking. He looked down at his lap and then back up at me. When I didn't move, he repeated the sequence.

"You want me to hold it for you?"

Pat just looked back down. As I observed his lap more closely, I saw what he was trying to show me. The front of his pants was sopping wet! We were too late!

"Oh great!" I groused, "What are we going to do now?"

Pat didn't miss a beat. "Get me back to my table, girl. My lobster tail's getting cold."

So back we went, a little slower this time. Once we arrived at our table, Pat didn't really attempt to eat his food. I could tell he knew he could not manage to do it, so I risked a rebuke.

"You want me to help you with that?"

He did not object. I reached over and cut up his food as nonchalantly as possible, so I wouldn't draw any more attention to us, then began to eat my own meal. Pat ate about three bites, then told me he was ready to go.

"I want a doggy bag to take this home to Mama."

Dolly was waiting to hear about our adventure. She laughed herself silly as I gave her a blow-by-blow description of what was more a wild escapade than an adventure.

"You are crazy as hell to have taken Pat out like that!"

"Wouldn't you have done it, Dolly, if he had asked you?"

"Hell no, I'm not that stupid! Wally, wait 'til you hear what Pat made Randolph do!"

Randolph was Dolly's nickname for me. If she couldn't think of that name fast enough, she called me "thing-a-ma-dooger."

One night, after Pat had gone to sleep, Dolly and I sat talking in the living room.

"You know you're going to have to preach Pat's funeral when the time comes, don't you?"

"You want me to?" I asked.

"Yes, you're the only minister I know who will not preach hellfire and damnation! You think you'll be able to do it? I know how close you are to Pat."

"Dolly, I would be honored."

"And I want you to sing something too. Just make sure you don't preach too long. If you do, Dolly's walking out!"

I knew she was only half joking.

On June 21, I met Dolly and Pat at the University Hospital for Pat's checkup. The doctor informed her that she didn't need to bring Pat back for more checkups. His condition was now beyond anything that could be done for him. It was now just a matter of time.

Pat wanted to ride with me back to the house, so Dolly helped me get him to my car. Pat had lost the ability to hold his head up. I had to drive and steady his head at the same time when we crossed the railroad tracks or bumps in the road so that Pat did not injure his neck. That drive home was one of the saddest rides of my life. I tried not to let Pat see my tears.

My parents had planned a family trip to Florida with their kids and grandkids. Dad had rented a condo on the white sand beach at Destin, Florida. I was looking forward to the trip, because I loved the ocean, although I had seen it only a few times. Now, I was not sure I should go because Pat was so ill. I was afraid he would die while I was gone. But Dolly insisted that I go. Since we were leaving the next day, I went to see Pat once more. When I arrived, Dolly told me that Pat had suffered a stroke and that he was much worse. At his bedside, I spoke to him. Pat opened his eyes.

"Pat, I rode on a party barge this afternoon at the lake with some friends from church. I kept wishing you were there with us."

"But I wasn't," he whispered. My heart broke. He was so young, and yet he looked like a weak, frail old man. When Dolly changed his pajama bottoms, I noticed a red spot on his backside.

"Pat, have you got bed bugs?" Dolly asked. "You have a bite on your bottom."

Pat rolled his eyes. "Randy bit me."

I prayed for Pat and said goodbye. I told Dolly one last time that I would stay if she wanted me to. She again refused.

"When you get to where you will be staying, call and give me your phone number. I will keep you updated on Pat's condition."

We hugged and I told her how much I loved her.

"I love you too, you scroungy old kid. Now, go have a good time with your family."

The first day I went for a long walk on the beach. There is something so healing about being at the ocean. I could not get enough of the waves, the emerald green water shimmering in the sunlight, and the bright reflection of the white sand. I called Dolly to give her the condo phone number. Crying, she said that Pat did not know her any more.

"Pat just looks at me and says, 'I ought to know you.'"

"Dolly, I wish I had stayed there with you. I am so sorry I am not there right now."

"No, it's okay. You aren't supposed to be here. You're where you're supposed to be."

The next day, when I telephoned, Pat was still alive. Later that evening, I called and Dolly told me his breathing was very quick and shallow. Dolly held the phone up to his ear.

"Pat, this is Randy. I am praying for you."

I found myself wanting to tell him I loved him, but I honored his wishes.

"Patrick Forbush, I sure do like you a lot."

After I hung up the phone, I walked on the beach in the moonlight.

"God, please be with Pat and Dolly and Wally and Michael tonight. And God be with me. I am so sad. I need your peace that passes understanding."

I looked ahead and there was a man walking towards me. He said, "Hello there, are you okay?"

"Yes, I'm just a little sad tonight."

"Would you like to talk about it?"

"Well, I am here on vacation with my family, and I have a friend back in Arkansas who is very sick and probably won't live through the night."

Then this nice looking stranger, with such a gentle voice, asked, "Does your friend have AIDS?"

I could not believe this. How could he possibly know?

"Yes, he does. I feel bad that I am not there with him and his family tonight."

The stranger then told me that he was on vacation with his partner, Steve.

"I am a therapist. I have seen many friends die of AIDS. Maybe what you need is to talk about your friend with me."

So we sat on the beach and I told him all the wacky things I had been through with Dolly and Pat. It felt good to talk. I felt that this stranger had been sent to me by God, since I could not openly talk to my family about my grief. I needed this therapy session.

It seemed to be a miracle, the chance meeting at a place where a gay couple would not normally vacation. It was mostly moms, dads, and kids. What are the odds that a gay therapist was staying at the same condos we were, and that he happened to be taking a late night stroll at the same time as me? There have been so many serendipities in my life that I do not believe they were just happenstances.

"Patrick Forbush, I sure do like you a lot!" turned out to be the last words I spoke to him. Early the next morning, Dolly called to tell me that Pat died ten minutes after midnight, about the time I was walking with the stranger on the beach. Dolly said that they planned the funeral for the following Tuesday, almost a week away, so that I would have time to get back to do the service. Pat's wish was to be cremated, so there was no rush, she said.

As soon as we arrived home, I went to Dolly and Wally's and we began planning Pat's funeral.

"What are you going to say?" Wally asked. I knew he probably wondered if I was capable of conducting a funeral. While I had given eulogies and sung at funerals before, I had never been in charge of the whole service. Dolly spoke before I had a chance to answer.

"He'll do fine. He knows what I *don't* want him to say."

Pat's funeral was bittersweet. I shared memories of him and paid tribute to the wonderful job his family had done in taking care of him. I looked out at the mourners and spotted my mom and dad. Their presence that day meant the world to me!

After the funeral, Dolly hosted a wake at her home with lots of laughter as everyone told their "Pat" stories. Then, Dolly showed me where she was going to place Pat's remains.

"Pat wanted to be on, or close to, the television, so he would always be a part of what we were doing as a family."

Wally had planned to bury his son's ashes, but after Pat made it clear what he wanted, Dolly would not hear of having it any other way. So Pat was literally at his own wake as we told of his many antics. There was so much warmth and love in that room. I think Pat would have approved. I miss him still, and I can only imagine what embarrassing outings he is planning for me upon my arrival to heaven.

I hoped to stay connected with the Forbush family after Pat's death. I did not have to worry. In the weeks ahead, Dolly had plenty of work for us to do. She would ask me to meet her at the hospital. We walked the halls, looking for red information cards on doors, which signified the required use of gloves and masks. This usually meant the patient had AIDS.

Dolly and I put together a loosely organized group of volunteers, composed of parents who had lost children to AIDS or whose children were suffering from AIDS, gay men who had lost partners to AIDS, and supportive medical professionals. We made friends with the nurses who took care of the AIDS patients and gave them our phone numbers. They called us when there was a new patient who was depressed, or did not have a supportive family. We visited patients being cared for at home, too. Dolly became every AIDS patient's "mom."

Darrell had given up. He was living at home and would not get out of bed, or eat. Dolly called me.

"I need you. Darrell is depressed. Let's go cheer him up. He won't come to group, so we're going to take group to him. Can you be ready in 30 minutes?"

It was hard to say no to Dolly. At Darrell's home, we walked into his bedroom.

"You old scroungy kid, what are you doing piled up in that bed?"

Darrell rolled over to see the "hurricane" that had just invaded his bedroom. "Hi, Dolly." Darrell's voice was soft and flat. He rolled over and pulled the covers over his head.

Dolly would have none of that. Oh no! She sauntered deliberately to his side of the bed and sat down, nudging Darrell over with little thrusts of her hips.

"Move over, gay boy, so Dolly can get her big fat butt up here in bed with you."

Darrell reluctantly made room. Who could say no to this irreverent, loving force? Once snugly embedded in Darrell's nest, Dolly turned to me.

"Come on, Randy. The more the merrier. Isn't that what they say?"

I was always afraid that we would be rebuked because of Dolly's forwardness, but the rebuke never came. Dolly's persuasiveness proved irresistible. Cautiously, I sat down on the foot of the bed. This was not good enough for Dolly.

"Get your sorry butt up here with us. We're going to have a party aren't we, Darrell?"

Before the visit was over, Darrell was laughing and eating the ice cream we had brought.

When families tried to figure out the relationship between Dolly and me she would answer, "Randy's mine. He's my kid. He's my minister. I carry him around in my hip pocket."

I loved Dolly's in-your-face irreverence. When you come from a family and religion that is stuffy and rule-oriented, you eventually enjoy the freedom of torpedoing those made-up strictures. Dolly had broken free years ago. She loved people. God loved her, too, but she did not believe it.

"Dolly," I said, "you are a saint in my eyes."

"Now, that is one thing Dolly has never been called!"

"Yes, you have. I just did. Dolly, don't you believe that you'll go to heaven?"

"No, I'm not good enough for that."

"But Dolly, I am learning that salvation isn't about being 'good enough,' even though you have many beautiful traits in the goodness department."

"You must be talking about somebody else. Dolly's rotten."

Dolly always referred to herself in the third person. And she found it impossible to accept a compliment.

"Dolly, I've seen how you minister to these guys. They love you…and why? Because they know you love *them*. That's what Jesus taught us to do—to love others, and to serve them. Dolly, you *are* a Christian, whether you ever admit it or not. You are, in the purest sense of the word. And you have such a welcome committee waiting for you in heaven when you get there. All these guys you are helping over to the other side are going to be there to get a Dolly-hug when you walk in the gate."

As always, whenever I said something that touched her heart, Dolly walked away so I would not see her tears.

Being around Dolly was opening my eyes to why Jesus enjoyed hanging out with irreverent characters in his day, and why he avoided the self-righteous religious leaders. They were the ones he rebuked.

If you wanted to locate Jesus, he was partying with the Dollys of his day, the poor in spirit, the ones who know they haven't got it all figured out. It was the poor in spirit whom Jesus proclaimed blessed. Jesus was far more comfortable around the "unchurched" because they didn't speak religiously. These plainspoken men and women were real and did not hide behind sanctimonious masks, or flaunt their religious standing. Thank God I was blessed to be adopted by Dolly, a servant who showed me how to be real. Dolly was committed to helping me loosen my mask. Masks can be as stuffy and cumbersome as closets! With Dolly, "what you see is what you get." I learned a great lesson from this special friend.

Randy with Dolly in 1992

Chapter 23
My Grace Teacher

During the last hot days of summer 1988 I was finishing work creating my one-man play, "The Life of St. Paul." Many who remembered my past work in church drama were looking forward to my new dramatic portrait. Pastors were calling to schedule a performance. The dream of being back in drama ministry was becoming reality.

After two years of abstinence and studying ex-gay literature, I was still battling with attraction to men. Except for my trip to Washington, D.C., and the week Gary came to visit in 1987, I had been pretty successful in not acting on my attractions. Yet, an internal war raged. When I masturbated, I tried imagining a woman's body, but I always had to switch gears in mid-stream because the idea of being with a woman did nothing for me. I was not progressing on the road to heterosexuality.

Gary was having the same experience. His frustrations were evident in his letters. In one, he wrote and told me he had given in to a former gay acquaintance, and had allowed things to get out of hand sexually. I wrote back,

Gary, I am very concerned about you. I know that it would be just as impossible for you to live happily in a gay lifestyle as it would for me to do so. We both KNOW THE TRUTH! Your confession made me sad. I love you with a pure and holy love, Gary. I have found that this love is so much greater than any sensual or sexual love the world has to offer. In my loving you through Christ, I love you selflessly. Mind you, I have not reached perfection yet. I am not about to make that bogus claim.

Gary responded back to me,

Randy, for some reason I seem to be struggling harder than you in giving up my identity. Although I finally realized THAT is what my problem is. It's not giving up men, or the lifestyle or anything else…it's giving up me. It may not be that special or honorable to be gay, but it is who I am, and I'm struggling to make God fully Lord of my life and return my identity to Him. Of course it doesn't make it any easier when guys from my past, who I thought were my past, write and call, wanting to get things going again. Anyway, my periods of depression are much more short-lived these days and I am learning many things about

God's nature and love. I have gotten to a place where homosexuality for me, Gary Eddy, a child of God, is a dead issue. It has no real significance. Old things have passed away and all has become new. It is a forgotten and forgiven issue as far as God is concerned and as far as I am too, now.

Gary seemed very sure of this, but then he ended the letter with this request.

Do continue to pray for me when God brings me to mind. It's a long journey back to build the spiritual habits again. I think I am still vulnerable a little! You take care and I love you, Gary.

I met Lois Hargrove, an amazing woman who taught the College and Career Sunday school class at church. This petite, pretty woman was something of a maverick theologically, at least in the world of the Assembly of God. Her teachings about God's love and grace were so different from my previous teachings. I confessed all my past to Lois, but she didn't seem to be phased by any of it. She could make me think outside the box. Grace, according to Lois, meant "unmerited favor." She loved what the Apostle Paul wrote in his letter to the Ephesians,

For it is by grace you have been saved, through faith—and this not from yourselves, it is the gift of God—not by works, so that no one can boast. (Ephesians 2:8-9 NIV)

I asked Lois if that meant that God loved me just as much when I failed as when I succeeded in doing what was right. She assured me that God's very nature is love, and that His love for His creation is constant and unconditional. This opened new doorways of theology for me. I could ask my questions without fear of reprisal. While this did not change my negative view of homosexuality, it allowed me to seek God's true will for my life without the constant fear of failing and getting zapped by God. I began to sing "Amazing Grace" with new feeling and conviction. I will be forever grateful for Lois, this precious, courageous teacher of grace.

Chapter 24

Looking For Mrs. Right

At this time, I was pursuing the dream of being heterosexual, and worried that I might be HIV positive. According to the experts, the virus could lie dormant for many years before any symptoms surfaced. I dreamed of having a wife and children. I ached to be a father.

I named my Christian work "Life Abundant Ministries," designing a little lamb with the letters L. A. M. under it for my logo. One day, thinking about my future, I tried to imagine what I would name my little boy. I had always loved the television show, *The Rifleman,* starring Chuck Connors. Aside from the fact that I found him very attractive, I loved his character's name, Lukas McCain. I decided I would name my future son Lukas. I would then give him my middle name, and he would be Lukas Allen McCain. His initials would be L.A.M., the same as my logo.

Adding to this happy train of thought, my initials were R.A.M. We would definitely keep it in the *sheep* family. I went out and purchased a stuffed toy lamb for my future son, as a step of faith. Sometimes, when I became uptight thinking about the possibility of dying of AIDS, I would walk out into my parent's backyard. Dad had hung a swing for his grandkids from one of the oak trees. I found it strangely calming to imagine swinging my little boy, Lukas. I even wrote messages to him in my journal.

Lukas Allen, son, I want you to know that Daddy's thinking about you today. I loved you before you were even born. I long to take you to the park, play ball with you, swing you on the swings and buy you ice cream. I can't wait till you arrive! Love, your Dad.

I also journaled about the future Mrs. McCain.

Hey, Mrs. McCain. I wonder if you're lonely tonight and wishing you were with me. I love you!

For Valentine's Day, I bought the prettiest card and signed it, "To my beautiful sweetheart. I dreamed you into existence. Love, your devoted husband, Randy."

One day, Lois, told me that a friend from her hometown was coming to visit.

"Randy, she's single and about your age. She's never been married and she plays the piano and sings. Also, she is a secretary with great typing skills. She could help you with your plays. Her name is Libby."

Wow! This certainly sounded like a "God thing." I couldn't wait to meet her.

One Saturday afternoon, Lois called to say that Libby had come for a visit. I primped and made sure I was looking my best before going to meet her. Lois introduced us and we connected immediately. I couldn't wait to hear Libby play the piano. When a young man goes to a Pentecostal Bible college, he is strongly encouraged to find a wife who can sing and play the piano. She needed these skills to be an asset to his ministry. From the moment Libby sat down at the piano and started playing, I knew that she had that Pentecostal touch. Even better, when we tried harmonizing, our voices blended perfectly. Wow!

Looking back, I did not pay much attention to her physical attributes. While I noticed that she was a pretty girl, and dressed nicely, I failed to be interested in her figure or her breast size. At the time, I told myself that this lack of interest was a work of God's grace, allowing me to develop my desire for any woman in a totally pure way, free of any carnal desires.

Libby and I started seeing a lot of each other, even though she lived two hours away. One day, I asked Lois if she had shared anything with Libby about my homosexual past. She said no, that should come from me. I was planning to visit Libby soon and decided that I had to face my fears and tell her, doing my best to choose the right time and place.

Libby lived in a town on the banks of the Mississippi River. One afternoon, we walked along the riverbank, to take in the mighty Mississippi.

"Libby, you know I've been very involved in a ministry to AIDS patients."

"Yes, I admire you for it, Randy."

"Well, there's something I need to tell you about me. Many of those guys were my friends before they got sick. You see, I…"

The words, so hard to form, stuck in my throat. Breathing a silent prayer, I forged on.

"I used to be gay, Libby, but I realized that this was not pleasing to God. I prayed for Him to take my homosexual desires away. I consider myself ex-gay now."

Libby did not say anything, but I could tell that inside she was reeling.

"I wanted you to know this because there are a lot of people who *do* know, and I was afraid they would tell you before I did. I wanted you to hear it from me, Libby. When I was gay, I had sex with a lot of men. I have had live-in relationships with men; one lasted four years. I have prayed to be delivered from this life, and I believe God has answered that prayer. I want more than anything to have a family, one day. I don't know how you will feel now about dating someone like me. You may not want a husband who, well, has been with men. I will totally understand if you never want to see me again, but I *had* to tell you."

Libby sat quietly for a long time, wrestling with her emotions. I sat beside her, silently praying and watching the river, giving her time to put her thoughts into words.

After what seemed like an eternity, she said, "Well, I must say that I am shocked. That was a lot to hear, all at one time. But Randy, I know God is in your life. I've seen the compassion you have for the guys you minister to. I've heard you sing in church, and I know you are anointed by God. But are you attracted to me?"

"I really feel good when I'm with you, Libby. I love it when we sit and talk about life. I love how you love the Lord. I enjoy singing with you. I want very much to pursue a relationship with you, if you're willing to take a chance on me."

"Randy, you have taught me so much about compassion and grace. I've been challenged by your life and your ministry. I come from a very prejudiced town. Yet, I see the love of Jesus in you as you embrace those whom society and the church have rejected. Your caring spirit makes *me* want to be more loving and more caring."

Even before my monumental revelation that afternoon, dating me had challenged Libby to live outside her comfort zone. She had met some of the guys from the AIDS group, and when I introduced her to Dolly, I had sensed Dolly's disapproval, and so had Libby. It went something like this.

"Dolly, this is Libby, the girl I've told you so much about."

"So he dragged you to group," was Dolly's greeting to Libby. There was no, "Good to meet you", or "I've heard wonderful things about you."

"Yes," Libby responded. "I've looked forward to meeting you. Randy has told me so much about you and the guys here."

"And you still came?" Dolly said with a smile.

Libby did not know how to respond.

Dolly added, "Randy McCain is *mine*. Nobody says anything bad about him around Dolly. He's my kid!"

Libby responded, "Thank you Dolly, for loving him. He sure thinks the world of you."

Dolly tried to like Libby ever since that first meeting, because she knew I wanted her to, but Dolly was not convinced that my attempts to "go straight" were heartfelt, or likely to be successful.

I was giving the relationship with Libby my best shot. I wanted to marry a girl who would love the people I loved. That is why I had taken Libby to meet Dolly and the guys with AIDS. Libby was getting quite a crash course on "the world according to Randy." She was a small town Assembly of God girl who had never wanted to live in a big city. Her family was her world. Libby was being wooed to slip outside the predictable strictures of that protective bubble. I believe she found it fascinating on one hand, odd and threatening on the other. I admired Libby for attempting to broaden her horizons. She said she wanted to love the people I loved, but I didn't know if she was ready for the *Randy McCain Express.*

Sitting on that river bank, I gave Libby another piece of the complicated puzzle she was trying to put together.

"Randy, God has forgiven you of your past. How could I do less? I love you, and although this is really hard for me to understand, I still want to date you." I was relieved. I felt I was making real progress on the road to heterosexuality.

One day, I decided to get back in touch with Roger, the former Methodist minister who had been fired for being gay. Roger seemed glad to see me again, but I sensed a little tension in the air.

"So, Randy, is it true what Jerry told me, that you are calling yourself straight now?"

"Yes, Roger, I am. I'm dating a girl. I really feel that this is what God wants me to do. I was never happy as a gay man."

"Then why are you here visiting me?"

"I want us to be friends."

"Randy, we can be friends on one condition—that you can look me in the eye and say that you accept me as a gay man, and that you do not judge me for being gay. Otherwise, we cannot be friends."

"Roger, I do not look down on you in any way. I love you. We've been friends in the past and I still want to be your friend."

"But can you say it, Randy? Can you truthfully say, 'Roger, I want to be your friend and it is perfectly fine with me that you are gay'?"

"You are asking me to be honest with you, Roger, so I have to tell you I do not believe that the homosexual lifestyle is an acceptable Christian alternative."

I felt bad saying this. I knew how it sounded to Roger, because I had been in his place back when people disapproved of me because *I* was gay. I wanted to get us off the subject of homosexuality.

"Roger, I did not come here to judge you in any way. I just came to assure you that I still want to be friends."

"Well, if you came over here with a hidden agenda, hoping you can get close to me again so you can 'save' me, you can forget it! I want no part of it. I have fought hard to get to a place where I could genuinely accept and respect the real me. And it wasn't easy after all the rejection I experienced from so called 'Christians.' Finally, I am experiencing true peace and I don't want anyone telling me they think I am a sinner for being gay."

Roger's voice softened. "Now honestly, Randy, I do not hear condemnation in your voice. But, I am feeling a certain amount of anger toward you, for some reason, and I'm not sure where that is coming from. You were the one I came to when I was so unsure of who I was. You were the one who helped me learn to accept myself as a healthy, gay man. Now you sit here, very self-assured, and tell me the exact opposite."

"I know, Roger. You have every reason to be skeptical. But I just want you to know that if you ever need me, I am here for you. We don't even have to discuss the gay issue. Here's my number. Call me any time."

I placed the paper with my phone number on his coffee table and stood to leave. As I walked towards the door, Roger came over to me.

"Randy, I want to be your friend. I've missed our friendship. But I hope you'll understand if I keep you at arm's length for a while."

"Roger, fair enough. I understand. I do."

I wrote about this later in my journal, and I spoke of my feelings of sadness. There was now a wall between me and my friends from the past. I learned from the ex-gay ministries that this was to be expected. Light and darkness do not mix.

"I guess sometimes the right road is lonely," I concluded at the end of the entry.

Libby and I started seeing each other as often as we could. I told her about a job she could apply for in Little Rock, and she set up an interview. We even began to flirt with the idea of marriage. We had long talks about what our future would look like. I told Libby all about little Lukas Allen.

Lois asked us to babysit her young grandson, Caleb, one night. Libby suggested I put him to bed, so I read to him and then tucked him in. We said our prayers, and as I heard him repeating, "Now I lay me down to sleep…" I thought of myself as a little boy saying those same words. Caleb looked a lot like I did when I was young. We had the same coloring, the same eyes…I even had people ask me if he was my child when we were out together in public. I so badly wanted to be a daddy! After our prayer, Caleb didn't want me to leave him, so I lay down beside him until he fell asleep.

Libby looked in on us. "Is little Lukas Allen asleep yet?" she whispered.

"Yes, just now."

I joined her in the den to watch a movie. We sat holding hands and snuggling. I was doing my best to be the "all-American guy." Even though I enjoyed Libby's company, and was thrilled with the thought of being a father, the kissing, holding hands, and sitting close together did not come naturally for me. I kept telling myself that this would develop over time.

In August of 1988, I was tested for AIDS. I had put it off because a part of me did not want to know. As long as I didn't know, I could imagine that I was healthy. I watched too many friends die an agonizing death, and it scared me to think I could be facing the same sentence. Now that Libby and I were talking about the possibility of marriage, I had to know. After making the appointment, I wrote in my journal,

It is really strange. The first thing I thought of when I woke up this morning was about getting tested. It is as though I have no control over my emotions. I mean, logically, I am not that worried. But these emotions are there, and I want to burst out crying all the time. I think, now that I know I'm going to get tested, I'm identifying closely with those who have tested positive. I just want to get it over with now!

I fought the urge to cancel my appointment. But I knew that I had to go through with it if I wanted to continue my plans for the future. When the day came, I walked into the testing room with determination. Finding individuals from my AIDS support group volunteering there was a little uncomfortable for me, but I stayed focused. I learned that it would take three weeks to get the results. Three weeks of waiting! Three weeks seemed like an eternity.

Since I had shared my decision with Mom and Dad, both were on pins and needles. I woke up every morning with fear. It felt like an elephant was sitting on my chest. As the date to find out the results got closer, Libby asked if I wanted her to go with me. I told her I wanted to do this alone. Driving to my appointment, I prayed for Jesus to give me peace to accept whatever the result. Inside the testing office, one of the nurses from group who knew me well greeted me. She held a folder containing my results. I wondered if she had looked at them yet.

"Hello, Randy, why don't we go upstairs to my office?"

I watched her closely for any signs that would give away my results. Friendship aside, she had a job to do. Once we entered the office, she asked me to close the door. As I sat down, she opened my records and looked over them.

"Well, Randy, I have good news. Your results are negative."

"YES!" I shouted. I didn't hear much more of what she said, something about, "I don't have to tell you what to do to stay negative."

I assured her that she did not. I practically glided down the stairs to my car. Driving down the freeway on my way home, I rolled down all the windows and felt the wind blowing in as I screamed at the top of my lungs. All the pressure, building for those three agonizing weeks, was gone! There were no words, just loud screams.

Mom and Dad were standing at the door, waiting for me. "I don't have it. I'm negative!" They started crying and we all hugged. I called Libby, Lois, Dolly, and several others who were praying. The next day, I called Gary, who was relieved for me.

"Oh, Randy, Thank God!"

Until that day, I had not really talked to Gary about Libby. Now, I told him all about her, and that we were thinking about marriage. I thought he would be excited for me, but I could tell he was not thrilled with my news.

"I know I probably shouldn't tell you this, Randy," Gary said, a twinge of disappointment in his voice. "But I am jealous of her."

"Why, Gary?"

"Because." There was a long pause. "I have had this fantasy that someday you and I would be together. If you get married, I will have to bury that dream. It has been precious to me, something that I could fantasize about in my loneliest times."

"But Gary, we are ex-gay now. God is healing us. We'll always be good friends. I'll always be there for you, and you'll always be there for me."

"I know, Randy, but it won't be the same. I'm sorry. I'll get used to it. I promise. I just wasn't ready to hear this."

It was sweet that Gary still had feelings for me. I tried to imagine a day in the future when he, too, would be married, and he and his wife would get together with Libby and me. Our kids could become friends. But I also experienced a little jealousy, thinking of him with a woman. I did my best to commit all this to God.

I started booking churches to present my drama, *The Life of St. Paul*. I was soon booked to perform every weekend. The churches loved drama as a tool of ministry and, because few were doing this, I was in demand. Libby and I continued our relationship long distance because she did not get the job in Little Rock.

I headed back to Grandma McCain's when I had a break in my schedule, where Libby joined me for the weekend. Grandma liked Libby, and Libby adored Grandma. I also introduced Libby to Arlene, a young widow who was the youth minister at Grandma's church. Because Arlene was easy to talk to, I had been honest with her about my life. Naturally, I had told her about Libby, and she was excited about meeting her.

When they did meet, the two women hit it off. A few days later, when Libby had gone home, Arlene grilled me with some penetrating questions.

"Randy, has God changed your physical desires? Are you turned on by women now, instead of men?"

"Well, I seem to be more attracted to women than I used to be. But I still don't look at women and wish I could see them naked, like I've done in the past with men."

"So, do you think that if you marry Libby, you will be able to have sexual relations with her?"

"I think so."

"What if Libby goes out and buys a real sexy nightgown, and surprises you with it when you come home from work? Would you be turned on by that?"

I had to think before answering. Quickly, I put myself into the fantasy, and walked in the front door of our house. I called out, "Honey, I'm home!" Then I imagined Libby, seductively entering the room in a sexy nightgown from Fredericks of Hollywood. I sensed myself cringing.

Immediately, I tried to slap the ex-gay spin on this. The ex-gay material taught men not to have sex with their new wives until their desire to be protected became a desire to protect. Also, ex-gay men were told to work out at the gym so that their own bodies would be hard and muscular and they would learn to appreciate a woman's "soft, squishy" body. Looking back, this sounds so ridiculous, but back then, I was grasping at straws.

I struggled for a way to answer Arlene.

"I don't think I would lust after her, because God is not going to give me lustful thoughts for any woman. God would not turn lustful thoughts for men into lustful thoughts for women. Lust is not godly. God will teach me to love my wife sexually, but without lustful thoughts."

"But Randy, if I ever got married again, I would want to know that I could turn my husband on. I would want him to desire me physically. I don't think I would want a husband who went through the motions with me sexually. I would want him to appreciate me physically."

Arlene planted important seeds of doubt in my mind.

Randy as the Apostle Paul in his one man play, The Life of St. Paul

Chapter 25
A Life-Changing Book

A Baptist church in town sponsored a Christian singles workshop that I decided to attend. The facilitator for the event was Dr. Harold Ivan Smith. The workshop was fascinating. Dr. Smith was mesmerizing as a speaker. In one of the sessions, he gave an impassioned plea for Christians to reach out in love to people with AIDS instead of judging them. His indictment against the church for failing to show Christ's love was powerful and convicting.

The church had been silent about AIDS, except to condemn and judge. Harold Ivan Smith's approach to the subject was unique, because he did not make the person with AIDS the villain. He reprimanded the church of Jesus Christ for not obeying Jesus' command to love. Afterwards, I spoke with Harold Ivan. I told him how much I appreciated his words, and how brave he was to say these things in the churches of America. He thanked me. Then, I told him about my ministry to AIDS patients. He encouraged me and also told me about Tony Campolo, who he said was very concerned about people with AIDS. Harold Ivan gave me Tony's address and encouraged me to write to him. He also strongly encouraged me to get a copy of Tony's latest book, *20 Hot Potatoes Christians Are Afraid to Touch*.

In my letter to Dr. Campolo, I shared some of my experiences ministering to AIDS patients. He wrote back, commending me on my compassionate approach toward those suffering with AIDS, and suggested that I read his latest book, the same book that Dr. Smith had recommended. I bought a copy and began reading it. In his chapter, "How Do We Answer the Challenge of AIDS?" Campolo writes:

I cannot believe that homosexuals are major league sinners deserving of major league sickness, while the rest of us are entitled to generally good health because we are minor league sinners who are therefore not so bad! …To make God into a spiteful deity diminishes His goodness in the eyes of many and makes Him something that He is not. …Two thousand years ago when Jesus was physically present among us, He reached out to lepers. He touched the untouchables. He showed special compassion toward those who had been treated in such a cruel manner by the people around them. His willingness to lovingly lay hands on those whom society deemed unclean should set an example for all of us who sing "I Would Be

Like Jesus."

Campolo's words on AIDS moved me. What a maverick! Tony and Harold Ivan were my new heroes of the faith! Next, I read Tony's chapter on homosexuality, "Does the Church Have Any Good News for Homosexuals?" The chapter set out Campolo's beliefs that while homosexual behavior is contrary to the will of God, he called upon the church to stop singling out homosexuals with such over the top hatred and condemnation. He wrote:

The fact that homosexuality has become such an overriding concern for many contemporary preachers may be more a reflection of the homophobia of the church than it is the result of the emphasis of scripture.

I agreed with him so far, but then he said something so unbelievable that I read it over to make sure I understood what he was saying.

...I do believe that a great proportion of both males and females who are homosexual in their orientation did not choose to be this way, and a significant number of them who desperately want to get out of this orientation are finding little hope or help from either science or religion... There must be good news for homosexuals. In the likelihood that most of them will still have their basic sexual orientation regardless of their efforts to change, we must do more than simply bid them be celibate. We must find ways for them to have fulfilling, loving experiences so that they might have their humanity affirmed and their incorporation into the Body of Christ insured. Homosexuals are our brothers and sisters and must be treated that way. To do less is sin.

I could not believe what I was reading! Here I was, desperately trying to change my sexual orientation because I had been convinced by preachers that I *chose* this sin of homosexuality, and Dr. Campolo was telling me that my chances of changing my orientation were practically zero. He also stated that gays do not *choose* to be gay.

In time, I realized that reading Campolo's words nudged me to question the manipulation-based theology of the ex-gay ministries. But at the time, paradoxically, I felt like I was being ridiculed by Dr. Campolo for my efforts to change my orientation.

A few months later, Harold Ivan Smith spoke at my home church's single adult conference. At the lunch break, I could not wait to get a moment to talk with Dr. Smith. I refreshed his memory about our previous meeting, and told him that I had read Tony's book but had strong negative reactions to it. Harold Ivan listened very closely. He had such a gentle way of making me feel he was genuinely interested in what I had to say. He asked me to join him for lunch. As we ate, he told me about the research that had been done, showing overwhelmingly that gay people do not choose to have same sex attraction. He also said that many of the ex-gay programs were taking a hard look at their reparative therapy, because the success rates were miserably low.

"Randy, perhaps you should write again to Tony and tell him of your feelings about his book. It helps writers to have feedback from readers."

I would not write again to Tony Campolo until 1994. By that time, I was in a far different place than in 1988.

Chapter 26

Cupid Goes on Strike

1989 and 1990 were strange years. While my drama ministry grew, I was becoming more disillusioned with churches in general. I was fighting so hard to be free of my homosexuality and spending more time with Libby. Invitations came for us to minister together. I felt safer having a girlfriend when I went to Baptist or Assembly of God churches to minister. It cut down on the speculation as to why I was in my 30s and not yet married. Keeping company with Libby also kept my hopes alive that someday little Lukas Allen would become real. But the longer Libby and I dated, the more uncomfortable I became with the intimacy of sitting alone together, kissing and holding hands.

I began to resent that Libby was very affectionate. It became more and more awkward for me. I enjoyed having Libby as my close friend, loved talking and shopping with her, and watching movies together. But the physical part smothered me. I tried to convince myself that this was because of my past homosexual experiences and that the more I was with Libby, the more comfortable I would become. The body and heart have minds of their own!

I usually closed my eyes when we kissed. That seemed the natural thing to do. One night, as I was kissing Libby, I opened my eyes. She was so into that kiss. She was blushing and her breath was fast and shallow, much as mine had been the night I had stood with Carlos in that city park in Arlington. Knowing what it felt like to be turned on by someone else, I recognized that she was, but *I wasn't*. The devastating realization occurred to me…I would never again experience the breathtaking thrill of rapture that comes from sexual ecstasy, of being with another human being who could cause me to respond with my spirit, mind, and body.

I would settle for making it happen for Libby. At least one of us would be fulfilled. But then I remembered Arlene questioning me. At some point, Libby would perceive my lack of interest. I remembered the joy I had received from knowing that another man was excited because of me. I loved being able to engender that response in someone I cared about. Was it fair to ask Libby to settle for a man who could never fully appreciate her womanliness, her femininity?

All of this came to a head in 1991. Libby and I took a long road trip to Kansas

City. Before we arrived home, it seemed that we had been together for an eternity! I have always been hyperactive, and I talk a lot and insist on sharing my favorite music with other passengers on a long car trip. I can be overbearing at times, and I was especially so on this trip. I was also trying to dodge Libby's questions about where our relationship was headed.

Recently, I had become impatient with Libby. I was often short with her, and I horrified myself at how thoughtless I could be. I was striking out at her because I resented having to settle for a relationship that was not sexually or romantically satisfying. It was not Libby's fault. She really loved me and was a beautiful, desirable woman. I was wrong to be involved with her, but I did it in an attempt to please God, my family, and my church.

The tension in the car on the way home intensified, mile after mile. The trip could not end soon enough for two "caged animals." She tried so hard to figure out why I was being distant. When she tried to hold my hand, I pulled it away. After all, good drivers keep both hands on the steering wheel. Surely she realized that things were not working between us. As we said our goodbyes, I hoped she would end our relationship so I would not have to.

Libby's church was having a Valentine Banquet the following weekend, and she invited me and another guy from my church, Donald, who was dating Janis, her best friend. This had been planned before our miserable trip and, since we were double dating, I did not see any way out of it. The thought of spending another weekend together was not romantic, to say the least. But since we would be with another couple, and we would be at a church function, there would be no "alone" time for us.

I really did not know why I was so agitated about Libby. I felt like a number one jerk for the way I was shutting down without offering her any explanation. But I was in the dark. Now I know a part of me was rebelling against the mandate of society and the church to deny my personhood. I was forced to play a role that went against my deep desire to be the gay man I was created to be.

I believe our bodies and our inner being know what is best for us. Our true identity will warn us before we make major wrong turns. I believe this is a God-given mechanism to protect us. When it is not understood, or is ignored, we become miserable. Like Cinderella's stepsisters, we try to force our foot into the appropriately sanctioned, yet ill-fitting glass slipper. How confusing my confusion must have been for Libby.

Donald and I went together to pick up the girls and gave them corsages, then we went for a Coke. Everything seemed to be going fine. There were no awkward moments. But everyone could tell I was not my chipper self, so I told them I had been sick earlier in the week and was not feeling up to par. In fact, I *had* been sick, but that was not the source of my uneasiness. It was a convenient excuse to hide behind.

Donald and Janis dropped us at Libby's parent's house to get dressed for the banquet. We would see them at the church. (Later, I remembered noticing a certain little grin and eye contact between Libby and Janice when I said that.) I was ready before Libby, so her father and I talked for a few minutes. Libby's parents were attending the banquet, too. Libby walked into the den.

"Are you ready?" I asked, hoping to get away from her dad before he asked me any embarrassing questions about my intentions toward his daughter. Libby's mother had already laid down the law to me earlier that afternoon that her kids were always expected to be at Mama's house for Thanksgiving and Christmas. I felt this was a little presumptuous, but tried to act pleasant. Libby hugged her mom and dad. We got into her car and headed down the street. As we passed her sister Carrie's house, she abruptly turned into the driveway.

"What are we doing Libby? I thought you were concerned that we were running late."

"I promised my sister that we would stop by so she could take a picture of us. She wanted to see what we were wearing."

Even as an actor, I was uncomfortable making like the happy couple, but I followed Libby to the front door.

"Knock, knock," Libby said as she opened the door. We walked into Carrie's dining room and I spotted the table, beautifully set for two. Candles flickered, and I heard soft music playing. Perhaps Carrie was expecting a male friend for the evening. Then I noticed, at one of the dinner settings, a card with "Randy" written on the outside of the envelope. That's when it hit me! Oh, no! Libby had planned all this to surprise me—a romantic evening for just the two of us! I had seen enough romance movies to know that this was the moment where I was expected to turn to Libby and sweep her off her feet, kiss her passionately, and tell her how much I loved her while the music swelled.

"Surprise!" Libby gushed. I had been ambushed! What I felt was anger. I was trying not to show it, but I knew I did not look thrilled. Libby tried to make the best of it.

"But won't they be expecting us at the church?" I asked, trying to buy time.

"No, they all know about this."

"They *all* knew?"

Libby nodded affirmatively. "Yes, Carrie is at a friend's house for the evening. Donald, Janis, Dad, and Mom know not to expect us tonight. This is my Valentine gift to you."

Conflicting emotions raced through me: rage, resentment, anger at myself for being unable to appreciate all that Libby had done just for me, and anger at her for putting me in this awkward place. Surely, she should have known by my actions since our trip that things were not going well. I was furious at Donald for not tipping me off. I wanted to bolt, but I had no car and was over a hundred miles from home. While these emotions were bombarding my brain, I felt deep sorrow for Libby, and the hurt I could see she was feeling.

The room filled with a palpable tension, but Libby was a real trooper. She stayed "on script" by serving a delicious meal. How many times had she heard "the way to a man's heart is through his stomach"? I was not hungry and I became a zombie, going through the motions of eating while feeling like a heel.

After dinner, Libby gave me gifts: candy, a beautiful card, and a stuffed bear. I had brought her only the corsage. My guilt multiplied. I prayed Donald would return soon, but that prayer went unanswered for another hour or so. I did my best to attribute my lack of response to still being weak from my illness, and kept apologizing for not eating very much and not having brought any gifts for Libby.

"I just haven't been myself all week."

Libby suggested that I watch television while she cleaned up the kitchen. When she finished, she came and joined me on the couch, but there was a wall between us. By this time, she was probably praying the same prayer as I was. She, too, wanted this nightmare over. Both of us were thankful when we heard the doorbell. I thanked Libby for all that she had done, and we hugged goodbye stiffly. I got into the car with Donald and, as we drove away, I breathed a sigh of relief.

A few days later, I wrote a letter to Libby. After thanking her for the dinner and gifts, I tried to tell her what I was feeling inside.

I have had to be very honest with myself to try to understand this wall that has come between us. You said to me that you have insecurities about where we stand in the relationship, specifically whether I love you in the same way you love me and whether I am ready for a life commitment. I do not feel I am able to make a lifetime commitment at this stage of my spiritual as well as emotional growth. I also cannot give you any guarantees for the future. Libby, I do love you, but the love I feel is more a close friendship love than a romantic love. I care about you and want the best for you; I'm just not sure that I am what's best for you. Only if I were convinced of that could I commit to a strong relationship. A lot of men would love to have a woman respond to them as totally as you are able to respond to me. I see that quality and admire it in you, but cannot receive it myself.

I ended the letter by telling her how much I respected her and that I wanted to remain friends and hoped that she would forgive me for my rudeness.

She answered a few days later. She appreciated having an honest response to a questionable situation. She admitted that she had been confused after the trip to Kansas City, because she didn't know whether I was hurt, angry, backing away, or just feeling bad physically. She noted my discomfort with being affectionate, and said she considered holding hands to be normal for two people who are dating and care about each other.

Then Libby brought up the horrible Valentine's Day fiasco. She had asked several of my friends if they thought I would enjoy a candlelit dinner, and they all said that I would love it. She had so wanted to do something special for me. She confessed that her dad had told her, while I was getting ready for the banquet, that he thought her surprise was poorly timed, and that we should just go with them to the church. Libby felt that if we were alone, we could talk about what had been bugging me and clear the air. She assured me that she had not meant to make me feel trapped or uneasy. Later, as she had been trying to make sense of my behavior, she wondered if I had purposely tried to make her day miserable. Libby ended the letter by saying that she respected my feelings and hoped I would respect hers. She cared deeply for me and wanted to continue the friendship, with no pressure of future commitments. In reality, it was over.

I regret how I treated Libby, but I thank God that I did not marry her. This would have compounded the pain. Some people criticize gay men for marrying women, but many gay men marry because they have been taught that this will "cure" them of their attraction to men. Sadly, when the change does not occur, they feel trapped in their marriages. If they do decide to be honest and take off the mask, they have horrible feelings of guilt and self-doubt, brought on by the wife's accusations.

"How could you have married me, knowing you were gay? You lied to me. Our whole marriage was a farce, because of your selfishness and deceit!"

Now, when I counsel married gay men, I always remind them, "You did not choose to be born into a homophobic society and a homophobic religion and a homophobic family. By marrying a woman, you were only doing what your church and your family taught you to do. You were trying to be normal."

Many preachers, and even some Christian counselors, say, "Marry the right woman and you will change." So, even though I totally understand why the wife would feel cheated, lied to, and used, I think the blame must be laid not at the feet of the gay husband, but at the door of the church. Tragic marriages should never happen because of the backward thinking or ignorance of pastors and counselors.

After four long years attempting to change, I was frustrated with my lack of progress. I felt the church and my family were trying to get me to live in denial of my feelings. It wasn't for lack of longing in my heart to fully experience romance in my life. I tried with Libby, but I finally had to admit that I was not attracted to women. I started resenting that people wanted me to pretend that I was cured.

As I traveled, performing two plays, *The Life of Paul* and *The Life of Christ*, I was receiving invitations from Catholic, Assembly of God, Baptist, and Methodist churches.

I was enjoying their acceptance and approval, but in the back of my mind the question haunted me. "If you knew the real me, would you still want me in your church?"

This all-consuming conflict culminated in the most honest prayer I had ever prayed.

"God, please! I want to know the truth about my homosexual desires. I really do. But I feel like I'm being tortured by the church and my family and my own conscience. Everybody is trying to manipulate me into seeing this issue their way. I refuse to be forced into believing someone else's theology, and I refuse to say I am *cured* when I know, deep inside, that I'm not. I want to know for myself. God, you know how much I love you! Please, just show me plain and simple, whether I should embrace my homosexual orientation or continue to fight it. But God, in showing me, please honor my plea not to do it by using guilt or shame to manipulate me into a certain way of thinking. Please, God, show me your will for my life, without jerking me around by my emotions. Gently show me your way, dear Father. I am so tired…so tired. Just show me the way. I want to do your will. Amen."

I journaled on May 25th, 1991:

God, why do I have this problem? Why did it happen to me? I loved you so much as a child, and I still love you. I just don't understand this whole impulse. Why do I still have to deal with it? Is it just sexual, or is it emotional, or psychological? Does anyone really know? On September 5th of this year, it will have been five years since I started my attempt at going straight. There is a lot that I hate about my lifestyle before that, and yet I still feel a certain amount of identity with it. A part of me aches for the hurt that those who are gay have to suffer. The church will not even mention the fact that they (we) exist. Why not? Is it that they are hoping homosexual people will just somehow disappear? I need to be in an atmosphere where I can get help without having to soft-shoe my way around the real issue.

God, help me! Deliver me from uncaring, hypocritical Christianity. Deliver me from preachers who say they speak for you but have "accents" that give them away. I am tired of making excuses for them while I am dying inside because of spiritual drought! Sometimes I feel as though no man cares for my soul. Sometimes I am tempted just to give up. And yet I love you Lord, and do not want to displease you.

My pastor at the Assembly of God church was not much help. When we talked about my past, he was very uncomfortable, shifting in his chair and frequently glancing at his watch. Admittedly, he appreciated my talents in drama and willingly allowed me to direct the plays in church, but would not give me a paid position for fear of reprisals from those who knew about my former life.

Chapter 27

Church for Misfits

One day, a local pastor called. He told me that he had been given my name by a friend.

"We have just started a new church in Sherwood and we need someone to help with the music. You were referred to me by someone who says you are very gifted in the area of church praise and worship music."

I asked him what denomination and he said it was a Cumberland Presbyterian Church. At the time, I did not know that there were different brands of Presbyterian churches. I discovered that there are liberal, moderate, and conservative branches. The Cumberland Presbyterians were considered moderate. I doubted that any Presbyterian church would respond to my style of worship music. However, Pastor Michael Qualls assured me.

"I've just finished a course out in California that teaches how to make your church *seeker-friendly*, and one thing that really draws the un-churched is lively praise music. The Assembly of God is known for their spirited worship music, and that is why I called you."

Pastor Qualls told me that most of the Cumberland Presbyterian churches primarily tended to use the old hymns in service instead of the new praise and worship choruses. His church needed someone to lead their music department and also to play the piano. Since I could do both, they were very interested in me. I was excited and amazed. The church's consideration of me could not have come at a better time.

The week before my "tryout," I went to talk with Pastor Qualls, who was personable and charming. We hit it off right away. His church, which had started only three months before, was meeting at the local YMCA. It had been launched using a telemarketing technique, with phone calls to all the homes in the North Little Rock area asking people if they would like to receive literature about an exciting new church that was just getting started. On its first Sunday, over 200 people attended to check it out. Now they were running about 70 attendees each Sunday.

The church name was catchy. It was "Friends of His," meaning "Friends of Jesus." The trend in new church development was choosing a name that did not sound "churchy." Friends of His was dedicated to being a safe place for the misfits, those who had not found a place in more traditional churches.

Michael's office was in his home. He introduced me to Marilyn, his wife. Michael said, "Randy, this is the most transparent woman you will ever meet." Marilyn was a tall, attractive woman with a welcoming smile and a winning personality. Her speech was punctuated with much laughter and rich with southern, country charm.

They were the parents of two daughters. Twelve-year-old Micah, the older girl, was energetic and loud! Micah never took time to ponder whether she should say something. She just said it. Melanie, her nine-year-old sister, was quieter than Micah, but both Qualls girls were what I considered to be rowdy. Their parents did not put many strictures on them, so the girls were free to develop their own styles and ideas. I was fascinated, and yet at times judgmental of the way they were being raised. The family functioned differently than any pastor's family I had ever experienced. I would grow to love them.

On my first visit with Michael, as we talked in his office, he became excited about my suggestion to incorporate drama into worship. I considered it important that I tell Michael about my past involvement in the gay community. There was no easy way to segue into this, so toward the end of our meeting, I broached the subject.

"Michael, there is something I need to tell you. This may make a difference as to whether or not you still want to consider me for this position. It has to do with certain things in my past."

"Randy, you will learn that I am not a judgmental person. We all have things in our past of which we are not proud. You can tell me anything."

"Well, Michael, for a time, I lived my life as a gay man. I have been ex-gay for over four years now. I am desperately trying to trust God to change me, but I must admit that I am still attracted to men more than I am to women. I am not acting on my desires and have been celibate for some time now."

I prepared myself for the rejection that I felt would surely come, but Michael had a nonchalant look on his face.

"So? Your point is?"

This surprised me. But since he remained calm, I went on.

"It is very difficult for a gay man to come out to a heterosexual acquaintance, because many straight men immediately assume a gay guy is going to hit on them. But that isn't true, Michael."

"So Randy, you are trying to say I don't have to be worried about you acting inappropriately towards me?"

"Yes, that is what I am saying. I wanted you to hear this from me instead of hearing it from someone else. I felt I owed it to you."

"I don't know that much about homosexuality, Randy. I have always thought that it is probably one of the most misunderstood problems that people face. Our society, and especially the church, seems to single this out as the worst of sins. But I have never looked at it that way. You will probably be able to help me understand more about the struggle. I know this has to be a painful thing for you to deal with. What I *can* offer you is to be your friend. If you need someone to listen, or walk with you through the hard times, or just to stand with you while you scream at the moon some night, I'll be there."

I was overwhelmed at the grace I sensed in this man. Michael was affecting me in a profound way that afternoon. I had never talked with a minister who seemed to have empathy for my situation. I felt that he would not sit in judgment of me. Being offered the position at Friends of His was the answer to the prayer I had written in my journal: "I need to be in an atmosphere where I can get help without having to soft-shoe my way around the real issue."

As I left our meeting, I was thrilled. God had taken notice of my predicament and was leading me to a place where I could finally seek truth, without condemnation.

The first Sunday, I led the music and sang two solos for my "audition." After the service, Michael said the job was mine if I felt led to take it. There was not a lot of money available, but if things worked out, they would find a way to pay me more. Finally, I had the opportunity to return to church ministry!

I knew from my past experiences that it was important for the pastor and the music minister to get along, and I felt that Michael and I would have no problem working together. I was in awe of this gentle, self-depreciating, sensitive, caring man of God. His sermons were filled with funny anecdotes and heartfelt stories from his own life that presented the Christian walk as possible by portraying God as a loving father who was *for* us and not *against* us.

The grace teaching that Lois had invested in my life was resurfacing. When I walked into my position at Friends of His, I longed for God's grace to free me from my self-loathing attitude. The interesting people who made up the congregation were not hung up on "church traditions." Too many times in my former denomination I felt we were pretending we had it all figured out. Many ornate masks were worn on Sunday mornings. But at Friends of His, the masks came off and you could show your true identity, warts and all. This was the initial, idealized view I had of Friends of His. Although in a less judgmental place, I did not disclose my "past" to the members, nor had I given myself permission to be gay. I had a backlog of internalized homophobia to deal with. Also, I was still holding out for a miracle, in case God decided to change the objects of my sexual attractions.

When I told Gary about my new church position, he was happy for me, but was experiencing a difficult time. His dad had died several years before, and now his mom was gravely ill. Gary's sister and brother lived too far away to help take care of her, so she became Gary's responsibility. When it became evident that she could no longer live alone, Gary moved her in with him.

He was only close to one member of his family, his sister Sherry. He had been afraid of his dad, and had little in common with him. Sadly, Gary's mom was never maternal. She had not enjoyed holding her children when they were babies, and never told them she loved them.

Gary's mom apparently lacked what most consider natural maternal instincts. Gary had a great gift for art. Teachers complimented him on his abilities, but his parents never encouraged his talent. In fact, they did not show interest in any of their children.

Gary's dad died at 60. When he was in college, his father made an attempt to connect with him, but Gary had no desire to reciprocate. By this time, he had learned to live life without a father. Doug, his brother, was eight years older and left home when Gary was young.

Gary never told his parents he was gay. After his two trips to Arkansas, his mother asked, "Is Randy a homosexual?" He remembers being surprised that his mother would say that word.

"Yes, he is, but he is trying to change his sexual orientation with the help of the Lord."

Then she asked, "Gary, are you a homosexual?"

Gary's whole world stopped turning for a split second. He panicked. A long pause must have spoken volumes to his mother before he replied, rather unconvincingly, "No."

Since his mom's death, Gary has regretted lying to her that day. He thought his mother knew he had not been honest. Shortly after this she went to a nursing home, although not willingly. Gary could no longer take care of her and work.

While things were looking up for me, I invited Gary to visit again, but he responded that his responsibilities to his mother would make it difficult for him to visit any time soon.

Chapter 28

Facing My Religious Demons

I was happy with my job and with having a new church home. Much of the worship style was not what I was accustomed to. I found it refreshing. I journaled:

I cannot pretend any more that the Assembly of God denomination has all the answers for me. They have been so totally silent where I am concerned. For them, I am a problem they just don't want to deal with. If they have so much of the power of God, the anointing of the Spirit, and the compassion of Christ, then why is it that I have had to suffer for five years in silence? I am enjoying Friends of His because there are no spiritual giants, simply struggling people who are giving God a chance to work in their lives.

God, I am seeking your truth, for truth shall set me free! Grant it Father, through Jesus name, Amen.

To help the musical part of worship, I put together a praise band consisting of keyboard, drums, a bass guitar, a saxophone, and three other singers. I led the worship at the keyboard. This contemporary style of music pleased the congregation. Michael lightheartedly poked fun at the loud colors in my unconventional wardrobe. I reacted with great comeback lines, and we became a comedy duo of sorts. He called me Doc Severinsen, after Johnny Carson's band leader and trumpeter who wore outrageously colorful clothes. Michael and I made a great team. He took a real interest in my life and included me in many of his activities, even taking me on a fishing trip with his buddies and teaching me how to jig fish.

Michael also supported my volunteer ministry to people with AIDS. Sometimes he would visit patients with me. Moreover, he invited Dolly to speak about her son Patrick's battle with AIDS in a Sunday service.

Michael firmly believed that to minister to today's un-churched crowd, entertaining services had to be offered in order to gain and to keep their attention. We certainly provided that. Michael preached eternal truths, but he followed Jesus' model of ministry by creating modern-day parables to translate those truths meaningfully to the modern listener. Some of his stories seemed to me to be inappropriate for church. I told Michael that he should run his stories by me before using them, if he thought they might be questionable.

Actually, most of the folk attending Friends of His were not hung up on church appropriateness. I, on the other hand, was ministering outside my comfort zone. In my old church, most of the thinking was done *for* me. Furthermore, I had plenty of preconceived beliefs about what a pastor should be. Michael messed with my concepts! Although he was loving and grace-filled, Michael sometimes pushed the envelope. I was battling some demons that I know now were disguising themselves as religious spirits. I needed to learn the difference between *true* Christianity and the religious facsimile, so common in America. Michael was *just* the pastor to teach me the difference.

I was hung up on a lot of religious baggage, acquired over the years. Differences between Michael and me in this area came to a head in a matter of days. I started feeling strong reservations about Michael. Late one Saturday evening, I dropped by his house to pick up something I needed for church the next day, expecting to find Michael studying his sermon. I assumed that *all* pastors spent Saturday evening on their knees with an open Bible in front of them, listening to hear the message God wanted them to preach the next morning. When Michael's daughter Micah came to the door, I asked to see her dad.

"He's in the living room, watching *Saturday Night Live*." She grinned. "It's so funny tonight!"

I was shocked! I found him glued to the TV with his family. They were roaring with laughter over this show that my former church had told me to boycott because of its lack of respect for God. I witnessed my pastor, on the night before church, rolling with laughter at these Christ-mockers, and worse, allowing his young, impressionable daughters to watch it, too! I did not say anything, but left in a huff.

The following week, I was at the Qualls' home, waiting for Michael to return from the grocery store so we could go on a visitation call. When he walked in the door, he had a sack full of groceries in one arm, and a six-pack of beer in the other! I felt the same shock I had experienced as a first grader, when I walked up to ask my beloved teacher, Miss Adams, a question. Her purse was sitting open on the desk, and I peeped in and saw a pack of Winston cigarettes inside. I remember going home in tears because Miss Adams was going to burn in hell for smoking cigarettes! The problem in my little mind, back then, was that I could not associate teachers with smoking cigarettes, and now the problem was I could not associate pastors with drinking beer or alcohol! I was so disappointed in Michael.

It became evident to him that I was pulling away, so one afternoon he asked, "Randy, is something wrong? Have I offended you?"

"Well, Michael, since you asked, yes, there is something wrong. You are different from any pastor I have ever known. First of all, I have never seen a pastor buy Coors

Light! Secondly, when I came over last week and found you engrossed in *Saturday Night Live*, I was appalled! You were to minister the following morning, and instead of preparing your heart in prayer and meditation, you were sitting there, laughing at those actors who constantly poke fun at Jesus and the church."

My religious spirit kicked into high gear.

"I believe, Michael, the spirit behind that ungodly show is the same spirit in those men who mocked Christ as He was hanging on the cross. When you laugh at their lewd, Christ-mocking humor, you are participating in the same spirit that influenced the men who crucified our Lord."

Michael was speechless. He had never known anyone like me. He stared in disbelief. Thank God he was kind.

"Randy, I don't know what to do with that. I'm sorry, but I am just not making the connection. I don't see it the same way you do. Obviously, I have upset you, and for that I am sorry."

At that moment, God pulled back a curtain and I was confronted with the ridiculousness of my piety. I saw my religious spirit for what it was.

For those unfamiliar with the term "religious spirit," let me say that it has nothing to do with the Holy Spirit. A religious spirit is a sickness that infects one with "churchianity." Those affected become increasingly legalistic in their approach to Christianity. The Apostle Paul wrote to the church in Galatia, infected by this condition. Today, the church is filled with religious spirits running around, loudly and pompously, using their rules to indict and judge others.

The four and a half years I spent daily sacrificing my longing for sexual intimacy drove me to be highly judgmental. I felt that if the church, filled with heterosexuals, could demand that I be celibate while they went home to their wives or husbands for marital bliss, then I had a right to judge them harshly in return.

"If I have to sacrifice all sexual enjoyment to be a Christian, I will do it. I will be celibate for the rest of my life, and say goodbye to my dreams of having a loving relationship with another man. But if I do, watch out, my heterosexual brother and sister. I will be watching you, and when you slip up and break one of the rules on *my* judgmental sheet, I will be just as hard on you as you have been on me!"

But that day, learning how unloving my words were to Michael, I decided I no longer wanted to carry this grudge in my heart toward those with whom I disagreed spiritually. I wanted to resign as judge and jury, and heed Jesus' words to "judge not lest I be judged." When I asked Michael to forgive me for being so judgmental, he graciously accepted my apology.

"Randy, you are trying so hard to please God. I see that in you, and I know it is coming from a sincere heart. But Randy, no one will live up to your set of rules, not even *you*." He was right.

I made a decision to join Friends of His and become a Cumberland Presbyterian. Maybe I could find my place in this unique new congregation who welcomed misfits. In this atmosphere of grace, I found myself wanting to draw closer to God, and I was beginning to believe God loved me unconditionally. Grace allowed me the freedom to seek and find my whole identity as a gay Christian man.

One night, as Michael and I drove home from a church service about two hours away, I opened up to him about my deepest struggles.

"Michael, I have so much romance in my heart. At the same time, I know that the only romantic relationship that is possible for me is with a man. If what the church has told me is true, the only way I can please God and also have a significant other in my life is to fall in love with a woman. I know now that this is *not* a possibility for me.

"So, according to the church's edict, the only way I can continue in ministry and remain a Christian is to be celibate. But what if God made me this way? What if I didn't choose this, Michael? I can remember getting hot and bothered seeing Tarzan in his loincloth back when I was nine. I didn't get excited at all by seeing Jane in her skimpy jungle dress. So, if I didn't choose to have these attractions, maybe God meant for me to be gay."

I could not believe I had the nerve to articulate that thought without the fear of being struck by lightning. It felt good to trust a God who was allowing me to explore truth. I have since discovered that we are closest to God when we question. The questioning shows our deep desire to know God, and I believe God responds joyfully to that desire.

"Michael, I don't want to live the rest of my life without a meaningful relationship. I enjoy ministry. I do. Ministry is very fulfilling. But there is a part of me that is not being fulfilled. I am not a whole person, and when people insist that I *have* to change, it feels like they are trying to do some kind of lobotomy on me. They are trying to remove a big chunk of who I am."

Michael listened intently, nodding affirmatively at times to let me know that he was following my logic.

"Randy," he said, after I stopped to catch my breath. "I try to put myself in your place. Could I be celibate for the rest of my life? Would I see that as fair, or even a possibility for me? No, I couldn't be celibate and live without an emotional bond with someone I loved. You know, I think all of us have a "cross" in our lives, obstacles each of us has to overcome before really getting on with life. When my older brother was killed in a car wreck, I almost lost my mind. I grieved big time. But his death really got me to thinking about so many things. I decided that my greatest fear in life was not death; my greatest fear was dying without ever having really lived."

That was it! That was what *I* was feeling too! Michael articulated what I could not put into words. I wanted to live *my* life, not the life everyone thought I should live.

"Michael, I don't want to have regrets someday. I want to find out who I really am. The God you preach about, the one I am getting to know, loves me enough to give me freedom to seek out truth. If I go in the wrong direction, God will still be there to love me and redirect me, gently. I can no longer deny that I am a gay man, and if God had wanted to change me, surely He would have done so in the past five years. No one has tried harder than I have. *No one!* I know it has to be different this time. I don't want to be promiscuous. I want to be a gay, Christian man, who is not ashamed of his love for Jesus, a gay man with values and morals. I would like to date a man who loves Jesus as I do. I want to see if it is possible."

Michael assured me that he understood and would not judge me.

"But what if I do find a man that I fall in love with, Michael, and decide to commit my life to him? What would that mean to my position at Friends of His?

"I can't say, Randy. I don't think it would make a difference for me, but I can't say how the rest of the church would see it. This is a really big issue right now in the churches of all denominations. I would hope that we would not allow this to become an issue, but if it did, who knows how it would turn out."

"Michael, I have been honest with you from the beginning and I want to continue that honesty. I see you as not only my boss and my pastor, but also as my friend. I really need a friend right now. Thanks for being there for me."

Randy McCain and Michael Qualls in 1992

Chapter 29

Is This a Date?

As Christmas approached, I started preparing my first musical program for Friends of His. Christmas is my favorite time of the year. I noticed in the newspaper that a traveling group was going to perform Dickens' *A Christmas Carol* at a local college, so I bought two tickets and called Dolly to see if she would go with me. Dolly already had plans, but knew a guy named Paul who was really down and could use some cheering up.

"Why don't you call Paul and ask him to go with you?"

"But Dolly, he might think it odd for a stranger to call him up and ask him to go to the theatre. Why don't *you* call him and see if he would be interested?"

"I'll call him."

She hung up without saying goodbye. In a few minutes my phone rang. It was Dolly.

"He said for you to call him. Here's his number."

I dialed the number slowly, wondering if this was the right thing to do. I paused before I pushed the last digit. "Randy," I said to myself. "This guy is lonely and so are you. It isn't a date. You just have an extra ticket."

Paul sounded very nice. He was a nurse who was also involved in theatre and dance. We decided to meet outside the theatre entrance. I got there and wondered if I would be able to pick him out from Dolly's description, and if I would find him attractive. I had never been on a blind date, but I reminded myself that this was *not* a date.

Paul came walking up. We exchanged hellos and he thanked me for offering the ticket. I could not believe how *cute* he was. He was taller than me and had a dancer's body. His beautiful eyes sparkled and danced with energy and personality. Yet, he seemed bashful.

The show was magical. The costumes were elaborate; the acting and singing were exceptional. By the end of the play, I was in the Christmas spirit and I was feeling more and more comfortable with Paul. As we walked to our cars, he again thanked me for the ticket and the invite.

Then he added, "You are welcome to come by my place for a drink. Oh that's right, you're a preacher. Dolly told me. Well, I have Cokes and hot chocolate."

A shiver ran up my spine. No matter how much I kept telling myself that this was not a date, it was starting to feel like one.

"I probably should be getting home, but thank you."

"You sure you won't stop by for a few minutes? I don't live far from here. It really is on your way home."

I thought it over. He was someone Dolly knew. That meant he wasn't a total stranger. I was attracted to him and was having a great time. I really didn't want the evening to end.

"I guess I could stop by for a little while."

When we got to his apartment, he put on some of his favorite music. He loved Bette Midler and so did I. He had all her music. He fixed hot chocolate, and I sat on the couch while Paul sat on the floor. We had no trouble finding things in common to discuss. We talked about our favorite Broadway musicals and movies.

Then, out of the blue, Paul asked me, "So, you don't want to be gay anymore?" I looked shocked. He saw this and added, quickly, "Oh, Dolly told me. Hey listen, I respect your decision. I'm just a little disappointed, that's all."

"You're disappointed?" I asked.

Paul started to blush and looked down, as though he had embarrassed himself.

"Yes, because I would very much like to be sitting next to you on the couch, holding your hand while we listen to Bette instead of being way over here."

"Well, there's plenty of room on the couch."

"I don't want to scare you."

I patted the seat beside me. Paul hopped up from the floor and scooted in next to me on the couch. It felt so natural. Unlike Libby, I didn't mind Paul invading my space, nor did I feel smothered by his attention. Rather, I was soaking it up like a dry sponge.

We talked some more, and before long, he said, "Randy, I'm going through a real sad time right now. I broke up with my boyfriend not long ago and I've been in a deep depression. This has been such a good thing for me tonight. You don't know how much your company has helped me."

His hand was next to mine on the couch. I instinctively reached over and held it. I looked at him and he looked at me. Our faces were close, and the moment seemed magical as we began to respond to each other and move with a choreographed grace. My hand moved toward the side of his face and he leaned in. Our lips met and suddenly I remembered how good it felt to kiss, and be kissed, by a man. My face was flushed, my palms were sweaty and my breath was shallow and fast, which felt so good and natural to me. After a while, I broke away and thanked Paul for a memorable evening. He thanked me in return.

"Maybe we can see a movie this week," Paul suggested.

"Sure, I'll call you."

We kissed once more at the door, and as I walked to my car, I didn't feel the cold. I was so *alive*! I was ME again. Driving away, I allowed all the excitement I had tried to keep in check to burst forth like fireworks on the Fourth of July. "Yes!" I screamed.

We decided to see a movie. I looked forward to seeing Paul again. We had talked on the phone several times. I thought how interesting it would be to date someone without it ending in sex. I wanted to see if it were possible for two gay men to date and develop mutual respect. I wanted to know more about Paul.

When I arrived for the date, he seemed happy to see me. I don't remember what movie we saw, but we went back to his place. I realized that Paul had more on his mind than hot chocolate. I found myself going with the flow, but then I remembered my promise to myself. I stopped things abruptly, in midstream. To Paul's credit, he did not make me feel embarrassed or bad.

"Randy, I'm just newly single myself. I'm probably not ready for this kind of intimacy, either."

After perhaps three dates, I sensed that things were not connecting for the two of us. Paul enjoyed spending time with me, but could not understand my intense struggle with my sexuality and my Christian faith. During one of our evenings together, Paul surprised me.

"Randy, I know you think I'm a terrible heathen because I curse and I don't feel a need to sing about Jesus all the time…but for your information, I am a Christian."

I was shocked. "You are?"

"Yes, I love Jesus and believe He died for my sins. I just don't understand your view of God. To you, God seems to be mean and judgmental. My mother taught me that God loves all His children…red, yellow, black, white, straight, gay…all His children. I respect your faith, but I can tell you right now I am not going to be a preacher's wife!"

Paul was not one to hide his feelings. He had put into words what I was sensing, but was afraid to admit. The two of us were not on the same spiritual wavelength. In hindsight, Paul was much farther along than I was in accepting his own gay orientation and God's love for him. His mother was so different than mine. She had instilled in Paul the truth of God's love, whereas my mother had taught me this other God, one that loved you one minute and hated you the next. Paul was not willing to take me on as a project. He was out and proud. I was in the closet, trying to convince myself that it was safe to leave the closet behind.

Although I had strong desires for Paul, he helped me see that it would never work out for us. If I did come out, I would need a partner who understood my need to be in the ministry.

Paul was a sweet, handsome, talented young man, and I will always be indebted to him for the reality check. His interest in me was the pin that burst my balloon of denial and allowed me to pursue the reality of being a gay, Christian man.

Gary in Arkansas

Chapter 30

My True Love, There All Along

In late January 1992, Gary wrote me that his mother was very ill. Her doctors did not hold out much hope. I wished I could be there with him during that time, but Gary said it was enough knowing that I cared and was praying for him.

I wrote Gary on February 5 that I felt free to really explore who I was and where I was going. The freedom I was experiencing is evident in one excerpt:

…The truth is, I am gay and Jesus loves me. I do not have to make excuses for what I am. I don't even have to understand why. I'm getting in touch with me, with who I am. I haven't made any decisions and still have a lot of questions, but at least now I have opened up the communication lines between me and the Father and I know He is faithful!!!

Gary wrote back,

I'm so glad you are breaking through to a deeper, more meaningful relationship… That is an answer to my prayers. Randy, I'm so privileged and joyful to have you as my dearest friend. I love you so much and care for you deeply. It's amazing to think that our present relationship perhaps hung on a very thin thread years ago when it was a matter of sending one letter which could so easily have been lost or misdirected. I'm sure God's hand delivered that letter to Mother's house using one of His angels. And I didn't have to respond to it either. But I'm glad I did. You have been a rock to me. My life's greatest meaning (apart from Jesus Himself) has been knowing you. I think you are my ministry sometimes…Well I'll sign off…I love you. I love you so much…

Dorothy Eddy died on February 3, 1992. Gary soon sent a letter enclosing a program from his mom's funeral. He spoke of how relieved he was to know that his mother was whole again and in heaven with his dad. Because Gary was the executor of his mom's estate, the next few weeks would be filled with stressful business matters, but he wrote,

I need a vacation soon, real soon…you may see me sooner than you think…I don't know if you will want me to visit or not…I'll be a basket case with the jitters and mush for brains! …I hope you are doing well. Please take care of yourself. I hope you discover that having a

significant other is ok. I want to be him to you! Actually, I think we are already significant others to each other now. But sometimes I'd like to express it differently. Sometimes I yearn to express my love for you intimately—at least—oh well, never mind...

I shared with Pastor Michael what Gary had written about wanting to be my significant other. In reply, Michael asked if I thought Gary and I would get together someday.

"Oh, I don't know. Gary is so persnickety. When I visited him during college, his side of the dorm room was immaculate! Everything had a place. His bed was so tightly made you could bounce a quarter on it. If we were to live together, we would drive each other crazy. It would be like Felix and Oscar in *The Odd Couple.*"

"Well, how do you feel towards him *other* than those differences?" Michael asked.

"Gary has been there for me more times than I can count. He has been a safe place for me to pour out my heart. I could always count on him for help. But I just don't know if we could make it together. We are such good friends, and there is a sexual attraction there between us. I don't know. We haven't had that much time together to see how we connect on a day-to-day basis. I just don't know if we could get along."

Later that evening, I started rereading some letters from Gary. All of them contained a recurring theme of love and respect for me and for God's work in my life. One letter, in November 1988, written while both of us were struggling to be ex-gay, ended with these words:

I love you dearly Randy—even though we don't talk as often or see each other we are still knit together, my love flows strong for you. You'll always have my support and you'll always be my dearest friend.

In a July 1989 letter, Gary wrote:

...You are often on my mind. I pray for you and always thank God you are a part of my life—a big part. We are kindred spirits. We understand each other as no one else can. Together we have learned the meaning of Christ's unconditional love. What a privilege I have to say you're my friend, to have graciously been given a role (however difficult it has been at times) in developing your life in Christ—the privilege that God uses us despite the danger, the clear possibility of my possible unwillingness to give you up at the early stage right after Jerry. God went ahead. That tells us He knew we'd make it, and that, in turn, bolsters my faith in the belief that He knows what He's doing and that He knows us fully.

Amazingly, even though we were trying to alter our sexual orientation back then, Gary still shared his honest feelings of love for me. I began to ask if Gary was the man that I had been looking for. I could not deny the divine intervention in our friendship. If we could just spend time together, exploring the possibilities, perhaps we could sense how God was leading.

Gary decided to come to Arkansas in May 1992. Both of us wanted to explore being together as a couple, and I wanted Gary to meet the important people in my life. I couldn't wait to introduce him to Dolly, although he said he felt he already knew her. Dolly was ready to meet him, too. Because Dolly's protective feelings for me were strong, Gary would have to pass the "Dolly test" before she bestowed her blessing.

I wanted Michael to meet Gary and was curious how he would deal with his worship leader having a boyfriend. Pastor Michael talked a good game, but how would he respond when the reality was staring at him every Sunday morning?

I chose not to tell Mother and Dad about Gary's visit. Lately, tension was building between my parents and me as they sensed the newfound freedom I felt exploring outside the box. They were afraid I was headed back into the lifestyle I had lived before I left Jerry. All they knew of the gay world was the underbelly they had seen through my experiences. I didn't know how I could explain to them that it was different this time and that I was much healthier than before, so it seemed easier not to tell them about Gary's visit.

I planned to pick Gary up at the Little Rock airport and then go directly to a state park about an hour's drive away. I had the car packed with camping equipment and food for cooking on the grill. This was the cheapest way that Gary and I could be together without having to worry about the distractions of family, friends, and church.

I arrived at the airport early and could not believe how good it felt to hug him. We had not been together in a number of years. I liked the way he was maturing, although I did want to make him an appointment with my hairdresser. His hair was way too conservative!

We headed for the country. It was nice holding his hand as we drove. Neither one of us could believe we were actually sitting next to each other, instead of talking on a phone. I loved camping. Gary, as it turned out, hated it. He felt it was dirty and unorganized, and he did not like taking cold showers. We felt a certain amount of tension between us the first few days. We were not very physical with each other. We knew that this was a very important time in our lives, and so much of our future could depend on how we got along during Gary's stay. And I might be facing the uncomfortable prospect of telling my parents I was going to live with a man again. I also was considering the impact a relationship with Gary would have on my position at Friends of His. This pressure, plus my growing awareness of Gary's aversion to camping, made for a strange mix of emotions.

We returned to Little Rock on Saturday in time for Gary's appointment with my hair stylist. I could not believe the transformation. His hair was short and sexy! He had also not shaved for the whole time we were on the camping trip, so he had that short stubble I find attractive.

When I took Gary to meet Dolly and Wally, Gary was surprised by Dolly's appearance. From the way I had described her, as a strong-willed, aggressive person, he had pictured Dolly as a large, tough-looking woman. Gary really enjoyed Dolly's eccentric mannerisms, and thought Wally was nice.

Sunday rolled around. I found it exciting to minister with Gary there. I had so much fun introducing him to everyone. Michael and Marilyn seemed to approve of him.

Gary and I went to eat with friends from church, and then took off for Eureka Springs, a unique little village nestled in the Ozark Mountains. The town was actually built on the side of a mountain and offers many bed and breakfasts and quaint little shops. Eureka Springs is also home to one of the most famous outdoor passion plays, dramatizing Jesus' life, death, and resurrection.

Gary and I were exhausted, so we spent the night in Harrison, about thirty miles from Eureka Springs. The next morning, I looked over at Gary. He is one of those people who wakes up perfect in the morning without having to comb his hair or anything. "Could he be any cuter?" I thought. Gary opened his eyes and we kissed tenderly. This all felt so right to me. He got up, dressed, went to the motel office, and came back with coffee for me. I was touched by his thoughtfulness.

In Eureka Springs, we stopped at one motel that had a very reasonable offer posted outside. Gary went in to get a room. He came out and told me that he had splurged on a room with a Jacuzzi for two! I had never been in a Jacuzzi before.

We decided to check out the cute little shops when it started raining. It was fun running from one store to another, and we both fell in love with this perfect setting for romance.

That evening we attended *The Great Passion Play*. As we sat next to each other, watching the story of Jesus come alive before our eyes, I found myself spiritually moved, and at the same time experiencing wonderful feelings for Gary. Actually, we had fallen in love years ago, but it was just now becoming clear how much I felt for this friend who had been there for me through thick and thin. For the first time, two parts of me that had been separate for so long were becoming one. I felt like I was finally whole, which equaled *holy*.

Later that evening, as we lay side by side on the bed, Gary said to me, "Randy, I want to move to Little Rock and spend the rest of my life loving you."

His words startled me. It was as though someone had suddenly put on the brakes in the middle of a thrilling joy ride. I did not respond right away, but tightened my hold on him as we lay there intertwined. I am sure Gary must have felt awkward with no response to his tender words, but I was not ready to consider the consequences of coming out as a gay man.

The next day, on the way home, I was quiet. Gary finally asked why I was not talking.

"I don't know, Gary. I really have enjoyed our time together, but what you said last night, about moving here and us being together...that is scaring the *hell* out of me." This was unusual. I never use profanity, but at that moment it was the only phrase that fit.

"Randy, I'm sorry. I don't want to scare you. There is no pressure from me, I promise."

"I know, Gary. I'm just thinking about what this would mean to my ministry. I need time to sort it all out."

The next day, when I took Gary to the airport, a part of me couldn't wait to get him on the plane. Perhaps distance would give me more clarity. Gary was a nervous wreck, trying to hide his troubled emotions. Even though I put up a good front, he could tell things were shaky between us. We kissed before we got out of the car, very quickly so as to not be seen by anyone. I waited with him until he boarded the plane. When I got back in my car, I sat missing my friend.

I cried as I drove home, remembering how safe, warm, and loved I had felt holding Gary. When I called later that evening to see if he had made it home safely, we chatted for a little while, and then Gary said shyly, "Randy, I want to say I love you but I don't want to make you nervous like I did the other night."

"It's okay Gary, you can say it." I heard Gary's relief.

"I do love you, Randy, and I miss you very much."

"I think I love you too, Gary. I really do."

As we ended the conversation, I felt a little more confident of my love for Gary Eddy. The next day I wrote:

Dearest Gary,

Just a few lines to tell you how much I enjoyed our 12 days together...Last night when we talked on the phone, I felt new warmth in our conversation. What was a wonderful friendship before the vacation has become even more wonderful!!! You have always been there for me, Gary. You were always my safe haven...

Gary wrote, sharing a fantasy about us being together:

Tonight is a beautiful night for romance. An intimate dinner, sitting on the sofa afterwards snuggled together, listening to each other's heartbeat, listening to the rain falling gently outside. It is raining here tonight, a gentle soft rain, a rain as light as the touch of my lips on yours, gentle as the love you have for me! I love you, Randy. You are more important to me now than before; our relationship has taken on a third dimension. We're real people to each other now. After our time of vacation and after the talks we had, I think I'm more inclined to relax in our love…

I look forward to being your very significant other. I want to be your friend, spend lots of time together, and I want to make love to you. I think of you often, and think of you in the mornings. I long to feel you beside me, the warmth of your body filling me with joy and strength. I also want to share your faith. The love you have for God is so real and palpable. It imparts even to me a new revelation of God and His love for me. I love that about our relationship. We have not just the physical passion, but we have the emotional tie. And the spiritual connection…we have so much going for us. So I think we have a very good chance of reaching old age together!"

I knew Gary was waiting for my invitation to move to Little Rock. What stopped me? It was concern for my ministry at Friends of His. As I thought and prayed about this, Gary kept coming to my mind. This man I had known for 18 years stood with me through good times as well as bad. Honest to a fault, he loved Jesus and sought to be in the center of God's will. He not only understood ministry, but also felt God might call him to be a missionary someday. As far as sexual attraction, there was no problem there. Admittedly, he was not tall and Hispanic, the characteristics that made up my fantasy man, but I knew from past experiences of being around him that there was a definite physical desire between us.

Moreover, he did not just love Jesus. He had survived the same spiritual, legalistic abuse. As I weighed these things in my mind, I asked, "Randy, where will you find so many positive building blocks for a relationship? A man like Gary does not come along every day."

I picked up the phone and called him.

"I have been praying and thinking a lot about my future. I have considered all the possibilities, and I have reached a conclusion. I want you, Gary, to be my partner for life…I want to accept your proposal of marriage."

Now, I am amazed how God brought us to this place. Timing was everything. Had we gotten together in 1985, we would have been unprepared for a solid relationship. But God's plan, though at certain points complicated by our lack of understanding, was always steering us toward this rendezvous with grace and love! How many times I had read, "For I know the plans I have for you,' declares the Lord, 'plans to prosper you and not to harm you, plans to give you hope and a future.'" (Jeremiah 29:11)

Once I made my decision, I wanted us to be together right away, but Gary told me that this was not possible. He couldn't move to Arkansas until the first of September. June, July, and August would prove to be the longest three months of my life! We ran up some expensive phone bills during this time of separation.

On June 7, 1992, the evening of my 36th birthday, I could not go to sleep. I needed to tell Michael about my decision to be Gary's partner. Michael once told me to call him if I needed to talk, regardless of the time. I called at midnight. Although he had been asleep, he told me to meet him at the YMCA where we met for church each Sunday. The minute I saw him, I got emotional.

"Michael, I have made a decision. You and I talked before about the possibility of me discovering that I could have romance in my life. Well, I can't pretend any longer. I *am* gay. This is who I am. I am a gay, Christian man and I love Gary Eddy."

Michael asked me how I was dealing with this spiritually.

"I am being really honest with God. I have told Him, 'God, you know my heart. You know that I have always loved you, even when I was a little child. You also know that I have always wanted to do your will. I asked you to change my sexual orientation, but you didn't. This is the way I am. I love Gary and he loves me. He and I both love you very much. Now when we die and stand before you, I believe that you will accept us as your children. But, if you tell us we can't enter heaven because of our love for each other, then we will have to accept that, because you are God. You get the final say. But I am learning, more and more, to trust your love and grace. So I am willing to place myself in your loving arms and allow you to rule on whether our love is acceptable to you or not. But with all that is within me, I believe that our love for each other is centered in you.'"

Years later, Michael told me he had been moved beyond words by my confession. He believes that if those who say derogatory things about gay people could have heard and experienced the depth of feeling coming from me that night, surely it would affect the way they feel about gays.

Michael assured me that he was my friend and would accept our relationship. This meant the world to me. He did not seem upset in the least that I was making the decision to live with Gary in a loving committed relationship. But he did caution me that, though we had his support, he was unsure about the rest of the church.

"So, are you asking me to lie about our relationship?"

"No," Michael said. "I would never ask you to lie. I would just caution you not to tell the *whole* truth."

I had no idea the challenge this would become, but I was willing to give it a shot. I found a small, two-bedroom apartment with a fireplace How romantic for our very first home together! Now, all it needed was Gary.

Gary, I found out, is a talented poet. He wrote several poems that reflected his emotions during the days that followed our decision to be together.

The love within my heart
Is like a newborn fawn,
A fragile dappled form
Struggling to stand
On unsteady legs
Already growing strong.

A companion poem from these days of waiting:

Out of the depths of my heart,
Up out of the still catacombs
Of a dormant soul,
Come strains of a new song.
Impossible to believe
Beneath the shadowed gauze of melancholy
Sunken deep beneath the dust of fear
That these once silent bows
Can slide across strings long out of tune.
The music wafting up on gentle frightened waves
Brings a mystery engaging my soul.
I listen, trembling
For I do not want this joy to end.

The depth of meaning that he captured in his poetry amazed me, and caused me to desire him more. Gary decided that he would come to Arkansas on the first of September. He sold most of his furniture and would bring what he could pack in his car. He planned to visit his sister in Pierre, South Dakota and then stop at his Grandmother Eddy's house in Kansas City on his way.

Gary had not had a vacation in 12 years, and now that he was free from his work obligations, he decided he would take at least six months to get settled in Arkansas before looking for work. He would live off the small inheritance he received following his mother's death.

I wanted him to get here as soon as he could, but was glad that he wanted to keep his ties with his family. His sister Sherry, who had been very affirming back in 1985 when Gary had decided to move in with me after my break-up with Jerry, now had reservations. She had resumed attending an Assembly of God church, and her attitude toward the gay issue had become more judgmental. She and Gary tried to avoid the subject to enjoy their time together. However, Sherry was unhappy her brother was moving so far away.

I didn't know Gary's exact arrival day, but I planned all kinds of things to welcome him to Arkansas, including a banner that said, "Welcome home Gary!" and a bottle of champagne. The first Friday in September he called saying he would be there in a few hours.

Soon, Gary would step into our apartment for the first time and I would be able to put my arms around him, hold him, and show him physically how glad I was that we had made the decision to spend the rest of our lives together. I fixed a big pot of chicken and dumplings to introduce Gary to my southern cooking skills. The champagne was chilled, the apartment was clean, and the welcome home banner was stretched across the room for Gary to see the minute he walked in the door.

He called from a nearby service station to say he would be right there. I spent those last few moments in high anticipation of his arrival. I wanted to totally be in the moment because this day would always be one of my fondest memories. I heard his car. He walked up the steps and I couldn't wait for him to knock. I opened the door, grabbed him, and we held each other close. I will never forget that moment. *Ever.*

Gary was wearing jeans and a flannel shirt. He smelled of gasoline, but it was like rich cologne to me. I could not let go and neither could he. We kissed and hugged and kissed again. It became apparent that we were not going to let each other go. We had waited 18 years for this moment, and we wanted it to last. We shuffled together, still intertwined, to the sofa and sat down. We eventually toasted our future life together with champagne, but we did not eat chicken and dumplings until about one in the morning!

The next day was the ultimate "show and tell." I have always been one to enjoy sharing things I love, with people I love…movies, food, restaurants, knick knacks, pictures. I am sure Gary Eddy got his fill. The next evening, I showed Gary off to some of my friends. Most were gay acquaintances. I wanted us to be in a social setting where we could be ourselves, without worrying about hiding the fact that we were a couple. Everyone welcomed Gary with open arms.

PART TWO

Chapter 31
A Spiritual Re-Awakening

Before his move, Gary had written to me that, as much as he loved the cassettes I had sent him of Michael's preaching, he felt it might be better if he attended a different church. That might protect my position at Friends of His. The more I thought about this, however, the more convinced I became that I wanted us to worship together.

The next Sunday, I introduced the congregation to my friend from college days, who had moved to Arkansas to avoid the cold winters of South Dakota and was going to share my apartment. This announcement was straight out of the textbook for the Michael Qualls' School of How to Avoid the Truth Without Telling a Lie, which would work for a while. But an event was about to take place that would make it harder for us to publicly deny our feelings for each other—a spiritual rendezvous at a gay and lesbian charismatic conference outside of Houston, Texas.

Bernard Jones, a gay man who was a member of Friends of His, told me about the conference. He felt that God wanted him to share this experience with Gary and me, and he offered to pay our way. I was a little troubled by the brochure for the conference. It explained that the gathering was being held at a rustic campground out in the woods. Those attending the conference were asked not to leave the compound for five days. What if it was a cult? Gay Pentecostals?! Could there be such a thing? Why was there a rule about not leaving the whole time?

I kidded Gary, "If they serve Kool-Aid I am not drinking it!"

Although I tried to bail out, Bernard insisted that we were in for a spiritual treat. Reluctantly, I committed us to go.

When we reached the campgrounds, Gary and I were greeted by friendly strangers. Most participants had attended the conference in years past, so we were the new kids on the block. There were classes offered on gay spirituality and ethics, one for gay couples dealing with problems unique to gay relationships, and one that Gary especially enjoyed, a workshop for spouses of ministers.

Friday night was the first worship service with over 200 Christians, most of them gay, praising and worshiping God. I wasn't quite prepared for how this would affect me as the lively worship music began. Individuals with tambourines were dancing up the aisle, carrying banners with Christian worship symbols and scriptures. I loved seeing my fellow outcasts, who had been driven out of churches all across America, now being welcomed into a place of worship. Thankful hearts overflowed with the joy of the Lord. Gay and lesbian believers, tears streaming down their cheeks, raised their hands in worship. My heart was moved beyond words! As I stood there looking at these sincere gay and lesbian Christians, I recognized a real *move of God*.

One thing my Pentecostal background had taught me, even as a child, was to recognize and honor the true moving of the Holy Spirit. Now, in this place, I had no doubt that this was an authentic move of God's Spirit in response to worship. My hands were raised and tears streamed down my face. This was the confirmation I had needed in my life. I thought I was already convinced that God had accepted me, but now there was no doubt. I was right smack dab in the middle of a powerful wave of the moving of God's Holy Spirit, where gays were in the majority. What was God thinking?

Later in the service, during a time of prayer and singing, an attractive white-haired lady came over to talk to us. Her name was Sister Evelyn Schave. She had been a Pentecostal evangelist for years. She and her husband, Dennis, were attending the conference, as they had for the past few years. When a gay friend invited them, they questioned if it was right for them to attend. She sought advice from one of her Pentecostal friends, saying, "I have been asked to preach at a gay and lesbian Christian Conference. What should I do?"

The minister friend responded, "Go and get them all saved and delivered!"

At the conference they attended, Sister Evelyn was astonished to realize that these gay and lesbian believers had the same Holy Spirit she had received. Her spirit bore witness with these precious children of God. She and Brother Dennis had returned every year to experience the move of God's Spirit.

Sister Evelyn came to Gary and me. She took our hands and said, "Randy, I sat under your ministry of drama last night when you portrayed the Apostle Paul. You are so gifted of the Holy Spirit. God has sent me to tell you that He has a very special work for you and Gary to do in the future. You are precious in His sight. I have been directed by God to pray for both of you."

She joined hands with us and began praying like only Pentecostal women can. Afterwards, as we thanked Sister Evelyn, she again took our hands.

"Randy and Gary, you are so anointed. I feel the Holy Spirit in you, even now. I know what demon possession feels like. I have seen people possessed of the devil. If you boys were demon possessed and as evil as many in the church say gays are, I would be able to discern it, believe me! But when I hold your hands, I feel the presence of the Holy Spirit all over you. Your union is precious to God and you are one couple I am so excited about. I know that God's hand is upon you, and don't you ever doubt that for one minute. Your family and others may say you'll never be used of God unless you change. They can say it, but that doesn't make it so. They will come to see that God's anointing is truly upon you. That is what will convince them. The anointing makes the difference. And you *are* anointed!"

Sister Evelyn's words and prayer deeply touched Gary and me. Later that night, as Gary and I walked around that rustic campground, we shared our thoughts. We were trying to process our experience. Apparently everyone had gone to sleep, but we couldn't because of the excitement we were experiencing.

"Gary, this is so overwhelming. I believe God wanted us to be here, don't you?"

"Yes, I do now. I had my doubts when we first arrived, but after that service, I am convinced that we are here to receive from God."

"I know that it is not possible for us to have a wedding ceremony that is legal, but I believe that God has blessed our union. This was confirmed tonight by what Sister Evelyn said to us. I want us to have a wedding ceremony sometime next year. I think it is important that we make our vows before God and witnesses, but tonight, I just want us to make those promises to each other."

We joined hands under a rustic pavilion and promised to love, honor, and cherish each other "'til death do us part."

In the final service of the conference, I sensed that God was speaking to me in much the same way He had that night I was called into the ministry, twenty years before. Yet this time, his words were even more specific.

Randy, for years you have been afraid to look into my face. You have walked around with your head down in shame, because you hated yourself. You felt that I was ashamed of you. But this weekend, you have looked fully into my glory, and there is no longer any shame. My Spirit has affirmed to your spirit, that you are my beloved son in whom I am well-pleased. Now that you are no longer ashamed, the anointing upon your life and upon your ministry will be greater than ever before, because now you are confident of my love for you, and for the world!

My tears flowed. Jesus was right there holding me the way He did in that bathroom years before, when I had been at my lowest point. It was an intimate moment with the resurrected Christ. I raised my hands and praised God. I was lost in worship! I would never be the same again because the truth had set me free.

Gary and I returned home on cloud nine! We will always be indebted to our dear friend, Bernard Jones, for providing us with such a great opportunity to re-establish our spiritual roots so early in our married life.

Chapter 32

Saying Goodbye to Grandma McCain

In October of 1992, when Grandma McCain discovered that she had adult on-set leukemia, Dad brought her to Little Rock to see a specialist. I was determined that Gary would meet Grandma. He knew the significant role she had played in my life because I had shared so much about her with him. Grandma always said that she did not fear death, but she was honest about not understanding everything about it. One day in 1990, while she and I visited the McCain family plot at the Warren cemetery, Grandma questioned why God had allowed Grandpa to die first.

"He was afraid of everything," Grandma remembered. "He especially was afraid of dying. I have always wondered why God didn't take me instead of your grandpa."

"God knew you had a very important role to play in so many lives, especially mine," I replied. "Grandma, you, more than anyone else, have shown me God's un-conditional love. I'm glad God didn't take you to heaven way back then. I needed you…and I still do."

"Well, I am 85 years old and I am ready for God to take me home. My greatest fear has always been that I would become a burden to my family, or that I would have to go to a nursing home. I have lived a good life. God has been so faithful to me. I still have my home and I can take care of myself. I just pray that God will take me home soon."

"But Grandma, I cannot imagine living in a world without you. And remember, you are supposed to attend my wedding someday."

"Randy, I have asked the Lord to send you someone very special to take care of you. That is probably why you haven't met *her* yet. It is taking God time to prepare her for the challenge of being your helpmate."

"That's why you can't go to heaven yet, Grandma. You have to pass the baton to my future wife. You have to make sure I have met that special someone before you go on to your reward."

We laughed that day. Some of what we said was in jest, but underlying our words was a thread of truth. I did need someone to go through life with. I was not the kind of person to face life alone. Grandma had always been there for me. She had been my encourager, my spiritual giant. There would be such an empty hole in my life when she died.

Grandma was always happy when one of her grandkids got married. She made most of her granddaughters' wedding dresses, and was always thrilled to be at Mc-Cain family weddings. I wanted her to be there for mine. Now that I had found the person I loved, and with whom I had vowed to spend the rest of my life, I wanted Grandma to meet him. Her prayers for me had been answered when God brought Gary into my life.

When I stopped by my parents' house to see Grandma, she was glad to see me, but I was troubled by her physical appearance. This disease had aged her. I asked Grandma if she would come hear me sing at Friends of His the next morning. She said she would talk to my dad and mom, and I figured this meant she would not be coming. My parents would not attend my church because Mom was angry at me for giving up on Project Heterosexual.

Mom made it clear that I was always welcome at their home, but not Gary. During the time I had attempted to be ex-gay, Mom had always been eager to attend services wherever I ministered. When I was first hired at Friends of His, Mom had come to our special services. But since Gary had moved here, she had refused to place her seal of approval on my ministry, and definitely not on our relationship.

I left Mom and Dad's house sure that Grandma would never meet the love of my life. The next morning, I got the thrill of a lifetime. While I was sitting at the piano, leading the first praise song in the Sunday service, in walked Grandma! Dad had taken her to his church for Sunday school, and then brought her to Friends of His. She wanted to hear her grandson sing, and see him in his role as Minister of Music and Assistant to the Pastor. Dad made sure she got safely inside, and then he left to rejoin Mom at the Assembly of God. He assured Grandma he would be back to pick her up after the service was over.

I cannot describe the joy that swept over me as I watched Grandma's entrance. She was very slow and had to be sure of every step, but she was making a statement by entering the forbidden zone. She was saying that *nothing* would come between her and me. After the service, Grandma McCain beamed as I introduced her to my friends and my pastor. Then Gary walked up.

"Grandma, this is Gary. We attended Evangel College together. He just moved here from South Dakota."

Grandma knew who Gary was to me. Mother had filled her in. They hugged. Grandma had lived to see me happy and settled and had met my special life partner.

When Dad walked in, I could tell that he would have attended with Grandma, but he would have been in deep trouble with Mom. Dad was friendly to everyone, especially to Gary, for which I was profoundly grateful.

Soon after Grandma returned to Warren, she developed pneumonia. When Dad called and told me that she was not expected to live through the week, I was devastated. I left the next morning to see her for what I knew would be the last time. How many times had I made that trip? What would life be like without Grandma's house to run to in times of trouble? By the time I arrived, she was no longer able to communicate. I hugged her and sat by her side most of the evening. I took her favorite Bible and read to her all the verses she had underlined. Then, remembering how much Grandma loved to hear me sing, I sang for her one last time. I sang all her favorite songs. Her breathing became shallow and fast. I had been present for the deaths of many young men with AIDS, so I recognized that the time was getting close for Grandma to make her heavenly journey.

When I could hear death coming in her breathing, I leaned over, hugged her, and whispered, "I am so proud to call you my grandma! You have been so good to me. But now it is time. You and I have talked about going to be with Jesus and seeing our beloved Savior face-to-face. Grandma, I know you are tired and ready to go, and it's okay. Just take the hand of Jesus. He is there for you, Grandma. We're here for you too. I love you so very much!"

I leaned forward and kissed her forehead. Her breathing slowed. Her weary body seemed to relax. In just a few moments, her chest stopped its up and down struggle. My mother looked at me. "Is she gone, Randy?" she asked.

As I gazed at the peaceful look on Grandma's face, I answered, "Yes, she's with Jesus."

I remembered saying to Grandma once, "Grandma, if you die before me..."

She interrupted me. "Oh honey, I *will* die before you. You can count on that."

"Okay then, when you get to heaven, will you put in a good word for me at the throne of God?"

"Oh Randy, Grandma will be there constantly saying, 'Lord, help little Randy. You know he gets himself into a lot of trouble. Keep him safe, Lord Jesus.'"

"And Grandma, another thing I would ask of you. When people have had near-death experiences, they say they are greeted by some of their beloved relatives who are already there, to help them make the transition. Will you be the one to meet me when my time comes?"

"Son, if there is any way, I will be there."

After Grandma's death, I went through many sad days missing her. But God provided me with a dear, sweet eighty-year-old grandma at Friends of His named Esther Smith, a retired Cumberland Presbyterian minister. Every Monday morning, Michael Qualls, Gary, and I met at Esther's house for prayer and planning sessions. Esther was a tall, large-boned woman with grandmotherly features. Her white hair was cut in a short, modern style. When she smiled she reminded me of Miss Lillian, Jimmy Carter's mother. When Esther laughed, her whole body shook. She loved Gary and me. When Grandma died, Esther told me that she would be my Grandma, if I wanted her to be. I accepted her offer gratefully.

Thanksgiving was approaching, and I faced a quandary as to what we would do for the holidays. I talked about this with a lesbian minister friend I met at the conference in Houston.

"My family always gets together at my parents' house, which is just two miles from where we live. They have made it clear that *I* am welcome in their home, but that Gary is *not*. I don't want to spend the holidays separate from Gary. He's my spouse. But it will be hard to miss my family's celebration."

She answered with words that I recognized as truth. "Randy, if you don't show your family that *you* respect your relationship, then how can you ever expect *them* to respect it? I wouldn't be rude about it, but I would respectfully decline the invitation as long as they insist on barring the one you love from sharing it with you."

That made a lot of sense, so I told Gary that I was not going home for Thanksgiving. My mom called and asked if they could expect me for the annual dinner, and I told her that unless Gary could come with me, I would not be there. She said that it wouldn't look good, nor would it set a good example for the grandkids to see Gary and me as a couple. Then Mom hung up.

Gary and I decided to spend the holiday at a local restaurant offering an all-you-can-eat Thanksgiving Buffet. We dressed up and celebrated by starting a new family tradition. Admittedly, several times during the day I tried to imagine how they were dealing with my absence. My dad came by the apartment with some leftovers. He didn't stay, but I got the message, loud and clear. Daddy could not go through Thanksgiving without seeing his one and only son. We survived our first holiday.

Christmas was exciting as we made the most of our first holiday season together. We built roaring fires in the fireplace and placed stockings on the mantel. Our greatest gift that Christmas was being together. Christmas 1992 was warm and special, even though we didn't join in my family's festivities. Gary Eddy was my family now.

Chapter 33

Planning Our Wedding

As a couple, 1993 gave us many opportunities to make a lot of adjustments. Gary's life in South Dakota was quiet and predictable. He worked at a hearing aid clinic. Although he had a degree in art, he realized that teaching was not for him after teaching one year in public school. His work at the clinic required interaction with older adults, and Gary had a winning way with them. Before life with me in Arkansas, his routine consisted of going to work each day and spending a quiet evening at home. When he prepared his evening meal, he delighted in garnishing the plate and making the presentation pretty as a treat for himself. I, on the other hand, was used to eating my meals out of the pots.

When Gary crossed the state line, he boarded the *Randy McCain Express.* Nothing about my life and ministry was predictable, other than the fact that I could count on it being unpredictable. Few of my evenings could be labeled "quiet." Our apartment was always filled with people, some nights for a church-sponsored weekly Bible study. Also, I received invitations to minister my plays around the state, and Gary was soon helping me with these productions.

He really didn't know what he was getting himself into. First, he had to adjust to leaving his beloved cats, Shandy and Tu-Lee, because I am allergic to cats. Secondly, Gary left his native state, and all his friends and family, and moved to a different region of the country, parting with most of his furniture and belongings. His new life demanded quite an adjustment, and there would be more.

Gary found the southern accent in Arkansas hard to understand. Moreover, as a neat freak, he was accustomed to everything having a place. He found himself living with an unorganized pack rat! There were times, that first year, when I was afraid he might just pack up and leave.

As is the case in many relationships, we were opposites. I loved to share my feelings and thoughts, while Gary was more private. He had lived alone and did not need people in his life. I did.

Slowly, we found things in common, such as Bette Davis movies and eating out.

When it came to communication skills, I was light years ahead of Gary. My new quest in life was to find a way to unlock the safe where Gary stored most of his feelings. On the other hand, his goal was to teach me how to enjoy quiet nights at home, spending time together, enjoying a nice meal, and watching television, but closing the door to the rest of the world.

We have made great strides in blending our agendas. Our differences have offered opportunities to grow and mature. One of my goals was setting a date for our wedding.

"Gary, I know it's not legal…but I don't want us to live our lives as just roommates. We need something to validate our love for each other. I want to say my vows of love to you in front of God and friends."

"Okay, if it's that important to you, let's do it."

We chose October 16, 1993, and asked the Rev. Tom Hirsch, the minister who headed up the conference in Houston, to perform the ceremony. We were pleased, since we had very little money, to find that we could rent the Unitarian church for seventy-five dollars.

Since we were not out at Friends of His, we did not purchase identical rings, but I insisted that we wear them on the traditional ring finger. Who, we pondered, should we invite to our wedding? For sure, we both wanted Dolly and Wally to be there, and Lorrene Wenzl, the mom of one of my gay friends. We both thought of our adopted Grandma, Esther Smith, but we had not come out to her yet. Actually, Gary and I were apprehensive about telling Esther. We spent hours at her house, playing dominoes and attending the weekly prayer and planning sessions. Surely, she would not judge us. But, at her age, would she accept something so radical? We decided we had to tell her, and Gary worked out how we should do it.

"Randy, we'll go to Esther's house and you can tell her while I mow her grass. I will be praying for you."

The day arrived. While Gary mowed the lawn, I told Esther I wanted to talk to her about something important.

"Esther, you have told me before that I could always talk to you about anything."

"Yes, Randy, and I mean it. I want you to feel free to share anything with me."

"Well, there is something I really need to tell you. I don't want you to hear it from somebody else."

Esther, sensing my nervousness and agitation, got a worried look. She moved her chair closer to mine and took my hand in hers. "What is it, Randy?"

"Well, there is something I am going to tell you and I don't know exactly how you are going to take it. I love you Esther, and you are like a grandma to me…"

I dragged it out. It was like I was trying to land an airplane, but every time I attempted a landing, my fear held me back and I circled the airport again.

186

Finally, I got up the nerve to say, "Esther, you know I have talked to you about the difficult time that gay people have in life, and about the burden I have for those who have AIDS. Well, there is a reason why I'm so concerned about gay people because, well, I'm gay and so is Gary. Gary and I, we love each other…we're in a relationship, and we are going to have a ceremony. We are going to get married…to each other."

Somehow, I got my thoughts out and braced myself for whatever reaction might follow. I studied the tired wrinkles in the face of this dear saint. I had taken her completely by surprise. Then, after what seemed forever, Esther looked at me with a twinkle in her eye and a sly grin.

"Am I invited?" was her reply.

I jumped up and threw my arms around her. As we cried for joy, in walked Gary.

"Are y'all talking about what I think you're talking about?"

"Yes, Gary, and Esther asked if she could attend our wedding."

Gary gasped in a burst of emotion. Esther put her arms around us and said, "I love you boys. You are the same boys I knew and loved before you told me this. God told Moses, 'I am who I am', and He expects us to be who we are."

What a beautiful response to our revelation. Esther's words have remained in a special place in my heart. How could I ever forget that holy moment, when Esther Smith made two frightened boys feel so loved and accepted?

We now had a list of people we wanted to invite. Several were friends from church who did not know about us, so the next days were filled with anxious moments. When I broached the subject with Michael Qualls, I honestly didn't know if he would attend the wedding. He had grown to love Gary. Gary was teaching a Sunday school class. We were frequent guests at the Qualls home. I chose a day when Michael and I were riding together, after a hospital visit.

"Michael, Gary and I have decided to have a wedding ceremony. I have taken your advice and I have not broadcast the truth about our relationship in the church. But now we would like to invite a few people from the congregation to our ceremony. We are choosing very carefully. We told Esther and she is totally supportive."

"Where are you going to have the ceremony?"

"We rented the Unitarian Church. Michael, I really would like you to attend. I know you can't marry us, because of your ties to the Cumberland Presbyterian denomination, but I'd love for you to pray a prayer of blessing over us. Could you do that?"

Michael was quiet for a moment. Then he said, "Well, I don't think I could take part in it."

After a short pause I allowed my feelings to come out. "I thought you would say that, and there's a part of me that understands. But there is another part of me that is angry and disappointed in you. Last month, you married a couple you didn't even know. The ceremony took place after we played a game of volleyball at the YMCA. You were in your shorts and t-shirt. You told me that you met with them and that you did not give their marriage 'a snowball's chance in hell.' Yet, you bestowed the church's blessing upon *them*."

I did not take time for a good breath.

"Gary and I work hard for this church. We come down to the YMCA every Saturday night and set up chairs and sound equipment. We host a Bible study every week in our home. Gary teaches a Sunday school class, and I am your associate and your music minister. You *know* how devoted we are to each other. We love Jesus and have a Christ-centered home. Yet, knowing all this about us, you will not give us the blessing of the church. There is something very wrong with that picture, Michael. I forgive you, but I still have a problem with your decision. And I just have to be honest with you, it hurts."

Michael didn't get defensive. He nodded his head in agreement with me. "I hear you, Randy. I understand why you would be upset."

Nothing else was said. We rode to my apartment in silence. Michael had disappointed me. I wanted him to stand with us.

Unfortunately, my dear friend had a strong need for everyone to love him. Michael told me once that if he had pastored in the south during the civil rights movement, he would not have taken a stand against segregation from the pulpit.

How could he be such a sensitive, liberal, intelligent man, and refuse to stand up for his beliefs? But as mad and frustrated as I got with Michael, I loved him and saw such good in him. He was the man I hoped would restore my faith in ministers.

Next we told Toni Morvant, a wonderful friend who attended Friends of His. She was originally from New Orleans and had been around gay people, which prepared her for our revelation. She told us how happy she was for us, and that she looked forward to being there.

Next, we went to the home of M.J. Fisk, who also attended Friends of His. She had recently fallen head-over-heels in love with a man. After a whirlwind romance, they married. The marriage lasted one month. Gary and I had stood by a devastated M.J. through her nightmare. We felt sure that she would not abandon us now over the gay issue. We broke the news to her about our relationship and our upcoming marriage.

"Wonderful!" she replied.

That one word was so important to us! M.J. had friends who were gay and she wondered about us, but since we did not talk about it, she respected our privacy by not prying. We were under the original "Don't Ask, Don't Tell."

We were elated that, so far, everyone had received the news well—even Michael, who was glad for us but had to juggle strong concerns about the church's reaction.

After our encounter with M.J., Gary teased, "Maybe we should stop while we're ahead. We've got a perfect score so far. Let's not press our luck."

Carol, a member of Friends of His who already knew about us, wanted to throw a wedding shower. Wow! I saw many wedding showers in the years I worked in churches, but never dreamed I would have one. This was almost too good to be true!

"Just be careful about who you invite," we warned her.

"You give me a list of who you want to attend and I'll contact them." She promised.

Eighteen brave souls showed for our shower. We read sweet cards aloud as we opened gifts. I think everyone wondered if this shower would feel different than a shower for a more traditional couple. It felt like we were doing something revolutionary and exciting. Besides, everyone needs Tupperware! After we finished opening presents, I thanked our friends.

"Gary and I cannot thank you enough for being here tonight and affirming us and our love for each other," I said. "What he and I are doing may be a little out of the ordinary, but we really feel strongly that since we both love God, and we both believe that God loves us, it is right that we declare that publicly. We know that we love each other, but it matters so much that we have a supportive network of friends. I will never forget this night. Thank you, Carol, for opening your heart and home to us, and for all you did to put this together. And to every one of you here, you will always have a special place in our hearts for sharing this important event with us. God bless you all."

As the evening drew to a close, Carol's friend Lou Ann, whom we had met recently, said she would like to share a song and dedicate it to us, since she would be out of town the weekend of our wedding. When she started singing, I got chill bumps. It was the song I had selected to sing to Gary at our wedding! Paul Johnson wrote "Make Us One" as part of a musical, *Here Comes the Son*, which our youth choir had performed in 1975. I was amazed that Lou Ann knew it, and even more that she wanted to sing it to us. I had chosen it because I felt it said, so beautifully, what I wanted our lives to say as a married gay couple.

Make us one Father God, make us one
So the world will know you gave your only son.
Fill us with the love you've given us to share
And protect us from the evil everywhere
For you have chosen that together we should be

A reflection of your love and unity

Cleanse us from our old nature of sin

That your image may be seen in man again.

Send us in the world to be a channel of

All the glorious riches of your son

And we'll tell the world the truth of how you feel

That the world may know your love for us is real.

"Make Us One" (Paul Johnson)
Lyrics reprinted by permission of Paul Johnson

The evening had been magical! We went home with presents in hand and memories of love and friendship in our hearts.

The next Monday morning, we were about ready to end the prayer and planning meeting when Esther remembered something.

"Just a minute, Randy and Gary. Before you leave, I have something to give you."

After disappearing down the hallway, she returned, carrying a wrapped box. Inside, I found two frilly garter belts. At first I was a little confused as to what this meant.

"Well…thank you, Esther. But what are they?"

"They're garter belts."

"I know that, but what are they for?"

"To wear at your wedding!" her hoarse voice barked at me.

"But, where do we wear them?"

Esther started to laugh and the laugh rippled through her body. "I don't know where gays wear theirs."

This 80-year-old Grandma's total acceptance amazed us! Later I questioned her. "Esther, why do so many people have a problem with this issue, and yet you seem to just accept us?"

"Well, I look at it this way: gay people are like people from another country or culture. I enjoy getting to know them."

Chapter 34

The Great Debate

One evening, Gary brought up the question we had been dodging.

"Are you going to invite your family?"

"I've been thinking about it and I'm going to invite Pam, and Mom and Dad."

"You don't think they will come, do you?"

"I don't know, but I do want to give them the opportunity. Whether they decide to come or not is up to them."

I went to Pam's house, figuring I would do the easy one first. Unfortunately, the conversation at her home did not go well. Pam was dead-set against giving me permission to reclaim my gay orientation, since she had seen how much damage it had caused in the past. Now, I had a ministry and, in her estimation, was well on my way to pursuing a happy, healthy life. She worried about the hurricane of rejection I would receive if I committed to a relationship with a man. She didn't totally refuse my invitation, but she didn't commit either.

The next afternoon, when I pulled the car into my parents' driveway, Dad's truck was gone. I almost turned around and left, but I had really prepared myself and want-ed to get it over with. I walked into the house, where Mother was watching television. I told her I needed to talk with her, so she pushed the mute button.

"Mom, I am going to tell you something, and please, just hear me out before you make any comments. I know that in the past we have had a really hard time com-municating. I'm sorry for that, and I accept a lot of the blame. I want you to know that I appreciate you and Dad and all you've done for me over the years. I know how difficult it has been for you to watch me struggle with my sexual orientation, and I want you to know that I really do want to please God. That has always been the most powerful desire in my heart. You raised me to seek after God, and I have always tried to do that."

"I do believe that, Randy," Mom assured me. "There is no question in my mind that you really do want to serve God."

"I want you to know that I have studied the scriptures, and I have prayed and prayed. The conclusion I have reached is that I am a gay man and God loves me and has called me to truth. This is my truth Mom. I am a gay, Christian man."

"Randy, I know you *think* you believe that, but surely you would not want to go back to the unfulfilled life you lived when you were in the gay lifestyle."

"No Mom, I don't want to go back to that way of living. This time I came out of the closet and I brought my values with me, the values that you and Dad instilled in me. Before when I first came out, I trampled on my values. I felt like God had rejected me. But this time I am assured of God's love. I know I did not choose to be gay."

"But Randy, homosexuality is a sin. We *choose* to sin."

Always before, when she made statements like this, it really pushed my buttons, but this time I remained calm.

"Mother, I do not believe that being gay is a sin. Now, I do believe that gay people can sin, just as heterosexuals can. Both gay and non-gay people can use their sexual orientation and desires wrongly. There are guidelines that are given to us in Christ's teachings that show us how to live fulfilling lives as couples. These guidelines are the same ones you and Dad have applied to your lives as a married couple. I don't ever want the empty life of casual sex with strangers and mere acquaintances. I want a rich, healthy, loving, Christ-centered relationship. This is what I have found with Gary."

"Oh Randy, no!" she moaned.

"Mother, just hear me out, please. I need to talk to you about Gary and me. Gary is a good man. He loves God. Ours is a Christ-centered relationship."

"No, Randy, it *can't* be. Surely you see that."

"Mother, I know what the presence of the Holy Spirit feels like, and I can sense the presence of Jesus in our home and in our relationship."

"Randy, Satan has deceived you."

"Mother, I know what Satan feels like. When I was running from God, when I abandoned all attempts to serve God because I felt unworthy, when I trampled all my emotions and spirituality, I felt the power of Satan. I know you watched me go through this difficult time.

"I don't blame you for having reservations now. But I'm here to share with you the truth I've learned, after trying for five years to change my sexuality. I wanted to surrender everything to Jesus and I did. I gave Him my sexuality. I thought Jesus would keep it or change it. Well, He didn't keep it. He gave it back to me. But He did change it; He transformed it into something beautiful, as He does with everything we give to Him."

Surprisingly, Mother did not interrupt me, or try to correct me. She seemed to actually be listening for a change. So I continued.

"When I chose Gary as my spouse, I was looking for the right things in a relationship. I wanted a man who would love and serve God right along beside me. Gary *is* that man, Mother. What I am trying to tell you is that there are as many gay lifestyles as there are heterosexual lifestyles. The lifestyle I lived when I first came out was not a lifestyle I'm proud of. I did things that I am ashamed of. I used people to fulfill my sexual addiction. Mother, the sexual drive is so powerful. That is why we teach young people self-control. But when I was discovering my sexuality and my attractions for men, there was no one there to give me any boundaries or guidelines. Everybody just told me that my sexual feelings were dirty and sinful. I tried to deny them, but it is impossible to deny that we are sexual creatures. When I realized I could no longer deny these desires, I tried to look to the church for guidance through the minefield of puberty and young adulthood. But there was no guidance to be found for a gay man. I was all alone."

"But we were here for you, Randy, why didn't you come to us?"

"Because, I knew how strongly you disapproved of homosexuality and how hard it is to reason with you when you feel you are right. That's why I felt so alone."

Mother did not argue that point, so I resumed my defense.

"I acted out in negative ways, along with all the others who had also been declared God-forsaken outcasts. We were not evil people, Mother. We were simply trying to get through life the best way we knew how. My lifestyle *now* is to seek God in my daily living, and in my relationship with Gary. It is so much better than the reckless one I lived before. Those five years that I spent trying to renounce my sexual orientation taught me to trust my heart. I learned about God's love and grace, and this gave me the courage to question God, without being afraid that He would punish me just for asking. And Mother, with all my heart, I believe that this is where God has brought me."

"Randy, I just cannot accept that. Look at Sodom and Gomorrah. God hates this sin, and look what He did to those cities that practiced it."

"Mother," I countered. "Those men who threatened the angels at Lot's houses were threatening to rape them. Rape is wrong, whether it is heterosexual or homosexual. And Mother, if you use that story as a standard for sexual ethics, what about Lot offering his daughters to those men for their sexual pleasure, or the events that took place when Lot and his two daughters escaped Sodom? They went up into the mountains and the daughters got their father drunk, had sex with him, and became pregnant by their own dad! Can't you see how radically different the culture was in that part of the world and in those ancient times? We don't identify with anything else in that story, why should we try and pin our beliefs about sexuality on it?"

"Randy, God's Law in the Old Testament says that 'you shall not lie with a man as with a woman; it is an abomination.'"

"Yes, Mother, and it also says that you shouldn't eat shrimp or pork, but I haven't seen Jerry Falwell boycotting Red Lobster or calling for a moratorium on eating bacon for breakfast.

"It says that you shouldn't plant two different kinds of seed in the same plot of ground. It tells parents to take disobedient children outside the city gates and stone them to death. Are you going to pick and choose which of those scriptures you are going to live by, and which ones you are going to throw away? Paul teaches that we are no longer under the Law. He said that Christ Jesus has freed us from the Law. We are not Jewish, Mother; we are *Christians!*"

I felt myself getting more and more comfortable with the conversation, which was something new for me. Always before, when we "discussed" the gay issue and scripture, Mother had been able to make me doubt my stance. This time, I felt secure in my understanding of God's love and acceptance, and nothing she said was shaking me.

"But Randy, in the New Testament, Paul says in Romans that God gave them up because their men left the natural desire for women and burned with lust for one another. *That* is New Testament."

"Yes, Mother, but if you read the whole chapter of Romans 1, you see that there is a progression that transpires. These people Paul speaks of denied God. They did not consider God worth knowing. They worshiped idols. Therefore, God gave them over to shameful lusts.

"Mother, you have watched me grow up. You know how much I have always loved God. When the kids were outside playing, I wanted to be with you and the grownups, in the Bible studies and prayer meetings. You raised me to always strive to put God first in my life. At what point did God look down at me and say, 'Little Randy doesn't consider me worth the knowing. He is worshiping idols. I think I will place in his heart a desire for shameful lusts and reject Him.'? Mother, it has always been natural for me to be attracted to men rather than women. When I was trying to convince myself that I was attracted to Libby, it felt so unnatural. I did not leave what was natural for me when I embraced Gary. The unnatural for me was when I dated Libby. I believe that what Paul is speaking about in this chapter of Romans is a reference to male prostitutes who worked in the temples of the pagan gods and goddesses. The worshipers would come to those temples to have sex with the men who were there. The sex was considered a form of worship.

Also, in the Roman culture, older men would have sex with young boys. Both of these acts were lust driven, and I believe they were what Paul had in mind when he wrote Romans 1. The Bible never speaks against loving, committed relationships between couples of the same gender. The only time sexual contact between same-gendered couples is spoken of in scripture, it refers to lust-driven or forcefully violent acts.

Lust and rape are wrong for heterosexuals as well as homosexuals. My relationship with Gary *should not* be compared to what Paul is referring to in Romans. Our relationship is founded on love, respect, and God-given principles. Lust is not the motivating force behind our relationship; love is."

"Well, Paul also lists homosexuality as one of the sins that will bar people from the Kingdom of God."

"Mother, that scripture is found in 1 Corinthians 6:9, where Paul says, 'Know you not that the unrighteous shall not inherit the Kingdom of God.' And then he goes on to list several sins. The original Greek words that are translated *homosexual*, in some translations of the Bible, are the words *malakos*, which means soft, and *arsenokoites*, which is a word that many believe Paul made up. It may have been understood by the people of his day, but not by those reading Paul's letter more than 2,000 years later. These words are found in the middle of a list of sins, so it is hard to decide their meaning to the rest of the sentence by reading them in context. The closest Greek translation of the compound word is 'male couch.' How in the world could the translators have come up with homosexuality out of 'soft' and 'male couch'? The word homosexuality did not even exist until 100 years ago."

"Randy! You are just twisting scripture to make it say what you want it to."

"But, Mother, aren't you doing the same thing? You go to the Assembly of God church. They ordain women ministers. Yet there is a scripture in the New Testament that says, 'Women should not speak in the church.' Paul also taught that women should not go into the church with their heads uncovered. Jesus, though not saying anything against homosexuality, taught that those who are divorced should not remarry. Yet there are members at First Assembly of God who have divorced and remarried.

"So, couldn't someone say that you and your denomination are twisting scripture to say what *you* want it to say? Mother, we have to take into consideration the culture when the Bible was written. Look at the differences today in the cultures of the United States and the Arab countries. The Middle East is where the Bible was written. Things have not changed that much since the days of the Bible. Women still have to cover their heads when they go out in public. Back when Paul was writing his letters to the churches, there was no knowledge about sexual orientation. Everyone was presumed to be heterosexual. The only time the Bible speaks of same-gender sex is in the context of lust and of using others for sexual gratification without love and without relationship. That culture did not understand that two men or two women could live together and love each other in a committed relationship."

"But, Randy, I have heard you say before that you knew that homosexuality was a sin."

"Mother, I have heard you say in the past that going to movies is a sin, but now YOU go to movies. We all grow in our understanding of ourselves and our faith. I remember a time when you would not wear pants. You thought it was a sin because of the scripture forbidding women to wear male clothing, but now *you* wear pants. Yes, when I was trying to change my sexual orientation and ordered material from the ex-gay ministries, I *did* say that I believed homosexuality was a sin. But now, I understand more fully the context in which those scriptures were written."

"Randy, I have prayed that God would give me a peace about this, if it really was His will for your life, but He hasn't."

"Well, Mother, there are people today who would tell you they still do not have peace about you going to movies, wearing lipstick, cutting your hair, and wearing pantsuits, but *you* seem to have a peace about it."

"Randy, can you truthfully tell me that you have no doubts in your mind about this issue? Can you tell me honestly that you don't fear dying and going to hell because of your relationship with a man?"

"Mother, I do not fear hell. I have an assurance in my heart that Jesus is my Savior and Lord. I don't understand everything yet about sexual orientation. I don't know why there are some people who are gay in a world where the majority are heterosexual. Maybe it is God's way of helping with overpopulation. I do, however, know what love is and what relationship and attraction feel like. I experience all that with Gary. I never felt that for a woman. I also know what it is like when the Holy Spirit tells me my life is spiraling out of control. But I can truthfully say I have peace in my heart about loving God and loving Gary. In fact, I am so sure of this that Gary and I are getting married."

"WHAT?!!" Mother was flabbergasted.

"Yes, we know it's not legal *yet*, but we want to make a covenant before God and before our friends to love and be faithful to one another for life. I came over to invite you and Daddy to our wedding."

"Randy, you know we would never come."

"Well Mom, that's up to you. I just wanted you to know that this is going to be one of the happiest days of my life and that you and Daddy are invited. Whether or not you feel you can attend is your decision."

"Well, I can tell you right now that we will not attend!"

"Okay."

As I got up to leave, we heard Dad drive up.

"Do you want to tell him, or do you want me to?" Mother asked.

"I'll tell him."

When Dad walked in the house, I broke the news about the wedding and that he and Mom were invited. I told him the date and the place it was being held.

He answered in his quiet, nervous voice. "Surely you know we would never attend such an event."

I told him, as I had told Mom, they would have to make that decision, but we wanted him to know they were invited.

As I walked out, I was amazed at the peace I felt in my spirit. "What was different?" I wondered. Then it hit me. I was now in a healthy relationship, one of which I could truly be proud. Living with and loving Gary had convinced me that it is possible for two men to spend their lives together in a healthy Christ-centered relationship. As I drove away, I was filled with thanksgiving to God for giving me understanding and peace.

Randy and Gary ... just married!

Chapter 35
Saying I Do

The plans for our ceremony were coming down to the wire. Rev. Hirsh would arrive on Friday and we would have a rehearsal at our apartment that evening. The service was scheduled for two o'clock the following afternoon.

Our dear friend Marvin Glass was making the cake, which was a three-tiered white cake with purple flowers, and surprise!—*two grooms* on top. The rehearsal on Friday went without a hitch. Gary and I kept the vows we had written to each other a secret. We decided that we could not afford flowers, but Dolly was *not* going to have "any of that nonsense," as she delicately put it. She made sure that we had two huge sprays of purple gladiolas. By Friday night after the rehearsal, we were exhausted! It felt like we were walking through a dream. Gary matter-of-factly got ready for bed, but I could not act like it was just any other night. I had a mixture of fear and excitement about tomorrow's events. Part of me was curious to see if God would really show up. I had never attended a wedding ceremony for two men and had no idea what to expect.

"Gary, can you believe we are actually getting married tomorrow?

"No, I can't."

"I really wish Grandma was going to be there."

"Do you think Grandma McCain would actually have attended if she were still alive?" he asked.

"Well, who knows?" I replied. "Grandma came to Friends of His when Mom and Dad refused to. I don't know at her age if she could have crossed a radically new cultural hurdle such as a gay wedding, but you know what? I believe that Grandma's spirit *will* be there tomorrow."

"I hope so Randy. I know that would mean a lot to you."

Gary and I were so happy that God blessed our wedding day with radiant sunshine. The flowers from Dolly were absolutely beautiful, the candle tree was in place, and the guests were arriving. We had invited 33 people, and 25 attended. I could not help watching to see if, by some miracle, *someone* from my family would show up. I also wondered if Pastor Michael would attend.

Tom Hirsch, the presiding minister, gathered those involved in the ceremony for prayer. Gary reached in his pocket for a Kleenex. He was already misty-eyed.

The ceremony began with a song and special poetry readings. As Gary and I walked to the front of the sanctuary, I saw that Michael Qualls had slipped in. Late, but present. Our friend Joe Terry performed a breathtakingly beautiful liturgical dance to the song "Lord, Make Me an Instrument of Your Peace." Pastor Hirsch exhorted us to love faithfully and to always base our home on the principles of Christ. Now it was time for us to read our vows. Gary went first.

"My dearest Randy, on this special day which we have set aside in history to seal our love and devotion to each other through word and deed, I pledge to you a lasting love. Although it will be imperfect, and sometimes I'll have to say, 'I'm sorry,' the love I pledge to you is a First Corinthians love. A love composed of all other pledges of loyalty and faithfulness, trust and honor, of patience and selflessness and understanding. Randy, I vow to give to you the best me…to draw out the best of you…and through this, create the best 'us'. This is a pledge I cannot fulfill apart from God, and therefore I pledge also my devotion and commitment to our Heavenly Father, by whom and for whom we are, and through whom we are one."

I was awed by Gary's tenderness as he spoke these words to me. His voice quivered and broke from time to time as tears flowed down his face.

Next it was my turn:

"I, Randy McCain, vow to you, Gary Eddy on this the 16th day of October 1993, to be a true and faithful friend. Just as Jonathan became one in spirit with David and loved him as himself, so shall I love you until death part us. I vow this before the Lord God, for He is witness between us. I vow to honor you always, to surround you with the comfort of my prayers, to give myself to you only, in the act of love's union. We enter this covenant through the veil of God's love, for it was His providence that brought us together. Therefore, I vow always to love God our Father first, for it was He who first loved us.

"Secondly, I shall love you above all others on earth. I choose to serve you with the heart of a bondservant, putting your desires above my own. A bondservant serves from a willing heart, not because such service is demanded. It is my desire that we shall become one heart that beats in worship to the Lord God our creator, that we shall be one in purpose to serve Christ in unity, and that we love each other in purity so that the world will see the fruit of God's Spirit coming forth from our union. These words of commitment come to you from a pure heart, my love.

"May God's Holy Spirit seal our union till the day we pass from this life into the riches of His heavenly kingdom; unto Him be glory forever, Amen."

After the vows were spoken, Gary and I lit the unity candle. Then, while the beautiful, sweeping strains of the soundtrack from *The Prince of Tides* played softly,

Gary read three poems he had written to me.

As a dim yellow glow
Lights the east with morn
And begins the quiet journey
To fill the sky with day
And
As a great orange dish
Rises slowly above a black horizon
And fills the evening
With a warm moon of romance
And
As a pure and holy light
Slowly filled a darkened world
Out of the silent streets of Bethlehem
So has your love come to me
A light awakening
The darkness of my lonely heart.

A petalled rose
Of deepest hue
High upon a boasting stalk
This scented joy unveiling
And with the earth rejoicing
At the one less painful moment
A rapture worth a pricking thorn
A beauty coveted
By nature's plainer seeds
So is our love to me.
A rare and priceless joy
A rapture worth all thorns on earth
Each soul of which
Would deign to buy

At any price
So dear a rose as is the love we share.

The pages of a thousand poems
Could not contain the love
Within the words
"I love you"
Nor could a thousand strokes
Of an artist's brush
Begin the story woven within a heart
Expressed with the words
"I love you"
And still a thousand symphonies
Strained from the notes of the sweetest reed
Could not attain the heights of meaning
In the words
"I love you"
These words I now speak to you.

I sang a love song to Gary. Everyone there, witnessing for the first time a wedding ceremony between two men, sensed the romance in the air. A sweet and awesome awareness of the Spirit of Christ permeated our wedding ceremony. Then it was time for Gary and me to exchange rings. Vows were spoken and a prayer of consecration was offered. We received Holy Communion and I sang the song that Lu Ann had sung to us at our shower.

After the service, all of us caravaned to the home of a friend for our reception. It was a very special moment for me when our adopted grandmother Esther took my hand and said that it had been a beautiful service. When another guest asked her if she thought "this couple would stay together," she replied, "I *know* they will!"

Chapter 36
The Sting of Family Rejection

As Thanksgiving approached, Grandma Esther invited us to come to her home for dinner. While grateful for the invitation, a dark cloud hovered overhead. I felt depressed. My sadness surprised me. I had handled not being included at my parent's home the previous year, but for some reason, the absence of an invitation this time ambushed my heart.

On Thanksgiving Day, Gary and I kept our new tradition by going back to the same charming restaurant for lunch. That evening we went to Esther's house. Though still stuffed from our noonday meal, we shoveled in more good food. After dinner, we visited with friends who filled Esther's home with laughter and light conversation.

Although the night was festive, I kept thinking about my family, just a few miles away…all together, except for me. Suddenly, aware that I was about to have a major meltdown, I headed for the front door and walked out into the cold night. I breathed the fresh air. I could not make myself go back inside. Then, without even thinking, I jumped in the car and drove off without telling Gary or anyone else, heading toward our apartment. As I neared home, I started crying so hard I could barely see the road. I pulled into our driveway and ran inside, knowing I needed somebody to be there with me, but who? Then I thought of Dolly. I picked up the phone and called her. When I heard Dolly's voice, I burst into tears.

"What's wrong with you, kid?"

"Do you…do you make house calls?" I sobbed, tears spilling off my face onto the receiver.

"You need me to come over to your house?"

"Could you?"

"Is Gary there?"

"Gary?"

For the first time I thought about him. I did not tell him I was leaving. What must he be thinking?

"We were at Esther's house eating dinner and I knew I was about to have a breakdown, so I just panicked and left without telling him where I was going."

"Well, don't you think I need to swing by and pick him up? Tell me where Esther lives, no, wait a minute, give me Esther's phone number. I'll call Gary and he can give me directions."

I walked into the bathroom and washed my face with cool water. I looked pitiful. The phone rang. It was Gary. I apologized for leaving without him.

"Randy, I just want to know what's wrong."

"Gary, I just miss my family so much," I sobbed. He assured me he and Dolly would be there in just a few minutes.

When they walked in, Dolly spoke in her usual brusque way. "What's all this crying about, you scroungy kid?"

When she sat down beside me, I hugged her. She wrapped her arms around me, and I laid my head on her chest and cried uncontrollably. Dolly just held me and let me cry.

"I know, kid. It hurts like hell. Just let it out."

"My family doesn't love me anymore, Dolly. If they did, they would have let me come home for Thanksgiving. It's not fair! I miss my family!"

Dolly continued holding me while I bled a mix of rage and sorrow. Gary sat on the other side of me, holding my hand, silently lending his support.

When at last my crying started to let up, Dolly said, "Gary might be jealous of Dolly. He might want you to cry on *his* shoulder."

"No, he's not jealous of you. I need a mama. I need some boobs to cry on right now!"

Dolly and Gary laughed. Their laughter made me laugh, and I realized that the crying had been good for me. The heaviness was gone. Once again, Dolly had been there for me. I marveled at her. The outer crustiness that she projected covered a heart of pure gold!

When Dolly prepared to leave, I told her I didn't know what I would have done without her.

"Well, I don't know what I would have done without you. It goes both ways."

That meltdown on Thanksgiving Day convinced me that I needed to deal responsibly with my family's rejection. Christmas was on the horizon and I didn't want to be a sitting duck for those same emotions to sabotage me again. After prayer and some major-league thinking, I wrote my mother. Her birthday was December 7, so I picked out a sweet birthday card and placed my letter inside.

Dear Mother,

I wanted to take this opportunity to wish you a happy birthday. I know I have been very much a part of your life for 37 years. We've experienced periods of separation, and periods of extreme closeness. I've sensed, at times, that you have withheld a part of yourself to show your disapproval of my actions, and I have done the same. You have not been a perfect mother, but I have not been a perfect son. We are family. We are in a grief process right now. You are grieving the loss of a dream…a dream you held in your heart of what you wanted me, your son, to be and to accomplish. I know these dreams were birthed in a heart of love. There is a part of me that cries out to make you and Daddy happy, make you proud of me. The part of the dream you are grieving is the loss of your desire for me to be a "healthy" heterosexual son, husband, and father. This is something that I wanted to give you so that your dream would be complete. But it is something that is impossible for me to do. If you demand this of me, and require this as a necessity for you to embrace me with your acceptance, then I will never have it.

I stated that we are both grieving. I, too, am grieving. I wanted so much to be all that you dreamed of as you held me and rocked me lovingly when I was a baby. I grieve the fact that I will never hold my own son or daughter. I grieve the fact that I must struggle against the tide of what is most accepted. But Mother, I also rejoice in the realization that I am a healthy gay man—not by choice, for I never chose this—but by design. You asked me how I could have peace with God when I was at odds with my family. If I had chosen to do something to purposely hurt my family and drive a wedge between myself and them, then I would not be able to approach God's throne with peace in my heart. But if my family rejects me, or finds me unacceptable because of something that is unchangeable and a part of who I am, then that is something I have no control over, and God knows that.

Mother, I have not chosen my life with Gary as opposed to my family. There is a special place in my heart, and always will be, that can only be filled by you; and there is also a place in my heart, and always will be, that can only be filled by Gary. I know that the last chapter in our relationship has not been written yet. I have hope.

Mother, you told me how much you have grieved and hurt inside since I shared my heart with you. I understand your grief. But I too grieve. But in my time of grief I have found great comfort in our heavenly Father, who does not take sides in this situation, but feels the pain of each of us, and comforts us both in our humanity. So in closing, let me just say that however you decide to deal with me, your son, I must accept it. I pray if the outcome is not what I hope for, I will not grow bitter. But please know that the communication lines are always open as far as I'm concerned and I am willing to try and work toward a mutual understanding. Happy Birthday, Mother.

I love you.

Your loving son, Randy

Mother chose not to respond, although Pam told me Mom read my letter. I believe the loving work that God had performed in my heart came across in the letter. I believe Mom's heart started to open when she read it, even though we were not invited to spend Christmas with them.

Pam had already dealt with her misgivings about our relationship and had made the decision to stick with her brother and his partner. Somehow, I had always known she would. She and her daughter came over on Christmas Eve, and we exchanged presents. I sent the gifts for the rest of my family with Pam. On each package I had written, "With love from Randy *and* Gary."

Gary and I spent a quiet Christmas. We cooked a turkey with the usual trimmings. Some things are not negotiable. Dad came by, bringing my presents from the family. He looked at our Christmas decorations. While he didn't stay long, by coming he had taken a big step. It was the last Christmas that Gary and I would not be invited to my parent's home for the holidays. Something beyond our imaginations would take place in the next year that would change the dynamics of our family life forever.

Chapter 37
A Birthday Invitation for One

1994 was a good year for Friends of His as the congregation grew. I enjoyed ministering with Michael. He and I held a few revivals out of state, at which I provided the special music and he preached. We were a great team, and people sensed this.

1994 was also a good year for Gary and me. We had grown closer, and the friction we had felt in our first year and a half was gone as we settled into a comfortable routine.

Close to my dad's birthday, January 27, my sister Linda sent a letter informing me that she was planning a family get-together at Mom and Dad's house on the Sunday afternoon of Dad's birthday. She said it would be nice if the whole family could be together. I wrote back that I would be glad to attend if Gary was welcome to come with me. I got no response. On the Sunday morning of Dad's birthday, he called me before church and asked if I was coming to the party.

"Dad, I would like to come, but you know how I feel about Gary not being invited. It's nothing personal. I love you. Gary and I have a present for you, and I will drop it by tomorrow."

Dad had emotion in his voice when he replied. "I understand, Son. We'll miss you."

"I'll miss being there, Dad. Happy Birthday. I love you."

"I love you too, Son."

After Dad's party, I wrote to Linda to make sure she understood why I did not attend.

Dear Linda,

Thank you for the invitation to Dad's birthday get-together. I wanted to come but was not sure you meant to include Gary. As I am sure you know by now, Gary and I are married, and I feel very strongly about him being included in any invitation to a family gathering. I know you probably have strong feelings against two men being married. We have committed ourselves to each other before God and our friends for life. So any future invitations should be addressed to both of us.

I added that I was at peace with God and loved my family. However, I told her that I felt her judgment and that she seemed to think she was a better person than me. I asked her to forgive me of these feelings. I ended the letter:

I am your brother. I am gay. I love Jesus with all my heart. I am a Christian. Christ is at work in my life and in my marriage. We have a Christian home and God is first in both our lives. Gary is a wonderful talented, loving, Christian man who is very good to me. I appeal to you out of your sense of Christ's teaching of love to include us in your life. But if you cannot, I must accept this, and with God's help, I will forgive you for your intolerance. I will always love you.

Your only brother,

Randy

Days later, Linda responded.

Dear Randy,

Your letter grieved my spirit greatly; not because I feel guilty of the "intolerance" and "judgmental attitude" of which you accused me. I know that God's word condemns the lifestyle you have chosen, and I know that you know this also. Let's be very clear about this: the words "Christian" and "gay" can never be used to describe the same person in my vocabulary, even if that person is very, very dear to me, even if that person is my brother whom I love with all my heart!

Linda continued the letter by explaining why she had not invited Gary. According to her, Mom and Dad had made it clear they did not want Gary in their home. She assured me she would have been friendly to him and would have talked to him as she would any guest.

I know you really believe what you are saying and feeling right now, but it is because you have been deceived by a lie of Satan.

Please believe that I love you and respect your right to live any way you choose. But please don't expect me to accept something that is absolutely contrary to everything I believe and trust in. That I cannot do! But I still love you!

Your sister,

Linda

After thinking over her words, I wrote back.

Dear Linda,

Thank you for answering my letter and sharing your feelings with me. I do not feel any condemnation from God because of my sexual orientation. I have the most beautiful sense of His presence in my life. The Lord has restored to me the joy of my salvation and I worship my Lord Jesus Christ in spirit and in truth!!! Linda, you said, 'but please don't expect me to accept something that is absolutely contrary to everything I believe and trust in.' I have accepted Jesus as my savior. Is that contrary to your belief? I love my family. Is that contrary to your belief system? I strive to put God first in my life. Is that contrary to your faith? I lead worship in church every Sunday and travel proclaiming the good news of Jesus through the avenue of drama and music. Is that such a terrible activity? Gary and I are gay Christians who believe in family values, regardless of what Pat Robertson and James Dobson believe and teach about us. We have a relationship that is Christ honoring, faithful, and trusting. We do not abuse alcohol or drugs. We host a Bible study in our home. Gary teaches a Sunday school class. So Linda, though you have a problem with my sexual orientation, I don't see why you would say that my "lifestyle" is absolutely contrary to everything you believe and trust in. Thank you for reading this letter, and let me say in closing that I love you with Christ-like love. And although it hurts that you do not accept my marriage to Gary, I still love and accept your marriage to Mike, and you and your children are always welcome in my home.

In Christ's love,

Randy

Linda and I would not discuss this issue again for years.

Chapter 38

Mom and Dad Struggle to Understand

We wanted to keep the door open to a relationship with my parents. That way, God could work a miracle. Gary and I tried to find ways to do things for them to let them know we loved them. We raked their leaves and bagged them, but never went inside their home. Dad appreciated this. He was getting older and no longer had the energy to take care of his yard.

One spring evening in 1994, I received a phone call from an associate minister of my parent's church, whom I considered a good friend. Although I had not come out to him, I was sure he had heard the rumors. In the phone conversation, he informed me that a young woman in the church was telling everyone that I had married a *man*. This same woman had once had a crush on me, and had been hurt when I did not return her advances. She seemed convinced that if she spread the news, everyone at church would understand why she had been spurned.

My minister friend did not ask if her words were true. He passed the information along, then added, "I just thought you would want to know that this is what is being said."

I thanked him for calling. I felt obligated to tell my parents that Gary and I were being talked about at the church they attended. I wanted them to hear it from me first.

The next day, Dad came by. I walked him out to his truck, struggling to find words to tell him.

"Dad, folks at First Assembly have found out about my marriage to Gary."

Dad was somber. "Well son, you have chosen a difficult road, being gay and in ministry."

"You're right. It is a difficult road, but I just want you to know…with all my heart, I do not believe I chose either. My sexual orientation and my decision to go into the ministry are both callings, not choices."

What Dad said next will always live in my heart as one of the most significant moments of my life.

"Well son, I'm beginning to understand. Whatever happens, whatever people say, I just want you to know…I'm your father and you are my son. I love you, and nothing will ever change that."

Waves of emotion swept over me. I hugged him tightly.

"Thanks Dad, you don't know how much it means to hear you say that."

I said goodbye and walked into the house. As Dad drove away I was aware that God was working in his life. He was an educated man who had an unshakable love for his children. Love caused him to look beyond the accepted norms and prejudices of his generation to learn about homosexuality. He was determined to find a way to stay connected to his son and believe the best of him.

I stopped in to see my parents regularly. One day, when Mother and I were sitting at her dining room table drinking coffee, the conversation was going well—until Mom noticed my wedding ring.

"Is that what you are *calling* your wedding ring?"

"This *is* my wedding ring."

"Randy, what a farce!

"Mother, we can sit here and talk, but if you insist on insulting my relationship with Gary, I am going to leave."

"How can you live in such a fantasy world? I can't believe they would allow you to be on staff at that church knowing you are living with a man in a homosexual relationship. Your ministry is going to blow up in your face!"

"Mother, I want us to get along, but I am not going to keep going over this issue with you. My relationship with Gary is not up for discussion as long as you feel this way about it. If I lose my job, and the churches stop asking me to do my dramas, God will open up a new door of ministry."

She continued her preachments, so I left. I didn't behave angrily but, having drawn my boundaries, I remained faithful to them. I would try to respect my mother, but I would not let her degrade me or my relationship with Gary.

A few days later, I stopped by to see my folks. We were visiting in their den when Mother started in on me again.

"Randy, I just pray for you and nothing seems to change. You have hardened your heart. I am worried for your eternal soul!"

"Mother, my eternal soul is just fine. You don't have to worry."

"But I do worry. Randy, if you were to die right now, you would be burning in hell. I can assure you of that!"

I had made myself a vow not to allow Mom to pull me into a heated discussion. But this time she had gone too far. I reminded her that Jesus commanded us not to judge others.

"You are judging me!" I exclaimed. "You are *not* my judge! God is! The God I serve is a God of love, and he knows my heart. Obviously you don't!"

Once again, I walked out.

The next day, I had to go by my parents home to pick up mail. Mother was there and I was not in the mood to have another scene, so I just ignored her. As I started to leave, she stopped me.

"Randy, wait."

Her voice was devoid of tenderness, very matter-of-fact and brusque. "I just want to say I'm sorry for judging you. Your dad said that I was wrong to talk to you that way."

"Thank you for acknowledging that," I said as I opened the car door.

"But I still worry about your eternal soul."

I did not respond.

A week before my 38th birthday I got a phone call from Mom.

"Randy, I was trying to decide what to get you for your birthday. I know one thing you really would enjoy would be a home-cooked meal. So why don't you and Gary come over Thursday night."

What a shock! Mother was inviting *Gary* to their house?! I would be able to go to my parents' house and sit at their dinner table with my spouse! This was huge!

When I told Gary, he was a little nervous. I could understand why.

"But Gary, mom is trying. I believe God is answering my prayer."

On my birthday, I brought roses for my mom and a card thanking her for the invitation. We had a wonderful time. My sister Pam and her daughter came, and also my mom's mother, Grandma Rhodes. Everyone was nice to Gary. It was becoming clearer to me now that my sister Linda and her family were the main barrier to being together as a family. Without them, Mom did not feel the need to hold up a standard of disapproval. Obviously, Mom showed some signs of stress. She seemed a little subdued, but overall it was a night of celebration.

When Gary and I returned home, he found a card from me waiting for him on his pillow. On the front, I printed the simple message, "I love you with all my heart."

Then on the inside I added,

I feel that God answered one of our prayers tonight by mother having us both over for my birthday dinner at her home. I was so proud of you sitting beside me. You will never know how much joy you have brought to my life! I am a very lucky and blessed 38-year-old gay Christian man. You are not only handsome, but a dear sweet man to love me so completely.

Your dearest,

Randy

Chapter 39

Something's Wrong with Mother

The last Saturday in October 1994, Pam called to tell me she thought something was wrong with Mother.

"What is it, Pam?"

"Well, she is just acting very strange. I was over at her house and she was stumbling around, saying silly things, almost like she was drunk. I've told Daddy we need to take her to the emergency room, but Mother keeps saying that there is nothing wrong with her."

I rushed to Mom and Dad's house. Dad seemed reluctant to take Mom to the hospital, but Pam and I insisted.

The staff in the emergency room ran a few tests and decided there was nothing wrong. It was then that Pam said to the nurse who had examined Mom, "There *is* something *wrong* with my mother. I know you don't know her and, to you, it may look like she is normal, but listen to me. My mother is *not* a jolly person! She doesn't drink. Yet she is acting like she is drunk and giddy!"

The staff checked her again and confirmed the decision to send her home. "Be sure and take an aspirin before you go to bed," the attending doctor said.

We took her home. Mom kept saying, "See, I told you I'm all right. There is nothing wrong with me. Y'all are just imagining things."

The next day I called Dad. He said that Mom had fallen in the living room that morning. She was slurring her words. She still had that silly grin on her face. It was weird, like an alien had taken over her body. She also seemed to be favoring her left side. My sisters and I insisted that Mother go back to the emergency room. This time, she was admitted immediately. I told Pam and Dad that I would spend the night with Mom.

Much later, as I dozed in the recliner next to her bed, I heard Mom get up.

"Mom, where are you going?" I asked.

"To the bathroom. I'm all right."

I was drowsy, and before I knew it I was nodding off again. Then, the sound of a crash woke me. I opened the door to the bathroom, and there was my very independent mother sprawled out on the floor, naked and helpless. This was very hard for me to see, but I went in and lifted her up and got her hospital gown back on. Then I had her sit on the toilet while I got the nurse. This was the beginning of our nightmare, one that many families have faced. The emergency room doctor had been unable to confirm that Mom had a stroke, but the symptoms pointed in that direction.

The next day, the doctor confirmed what we all feared.

"Mrs. McCain, I am Doctor Grimes. I have looked at your tests and they show that you have had a very serious stroke."

"Oh, no!" Mother almost yelled it. All this time she had been telling us that there was nothing wrong. But now she was truly frightened!

"Doctor, you must be mistaken."

"No, Mrs. McCain, I have seen the x-rays. Not only have you had a stroke, but you have had a massive stroke that has affected the right side of your brain."

Mom started to cry. My mother *never* cried. The doctor said there was a chance that, with rehabilitation, she might get back some movement on her left side, but stressed that there had been extensive damage.

Dad was so worried about Mom. It was sweet to watch him tenderly fussing over her. Mother had retired the year before, and she and Dad had made plans to travel. I thought how unfair life is sometimes, but none of us could see just how different life would be from here on out for our family.

Cindy, one of the activity directors at Mom's rehab, was a really nice woman who was acquainted with Mother before her stroke. Mom had attended a water aerobics class that Cindy taught. I decided to confide in her about the struggle Mother and I had been having over my sexual orientation. Cindy was very nonjudgmental as she explained to me that my mother was at a stage where, for the next few months, she would have to be reeducated. Cindy felt that this would be a good time to try to reestablish our relationship in a positive way.

Gary stayed in the background during the first days after Mom's stroke, but one evening I needed him to come with me. It was time to see how this "new" Mom would react to him. When we walked into her room, Mom had a visitor from her church. To my delight, Mom looked genuinely happy we were there.

"Well, there's my good friend *Gary*," she greeted. We were both in shock. What, Gary wondered, had they done with the old Marcelle?

"Hello Marcelle," he responded. "How are you doing?" The two of them conversed with no hint of disdain in Mom's voice. Obviously, Gary and I talked about that on the way home.

"Well, it was amazing," Gary said with wonder in his voice.

"I got goose bumps when she called you her friend."

"Well, don't get used to it, Randy. The old Marcelle could resurface at any moment."

"I know, but I am going to enjoy this one while she's here!"

Randy's mom and dad with Gary and Randy

Chapter 40

A Phone Call from Saint Peggy

I have never been one to try to meet famous people. I assume they get tired of fans constantly wanting to get a little piece of them. For some reason, Tony Campolo was an exception. I became fascinated by his powerful delivery as I listened to cassette tapes of his preaching,. He had a way of challenging his listeners by making controversial statements that made them feel uncomfortable. I mentioned to a friend that I felt led to write to Tony again, telling him of my journey.

"I just feel that he will listen to me without being judgmental. He may not agree with me, but I really feel a strong urging that I am supposed to write to him."

"Then Randy, you should do it," the friend encouraged. "There is obviously something God wants to accomplish through your letter."

There were only a few times in my life when I felt such a strong nudge from the Holy Spirit to do something specific. But over the years, I had become very sensitive to this strong intuition. I no longer had Tony's address and wondered where to find it. Then one morning, as we were gathered at Esther's for our planning and prayer time, she showed us a book she had just read: *Carpe Diem*, by Tony Campolo.

"I think you would enjoy reading it, Randy," Esther said as she handed me the book.

I found Tony's writing both fascinating and controversial. At the end of the book, Tony asks his readers to write and tell him what they thought of it. So one afternoon I shared my heart in a letter to Tony.

I introduced myself and told him about having read his book, *Twenty Hot Potatoes Christians Are Afraid To Touch*, and feeling betrayed by his statements about gays not choosing their sexual orientation and the inability of gays to change.

Tony, I was trying so hard to believe I could change my sexuality through the church and the power of Christ. You seemed to be saying in your book that this was not going to happen. You suggested that gays find a man to love and care about, make a commitment to live together, take care of one another, but not have sex!

To me this was like suggesting to someone on a diet that they should live in a bakery, because in my mind the most exciting sexual fantasy was one in which I lived in a loving, caring Christ-centered relationship with another man. (Not that sex was everything, but when you love someone and are attracted to them it is only natural that you would want to express yourself sexually in a very loving way.)

As I read your book, I felt you were betraying me and all others who were trying to change. I cannot tell you how hopeless this made me feel. But now that I look back, it was a turning point for me. I had to realistically look at my walk with the Lord. I was not any different after four years of Christian counseling. I was still gay.

This started me on a spiritual quest that has led both Gary and me to where we are now— two gay Christian men who love Jesus with all their hearts and who love each other with a pure, Christ-centered love. Tony, I challenge you to see for yourself what God is doing in the gay lesbian community. I would love to dialog with you on this subject. I would like for you to write to me. Ask me anything. Gary and I are open books to you. Please know that you and your wife Peggy are welcome to visit us here in North Little Rock, as our home is open to you, or we could meet somewhere else. Your books have blessed me so! Keep up the good work! God bless you, Tony, and I hope to hear from you soon.

> *Yours in Christ,*
>
> *Randy McCain*

I sent the letter after praying over it, and asked God to bring it to Rev. Campolo's attention. I did not have to wait long. He did read my letter, and on November 11, 1994 he responded.

Dear Randy,

Thanks so very much for taking the time to write to me.

I am sorry you feel betrayed by the things that I wrote in my book. I assume that you and your partner are in a relationship that involves going beyond the marks that I have indicated in my book, Twenty Hot Potatoes. In that book I was really advocating nothing. I was merely describing what many homosexuals I had interviewed were doing to resolve the conflict in their lives. Contrary to my critics who are taking shots at me, I am a conservative in terms of the Bible, and my views on homosexuality tend to reflect that. I am a strong advocate of gay/lesbian rights and I strongly communicate that my views on the homosexual issue are not the final word on the subject.

As you know, my wife, Peggy, differs from me on the subject. I'm going to ask her to write to you.

I appreciate where you are coming from and your sense of betrayal when analyzing my position. However, you have to learn to respect positions other than your own. I'm learning to do that, too. Stay alive in Christ. Stay strong in your faith.

Yours in Christ,

Tony Campolo

I was thrilled that this man, whom I considered to be the greatest preacher and Christian writer of our day, would take time to read my letter and answer so promptly! I was also excited to think that his wife Peggy would write me.

On the Monday before Thanksgiving, when I checked messages on our answering machine, I heard: "Hello, this is Peggy Campolo, Tony Campolo's wife, and I am calling Randy McCain. I would like very much to talk to you. Tony shared with me about you writing to him. And I would like to talk to you a lot after reading your letter. You could call our office number and leave a message for Peggy with my husband's secretary about when would be a good time to call you. I appreciate it very much."

On Thanksgiving Eve, Peggy called. The phone rang. I recognized the same sweet voice with the northeastern accent from Peggy's message.

"Hi, it's Peggy Campolo, is this Randy?"

I was so excited. "Yes, it is."

Peggy told me how much she loved my letter. We talked for about 20 minutes. She said that Gary and I sounded like the nicest couple and she could not wait to meet us in person someday. She asked me more about my ministry and said she would love for me to send her a video of my dramatic performance and a cassette of my music. She also was interested in Gary's artwork. Peggy told me about Evangelicals Concerned, an organization founded by Dr. Ralph Blair to educate the evangelical church world about the need to include gay and lesbian people in their churches. I soon discovered that Peggy was very good at networking and connecting people she felt could help each other.

When I hung up the phone, I was giddy. The wife of my favorite preacher and writer had talked to me like we could be good friends! She sounded amazing. I could not wait to hear from her again. Our conversation would later prove to be one of those rare moments in time that a phone call changed a life.

Chapter 41

A Holiday Season of Miracles

Thanksgiving Day, we planned to have the family meal at Mom and Dad's. Mother would not be able to attend, so early in the day Dad, my sisters, and I went to visit her while she ate her Thanksgiving meal at the rehab center. She was glad to say goodbye when we saw her back to her room, because the activities of the day had sapped her energy.

Then we went to Mom and Dad's house. Linda's family, Pam and Leandra, and Gary joined us for the traditional holiday dinner. Gary and I provided the turkey and dressing, and Dad made sure that Gary knew he was welcome. Never again would my partner and I be barred from my parent's home. Mom's stroke had changed the family dynamics.

On December 7, we threw a birthday party for Mom at her own house. She was still in the rehab center but had been given a pass to come home for the evening. It was her first attempt going out. She didn't spend the night, but her church friends joined us to celebrate her 68th birthday and all the progress she'd made in recovering from the devastating effects of her stroke. The night was magical. It seemed surreal bringing Mother home to visit her own house, but she was so excited. After a wonderful meal, Mom opened her presents. When one friend asked when she would be released from the rehab hospital, she replied, "They tell me that, if all goes well, I could be home just in time for Christmas."

"Won't that be wonderful?" her Sunday school teacher exclaimed. "Now *that* will be the time to really celebrate."

"Yes," Mom responded. "I think we should toast my coming home with champagne!"

Everyone was shocked as Mother had always been a teetotaler. Her Sunday school teacher responded quickly, "Marcelle you *don't* mean that."

"Yes I do, Dorothy. Isn't that what people drink to celebrate a special occasion?"

"Yes, but Marcelle, it has *alcohol* in it."

"I know!" Mom said with gusto and a smile.

Her church friends responded with nervous laughter, but her son made a mental note. If Mom wanted champagne, then, by George, she was going to have it.

The next weeks held many firsts for me. Friends of His put on a special Christmas musical program, and Daddy brought Mother. I felt so proud to announce to the congregation that *both* of my parents were there.

On Friday, December 23, 1994, Mom was released from rehab and we brought her home that night. Gary and I arrived with a bottle of champagne. All of us—Gary, Mom, Dad, Pam, and me—toasted Mother with a drink. Mom was so excited that I had remembered the champagne. So was Daddy! He always enjoyed a drink, but had abstained for years because of Mom's moratorium against drinking. Gary popped the cork and poured the champagne all around.

Mom was so funny. From her recliner she lifted the glass to her lips and exclaimed, "The bubbles tickle my nose!" I had the video camera going. I knew I would need to document this moment as proof that it really did happen. Mom drank her glass pretty fast. "Gary, is there any left? I need some more."

"Marcelle, you better drink this second glass a little slower." Gary warned. "Champagne will slip up on you and you'll be drunk before you know it."

"You sound like an old pro at this, Gary," Mom giggled. He poured her some more. She started to drink it but because of her reclining position, spilled some.

Gary got a kick out of this. "Marcelle, you are a sloppy drunk."

This really tickled Mom and we all laughed. It was a night like none I had ever experienced: my teetotaling Assembly of God family sharing a bottle of champagne! Never in my wildest dreams would I have believed this could happen. But we had something to celebrate!

On Christmas Eve, the latest remake of *Miracle on 34th Street* was showing at the theatre. My mom, Pam, Leandra, and I went to see it. This was the first time Mother and I had ever gone to a movie together. With so many firsts, the McCains were on a roll! But the best was yet to come.

That evening, I fired up a big pot of my famous homemade chili and invited Mom and Dad, Pam, and Leandra to eat at our apartment. Mother said she wanted to decorate Christmas cookies. I told her that Gary would be baking some cookies that night, and she could help him decorate them after we ate.

The candles were lit. The Christmas tree was decorated beautifully, thanks to Gary's expertise. The video camera was rolling as my parents walked in. I got an overwhelming sense of God's presence, witnessing the miracle of Mom walking through the front door of our home, the place she had mockingly called our "love nest" and assured me she would never step foot in. We ate together and then Mom sat at the dining room table, decorating cookies with Gary and Leandra.

The next day Gary and I went to my parents' house early to help Daddy get the turkey in the oven. We set the table where we would eat Christmas dinner together as a family. When Linda's family arrived, they were not very friendly to Gary and me, but the family was all in one room together. After dinner, we opened gifts around the Christmas tree.

The weekend would be a series of precious emotional moments. One came when I discovered the gift under the tree addressed, "To Gary, from Randall and Marcelle." It was the most enchanted Christmas I ever experienced, and one that reconfirmed my belief in miracles.

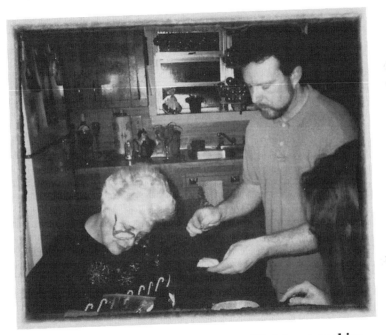

Randy's mom helping Gary decorate Christmas cookies

Chapter 42

Come Out, Wherever You Are

With Valentine's Day 1995 approaching, I was ready to start making certain moves toward validating our relationship. First step, wearing matching rings. I went to the department store where we had purchased my golden band with the cross and bought an identical ring for Gary.

I also bought a white stuffed puppy dog with a heart-shaped pillow in his mouth that said, "I love you." I pinned Gary's ring on the back of the pillow, then placed the dog on the dining room table along with a rose and a heart-shaped box of chocolates and a card that said,

You have made my dreams come true! I'm glad God protected us and brought us together at just the right time. I want to live the rest of my life showing you how grateful I am to God and to you for such a warm, happy relationship. You are the man of my dreams!

Gary smiled when he saw the table. After reading the card, he picked up the dog. Noticing something gleaming, he spotted the ring and immediately knew the significance of this gift. I was saying, "I refuse to hide my love for you." He gasped as tears welled up in his eyes. I unpinned the ring, slipped off his old one, and placed the new matching ring on his finger.

"What if people at church notice that we are wearing matching wedding bands?" Gary asked.

"I'm not ashamed of our love. I am getting so tired of having to constantly make sure no one finds out about us. I am *proud* of what we have. I don't know if this will cause people to ask questions or not, but what if they do? What if they find out? I'm ready to know if they love us for who we really are, or if they just love us for who they want us to be."

Neither Gary nor I could have envisioned the furor on the horizon. Friends of His was growing, and the future looked bright. The only area with which I felt uncomfortable was the fact that I was hedging about our relationship. When we hosted the Bible study for the church at our apartment, we had to "straighten up." We hid every object that might signal that Gary and I were a couple, especially our wedding picture and photos of us together.

One night while I soaked in the tub, I sensed God saying that it was time to be honest with the church board. My belief that I had heard from God was very strong. I told Gary that I was going to write a "coming out" letter to the elders, explaining why I did not feel that our loving, Christ-centered relationship should disqualify me from ministry.

"Are you sure you're ready for this?" Gary asked.

"I don't know. I just feel certain that I heard from God."

"Well, if you feel that strongly, then I support you."

The next day I wrote the letter. When I met with Michael, I gave him a copy and shared my intent. He asked how I wanted to present the letter. I asked if he would read it to the elders at the next board meeting scheduled in a couple of weeks. I also said that I thought it would be good for Gary and me to be present in case the board had any questions they wanted to ask. Michael agreed to this.

The next evening I received a call from Michael, saying that he would like me to take a trip with him to the Cumberland Presbyterian denominational headquarters in Memphis and talk to George Estes, head of the Board of Missions. George, a soft-spoken man, had asked me to lead worship at the denomination's New Church Development retreat, and had always been very supportive of the style of worship I was introducing to Cumberland Presbyterian churches.

Michael presented the idea of our talking with George as a fact-finding mission. We would ask George for his advice about how to handle the minefield we anticipated. I felt Michael was working hard on my behalf to help save my position. We needed to see George because Friends of His was under the leadership of the Board of Missions.

Michael and I mulled over the different approaches we could take in the next few weeks before heading to Memphis. He had been studying *In the Crossfire* by Sally B. Geis and Donald E. Messer, which contained divergent views on the role of gays in the church. The book had been designed to help churches debate this "hot potato" issue. Michael hoped the elders would not make a snap judgment. Perhaps we could arrange to have a dialogue series on the subject. I had no problem with giving the issue a full airing.

When we walked into George's office, I knew immediately that things were not right. George was not his usual warm, congenial self. He had shifted into his role of a church bureaucrat. He got to the point quickly. George, aware of my letter, had asked me to meet with him so that he could encourage me to prayerfully consider resigning. The fact that he was already aware of my letter was a surprise to me. I felt I had been set up!

"Randy, Friends of His is not at a stage of development where the people are ready to deal with this issue. I feel that if they are asked to wrestle with it now, it may do irreparable damage to the church."

"George," I said. "I have already 'prayerfully' considered my actions in coming out to the board. I have been praying and wrestling with this issue for a long time. It has taken years for me to come to a place of respecting myself as a gay Christian man. I know this is an issue that the church does not feel it is ready to handle, but George, when *is* it going to be ready? I know that this is a cutting-edge issue in the church and I don't like being on the cutting edge. It is very painful. But I find myself there simply because of who I am."

"Randy," George pleaded. "Please take into consideration what you are asking the church to do. Not long ago, I personally had to deal with this issue because some-one very dear to me came out. At the time, I wrestled with the scriptures. I studied diligently and found that gay people do have a place of hope in scripture and the church. But Randy, this just is not the time for this battle to be fought at Friends of His."

"George, once again, when *will* it be a good time? I hear of many gay and lesbi-an teens committing suicide after turning to the church—the last place of hope they felt they had in this world—and receiving nothing but judgment and rejection. I feel a responsibility to those nameless faces, those depressed and hopeless kids. I do not believe that my loving, Christ-centered, monogamous relationship with Gary Eddy disqualifies me from ministry. You, yourself have told me that I have been 'a blessing,' and that it is evident that God has placed ministry gifts into my life."

"So, Randy, you are telling me that you will not prayerfully consider stepping down…perhaps even continuing in the church without pay?"

"George, what I get paid is precious little, a part-time salary for a full-time job, and you would ask me to do this work for no compensation? Don't you think that is just a little unfair?"

"Randy, I am simply asking you to prayerfully *consider* doing this."

"George, I have no problem in praying for God's guidance. I truly believe that is what I have been doing all along."

"Well, that is all I am asking you to do today, Randy. Just think this through and see if you can find it in your heart to resign for the good of the church."

"I promise you that I will continue to pray for God's guidance, George."

The meeting was over. I suspected that Michael was being strong-armed into aligning himself with the denomination. I couldn't help feeling like George and Mi-chael ganged up on me. Michael said little in the meeting.

Driving home, he told me that I should not resign and that it was unfair to ask me to work without compensation. Michael seemed to be supporting me, so we went ahead with the plan for him to read my letter to the board.

I called one elder to tell him about my letter and what to expect at the next board meeting. This elder was a gay man and in a relationship, but his partner did not attend Friends of His. The others on the board were unaware of his sexual orientation.

I assured him that I did not want him to feel that he had to come out to fight for me. I would understand if he chose to miss the meeting, if he felt that it would be too uncomfortable for him. Not to worry. He assured me that he would attend.

I went to break the news to Mom and Dad. They read my letter and said it was good. Both warned me of the storm that would probably hit, but they also told me they were proud of me for being honest.

The difference in Mom's attitude amazed and pleased me. She gave me a hug and prayed with me, asking God to be with Gary and me through whatever would come. Looking back, I do not know what outcome I expected, but I have always been an optimist. One of my favorite quotations of George Bernard Shaw, so loved by Robert Kennedy, is: "Some men see things as they are and ask 'why?' I dream things that never were and ask, why not?"

That was the filter through which I always looked at life. I loved the members of Friends of His and I believed that they loved me. Yet, I had to know if they truly loved the *real* me. So I balanced an optimistic feeling with a certain amount of fear.

On the night the board met, Gary waited in the Pastor's office during the first part of the meeting. When it came time for new business, he joined us in the board-room to sit beside me as Michael read the letter. I kept my eyes on Michael. I did not want to watch the expressions of those around the table.

August 2, 1995

To the pastor and the members of the Session of Friends of His, Cumberland Presbyterian Church.

My dear sisters and brothers in Christ, I would like to take this opportunity to tell you how blessed I have been to serve this church for the past four years as Minister of Music and Assistant to the Pastor. The joys and sorrows we have shared have bonded us together in love. I believe very strongly in the mission statement of Friends of His, and the lives that I have seen changed in the past four years are evidence of the fact that the kind of ministry that Friends of His offers is needed here in Sherwood.

What I am about to tell you has been shared with the Pastor from the beginning of my association with this church. I have never lied about it and I am not ashamed of it. I am a gay Christian man. I am in a loving, caring, God-centered covenant relationship with Gary Eddy, also a member of this church. We are both aware of the stance of many in the evangelical world on this issue. There are many who believe that gay people choose their gayness. I do not say lifestyle, for this is a misnomer. There are as many homosexual lifestyles as there are heterosexual lifestyles. We know for a fact that we did not choose to be homosexual, and therefore we cannot choose to be heterosexual.

Many in the church world believe that a gay or lesbian has no place in the church and cannot be considered a Christian. Gary and I know that just isn't true. We both have been a vital part of this church, and although we struggle with the demands of Christ in our lives and many times fall short of the mark (to which I am sure we can all relate), both of us can see the fruit of the Holy Spirit in our lives individually and as a couple.

This journey has not been an easy one, and both Gary and I spent years poring over scripture and seeking counseling. Prayer has been a constant in our struggle. I remember shortly before coming to Friends of His, crying out to God for a church that would let me work through this maze without constantly making me feel damned from the outset. Friends of His called the next week and asked me to help with the music.

Here I have sensed God's wonderful love and grace as I never felt it demonstrated before. Through Michael, and through the wonderful friends that make up this faith community, it is here that I know I have wrestled with the angel of the Lord and have received blessing! Thank you for giving me that freedom.

Gary and I felt that we should share this with you. We will be glad to answer any questions that you may have as best we can. We feel strongly that we would love to continue in service to the Lord here at Friends of His and we commend ourselves as servants of the Lord. We believe that Friends of His can be a safe haven for ALL God's children: black, white, Hispanic, Asian, gay, straight, young, old, married, divorced, single...as Paul said in Galatians 3:27-28,

'For all of you who were baptized into Christ have clothed yourselves with Christ. There is neither Jew nor Greek, slave nor free, male nor female, for you are all one in Christ Jesus.'

We feel that the scripture assures us of our place at God's table. We are not ashamed of the Gospel of Christ nor are we ashamed of our love for each other. We also feel strongly that if we as a church have an open door to the oppressed and the hungry, God will help us grow and prosper as a church and as a people. Please prayerfully consider what we have shared *with you. We love you and will always care very deeply for our church family.*

In God's grace,

Randy McCain and Gary Eddy

You could have heard a pin drop when Michael finished reading. He asked if the elders had any questions for Gary and me, or any comments. Billy, a conservative member, spoke first, saying that the Bible was clear on the issue of homosexuality. He voiced his opposition to our church embracing a tolerant view on this subject.

"But Billy, it is not as easy as saying, 'The Bible says,'" I responded. "You can interpret the Bible many different ways. What about the fact that Jesus says nothing at all against homosexuality, but he does say quite a bit against divorce and remarriage?"

A female elder spoke up. "That is true," she said, "I know that there are two of us on this board who are divorced and remarried. So if we are going by a strict inter-pretation of the Bible, perhaps the two of *us* should resign."

"But aren't there *gay* churches?" Billy asked.

"Yes Billy, there are *gay* churches, but I don't want to attend a church that is made up only of gay people. I do not believe that God wants to divide churches up into gay, straight, black, white. I believe sincerely that God wants us all to worship together, like we have been doing here at Friends of His."

Then the gay elder spoke up.

"You may not know this, but I am gay myself. I am in a relationship with another man and I serve on this board. I wholeheartedly support Randy staying on as our Minister of Music and Assistant to the Pastor."

Jim Whitten, a retired pharmacist in his 70s, spoke next. "I love these boys. They are a part of us. I think Randy does a great job with the music and helping Michael. I think he and Michael make a great team. This information tonight doesn't change my feelings about Randy at all. These are good boys."

I was moved by Jim's support, and also by the courage of the gay elder to out himself and to take a stand for me. Out of the five members on the board, I could count on two for support. I suggested that we allow people in the congregation to dialog on the subject.

"We could actually schedule a night to discuss the issues surrounding all of this before a decision is made about my future. Gary and I are open books to you. We will be glad to talk about the process we have been through, to come to a place of understanding."

Michael wrapped up the meeting by suggesting that we keep this to ourselves for a week and pray about it. "We will then come back a week from tonight and talk about it further."

After we dismissed with prayer, Billy came to me and shook my hand. "I will say this, Randy. I know it took a lot of guts to do what you did tonight."

"Thank you, Billy."

The older elder, Jim, came over and hugged Gary and me.

"It's going to be all right, boys. Don't worry. It will be all right."

Although I was encouraged, Michael afterwards warned me against too much optimism. He did think that, overall, the meeting had gone well. What I didn't know at the time was that Michael knew that even if the session voted to keep me, the denominational headquarters would find a way to demand termination. The battle was not to be just within our congregation.

The Cumberland Presbyterian denomination did not have any rules barring gay people from serving the church as music ministers or associates. While they did not ordain openly gay people to the ministry, I was not in a position requiring ordination. This was going to be a tricky situation even though my ministry was well received by the congregation, and I had been a part of the Friends of His ministry team for over four years. The church itself had only been in existence three months when I came on board. Since I had been there from the beginning, it would be difficult for the congregation to envision the ministry team without me. Plus, the denomination had boldly birthed a church to attract those turned off by the traditional-style churches. The ministry style of Friends of His had attracted people who were not life-long Cumberland Presbyterians. The members were mostly baby boomers who felt no real allegiance to institutions and were more freethinking church-goers.

Still, Friends of His was a "mission church" of the Cumberland denomination. We had not yet become a fully fledged independent congregation. Since the denomination provided financial assistance, it had a certain amount of oversight. Yet, church members had been led to believe Friends of His was an independent church.

Michael knew that once the headquarters bureaucrats found out about me, panic would ripple throughout the top levels of the denomination. Unfortunately, he chose not to share this with me. He had telephoned ministers who had dealt with the "gay issue" in their churches and had found out that some congregations called themselves "open and affirming," meaning they not only welcomed gay people, but affirmed their personhood. Michael then started developing a plan that he hoped would allow our church to work things out without splitting. The plan was two different congregations: one open and affirming, and the other tolerant, or possibly even non-tolerant.

What about me? I would continue to lead music for the "open and affirming" wing of the church. Michael tried to formulate a policy everyone could live with, but when he pitched it to me it seemed ridiculous. It sounded like two Koreas, North and South.

I responded that his solution sounded like the separate yet equal policy that had never been satisfactory or effective. What if a gay person stumbled into the wrong service? How could two congregations exist as one, under policies to protect one group from the other? (Years later, Michael told me that, at the time, I hurt him deeply by so easily and quickly vetoing his concept.)

Michael was frightened. He knew that we were best friends. He also felt comfortable ministering with me and our ministry was being well received, both at Friends of His and at the churches around the country where we held revivals. Yet he could see that he would eventually have to take some pretty major risks to save my position and my self-esteem. He was afraid to do what it would take to save his friend's ministry. Rather, he tried to head off a major showdown with the denominational leadership in Memphis.

On Saturday, when Gary and I went to the YMCA to set up chairs for the Sunday service, Michael seemed very distant. As we finished, I confronted him.

"Michael, is something wrong?"

"No," he answered. "Why?"

"Well, you seem distracted tonight, and distant."

"No, nothing's wrong."

"Have you heard something? Has George called?"

"Yes, he did."

"What did he have to say?"

"He was disappointed that you had not resigned."

"What else did he say?" I asked.

"He brought up the fact that this could turn into a real scandal for the church and for the denomination—a scandal that might cause those churches in the state that had been financially supporting Friends of His as a mission work to withhold their support."

"I can see that George's call has you worried. Are you having second thoughts about supporting me through this, Michael?"

He did not answer. This compassionate man was shutting down emotionally toward me. For the first time, I began to realize that not only was I in for the fight of my life, but I would also fight without the help of my trusted friend and pastor. Heavy and unspeakable pain gripped my heart. I was stunned by this sudden change in Michael, stunned *and* frightened. He was deserting me before the major battle.

For four years, Michael was my close friend who was always there in my darkest hours. He comforted me when I lost a friend to AIDS and when Grandma died. He was also my confidant as I struggled to a place of understanding God's grace and my own sexuality. Now I was on the eve of one of the toughest struggles I had ever faced, and my good friend, my pastor, was deserting me.

When Gary and I got home, I went to our bedroom, fell on the bed, and cried a deep wail of betrayal and rejection. I wished I could turn off my emotions, because their weight was almost more than I could bear. Gary came in, sat on the edge of the bed, and wrapped his arms around me.

"I don't have a pastor anymore, Gary. I know now I will not be able to count on Michael for support on Wednesday night. Someone has gotten to him."

Indeed, Michael was not there anymore. It was as if an alien force had extracted the Michael I knew, and deposited in his body an unrecognizable being, devoid of feelings and emotions.

The next morning, as I dressed for church, I tried to prepare myself emotionally to minister in music. This would not be easy. I felt strongly this would be my final service at Friends of His.

As I sat at the piano, playing worship music, the people started arriving. Michael walked over to me and, to my surprise, acted as if nothing were wrong. Jolly and upbeat, he patted me on the back, asking if I was ready for the service. Although confused at first, I recognized a technique I had seen Michael employ in certain situations. He had a way of getting through must-do public events when dealing privately with difficult personal issues by acting as if nothing were amiss. I cringed when he patted me on the back.

That morning, it was not easy to get through the fast, upbeat praise choruses. My heart did not feel like rejoicing in the day that the Lord had made, much less inspiring others to do so. How could I pretend? When we sang slower choruses, I felt the tears starting to flow. As I lead the congregation, I looked at the people I had ministered to for four years. I saw them, knowing that very likely I would never have this opportunity again. My heart ached. I remembered how happy I had been the first Sunday I led worship at Friends of His. I thought about the long talks Michael and I had as we opened our hearts to each other about personal wounds in our lives. And now, the ministry that I loved so much, and the friendship I had enjoyed with my pastor, was about to be ripped from my heart.

After the service, Gary and I left as soon as we could. We didn't know who knew about my letter, and I didn't want to handle any awkward questions.

On Monday, we met at Esther's for our weekly prayer and planning session. It was difficult to act as though nothing were wrong. Clearly, I was disappointed in Michael. Now we were in a small group, forced to interact and pray together. I said little to him. Esther was very concerned for Gary and me, and also for Michael and the church. She was caught in the middle. I hated this, because Esther was experiencing bad health and recently had some severe panic attacks.

When we opened the meeting, Michael said, "I think Randy is angry at me and I don't know why. Randy, it hurts me to think that you could be mad at me or think that I have abandoned you."

"Michael, that *is* the way I feel. You told me that you didn't think I should resign. You also told me that you would stand by me, even if we had to go to the state head-quarters for the Cumberland Presbyterians. And now I feel you shutting down on me. Yes, that does hurt, and yes, I think I have good reason to feel abandoned!"

"Well, what do you want me to do, Randy?"

"I want you to stand up for me, Michael. I want you to tell George and the session that you support me as your associate, and you, personally, do not feel that my homosexuality should disqualify me from being in a leadership position."

"Randy, I can do that. I *will* do that, but if they vote to terminate you, I will have to go along with their decision."

"Michael, I know you can't save me yourself. All I am asking you to do is let George and the session know that you are standing with me."

Michael nodded that he would.

"I'm sorry for my feelings of anger toward you, Michael. I am just under a lot of pressure right now, and I need to know that you are with me in this."

We hugged and I told Michael that I loved him. By the time the meeting ended, I had hope in my heart that Michael would support me.

Gary and I had reported to some trusted friends what had already transpired, and we got calls from several of them reassuring us that, whatever happened in the meeting on Wednesday, we could count on their support. I also called my friend, Peggy Campolo, and alerted her to what was happening. She assured me she would "tuck me into her prayers" that night, and told me she would call to see how things had gone.

I called Chris Glasser, a gay Christian author whose devotional book for gay and lesbian Christians I had read. I was impressed with his intellect and spirituality, and I wanted to get his advice. When I explained to Chris that the denominational headquarters was pressuring me to resign for the good of the church, telling me that I would do damage to the church by refusing to step down, Chris was unconvinced by their arguments.

"Randy, your coming out to the congregation is not an act of violence, it is an act of vulnerability. Do not let anyone make you feel like 'the heavy' in this situation. You are the one who has been willing to take off your mask and be real. Church should be the last place where people have to be afraid to tell the truth."

His wisdom gave me fresh courage. How dare those denominational bureaucrats question my love for the church I had served faithfully for over four years? Chris' words inspired me to not back down. I would not allow them to make me feel like the villain.

On Wednesday morning, Michael called and told me that George Estes would be at the meeting that evening.

"Randy, he has asked to see you alone. He wants to have a separate meeting with you before the board meeting."

When I told Gary about the meeting with George, he asked what I thought this meant.

"He's probably going to ask me again to resign," I replied.

I prepared for the meeting by listening to some of my favorite Christian worship music. I prayed and meditated so I would be peaceful and open to the Holy Spirit's guidance. At four o'clock, I walked into Michael's office to find George sitting at Michael's desk. His manner was cold, even though he thanked me for my willingness to meet him.

"Randy, have you prayerfully considered my request for you to offer your resignation?"

"George, I have considered it and prayed about it, and I feel strongly that it would be wrong for me to resign when I believe that God brought me here to Friends of His. George, I love this church. I have placed my intentions under a microscope and I know I am not doing this out of stubbornness or arrogance, or to in any way hurt the people I genuinely love. It's just that it would be wrong not to be true to myself."

"So you will not resign."

"I will not resign, George."

"I was afraid you were going to say that. Well, thank you for meeting with me."

I asked if he would join me for a short tour of our new prayer garden that I had designed. His refusal was cold. George knew he was about to "execute" me, and he didn't want to have to pretend everything was okay between us.

When I returned with Gary for the board meeting, everyone was uncomfortable. (The board of each *Cumberland Presbyterian* church is referred to as "the session.") The session members were milling around in the kitchen area of the office building where Marilyn, Michael's wife, was serving coffee and refreshments. I thought this odd. Michael assured me that Marilyn would not be staying, but when the meeting was finally called to order, Marilyn was still there.

For me, that night will always be a dark memory, filled with pain and anguish. The meeting began with everyone having the opportunity to say whatever they wished. Gary and I were totally exposed in front of them, as though we were laid out on the table naked, and they were operating on us without anesthesia. I listened as people I loved spoke very coldly about us, as if we were just an issue and not their friends and brothers in Christ. Doc Whitten spoke in favor of us. The gay elder again affirmed his support. But the others made negative statements that still ring in my ears.

"The Bible says homosexuality is a sin and an unacceptable lifestyle for a Christian."

"We have to take into consideration the reputation of our church."

One woman said that she was not in favor of a series of discussions on this issue. She wanted, rather, to "get *this* behind us" because she was not willing to suffer through another painful week.

I thought, "What about the gay people who have suffered for years, without any help from the churches?" But I remained quiet.

The mood became even more tense when an elder asked if Michael had known about this before I came out to them. Michael admitted that he had. Why then, had Michael not brought this to their attention? Michael, usually very smooth and easy going at session meetings, hedged to avoid saying anything that would sway the vote either way. He admitted knowing the truth about me, but never gave a real reason why he had not told the elders. I kept waiting for Michael to say, *"The reason I have not said anything to you about this is because I personally do not have a problem with Randy being gay. I believe in him. He is not just my associate; he is a trusted friend. I have seen his devotion to God and to this church. As my associate in ministry, Randy has faithfully fulfilled his duties to me and to this church community."*

I waited for his affirmation, but an endorsement of me and of my ministry never came. As I twisted in the wind, Michael chose to remain silent. What about that promise he had made at Esther's two days earlier, that he would tell the session that he had no problem with my relationship with Gary?

After the elders spoke, Gary and I were asked if we had anything to say. Gary declined. I struggled to put into words what I was feeling. I knew I should speak, and silently prayed that the Holy Spirit would help me choose my words carefully so I would not be speaking from a place of anger and hurt, but from my heart.

"I just want to say that it has been very painful to sit here and listen as some of you have judged Gary and me unfit to serve this congregation. I want you to know that we love this church and we love each of you. I have prayed with you. I have grieved with you in sad times, and celebrated with you in happy times. I can truthfully say that if any of you were being discriminated against at work, I would go to the mat for you. But the majority of you are not willing to do this for me. Friends of His has marketed itself as a church for the misfit, a church for those who have not found their place in mainline churches. If you fire me, you will be going against the very mission statement on which this church was established.

"There is a very special blessing that God reserves for those churches that stand with the outcast. He tells us that if we will do this, He will cause our light to shine out of obscurity. Many have come here to this community of believers because they felt that, finally, they had found a safe place to worship. If you fire me then they will fear for their own safety. They may not be gay. Their rejection from other churches and family and friends may have been for other reasons. But the message you send to each of them by firing me will be, 'They found something in Randy's life that was unacceptable to them, and it may be just a matter of time before they find something unacceptable in me.'

"People will never again feel they can be vulnerable in this place of worship. Some of us who are members of this church have been wounded by other churches, and we felt we had found a safe place here at Friends of His. If you fire me, we will be wounded yet again. God will provide a place for us to worship if you turn us away. God is faithful. But Friends of His will lose the special, fresh innocence and blessing that it has enjoyed since its birth four years ago. The blessing God has given to us because we have opened our arms to the disenfranchised will be removed. I love this church, and I do not feel that Gary's and my loving, committed, Christ-centered relationship disqualifies us from ministry here. I have asked that you not make a rash decision. I have asked that we have meetings and dialogue about this issue. How could it be wrong to take time to make sure you are doing God's will? Gary and I love you. We love this church. Please think about what you are doing here tonight."

At this point, Marilyn Qualls spoke up.

"Randy, Mike and I have served this church for five years. We have sacrificed and worked to build it. If there was something in our lives that we felt would harm the church, we would resign. Do you not see that your unwillingness to resign could cause the church to split?"

She began to cry. "If you love this church Randy, *please*, step down. "

I remained calm and repeated my convictions.

"Marilyn, I cannot ethically resign because I do not believe that my loving, monogamous, Christ-centered relationship with Gary Eddy disqualifies me from ministry."

"But Randy," Marilyn persisted. "Gay people are such a small minority in our church, and we have to think about the majority and how this will affect them. We can't make a decision based on a few people in the church."

Later, I thought about the story of the good shepherd who goes out looking for the one lost lamb, even though 99 were safe in the fold. But at the time, I simply repeated, calmly, what I had said before. A third time, Marilyn begged me to resign.

I could feel anger building inside me towards her. First of all, she wasn't even supposed to be there. Secondly, she would not stop. She made her point and I responded twice. I saw no need to be badgered over and over. The third time she questioned me as to why I would not resign, one of the women on the session spoke up.

"Marilyn, if Randy truly believes God has accepted his relationship with Gary, I can understand why he feels he can't resign."

At this point in the meeting, George weighed in.

"I want to say that I know there is a lot of love for Randy in this church. I know his ministry has been appreciated by many of the members. Randy led worship at our new church development retreat recently, and I experienced personally his sincere ministry. I feel convicted for asking you to do this, but because of my position, I must ask you to terminate Randy's position as minister of music and assistant to the pastor. Now I know this may not be a popular decision. If there has to be a heavy, blame me and the Board of Missions. I understand that there are other gay people in the church. I would ask that you encourage our gay brother who has been elected by this church to stay on the session as an elder. That is my advice to you."

Wow! I was amazed that this man could sit there and say that he felt what he was asking them to do was wrong. He used the word "convicted," which means proven guilty. So he seemed to be saying in effect, "I feel guilty and judged in asking you to do this, but because of my position, I must do the wrong thing."

Doc Whitten, seeing that I was about to go down, started pleading my case. "Are we saying that these boys are wicked? Is that what we are saying? Have you walked out in that prayer garden? I have. I come down here during the day and I commune with God out there in those woods, thanks to Randy's dream and vision. I was very fortunate to be able to help Randy clear the path when he first marked out the plans for the garden walk. When you stroll down those paths and see the crosses and read the scriptures, you feel the presence of God. That garden was Randy's dream… and you are going to call these boys wicked? They are a part of us. They are members of this church. Are we calling them wicked? We can't throw them away."

I looked at this dear man, the oldest member of the session. With tears in his eyes, he stood and waved his hands in the air to punctuate his heartfelt support for us. I knew that they were coming to a vote, and that more things were going to be said that I didn't feel Gary and I should have to endure. So I stood.

"Gary and I have spoken our hearts to you, and I don't think we need to be here any longer."

Gary was so relieved when I decided it was time for us to leave. Although he had remained silent through this whole meeting, Gary felt every attack that had been aimed at me. I believe that a minister's spouse is hurt even more than the minister in situations like this. It is difficult to see the person you love being attacked, and at the same time to know that anything you might do to protect him could make the outcome worse. As we stood to leave, Doc Whitten jumped up and hugged us both.

"I'm proud of you boys. I am sorry you had to go through this mess."

We walked out the door and into the night. Suddenly, I felt as if my legs were about to give way. The tension I went through in that room felt like it sheared ten years off my life. Gary and I were too numb to say much on the way home.

About an hour later, the doorbell rang. Michael and Marilyn had stopped by to tell us the outcome of the meeting. I invited them in.

"Well, they voted to terminate your employment at Friends of His and to give you two months of severance pay."

There was silence in the room. I honestly did not know what Michael wanted me to say. "Thank you," or, "Gosh, how generous." Choice curse words were not in my vocabulary, so I just sat there. Michael broke the embarrassing silence.

"I feel like my right arm, the very person that God gave to our church to continue our growth, has been taken away from us, and I don't know how we will go on from here."

More silence filled our apartment. I was numb, and certainly not feeling up to dispensing any warm fuzzies toward our two guests. I was reeling from Marilyn's continued questioning of my love for Friends of His, and from Michael's total lack of support. I had made a vow to myself, and to the Lord, not to react in a negative way, but this was being put to the test. Michael interrupted the silence.

"This was a very tough thing for the session to deal with, but surely you could feel the love for you around that table."

I could not believe my ears! Love? That was definitely NOT what I felt! I marveled at his ability to rationalize cowardice into some twisted imitation of love.

"No, Michael," I broke in. "I did *not* feel love around that table. I felt attacked."

"Well, I would hope that you guys would remain at the church."

"Michael, that's not going to happen. I am not going to remain a member of a church that does not consider me *Christian* enough to serve because of my marriage to Gary."

"Well, I can see where you would feel that way. Do you have any suggestions how I should handle telling the congregation Sunday morning?"

"That is your problem Michael, not mine."

This time the silence was an exclamation mark. How *dare* he ask me for help when he had silently watched as I was fired, without any words of support for me! Now, for him to ask me for help in figuring out how to save face in front of the congregation? I was outraged! Gary's body language communicated that he was more than ready for the conversation to end, and for Michael and Marilyn to leave.

Michael mumbled, "I don't know what else to say."

"Say 'good night, Gracie.'" Gary snapped, with a definite edge.

I was so proud of him at that moment. Michael responded by asking if we could have prayer. I nodded yes. "Could we could join hands?"

I stood. We started to form the circle, but Marilyn was standing to the side. She was unsure if I would want her to be a part of the prayer chain. Michael tried to give voice to Marilyn's hesitancy.

"Marilyn wants you to know, Randy, that she does love you, she just doesn't understand you sometimes."

I forced myself to look over at her and offered her my hand which she accepted, completing the circle.

Michael prayed, "God, how it must break your heart when we do not do what is right."

I did not hear much more. In those words, Michael confessed that what had taken place earlier was wrong. But this would be the last time he would be so transparent until years later.

As Michael and Marilyn were leaving, he turned to me, still trying to make an awkward situation less awkward with humor. "Well, let's look on the bright side. We can take vacations together now since one of us doesn't have to be at Friends of His while the other is away."

"Goodnight, Michael." I said and closed the door.

He and Marilyn spun into "damage control" mode the next day, visiting members of the church to give a heads-up about the announcement coming on Sunday.

Chapter 43

An Eight-Legged Night Visitor

When I woke up the next morning, I seemed to remember being stung in the middle of the night. Pulling back the top covers, we found a dead spider. I must have rolled over on it in my sleep. By evening, I had a fever of 101 degrees, and the place on my back where I had been bitten had turned red and was spreading. We headed to the hospital emergency room. I was beside myself with grief and hopelessness.

The thought occurred to me—what would Jerry Falwell say about this spider bite? I could just hear him now: "Sure, you come out to the elders of the church and then you go home to your *marriage bed* and get bit by a spider! Don't you think God is trying to tell you something?"

My thoughts were all negative. My ministry was over. I would never have another happy day. Still, deep inside my heart God whispered, "Trust me Randy. Trust me."

At the emergency room, the front desk receptionist asked if I had insurance. After I answered no, she asked, *"Marital status?"*

I didn't know what to say. In my mind, this whole firing had been over my marriage to Gary. Yet the state of Arkansas did not recognize us as a married couple. So how was I supposed to answer?

Gary answered *for* me. "Single."

This hurt. Another slap in the face. How unfair that I could not let the nurse know that Gary was my spouse and would be taking care of me.

"Church affiliation?"

I hesitated before emotionally blurting out, "None."

"Pastor?"

"No," I responded as tears started rolling down my cheeks. I had not anticipated how painful a simple questionnaire for admittance to the emergency room could be. When the doctor came into the examining room, he looked at my back and immediately identified the bite.

"That was definitely a brown recluse spider. In fact, it is one of the worst bites I have ever seen."

He told me to sit tight and he would be right back. When he returned, he brought with him another doctor and a young intern.

"I want them to see what kind of damage one of these little fellows can cause."

They were all stunned by what they saw. The doctor then told me that I would need a series of treatments in a hyperbaric oxygen tank to speed up the healing process. He said that if I did not have the treatments, the area on my back that had turned red would start decomposing and I would have to have skin grafts to replace the rotted tissue. The oxygen treatments would heal the area and leave me with just a small scar.

I asked if this would be expensive and he said yes, but not as costly as skin grafts. I was to report to the hospital the next morning at 8:00 a.m. for my first treatment. Where were we going to get the money for these treatments? I didn't even have a job!

When we got home, our dear friends from church, Tony Morvant and her daughter Angel, dropped by with ice cream and Oreo cookies. They were very concerned about me. Peggy Campolo also called to let me know that she had received my message about my termination and the spider bite. She was so angry at the elders and the pastor for the way the meeting turned out. She assured me of her support. I was overwhelmed with her generosity. Peggy and her husband Tony were on vacation, and yet she called regularly to check on me.

The next day we went to the hospital for my first hyperbaric oxygen treatment. I put on the cotton scrubs they gave me to wear. I was wheeled on a gurney up to one end of a cylinder-shaped clear chamber and slid inside. When the end of the cylinder was closed, I was glad I wasn't claustrophobic, because I had to stay in this device for two hours. Knowing that Gary was in the room calmed me.

When the treatment was finished, I was told that the process would probably affect my vocal chords and cause some hoarseness for a few days, and that the steroid I had to take could cause me some feelings of anxiety. Great timing! This was all I needed, anxiety on top of all the stress. In two days, I was scheduled to perform *The Life of Christ* drama in a Baptist church. In my depressed state, I feared that we would drive up to the church and see picket signs saying, "Go home, faggots."

The nurse told me I could go home, but had to come back that afternoon for another treatment. Gary and I decided to clean out my desk and pick up my personal belongings at the church. It had to be done, and I was ready to get it behind me.

We arrived at the church office to find both Doc Whitten and Michael. Doc was so happy to see us and informed me that he was trying to come up with a way to fight the decision of the elders. Michael, clearly uncomfortable, asked how I was feeling. I told them about the spider bite, and Doc asked to see it, so I raised my shirt and showed it to them. I told about the treatments that I would have to undertake for the next six days. Both men seemed empathetic. Then Doc turned to Michael and asked if there was something the church could do to save my position at Friends of His. Michael said nothing.

As Gary started cleaning out my office, I told Michael I wanted to talk to him for a few minutes.

"Michael, how do you feel about the outcome? How do you *really* feel?"

"Well, I believe the board wrestled with this issue and made the only decision they could, under the circumstances."

"So you think this outcome is the right one?"

"I am not saying it's 'the right one,' but I am saying that the board really had no choice other than to terminate you. The denominational Board of Missions took the decision out of their hands."

"Michael, what if you had had a vote? Would you have voted to keep me on?"

Michael was silent for a long time, then said, "I don't think I would have, in light of the situation."

I turned to leave.

"Randy, have you thought any more about how I should announce this to the congregation?"

"Michael, I told you, this is *your* problem. You deal with the mess. Whatever you do, I am sure you are going to cover your own butt!"

I was angry and hurt. Gary and I started carrying my stuff to the car. Feeling betrayed by my pastor and friend, I wanted to get out of there as quickly as possible and shake the dust off my shoes!

Later that day, as I lay in the cylinder, Michael's words came back to me. He was giving me an opportunity to shape the way my firing would be announced to the congregation. I didn't want him to give the impression I was leaving with my head down in shame. I wanted my church family to know my side of the issue. As I pondered this, I came up with a creative way to tell my side of the story. After the treatment, I called Michael.

"Does the offer still stand for me to have input into how you announce my firing?"

Michael assured me that he would do his best to carry out any special requests I had.

"I would like for you to read the letter I wrote to the elders when you make the announcement to the church. Then I want you to play a song from the cassette I recorded last year, 'I Know Where I Stand.' Will you do that?"

He told me he would read the letter and play the song on Sunday. The song was a confident affirmation of knowing my place in God's arms of grace and love.

The next day I had two treatments. The second one was difficult. It was stuffy and hot in the cylinder, and my rash did not respond well to the moisture from the sweat. It burned and itched, yet I had to lie very still. I was made even more miserable because I had plenty of time to think, and thinking was not something I enjoyed doing at a time when I had so many negative thoughts.

In desperation, I prayed. "Please, Jesus, don't let me grow bitter through this. I am hurting so badly right now. Don't let me do or say anything I will regret later. Let me somehow get to a place where I can forgive these people for what they have done to me. I know that you forgave the men who crucified you, even as you hung in agony on the cross. Please Jesus, help me find a way to forgive. Heal my broken heart."

When I got home, Peggy Campolo called. I reported what I had asked Michael to do.

Peggy listened and then said, "Randy, I wish you and Gary would be in the service when he reads the letter. I know if I were a member of that church, I would want you to be there, so that after the service I could ask you where we would be meeting for church next Sunday."

I relayed the idea to Gary.

"I don't think that's a good idea, but you can go if you feel you should. Just don't ask me to go. I refuse!"

He was angry with the church and with Michael for hurting me. Moreover, Gary was mad at God. Where had God been in this?

An hour later, Gary came back to me and said, "Well, God and I had a little talk, and even though I still don't think you should put yourself through the ordeal of sitting in church as they announce your firing, if you do decide to go, I will go with you."

What a loving, caring spouse God had given to me. "Thank you honey, but I have decided against going."

Gary uttered a big sigh of relief.

"I don't think God would require that of me," I added, "but I do want to find a way to show love in response to their unloving act."

Later that day, the idea came to me. I bought a bouquet of flowers and asked Gary to arrange them. The next morning, on our way to the hospital for my treatment, we slipped into Friends of His before anyone had arrived and placed the flowers on the altar table with a card that read, *"To our church family. We love you, Randy and Gary."*

As I lay in the tube during the treatment, I watched the clock tick away the minutes until it was time for the announcement. When we got home, I collapsed on the couch. As Gary handed me my expensive meds, the horror of our situation overwhelmed me. I began to cry. Gary reached out and held me as we both gave way to our grief in a flood of tears.

My friend Tony Morvant had gone to Friends of His that morning. She reported to me that the whole service had been like my funeral. The music lacked emotion, and the sermon was not memorable. Michael announced that after the service the church had to take care of a little business. Michael told visitors they were welcome to leave. Most of the members stayed. Michael told the congregation about my firing, then recognized the ministry that I had shared with the church for four years and said that I would be missed.

He acknowledged that there were gay and lesbian members and said he wanted them to know they were welcome to serve the church in voluntary positions. Then he read my letter. When he finished, the tape began and the congregation heard me singing one last time, a song by Bruce Carroll.

Just like an actor, unsure of my lines,
I lived my life for other people, one lie at a time.
Desperate for approval, always tryin' to look good,
Never sure of who I was or where I stood.
Till You came into my heart, and exposed me with Your light,
Till You touched me with Your love,
And You healed me with Your life.

I know where I stand, strong and secure,
I finally know who I am, I'm myself and I'm Yours.
When I stand on Your promise, I always stand tall,
Even when I fall, I know where I stand.

So good to be real now, to know and be known,
Resting in Your perfect love, my heart is finally home.
Completely forgiven of all that I've done,
Now I'm living my life for an audience of one.
Finally sure of who I am, and I'm sure of who I'm not,
The insecurity is gone, because I live on the Rock.

I no longer live my life by what other people say
But I only live for You, 'cause Your love will never change.
And though people let me down, You'll never turn away,
No You'll never turn away, that's why I know where I stand.

"I Know Where I Stand" (Bruce Carroll & Claire D. Cloninger)
Lyrics reprinted by permission of Word Music Publishing,
25 Music Square West, Nashville, TN 37203

People began weeping. A young woman stood to her feet. Micah, the pastor's daughter, joined her. One by one, the whole youth group stood, followed by almost everyone in the congregation. As the song continued, those standing formed a circle and joined hands. When the music ended, everyone walked out in silence.

My friends Michael and Suzanne told me they sent their young son and daughter to the gym area to play ball until the meeting ended. The children, however, had slipped back in while Michael read my letter and announced my termination.

On the way home, they asked why the church had fired me. Suzanne struggled for the right words. Finally she said, "You know how Randy and Gary live together? Well, they love each other the way Mommy and Daddy love each other and the church thinks that is wrong, so they fired Randy."

Suzanne said the kids were quiet for a few miles, and then their 10-year-old spoke up. "Well, I don't understand what the big deal is! Randy is still Randy!"

Randy and Peggy Campolo

Chapter 44

Fallout from Being Fired

Gary and I attended monthly meetings of PFLAG, (Parents, Family and Friends of Lesbians and Gays), a support group. We shared the pain of my firing with our PFLAG friends. They were amazed that people who call themselves Christians could treat me this way. Esther, a heterosexual, orthodox Jewish woman was so kind to Gary and me. She sent cards and had us over for dinner. She decided to write Michael.

Dear Reverend Qualls,

I am writing this letter after lengthy and careful consideration. It is not an easy, or pleasant, letter for me to write. However I found I could not sit back and remain quiet…The subject of my letter is Randy McCain. As you well know, Randy was an honest, loyal and hard-working member of your church. He was dedicated to you as his boss, his pastor, and his friend. He felt a special and unique bond with the members [of Friends of His]. He never tired of praising you and the work being done within your church.

As a friend of Randy's and Gary's, I share not only their pain, but also their feelings of anger and betrayal toward you. …You chose to take the easiest and safest route for yourself by firing Randy. …Your reason for doing so—to avoid a scandal—is unacceptable. Someone in your position should be more aware of and sensitive to human needs and conditions. As someone unfamiliar with the Christian Bible, I am curious to learn what parts of your Bible justify the action you chose to take.

It is disappointing to realize that, over the past 2,000 years, the Christian church has not advanced much further than the dogma which spawned the Crusades.

Esther mailed me a copy of the letter she had sent Michael. It made me feel good to know of her support, but sad that someone outside of Christianity had to see such an ugly display of intolerance.

Peggy Campolo kept in close touch by phone. She sent me a gift, along with a letter that has become one of my most cherished possessions. Inside a small wooden box was a brown recluse spider! I was startled because the spider looked so real. On closer inspection, I realized it was a lapel pin. The letter contained things I needed to hear.

Dear Randy,

You have been on my mind and in my prayers, and I hope so much you are feeling better. I am well aware that, when the focus is off the damage that the little brown spider did to you, you will have to fight being weighed down by the grave injustice that has been done to you, and thoughts of future plans. I want you to know that I think that you have been a brave and loving person to come out as you have. It is a sad fact of life that no cause, however just, gets anywhere without the sacrifices of real people who hurt and bleed. I give thanks to God that you, and Gary too, are willing to stand firm. Someone has said that all great truths are doomed to begin their lives as heresies.

As I told you on the phone, Tony had some doubts about my sending you this gift. But as soon as I saw it, in a wonderful little gift shop in Provincetown, I knew that it would look great on your coffee table or your lapel. What I want is for you to look at it, remembering last weekend, and to see that weekend in all of the horror you could not prevent, but also to see, in the spider, how something very small could change so very much and affect something (in this case, somebody—you) so much bigger than itself. The spider's effect was bad, but I see what you have done as something very big that matters very much for ultimate good. Don't lose sight of that.

You and Gary need to remember how the ugly scene at the bridge in Alabama turned the civil rights movement around, and of course we all know the great glory and good that came from Calvary. I know that these days are a Calvary for you, and our Lord knows too. Be comforted by that and don't lose your hope. Please keep in touch—even a post card with news of how you are doing will be very welcome.

Peace and love,

Peggy

I liked Peggy's take on the spider incident a lot more than the one I had imagined I would get from Jerry Falwell.

A minister friend also gave me his thoughts on the spider bite. "You were in a place where you should feel safe, your bed, when you were attacked by the spider. To me, this is an analogy of what happened to you at your church. You were attacked by the board in a place where you should have been safe—the church."

As the days turned into weeks, I wrestled with my feelings for my former pastor and friend, Michael. He dropped by our house unexpectedly one afternoon to see how we were doing. Gary was mowing the lawn. Michael asked me what he could do for us.

"You can get me my job back."

"I can't do that, Randy."

"Then you can admit to me that you did not stand up for me and you are sorry."

"But Randy, how can I say I am sorry for something I do not feel I did to you?"

"Michael, do you really think you did everything possible to save my position?"

"I think I did everything I *could* do, yes."

"Then we don't have anything else to talk about."

"Randy, why are you so angry at me? I'm your friend. I am not the enemy."

"Well, right now you feel like the enemy to me. Why shouldn't I be angry and disappointed in you? Here you are, safe in your job, because you did not take a stand for me. On the other hand, I am unemployed and wounded. Michael, you say that you have no problem with my ministry. You say that God's hand is on me and has blessed me with ministry gifts."

"Yes, I do… "

"Well," I interrupted. "Don't you think it is hypocritical to fire me, and yet ask the gay elder to stay on?"

"Yes, it is hypocritical, but it is the only possible stand the church can take, a stand *not* to take a stand. Randy, I believe in you and your gifts. I am convinced that gays should be able to hold positions of ministry in the church."

"Then Michael, *say* that in the pulpit. Preach your convictions for a change! Take a stand!"

"You know I can't do that."

"Michael, listen to what you are saying. You are telling me you cannot preach your convictions."

"Randy, even if I had taken a stand for you, it wouldn't have changed the outcome. You would have still lost your job."

"But Michael, I would have still had my pastor and good friend to go to for help and support."

Gary walked in, most unhappy to find Michael sitting there. Michael continued trying to defend himself to me.

"Randy, again, how can I apologize when I don't feel guilty? You are asking me to do the same thing the conservative members are asking me to do. You are asking me to take sides."

"So Michael, do you not believe that there is a right and wrong in this situation?"

"No, there is no heavy or enemy in this. I am sorry that you see the church as your adversary. I am proud of the way our board handled this situation. They made the only decision they could. Friends of His will remain a safe place for gay and lesbian people and they are welcome to serve in any *voluntary* position they wish."

"Michael, the reputation of Friends of His as a safe place for the outcast has been badly damaged. I cannot believe you can sit there with a straight face and say that gays are safe there after what the church has done to me."

Gary spoke up. "Michael, there are young people at Friends of His who, in the past, have made derogatory statements about gay people. What you and the elders have done gives them permission to say ugly things about gays, and even to do physical violence to them."

"Well, interestingly enough Gary, Chris, who is one of the ringleaders for that kind of remark, asked me what happened to Randy. When I told him, he said to me, 'That's not right.' I said to him, 'But Chris, you're the one who is always talking about beating up queers.' 'Yes,' Chris answered, 'but that's me. The church should be different!'"

"See Michael," Gary continued. "The church is still giving him that message, that gays are defective and not as good as everyone else. In fact, the message you give these kids is that there is something terribly wrong with gays. I don't even know why you are here in our home, Michael."

"I came by to see how you are doing."

"Look," Gary said. "We don't need your kind of help. We can't trust your help."

Michael stood up. "Well, I see that my presence here is just making the situation worse. Maybe it would be a good thing if I do not come by for a while."

"Maybe so, Michael." I responded.

Michael walked over, shook both our hands, and walked out the door. I honestly wanted to forgive Michael, because I hate holding grudges, but the wound was too fresh. I needed time to work through my confusion and pain. While I didn't know what the future would be for Gary and me, I knew that I had been called to ministry. Yet, how could I fulfill this call if there were no place for me to use my gifts in the church?

One evening as I chatted with Peggy Campolo on the phone, she said to me, "I believe that you have the gifts to pastor. You have a pastor's heart. I think you need to prayerfully consider the possibility that God is calling you to begin a new work, a church where *everyone* is welcome."

I prayed, and soon wrote Peggy.

I feel that, in the past, I have used my pastoral gifts as an assistant pastor. I have made hospital calls to pray for the sick and I have preached when the pastor was out of town, and, while ministering to those with AIDS, officiated at many funerals. I have done Christian counseling. But, as to whether the pastoral ministry is the plan of God for me at this point in my life, I honestly cannot say. I have decided to carry on the weekly Bible studies in our home that Gary and I have been hosting for the past two years, although not as a part of the ministry of Friends of His as it has been in the past. I do have a tremendous burden for those who have no place to worship. Please be in prayer with me about this. I will keep you posted.

Gary went along with continuing the Wednesday night Bible study, but he was not overly enthused about ministry. I understood his hesitancy. Both of us had been wounded, and we didn't really want to go through anything like that again. Gary was not excited about the thought of starting a church and neither was I. I had never in my wildest dreams imagined founding a new church.

Chapter 45

God's Provision in a Card

Even though my position at Friends of His had ended, I still had avenues for ministry. I was singing at a Christian coffee house in town and receiving invitations to minister in churches around the state. At one such church in eastern Arkansas, the pastor Mark and his wife Sherry were old friends of mine. I was influential in getting the two of them together and served as best man at their wedding.

Mark and Sherry supported me back when I was fighting homosexuality. I performed my play, *The Life of St. Paul*, at their church right before Gary moved to Arkansas. I had not spoken to them since then, except to set up a return date for a performance of my play, *The Life of Christ*. Two weeks before I was to appear at their church, the phone rang early one morning, just after breakfast.

"Randy, this is Mark, and I need to talk with you. I have been troubled in my spirit about something and I just need to ask you a question."

Immediately I knew what was coming. I didn't know if I was prepared to answer an inquisition. I panicked and pushed the *off* button on the phone, ending the call. I stood there in shock for a minute or two. Then I rushed to the kitchen and told Gary what had happened.

"You just hung up on him?"

"Yes, I wasn't prepared to be confronted this early in the morning. I needed a minute to decide what I wanted to say. Now I'm going to call him back. Please be praying for me that I will say the right thing."

I went back into the bedroom and dialed Mark's number. When he heard my voice he said,

"Randy, we got disconnected."

"Yes, I know," I responded, trying to sound casual.

Mark told me that he had called my house a few days ago, and that afterwards the Holy Spirit had revealed to him that I was struggling with homosexuality again. Not for a moment did I believe that the Holy Spirit was outing me! When Mark called, he heard the message on the answering machine, "You have reached the home of Randy McCain and Gary Eddy."

Knowing my past struggles with my sexuality, and finding out that I was now living with a man, Mark put two and two together. Thus, his knowledge was hardly supernatural.

"Randy, I must ask you…are you *again* struggling with the sin of homosexuality?"

"Well Mark, I have struggled in the past with my sexual orientation. I wanted to be heterosexual. But Mark, I have come to the conclusion that I am a gay man, and God loves and accepts me for who I am. I'm committed to Christ and I'm no longer struggling with my homosexuality. For the first time in my life, I truly know who I am in Christ Jesus."

Mark lost his composure, comparing me to Jimmy Swaggart and Jim Bakker, two televangelists who had been through public scandals because of their sexual misconduct.

"You are giving into lustful desires! Randy, I have struggled personally with an addiction to porn. I know that God can deliver you from your sexual addiction because He delivered me."

"Mark, God has delivered me from sexual addiction. My relationship with Gary is not an unhealthy lifestyle. Our relationship is based on love and mutual respect. This is so different from one-night stands with anonymous men. My love for Gary is based on my love for Jesus. I have never loved Jesus more!"

"Randy, you are so deceived! I cannot have you minister to my congregation. You should never go into a church without confessing your sin to the pastor."

"But Mark, I do not believe that my loving, committed, Christ-centered relationship with Gary is a sin."

"Randy, Satan has you so blinded to the truth. I'm telling you right now that I will tell as many ministers as I can about you so they will not invite into their church someone who is living in open rebellion to God!"

I was amazed at how calm I was while Mark was confronting me, but the moment I hung up the receiver, I started getting shaky inside. I walked into the kitchen and calmly reported to Gary what had happened.

"Well, I guess this is what we expected, Randy."

"I know, but it *hurts*, and it brings back so many painful memories. All I've ever wanted to do is share the good news of Jesus with others, but now every door of ministry seems to be slamming shut."

On the way to the post office, I poured out my frustrations to God. "God, I really felt that I heard you tell me that it was time to come out and be the Christian gay man you created me to be. But since I obeyed you, I've been fired from my job at *Friends of His* and now my performances are starting to be cancelled. GOD, WHERE ARE YOU RIGHT NOW?! Are you going to protect Gary and me? I need to know that you are going to be there for us. Please don't ask us to go out on a limb and then saw it off behind us. I need to know that you are aware of our situation and that you are going to take care of us."

I turned on the radio. At that moment, Sandi Patti was singing, "There's a hand on my shoulder, through the storm, however it blows. There's a hand—a hand on my shoulder. Stays with me wherever I go."

I began to weep and thank God for this little heaven-sent assurance. Little did I know an even more dramatic answer to my prayer was on its way. God was going to make sure I knew He heard my cry.

Two weeks later, when Gary and I went to pick up our mail, we had received a card sent by two-day priority mail. It was from Lillian Lobb, a sweet lesbian pastor in California. We met Lillian while at the Houston conference, and she had shown a great appreciation for my ministry in drama. The card read,

Randy and Gary, I have no idea what is going on in your lives right now, but the Lord has instructed me to send you this check. I trust that there is a need that needs to be met. God wants you to know that He knows your needs.

The check was for $500! I became very emotional, right there in the post office. I was so demanding of the Lord, asking him to assure me that He would take care of us. Now, I wept as I realized that, on the exact day we would have deposited the love offering we would have received at Mark's church, God had arranged for us to receive a check for twice the amount I had been paid the last time I had ministered there! I showed the card to Gary and he shared my awareness of the timing. We both felt that Lillian's message was an unmistakable response from God to my prayer. I had asked God not to forget us in our hour of need, and God had responded through his servant Lillian. We thanked God for His loving conformation that we were headed in the right direction. When I called Lillian to thank her, I let her in on how God used her in His conspiracy of grace.

Right after this exhilarating experience, we were to face more rejection, and also an opportunity to cause damage and hurt to the church that had wronged me. A reporter from a local newspaper wanted to run a story about my firing. He pressured me to name the church and the pastor in the article. I told the reporter that I would agree to be interviewed as long as the name of the church was not included. Jesus had said to bless those who curse you and to pray for those who despitefully use you. I found it easier to *quote* Jesus than to put His words into practice, yet I managed to refrain from allowing the paper to write an exposé on Friends of His. The story did not name the church and gave me a fictitious name.

The reporter quoted Michael without revealing his name. Michael's response surprised me: "'It's beyond tough, way beyond tough,' said the pastor, who feels "nothing but compassion and acceptance and warmth" for gay Christians. His hope is that homosexuality will one day cease to be an issue in church."

Soon after the article ran, I was told I could no longer minister at the Christian coffee house where I had been a headliner for the past three years. When the owner, John, called saying he needed to talk to me, I somehow knew what the meeting would be about.

"Randy," John started out. "There have been rumors going around that you are gay. I want you to tell me the truth. Are you gay?"

"Yes, John, I am gay."

"Well Randy, people are calling and saying that if I continue to let a gay man sing, they will boycott my store. I've received calls from some of the other singers saying that they will no longer sing at my place if I allow you to minister here. As much as I hate to do this, I must ask you to not sing."

I went home and wept as I told Gary about my latest trial.

In the midst of my pain, I found comfort in a quote: *I would rather be hated for who I am than to be loved for who I am not.*

Although the rejection one suffers after coming out of the closet is painful, the freedom of not having to hide one's true identity far outweighs the pain. I have spoken to many who are questioning whether or not they should take that first step outside the closet. Although I cannot tell them what to do, I can testify to the night-and-day difference *coming out* has made in my own life. There are so many miracles I never would have experienced had I stayed in the closet. I would have spent my whole life wondering if the people who loved the Randy I pretended to be would have loved the real me. And I would never have known the healthy, loving relationship I enjoy with Gary. Never would I trade this open and unashamed life for my old life of shadows, fear, and half-truths. Jesus spoke powerfully to this when He said, "You shall know the truth and the truth shall set you free!" (John 8:32)

In the tsunami-like waves of rejection and ostracism we were experiencing at the end of 1995, it was hard to see, let alone imagine, anything positive coming out of it. Yet, in my pain, God's Holy Spirit kept speaking to my heart about forgiveness. Each day as I walked in the neighborhood for exercise, God challenged me to forgive those who had hurt me. I sensed God's Spirit saying, "Randy, you need to pray a blessing on Friends of His and on those who fired you."

At first, this seemed impossible. But after several days of the Holy Spirit's prodding, I gave in to the Lord's leading. I prayed a simple prayer asking God to bless the church and those members of the board who had voted against me, and to bless their families.

Though I had experienced a breakthrough with my feelings towards Friends of His, Gary was tightly holding onto a lot of hurt and anger. As he drove by Friends of

His each morning on his way to work, God nudged him, saying, "*Gary, bless them as you go by.*" Gary refused. He did not curse them, but he would not bless them.

I wanted him to experience the freedom I had found in forgiveness. One day I said to him, "I sure wish you and God would make up."

That week, as Gary drove past our old church, God's Spirit, again nudged him to pray a blessing, and this time Gary gave in.

"Oh, all right! God bless Friends of His. I forgive them for what they did to Randy and me."

That, for Gary, was a major breakthrough!

Chapter 46

Birth of a New Church

During the four months after I was terminated, Gary and I did not attend church. Our Wednesday night Bible study took the place of Sunday worship. That group was a wonderful mix of people.

When someone would ask me where I worshiped, I said, "I attend a home church." The group began to feel like a church. But to actually say that we were starting one seemed scary. Was that what God wanted? I knew that I did not know the first thing about starting a church. God led me to Friends of His, where I worked more than four years for a pastor who was pioneering a new church development. I learned much as Michael's apprentice and associate. But I never envisioned myself as anything but a pastor's assistant or an evangelist. Now I found myself face-to-face with spiritually hungry people needing a pastor-shepherd.

My prayers were filled with questions. God's answer came on December 26, 1995. I was meditating in prayer on what to speak about in our Bible study that week, when I sensed God say, "Randy, it is time to step out in faith. It is time to give birth to a new church."

The message was so real to me that I immediately shared the exciting news with Gary. He promised to support me. We called the individuals who attended our Bible study to tell them that Sunday morning, January 7, 1996, would be the first official worship service of Open Door Community Church. The name was inspired by the church my Grandma McCain had joined, which wanted people to know that its doors were open to *all* who would follow Jesus.

At this same time, God brought two wonderful men into our lives who would be co-laborers in developing Open Door, even though they lived over 900 miles away from us. Tim Malfo and David Plunkett were introduced to us by a pastor friend from Denver. Coincidentally, they were in Little Rock the weekend before our first service. They came to pick up equipment they purchased for the new print shop they were opening in Denver. Our pastor friend had asked if they could stay with us. We instantly felt a true kinship.

David had been in ministry before and Tim was a down to earth guy who had never been in ministry, but loved Jesus. David and I started talking theology right off the bat, while Gary and Tim talked about their favorite movies and less "spiritual" matters. David loved the message of God's grace as much as I did. We talked non-stop about how grace had first changed our lives, then our theology.

Given what we were going through, Gary and I were struggling financially, and were thrilled when Tim and David treated us to dinner and a movie. I had the distinct impression that our meeting had been ordained by God.

Our new friends were interested in our commitment to start Open Door. They vowed to be partners with us in prayer and to help us in any way they could. Tim and David would prove to be important to us in the years that followed. Their printing business would become very successful, and they provided Open Door Community Church with thousands of dollars in free printing.

On Sunday, January 7, 1996, Gary and I met together for worship with one other person. The next week we had five! I will never forget how awkward I felt getting up to preach to my spouse and a few of our friends, but from the first Sunday we had worship bulletins and structure to our services. God impressed on my heart, that we were never to refer to ourselves as a *gay* church. We were to worship so that all would feel welcome. This meant that we would be sensitive to the minorities in our group. From the beginning, non-gay individuals worshiped with those who were gay. I took heat for refusing to refer to Open Door as a gay church. The naysayers were many.

"You are a gay man and you are the pastor," critics would tell me. "So you should expect to have a church full of gay males. The straight folk won't come because you are gay, and the lesbian women won't come because you are male."

"But those dividing walls need to come down," I replied.

God showed me a vision of the church He wanted it to be: a place where everyone was welcome, a church filled with grannies and babies, with gay sons and daughters, their parents, and their friends and neighbors.

I knew many non-gay people were tired of attending churches where they heard the pastor ridicule and demonize other people. Gay people were not the only ones who needed a place to worship where they did not have to wear armor to protect themselves from hate-filled statements from the pulpit. People were hungry to worship in an atmosphere of God's extravagant love.

As I prepared my sermons, I focused the message on the struggles that we all have in common. God kept encouraging my heart, despite criticism and questioning from others, of my ability to launch a church from scratch. I wrote Peggy to share the news of the new church.

Dear Peggy,

Well, Open Door Community Church has started meeting on Sunday mornings! We have eight who are attending. We are few, but we share a sweet awareness of Jesus! There is a lot of talk about the church within the gay community and I think that as soon as we can find a public place to meet, more will come.

One day, I received a call informing me that a young man who attended Friends of His was in the hospital. His family wanted me to visit him. On my way, I prepared myself for the chance I might run into Michael. When I arrived, there stood my former pastor and friend. I visited and prayed with the patient and family. After I said goodbye and headed out the door, I realized that Michael was following me.

"It's my 40th birthday today, and I would like to have someone to eat lunch with. Can I buy your lunch?"

How could I say no to that? I walked with Michael to his car and we drove to a nice restaurant not far from the hospital.

"So what are you going to do to celebrate the big forty?" I asked.

"This is it."

"You mean the church isn't throwing you a big party? Forty is a major milestone."

"No, and frankly that is okay by me."

The combination of being tired and feeling sorry for this man, who did so much for people and received very little back, put me in the right mindset to begin the journey to a renewed friendship with Michael.

"Michael, I have missed you."

"Well, I've missed you too, Randy. I really have. Look, I am sorry I have hurt you. It's obvious that I let you down."

"You know Michael, I have tried to figure out what it was that you did that hurt me so deeply. I think it boils down to this: you treated me like an issue instead of a person who was your friend."

"Randy, you know me better than anyone on the planet and I have truly missed our talks. I've missed our friendship."

"Michael, I have heard rumors that the folks at Friends of His are saying that they think I am bitter, but I can truthfully tell you that I am not bitter. Hurt, yes, but not bitter. I am well aware of how damaging bitterness can be to the person harboring it. So when the bitter feelings came, I confessed them to Jesus. You know, to me true forgiveness is not retaliating."

"Randy, I know there were ways you could have hurt the church, but you didn't, and for that I am thankful. I have been given a rare glimpse into the hurt and rejection that gay people go through."

"Yes you have, but Michael, with that knowledge and insight comes a responsibility to act."

"But Randy, that's just it. I know that if the same thing happened tomorrow, my response would be the same."

"Well Michael, I'll just keep on praying that one day you will step up to the plate when given the chance."

Our salads had arrived. As I started to eat, I looked over at Michael. He was the man who had helped me move from legalism to grace in my theology, and yet he was running scared. I honestly believed that he loved me as a friend, but he knew as well as I that he could not be trusted to stand up for me at the risk of losing the support of those whose acceptance meant a great deal to him. I sensed that he could see this flaw in himself, and that it saddened him as much as it did me.

"Michael," I said, "I love you, and I will always be so thankful to you for helping me understand grace. Many times I have driven by the church office and felt a strong urge to pull in, get out of the car, walk into your office and give you a hug, then tell you I had forgiven you. Until today, I was afraid that you would not let your protective walls down long enough for me to be that vulnerable to you. Thank you for today, Michael. I do forgive you."

"Randy, what really got to me was the hypocrisy I saw in myself when I got so angry at John for barring you from your music ministry at the coffee house. I was painfully aware that what he did to you was exactly the same as what *we* had done to you."

Michael's words seemed to be very close to a confession of guilt. Then, on the way back to the hospital, he started saying things that sounded like he was trying to take back any admission of wrongdoing. I stopped him.

"Michael, please don't take it back. I am going to remember you said you were sorry, and I said I had forgiven you. Let's just go on from there."

Having lunch on his birthday opened the door to renewing our friendship. I was genuinely happy.

Money was tight at our house. While Gary's housecleaning business was becoming more successful, we were not keeping up with the bills. I started singing and playing piano at a restaurant in town for free food and tips, and I also auditioned for the musical *Some Like it Hot* at the same dinner theatre where I performed 15 years before. When the director, Glen Gilbert, spoke to me afterwards, I told him that I had been fired from my church position because I was gay. He was kind and told me that I would be hearing from him. A few days later, he called and offered me a part in the chorus.

That theatre experience was magical and healing. Plus I made a new friend, Martin McGeachy, who was starring in the play and was the founding pastor of a home church dedicated to reaching out to the arts community in Little Rock. Martin and I hit it off instantly. Ordained in the *Presbyterian USA* denomination, he had no problem with my sexual orientation. He told me that several members of his church were gay.

It was great doing the plays with Martin. On Saturday nights, both of us would cram for our sermons the next day, and the director would make comments about us being "the resident ministers." I was glad to be a part of the theatre community once again.

On June 7, 1996, I turned the big 4-0! Gary had survived this milestone two years before. The most wonderful gift I received was a poem written by Gary:

> *There come those moments,*
>
> *Not infrequent,*
>
> *When words fail*
>
> *And emotion constrains me*
>
> *With a feeling*
>
> *Of intense sweetness.*
>
> *Your vulnerability,*
>
> *Your boyish charm*
>
> *Cause my heart*
>
> *To wring itself out*
>
> *In an intensity of protective motherhood.*
>
> *Yet also come moments of desire*
>
> *With red light district feelings*
>
> *Though of purer aspect.*
>
> *Just such a moment came,*
>
> *Realizing as I did,*
>
> *That I have known you for over half your life.*
>
> *As we celebrate your earthly entrance,*
>
> *I look forward to our second half*
>
> *Knowing the first was a mere shadow of practice.*
>
> *Happy 40th Birthday*
>
> *Love always,*
>
> *Gary*

The weekly church services at our home were growing slowly. Word was getting out that there was a new church in town, and some Sundays we had 15 or 20 people! In November and December, we planned special events for the holidays because we were acutely aware of how lonely the holidays can be for gay and lesbian people. We had a potluck the Sunday before Thanksgiving. We went Christmas caroling at local hospitals and rehab facilities. We had a church Christmas party, and a special Christmas Eve service.

My salary was half the offering each week, not to exceed $50. Many weeks I did not get my full $50. Tim and David from Denver started sending us monthly offerings. One check was to the church and one was to Gary and me. They knew that the church did not pay much, nor assist with our utility bills even though the church activities were in our home. These dear friends wanted us to be able to count on a certain amount of financial help each month. Gary was getting more offers to clean houses, so I started cleaning houses too. We always seemed to have just enough to pay the bills, but hardly any surplus.

One week, Gary said to me, "Randy, you know when we stepped out in faith and committed to this ministry, you said we would trust God to help us find a way to make it financially. Well, this month there is just not going to be enough money to pay the rent. What do we do if God doesn't come through for us?"

I knew that Gary expected me to allay his fears, but I could only say, "Gary, I don't know."

"You don't know? We are going to be $400 short next week in paying our bills."

"Gary, if God doesn't come through for us, then we will not have the money. But God has shown us so many times that He will take care of us if we follow His calling on our lives. I am still going to trust Him."

Gary was not satisfied with that response. "Well, if God doesn't come through, I am really going to have a bone to pick with Him!"

I left and went to the post office to pick up the mail. I found a letter from David and Tim.

Dear Randy and Gary,

Tim got a great bonus this month and we wanted to share it with you. We know that you have a lot of bills, but please take at least $100 of this and spend it on something fun.

I unfolded the check and looked at the amount: $500! Just what we needed to pay our bills, plus $100 for something fun. I rushed home and handed the letter to Gary. He opened and read it, then unfolded the check. I saw amazement spread across his face.

"Oh man!" Gary finally exclaimed, "Now I am going to have to take back all those bad things I said about God!"

God had come through again thanks to our friends in Colorado!

As I ministered in the gay community, I became painfully aware of many wounded people who had been so abused by the church that it was hard for me to convince them of God's love, or even my own love and concern for them. Angry and hurt individuals lashed out at me because of treatment they had received at the hands of judgmental pastors. Several gay individuals attending *Open Door* wanted us to call ourselves a gay church and accused me of bending over backwards to accommodate the non-gays who also attended.

"Why not have a gay church for gay people? The straights have plenty of churches."

"Well," I tried to explain, "There are certain congregations that present themselves as gay churches, but that is not the vision God has given to me. God wants us all to sit at the table together and not be divided into gay churches and straight churches, black churches, white churches, and Hispanic churches. It has to start somewhere. I believe God wants to show the evangelical church-world how to be inclusive, and I am hoping and praying that He will use Open Door to get that message across."

Many in the gay community attacked me for having anything at all to do with Christianity. They had come to see all Christian churches as hate groups and couldn't figure out why I would still call myself a Christian. I assured them that the reason I was a disciple of Christ was because *Jesus* never did anything bad to me. The rejection I suffered was from some of His followers. "I refuse to allow them to take my Jesus away from me," I told them. "He loves me no matter what they say or do."

At times, I thought of myself as a man without a country. I was too gay for the Christian community, and too Christian for the gay community. Still, I stayed excited about the possibilities of bringing the church world together on this divisive issue. Open Door's affirmation of faith that we recite each Sunday affirms that we can change the world with God's help. I believe in the God of miracles and in Dr. Martin Luther King Jr.'s assessment that "the universe is on the side of justice."

It was challenging at times to imagine how a small church, meeting in our living room, could have such big ambitions. Yet I began to see the possibility that if gays and non-gays could worship together at Open Door, it could start a ripple effect. If it ever happened once, it would prove that it could happen all over the world. So I continued believing God, and praying for more non-gay people to attend. I believed when gay people, who had been put down and abused, could share from the same communion table with representatives of the group that had hurt them, a special healing would take place. Whenever anyone asked me if Open Door had an outreach to the gay community, I liked to say, "Well, actually gays are the majority in our church family, so we have an outreach to the non-gay community. That's important, because they need us as much as we need them."

Chapter 47

A Mother's Love

When Open Door was two years old, God sent a special gift in the person of a non-gay woman named Sheryl Myers who lived 70 miles from us in Hot Springs and taught kindergarten there for 25 years. She came to Open Door because she had just learned that her sixteen-year-old son Craig was gay. Sheryl began questioning her own faith as she and her football coach husband Jack struggled to accept their son. She began reading the hateful letters Christians wrote to the editor in the state's largest newspaper with new eyes. She read the ranting of individuals condemning her son to hell for being gay, and also judging her worthy of hell for accepting him. Christian churches started looking like hate groups to Sheryl. She felt they were asking her to sacrifice her gay son on the altar of religion, which she was not willing to do. Sheryl doubted she could be a member of the "Christian Club" any longer. Her faith seemed to be evaporating before her very eyes.

In desperation, Sheryl contacted Susan May, who led the Little Rock chapter of PFLAG, a support group for parents, family and friends of gay, lesbian, bisexual and transgender children. The first night she attended, I was not present. When she spoke of her spiritual crisis, everyone in the group told her she needed to talk to Randy McCain.

Sheryl rushed over to me as soon as the next PFLAG meeting ended. She described her disillusionment with Christians because of their hostility toward gay people. She asked how I kept my faith.

I was immediately drawn to this pretty, petite, sensitive mom. Her stylish clothes and features put me in mind of Jackie Kennedy, and her kindheartedness was so evident.

"Sheryl, Jesus never did anything mean to gay people. In fact He never said anything negative about homosexuality. You can embrace your gay son *and* your Christian faith. I pastor a church where this is possible. Maybe you could visit sometime."

"Where is the church?"

"We meet in our home."

Sheryl later told me that she thought, "How sad and depressing to have to meet in someone's home for church."

"And where is your house?" she asked.

"In Sherwood."

"And where is that?"

"On the other side of North Little Rock."

Since she lived 70 miles away, this didn't strike her as a practical solution for her faith crisis. As we were driving home, I told Gary that I felt such a love for this mom. Little did I know that Sheryl would become one of my most loyal supporters, a dear friend, and a colleague in ministry.

Months after we met her, Gary and I ran into Sheryl and Craig's older brother Matt at an art exhibition. We exchanged pleasantries and then, before we walked away, she asked for my email address. She emailed me that night:

This is Sheryl Myers, just trying out my email skills. Please let me know if you received this.

I wrote back that I had received her email, and also told her about the sermon I preached that morning on the love of God, including my sermon notes. She emailed me back:

Wow! What a beautiful sermon, Randy! The preacher was speaking to me. Maybe you are restoring my faith. It's been breaking my heart to lose it. I have been feeling like a child who just found out about the Easter Bunny and the Tooth Fairy, and knows Santa Claus is next. That sounds like a sacrilege doesn't it? I have been bothered by the scripture that says I can't love my child more than God, but maybe loving my child fiercely is loving God. God is Love. The rest is too difficult for me to understand.

Sheryl, like many parents of gays and lesbians, was on a spiritual odyssey. God was deconstructing the old views she had of Him so she could see a new, more complete picture of God's grace and love. A few days later, she called.

"Randy, I cannot tell you how much your sermon touched me. I have been giddy all day. I loved my family more. I loved my kindergarten kids more. I just saw them all as precious little examples of God's love. The God you preached about is the God I want to love."

"Thank you, Sheryl, for sharing that with me," I said. "You know, I would love for you to give that testimony at our church. Right now, our congregation is mostly men whose mothers do not accept them. It would mean so much for you to share what God has done in your life, and in the life of your family."

"I would love to do that, Randy."

We set a date. I explained that our worship was informal, sort of like PFLAG. Well, I guess I should have described it in more detail, because when Sheryl arrived for service that first Sunday, she was surprised that we actually had church bulletins. More than that, she was shocked when I said to her, "You speak right here, where it says 'sermon.'"

At first, she felt hoodwinked. She could not imagine in her wildest dreams giving a sermon! But the presence of God overwhelmed her as she experienced our music and worship time. Then, she began her testimony.

"I have been a Disciples of Christ and also a Methodist but I was never an every week attendee. But I think I could be an every week Open Door person. I love the worship here."

Sheryl said this somewhat in jest, considering coming to *Open Door* was a 140 mile round trip! As she shared her experience of accepting her gay son, there was not a dry eye in the place. I was immediately impressed by Sheryl's humorous yet meaningful, Erma Bombeck-style delivery. She would say something funny, then launch into a heartwarming story of family life. I wondered if she could be the one whom I had been asking God to send to help make our church more blended and build bridges to the non-gay community.

Sheryl went to lunch with some of us after church. She told me again how amazed she was by the worship. Two weeks later she returned to Open Door, this time with a friend named Carol, who also taught kindergarten at her school. Carol also fell in love with our congregation. Sheryl told me that she was going to invite her gay son Craig to attend our Easter service with her. Craig was angry at all churches, and could not understand why his mother wanted to drive so far to attend one. Craig was dating Brad, a young man who lived in Sherwood. Both of them, still in high school, were blessed to have families that were supportive and accepting. Given my own difficult journey with my family, this amazed me.

Sheryl invited Brad and his mother to join her and Craig on Easter Sunday morning. What a thrill to look over the congregation and see two gay teenage boys sitting between their moms. It touched me profoundly. This was the first physical manifestation of the vision of the church for *all* people that God had birthed in my heart.

I wrote Craig, thanking him for sharing Easter worship with us. Craig wrote back and said that he was very appreciative for what Gary and I were doing for gays and their families, and that he could see how much the church meant to his mom. He added:

I hope I don't offend you, but I don't really know if I believe in God. I want to, but I just have a hard time believing.

I wrote back assuring him that I was not offended, and that seekers were welcome at Open Door. No one had to believe any certain way to worship with us.

Sheryl became an every week attendee. On Mother's Day 1998, I asked her to give a talk on being a mom. I invited my parents. In the past when I had invited them, Mom said that she could not attend our church because we didn't believe the same way she did. I explained that we believed Jesus is the Son of God and that He died for the sins of the whole world, then asked her how that was so different from what she believed. Mom really didn't have an answer. She was curious about the church, but feared what my sister Linda would say if she attended a service. I wanted my parents to hear Sheryl. They had met her and thought she was a very nice person.

I gathered my courage and went to my parents' house to invite them. To my surprise, they did not say no, but promised to think about it. Saturday night before Mother's Day, Mom called and told me that they would be there the next day. I could hardly contain my joy and couldn't wait to tell Gary. He was amazed.

We had a crowd the next morning. Ten moms attended, and each received a gift from the church. Mom and Dad arrived late and the only seats left were on the front row. Sheryl did a wonderful job as she talked about the great privilege of being a mom and shared certain mementos from her special box of memories. Over the years she saved all the "mom gifts" her sons had given her, like cards, poems, and artwork, in a special box.

As Dad listened to Sheryl, he teared up. He missed his mom so much. He re-membered that Grandma McCain had a special place, a cedar chest, where she kept her "mom memories." Then Dad noticed his mother's cedar chest right in front of him. Grandma had given it to me, and we were using it as our altar table. Later Dad shared with me that he had received a message from Grandma telling him that he was in the right place. Grandma was still reaching out to build bridges.

When Sheryl finished, Craig got up and tried to talk about his mom, but her words had moved him so that he could hardly talk for crying.

"It just means so much to know that, after being afraid that my parents would reject me when I came out to them, my mom is here, loving me, and also sharing that love with all of you who don't have supportive moms."

We passed the Kleenex box that morning! At the end of the service, my mom hugged me and told me she loved me. "I could really feel the presence of the Lord here this morning," Mom said. "I now understand that there is a real need for this church and the ministry you are doing."

I was so happy I didn't stop smiling all day. The miracle of Open Door was com-ing to life before our eyes, and we just stood in amazement at what we were seeing and experiencing.

Chapter 48

Randy, the Gay Activist

Shortly after Mother's Day, Susan May, the facilitator for the local PFLAG chapter, informed us that Lambda, the nation's oldest and largest legal organization serving lesbians, gay men, and people with HIV and AIDS, was looking for plaintiffs to sue the state of Arkansas over the state's sodomy law.

The sodomy law had at one time applied to all couples, because it prohibited any kind of sexual expression except for actual intercourse between a man and a woman. In the mid-seventies, the state decided that the law was outdated and took it off the books. In 1977, the state legislature resurrected the law, but it would only apply to same-gender couples. This was clearly a blatant attack on the civil rights of gay individuals. Also, to add insult to injury, the law was packaged with a prohibition against bestiality. Susan thought Gary and I would make good plaintiffs to challenge this law in court.

"But," Susan added. "You will be publicly scrutinized, and you will have to admit to performing sodomy as it is described in the law books, which makes you a criminal in this state."

"Could we be arrested if we admit to this?"

"Yes you could, but you probably won't be. That would hurt the state's case, because they will say that since the law has not been enforced, it should not be taken off the books. So if they were to arrest you, they would be shooting down their own argument. But still, you will be outed to the whole state. I think the fact that you are able to express yourself clearly in front of people, and that you are a Christian minister, would make Lambda very interested in having you become a plaintiff in this case. So think about it, Randy."

Gary did not want to be a plaintiff himself, but had no problem with me getting involved. I asked him if any of his clients would have a problem with this. He said he really didn't think so, then added, "But if they do, then I don't need to be working for them anyway."

I began to pray about what I should do. I did a lot of thinking about why it was bad to have the sodomy law on the books. My concern was for all the young gay and lesbian teenagers, and even the little kids now in elementary school, who would one day grow up and discover that their sexual orientation was considered illegal by their state. I was horrified by the number of gay adolescents who were dying by suicide. Out of my heartfelt concern for young people, I agreed to be a plaintiff in what turned out to be a historic case.

When I attended my first meeting with a representative from Lambda, I learned that seven residents of Arkansas were going to be named as plaintiffs. Elena Picado, a courageous lady who taught in the Little Rock School district, agreed to lend her name to the title of the lawsuit. The actual lawsuit was titled: Picado v. Bryant.

Suzanne B. Goldberg, representing the Lambda legal defense team, made sure we understood we were getting into a long, drawn out process that could last up to five years, and that it would not be easy. She thanked us for having the courage to challenge the law, and assured us that Lambda would assume any legal fees associated with the lawsuit. Lambda's professional approach to their mission impressed me. We were informed that we should prepare ourselves for public scrutiny. Our names and faces would be in the newspaper and on television.

When Gary and I discussed the lawsuit that evening, I told him that I needed to inform my parents. I wanted them to hear it from me and not on the six o' clock news. The next day, I ran into Dad at the local library and asked if we could go for a cup of coffee.

In a little café, I told him about the lawsuit and the reasons why I felt I had a responsibility to be part of it.

When I finished, Dad set his coffee cup down and replied, "Well son, it *is* a bad law and somebody ought to do something about it. If you feel that you are being called to do this, then I think you should."

I was relieved by Dad's words and spent a long time reflecting upon my father that day. I had always appreciated my dad's concern for the outcast and the neglected. In his work for the federal agency The Farmers Home Administration, Dad was the champion for poor people and black people. I could remember him going into the black community in Walnut Ridge in the sixties and encouraging black families who were raising children in homes that were falling down around them to apply for government loans so that they could live in nice, new brick homes. Because of my father's initiative, the slums of Walnut Ridge started changing into a nice residential area where families could be proud to live.

I went with Daddy when the black families would have an open house. There was always good food, punch, and cookies. Raised in a segregated society and church, I loved watching my dad interact with people I knew little about.

Dad had a special place in his heart for a wonderful elderly black lady named Miss Lil, who had been the first one to hold him as a newborn baby. Dad used to take me to her home when I was a young child. I remember being scared the first time. I had absorbed the bigoted philosophies, then prevalent in the south.

"Daddy, I don't want to go to Lil's house. It will be dirty."

"Son, Lil's house may look like a shanty on the outside, but I promise you, it is one of the cleanest houses in Warren on the inside."

Out walked a thin wisp of a lady with white hair and a smile that pushed the wrinkles up on each side of her face until you could hardly make out her eyes. From the moment I laid eyes on her, I loved her. She scooped me up in her arms and hugged me close.

"Look at this little gentleman. Why, I was the first one to hold your daddy when he was born, and now I'm holding his son. What a fine boy you are!"

From that day on, Lil had put a face on black people for me, and now I could see why Daddy cared about them the way he did. It was all because of a sweet little lady who did not allow herself to be tainted by prejudice toward white people. She could have been very bitter, but her heart remained soft, and because of her loving spirit, Lil built a bridge and changed the lives of my dad and me. At an early age, I saw how much good one person can do by living out Christ's message of unconditional love.

When Dad made loans to the black community, he received strong criticism from whites in our town. After observing my dad's willingness to stand up for our black neighbors, I spoke up in favor of them at school. I was called a horrible name that white boys called other white boys who were kind to black people. I learned as a child that there was a price to be paid for standing with the outcast. My dad's loving heart taught me to disregard criticism, and to love and accept people who were different from me.

That day in the coffee shop, I realized that I had watched my dad become more liberal as he got older. Usually a person becomes more conservative as he ages. As we sat there, talking man-to-man about my participation in the controversial lawsuit, I could not have been more proud to be his son. Even though he would have to face his conservative friends, especially at church, after they read what the papers wrote and watched television news footage of his gay activist son, he still was proud of me for standing up for my beliefs.

"Dad, how will we tell Mom?"

"We won't."

"So, what if I am on the news and she sees it?"

"Then I will talk to her about it. But if she doesn't see you, there is no reason to tell her."

I felt this was good logic. Our lawsuit was entered in the Chancery Court of Pulaski County in Little Rock. The efficiency of the Lambda team amazed me, and

I was also pleased with our three local attorneys, Gary Sullivan, David Ivers, and Emily Sneddon, who provided helpful information to the Lambda legal team about state law and court procedures. Our lawsuit asked the state of Arkansas to declare the sodomy law unconstitutional because it denied gay and lesbian Arkansans equal rights, equal treatment, and privacy.

The government should not be in the business of policing the private behavior of consenting adults," said Suzanne Goldberg, Lambda's staff attorney who argued the case in court. "This law creates second-class status for lesbians and gay men, criminalizing intimate, sexual behavior that is perfectly legal for non-gay people. The Arkansas sodomy statute is used to cause terrible harm to gay people, depriving gay parents of custody of their children and putting people at risk of losing their professional licenses, their jobs, and their homes, simply for engaging in sexual intimacy with a loved one."

I was honored and humbled to be one of the seven who were challenging the state on behalf of all gay and lesbian Arkansans. It felt like we were a part of a movement that was larger than ourselves. At the end of that day, I felt good about the decision to be a part of this lawsuit. I never envisioned myself as a gay activist, but as a follower of Christ, trying to do what Jesus taught. This had been a good day.

Miss Lil Taught Randy to Love His black brothers and sisters

Chapter 49

Ordination

Another monumental event in my life took place October 10, 1998. I was ordained as a minister of the gospel. Ordination, as described in the New Testament, is the act of the church choosing, appointing, and setting apart, through the laying on of hands, certain individuals to perform specific functions on behalf of the church.

I faced a hurdle: no denomination would recognize me in the role as pastor or minister because of my sexual orientation. I asked Open Door Community Church to ordain me when a minister friend informed me that a local church has the right to ordain individuals to the office of pastor or minister. Who would be better qualified than those I had been shepherding?

When I made my request, members of the congregation happily went about the task of planning my ordination service. My friend, fellow actor, and Presbyterian pastor Martin McGeachy was an invaluable local resource. He was happy to assist the committee, and offered to provide the liturgy and oversee the proceedings of ordination. I recognized he was taking a risk, since the Presbyterian Church USA did not at that time allow their ministers to ordain openly gay people to the office of pastor. But Martin was a rebel in many ways. He offered his church to hold the ordination since 150 people were expected. Our living room would only hold 40.

I was kept in the dark about all the plans, but my mom let the cat out of the bag about one aspect of the ceremony. I stopped in to visit my parents a few days before the service. Mom had been talking with my sister Linda and was really stirred up when I arrived.

"I really don't think I can do what your church has asked me," she said unpleasantly.

"What would that be, Mother?"

"They have asked me to present you with a Bible at your ordination service, and I just don't know if I can do that."

"Why not, Mom?"

"Because, I just do not think you are qualified to be ordained as a minister of the gospel." Like an arrow seeking a bull's-eye, my mother could not have chosen more painful words.

"Mother, why do you think I am not qualified to be a minister?"

"Because you are in open rebellion against God by living a gay lifestyle!"

As Mom and I talked in the den, Dad was at his desk in the corner, reading his mail, trying to stay out of the conversation. I felt frustrated. Mother had been to our church and had worshiped with us. She told me how God had showed her that our church had a useful calling. But Linda chastised her for attending Open Door, and Mother was reverting to her judgmental habits.

"Mother, if you feel uncomfortable about giving your blessing to me as a minister, then I am sure the committee will find someone else to present me with the Bible."

"Oh, I'll do what they have asked me to, I just don't feel good about it."

It was as though she didn't want to look mean-spirited in the eyes of the committee, but she wanted to communicate her disapproval to me.

"No Mother, if you honestly feel that I am not qualified to be a minister, I don't want you to present the Bible to me."

Then I thought of Dad, who surely had heard the conversation. I spoke before I thought about the uncomfortable position I was placing him in.

"Dad, would you be willing to present me with the Bible?"

He hesitated for a moment. "Well, I suppose I could."

Mother again said that she would do it.

"No, Mother, Dad said he would present the Bible to me. But I want you to know something. I am very hurt by what you just said. You are the one who dedicated me to the Lord back when I was only five years old. I believe God heard your prayer, Mom. And now God is fulfilling that request, and you have lived to see this day. Yet you cannot even rejoice that God answered your prayer. One day, Mother, you are going to stand before God, and He is going to ask you, 'Marcelle, why weren't you more proud of your son Randy?'"

I walked out of the house. I surprised myself by holding my own against Mom's painful words. That conversation demonstrated how far I had come in my journey toward accepting myself. My mother's disapproval no longer made me doubt God's approval. I was in a healthy place, taking ownership of my own life and my relationship with God. I felt whole. It felt *holy*.

The morning of my ordination, I awoke with an awesome awareness of the significance of the day. When Gary and I walked into the sanctuary at Baker House Presbyterian Church, we were amazed at how much work had gone into the service. Four huge flower arrangements decorated the front of the sanctuary. A candelabra, holding 15 candles and decorated with ivy and purple bows, graced each side of the platform. I felt as though I was getting married all over again!

When folks started to arrive, I was touched as I recognized people from our church and from Martin's congregation. They were joined by others from Friends of His, and friends I made through my ministry to people with AIDS. More than 150 people gathered to celebrate the ordination of a gay man to the Christian ministry. My parents arrived with my sister Pam.

I sat on the front row next to Gary. Bill Prickett, a dear friend who was the pastor of an independent church in Fort Worth, Texas, spoke of the responsibilities that come with ordination. Martin asked me to come forward and answer questions as a candidate for ordination.

Dad walked up and handed me the Bible, then admonished me to look to God's word for guidance as I ministered to the people. He hugged me before he walked away, and the camera filming the event recorded a proud, smiling father. The most emotional moment came when Gary walked to the pulpit.

"I have written something that I would like to share now. I would like to dedicate this, first and foremost of course, to my spouse whom I love dearly. Also, I would like to dedicate this to his mom and dad. They have managed to raise a son who truly loves God and wants only to serve Him. They have every right to be proud of him. Equally, I want to dedicate it to Randy's Grandmother McCain, truly a rock in his life."

Tonight, let the bells ring out! Let the people gather rejoicing. Let the doors of heaven swing wide, and at them gather a great cloud of witnesses. At the forefront, leading them with a fair face filled with a righteous pride for this one honored here tonight, is Emma, a grandmother so dearly loved, her warmth of spirit so dearly missed that her memory alone is tangible. The mere touch of her walking stick brings fond remembrances and comfort. Out from the door of heaven, shadowed by the presence of God, are heard these words spoken to Emma as she gazed down on this scene of joy: "Before I laid the foundation of the world I knew this one, this apple of my eye. Before the multitude of suns began to shine did I pour the anointing oil upon my servant. This night is only the physical fulfillment of a grand design for Randy's life, Emma. Let me now say the words I uttered years ago and tonight repeat. 'Behold my son, adopted by grace, in whom I am well-pleased.'"

With pure tears of joy coursing down her cheeks, this grandmother, now eternally young, speaks with a voice strong with emotion and love. "I always knew Randy was special. I always knew your plan for him was good and holy. Behind the vale, I wasn't sure how. I didn't know the who, or when, or where. But now I see all things clearly, and my prayers have been justified. Randy, my grandson, I know you can't hear my words, but you can feel them. You can't touch me, but I know you are feeling my love surrounding you, holding you up, and sustaining your weary spirit. Know this, Randy; God is always with you, and so am I. His Spirit fills yours with love and that love is boundless, and through you, His love will spread to all the world one person at a time. Never give in to fear. Look always to God and know that I am proud of you."

A last word, simple and not from heaven, but a word from right here, from me. My love for you will one day be perfected and we will spend eternity sharing it. But until then, take this imperfect love of mine. Know it to be true and lasting and, along with God, let me say that in you I am well pleased, and this night is but the beginning of a road to great adventure and I will travel it with you to the end.

Gary delivered the reading with much emotion, slowing at times to gain composure. My face was awash with tears. I could hear my dad in the audience. I could always tell his sniff from everyone else's. Gary descended the platform and came over and hugged me. I could not get over the beautiful way he had captured my grandma in his presentation. He had truly been heavenly inspired. I thought how proud I was of this dear man with whom God had blessed me.

Years ago, he would have had such a difficult time speaking in public. But he was finding his voice in this new world of ministry. Also, I felt that we as a couple were being affirmed by so many that night. Few witness a man being ordained who is the partner of another man. Our love for each other was so visible, and those present were acknowledging God's presence working through us, a gay couple. It was very empowering.

Martin invited as many as could to come forward and lay hands on me as he prayed a prayer of ordination. Many flowed forward to touch me, and those who could not reach me touched those touching me. To be surrounded by so much prayer and love in this centuries-old ritual was emotionally overwhelming.

My thoughts wandered back through the difficult moments in my life, like those nights of walking the grounds of the Bible college, feeling so scared and alone. The times when my parents and I had butted heads over my sexual orientation, and the times when I felt that I would never minister again in the wake of being fired from Friends of His. It was indescribable to be surrounded by so much love and affirmation.

After Martin prayed, the congregation was told that they could come forward and congratulate me. The long line moved slowly. I got a lot of hugs and many kind words. My mother put her arms around me and told me how proud she was. She also said that the service had been beautiful, and that she had felt the Holy Spirit. That was quite a change from her words just days before.

To this day, I am in awe of how much support I received from so many areas of my life the night I was ordained into ministry.

Randy and his dad at the ordination

Chapter 50

Angels Unaware

One day I got a phone call that was to be the start of a very memorable friendship. The caller had a very distinctive speech impediment.

"I wa gibben you numba by my therapis who tol me I would be welcome at you chuch. I am twansgendad. And I dwess like a woman. I cannot dwess this way and go to my Batist chuch. But my therapis want me to twy and live as a woman fo a yea to see if I willy wan to be a woman. Could I atten you chuch?"

At first, I thought, "One of my friends is playing a joke on me." Thankfully, I restrained the urge to laugh. I told the caller that they would be welcome to come to our service on Sunday morning, but also suggested that we meet at my home. The caller agreed.

The next day, at the appointed time, a big pickup truck pulled in front of our house. I watched from the window as a very strange figure opened the door of the truck and waddled out. I first noticed the hideous wig, the kind of cheap fright wig you buy at Halloween for a few bucks. The next thing I noticed was the dress. It was one piece, but gave the appearance of being a blouse and long denim skirt. The breasts were obviously padded and were uneven. Moreover, they were not where breasts would normally be on a woman's chest. The individual had a large tummy and the dress was anything but flattering.

I breathed a prayer that God would help me understand this person. If I was supposed to help them in some way, I asked God to give me insight *immediately*. I could soon make out the facial features, especially stubble poking through thick makeup that had been applied unevenly. There was way too much lipstick, and the blush looked like it had exploded all over this odd face. I was reminded of a comedic character from a *Saturday Night Live* sketch. Little did I know I was about to open the door for one of God's angels.

One of the greatest lessons my mother ever taught me was that we should be on the lookout for angels that God would send to us, incognito, to see how we would respond to the stranger in our midst. I first learned this through an experience I had when I was eleven years old, and it has stayed with me all my life.

It all had to do with Hardy, a strange, mentally challenged man who lived in the country outside Walnut Ridge. My dad, as a deacon in the church, picked up individuals who needed a ride. I always dreaded when we had to pick up Hardy. He looked strange in his ill-fitting overalls, and he always smelled like he had not bathed in weeks. Also, Hardy would wet his pants in our car on the way to church. Then, during the sermon on Sunday mornings, he would stand up and shake hands with people.

Pastor Rorex would have to stop and say, "Hardy, you need to sit down until church is over. You can shake hands then."

Hardy was very obedient and immediately sat down.

I was so embarrassed when we drove up to church with Hardy. One Sunday morning, on our way to Hardy's little shack, I let out my frustrations to my parents.

"Daddy, why do we have to be the ones to always pick up Hardy?"

"Well, Son, Hardy wants to come to church and he doesn't have a car."

"Well, he couldn't drive one if he had it. He's retarded!"

"Now, Son, he can't help being the way he is."

"I know! But it embarrasses me when he gets out of our car. Visitors are going to think he's kin to us."

Mom spoke up. "Son, you need to be careful talking like that. We are told in the Bible that 'some have entertained angels unaware.'"

"What does that mean, Mama?"

"That means that sometimes we may see people as human beings, but they may actually be angels sent from heaven."

This was interesting information, but how did it apply to Hardy? "Mama, are you trying to tell me that Hardy is an angel?"

"Well, he *could* be."

"No, Mama, Hardy is no angel."

"How do you know Randy?"

"Because, angels don't smell like Hardy, and angels wouldn't wet their pants in the back seat of our car."

"God might just send an angel who didn't smell good and who wets their pants to see how we would treat them. Jesus says that when you do something for the least accepted person, you have done it unto Him. That means when we go and pick up Hardy, it's like picking up Jesus."

Mom's words have never left me. I have always looked for the "Hardy angels" who might drop into my life. So that day, as the strange caller approached my front door, I reminded myself of my past interactions with God's undercover visitors as I opened the door. After I introduced myself, I got this response.

"My name is Wobet but when I dwess like this, I am Wobeta."

I invited Roberta in and we began to talk. Thankfully, I knew a little about transgender people. There was a person at PFLAG who was transgender, and through her I learned quite a bit about this difficult life journey. A transgender person is born biologically one gender, but inwardly identifies with the opposite gender. This causes great inner conflict. Many transgender individuals long for a day when their outside matches their inside. Many have reassignment operations to correct what they see as a birth defect. Before they can actually have the surgery, however, the individual must first go through intensive counseling and live as the inside gender for at least one year. Roberta informed me that she was in the process of actually living as a woman so she and her therapist could evaluate whether she was truly transgender or simply a cross-dresser. A cross-dresser enjoys dressing in the attire of the opposite sex, but does not have the desire to *be* the opposite sex anatomically.

Obviously, Roberta was mentally challenged, but it was hard to estimate the severity of her handicap. The important thing was for me to let her know that Open Door would be a safe place for her. While I didn't know how her presence would affect the others at Open Door, I knew that we were called by Jesus to reach out to *all*.

Roberta reported that she had suffered a lot of public ridicule. I could see how that would probably be a daily occurrence for her. She was a member of a prominent local Baptist congregation that would not allow her in the door dressed as Roberta. I told her that Jesus loved Robert and Jesus loved Roberta. Both would be welcome at Open Door. After we visited for about 30 minutes, I asked Roberta if we could have prayer. She nodded. As I held Roberta's callused, oversized hands, I felt the most awesome presence of the loving Christ. When I finished the prayer, I opened my eyes and saw the tears in Roberta's eyes. I asked if it would be okay to give her a hug. She again nodded yes, so I reached out and gave her a warm embrace. When I pulled back, Roberta had a startled look on her face. I thought perhaps I had invaded her personal space.

"Are you okay?" I asked.

"Yes, it's just that nobody has evah done dat befoe."

I understood immediately that no one had ever treated Roberta with respect. I was moved beyond words. I imagined that Roberta's parents had been very protective of her when they were alive. Since their deaths, she probably felt like an abandoned puppy, struggling through life without much help from anyone. Already, I was beginning to feel very protective of this little lost lamb.

Before leaving, Roberta wanted to pay me something for my time. I told her that was not necessary, but she kept insisting. I told her that we had an offering box and she was welcome to give a donation, but that payment was not required. I was to learn that Roberta was not going to let anyone out-give her, and she never wanted to be beholden to anyone.

When Gary got home, I told him about my encounter with this fascinating person. He asked if I thought our church members would be kind to her.

"I hope so Gary, and if they are not, then this is a good time for them to find out how committed I am to the name Open Door and to our church's open door policy."

The next Sunday morning, I was going over the music for the morning's service when Roberta's truck pulled up, 20 minutes before service time. The people who regularly attended Open Door always arrived right at the starting time or a little after, but not Roberta. She was so excited about having a church she could attend! I had called a few members ahead of time to give them a heads up about Roberta so they would not be caught off guard. To my great joy, everyone was very kind to her.

Open Door had a tradition of going out to eat as a group after service, and I wondered if Roberta would want to join us. Was I ready for the stares we would surely receive with her at our table? I told myself to not worry about it, and at the same time promised myself and God that if she decided to join us, I would make sure that Roberta felt totally welcome in our group. I confess feeling relieved when she made some excuse as to why she could not join us.

Roberta left almost as soon as church was over, but not before telling me how much she had enjoyed the service. This went on for several Sundays. I would ask her to join us for lunch and she would decline. We had a potluck one Sunday after church and Roberta brought drinks and chips, but would not stay and eat with us. I told Gary that if we didn't find some way to connect with her, she would eventually stop coming altogether.

"There is a part of me that is almost glad that Roberta doesn't accept our invitations to go out to eat after church. I admit I'm afraid of the scenes that might take place. But then I think about how she faces rejection alone, every day of her life. I believe that God led Roberta to us for a reason. I want to try and find out how we can help her, but first I need to know to what extent she is challenged, mentally. I'm thinking about asking Roberta to allow me to go along with her to one of her therapy sessions."

Gary thought this was a good idea. The next Sunday, I asked Roberta if she would feel comfortable having me accompany her to one of her sessions. She looked puzzled, but then said that she would have to clear it with her therapist first. I told her I understood. The Sunday after that, Roberta told me she had asked her therapist and he thought my coming with her was a great idea. I arranged to meet her at the therapist's office the following week. When I got there, Roberta was waiting in the outer office. I sat down beside her and she seemed a little nervous.

"Roberta, are you sure this is okay with you, for me to be here?"

"Yes, it's just dat I neva had a pasta dat caed bout me."

It was obvious to me that what I had first read as nervousness was more like the kind of excitement a young child would experience when bringing a visitor to Sunday school.

During the session, I learned some very valuable information about Robert and Roberta. When Robert was a little boy, he had fallen from the top of a school playground slide and landed on his head. The accident had caused some brain damage, one of the manifestations of which was his speech impediment. The therapist was not convinced as to whether Robert was actually Roberta, or just Robert wanting to dress in women's clothes. Roberta had a few relatives who would invite Robert to their family get-togethers from time to time, but since the death of Roberta's mother and dad, she had lived alone in her parent's house. Roberta was a hard worker, and there was not a lazy bone in her body. She regularly checked in on an elderly uncle and often took him out to eat catfish. None of the family knew about Roberta; they only saw Robert.

Robert used to have a job bagging groceries at Kroger. He was well-liked by the customers because he always remembered their names and spoke kindly to them. But he had had to give up his job at Kroger because they would not let him dress as Roberta. At the end of the therapy session, Roberta's therapist Bill thanked me and asked if he and I could have lunch together soon. I told him I would like that very much.

When we met for lunch, Bill said that he had Robert's permission to discuss his case with me. Bill always referred to Roberta as Robert.

"Could your church members help Robert learn how to dress as a woman, and how to properly apply makeup?" he asked me.

I told Bill that I would see if I could get her some help. He thanked me and told me that he was trying to determine the extent of Robert's brain damage. In some areas, Robert was very intelligent, but in others, he was like a little child.

"Randy," Bill said to me. "Your church is the only real personal support that Robert has in his life. He just loves Open Door. I am not yet convinced that Robert is truly transgender. I am leaning toward the diagnosis of cross-dresser, but since *he* believes he is transgender, we are going to give this a try. If I can observe Robert dressing like a woman for a year, hopefully I will be able to tell."

I assured Bill that we at Open Door would do everything we could to help Robert *or* Roberta.

The fact that I had gone with Roberta to her therapy session, and taken time to talk about her with Bill, seemed to bring her out of her shell. The following Sunday, Roberta informed me that she was going to go out to eat with us after service. I was both glad and apprehensive, but all my fears proved unnecessary. The lunch went without incident. Yes, we got a few looks, but no one treated Roberta badly. After that, she always joined us when we ate out.

One Sunday, about 15 of us from the church were eating together at a local restaurant when I noticed a prim and proper lady, who had obviously just left her church service, staring at Roberta with a look of disdain and repulsion. This made me so angry! I made a point of staring back at the woman as sternly as I could. Eventually, she gazed over at me, and immediately became visibly uncomfortable. She stopped staring at Roberta after she got a little taste of her own pharisaic medicine!

After Roberta had been attending Open Door for a few months, she volunteered to serve as a greeter at the door on Sunday mornings. Being a greeter was a ministry that I felt was very important. I wanted people to feel welcome right from the beginning when they came to worship with us. To be greeted by someone like Roberta could prove to be a frightening experience for a first-time visitor. Plus, with her speech impediment, folks would have trouble understanding her. However, she was so persistent that I finally said yes. I stressed to her the importance of being early, but I failed to give her a specific time.

The next Sunday, Roberta arrived over an hour early! I was still in my pajamas when she showed up and rang the doorbell. As people began to arrive, I observed Roberta's greeting style. Her years of working at the grocery store had given her a natural ease with greeting people. She always had a big smile and a kind word.

Our greeter still needed a makeover, but I didn't know the first thing about how women applied makeup. "Who could I get to help Roberta?" I wondered. At the time, I was performing in a play at the dinner theatre. One night, between scenes, I brought up the problem of Roberta's makeup. Joe Terry, a fellow actor and friend, spoke up and said he had learned many makeup techniques during his years of performing on stage, and he would love to help Roberta. Her story had touched him deeply.

So, one Tuesday morning Roberta came by and picked me up in her monster truck, and off we went for a lesson in cosmetics. Joe was patient with Roberta and offered some wonderful, practical tips. By the time he finished with the makeover, she actually resembled a woman. I told Roberta we were going to go to the wig store. When I told her that the church wanted to buy her a wig, Roberta insisted that she would pay for it herself.

"No, Roberta," I said. "You give to others, and now you need to learn how to receive a gift. Let us buy this for *you*." Reluctantly, she agreed. When we got to the store, I told the little Korean woman behind the counter that we were there to buy Roberta a wig. Then, an amazing thing happened. When the shop keeper heard Roberta speak, a look of recognition came across her face.

"I know you!" she said, with a heavy Asian accent. "You Robert that help me with my groceries. What happen you?"

I explained to her that Robert was becoming Roberta, and that our church wanted to help by purchasing a nice wig for her. The woman looked at me as though I had three heads.

"Who are *you*?"

"I am Roberta's pastor."

"You a pastor?!"

"Yes."

"What church you pastor?"

"Open Door Community Church."

She then wanted to know where I had gone to Bible school. No doubt she was having a difficult time thinking about a church helping Roberta with such a controversial challenge. But when she finished with her interrogation, she surprised me by saying, "Well, come on Roberta, let's find you wig. I think you look good in red wig."

We found one, and what a difference it made! Roberta had a look of sheer glee on her face as she looked at herself in the mirror. I had to wonder if she could ever make herself look like this again, but for that one moment, she looked…not exactly pretty, but not so very odd either.

The following Sunday, when Roberta arrived to fill her greeter position, it was apparent that she had not retained much from Joe's makeup lessons. And it did not get any better in the weeks to come. Gary tried to assist Roberta each week when she arrived early for church.

"Roberta," he would say to her. "That wind has really done a number on your wig. Come in the bathroom and let me help you brush it."

Or he would say, "I believe you need to blend your makeup a little this morning, Roberta. Have you got your makeup case with you?"

There were times when we had to act as parents to Roberta, like the morning she showed up in a terrycloth mini skirt, made even shorter by having to be pulled over her substantial belly. Gary was horrified! He told her that she needed to go home and change. She left, but did not come back. I knew her feelings had been hurt, so I called Roberta after church and asked if I could come by to talk. She said I could.

Her home was a very nice, brick three-bedroom house. I entered through the carport door into a kitchen that was in total disarray. The kitchen table was piled high with stacks of mail, potato chip bags, candy, and soft drinks. Roberta gave me a tour of the house. Her parent's bedroom was still kept as it had been the day her mother died. The living room was filled with big remote control cars, expensive bass guitar equipment, and photography accessories. It seemed to me like a house a 12-year-old would live in, if he had plenty of money and no adult supervision.

When we sat down in the living room, I could tell that Roberta was excited to have a visitor. She showed me lots of her favorite gadgets, which she assured me were all top of the line. Visiting Roberta was like watching a child's show-and-tell presentation. Finally, I got around to the reason I had come to see her.

"Roberta, I think you were a little upset with Gary this morning, when he asked you to go home and change. Do you know why he asked you to do that?"

She did not answer.

"Roberta, listen. We love you very much, and we want you to come to church. But there is a certain way a lady dresses for church. The skirt you were wearing this morning was way too short to be worn in public, much less in church."

"I got a skut dat is shotta dan dat one."

I couldn't imagine that in a million years, but Roberta jumped up with glee and ran into her bedroom to bring it out as proof. She came back with something that resembled a tube top and told me it was a skirt.

"Roberta, honey, please tell me you have not worn that out in public."

"I have a fu times, like when I went to Pizza Hut or Wa-Mat."

I was horrified.

"Listen to me," I begged her, trying to find words Roberta could understand to explain why that skirt was totally inappropriate. "Roberta, it would be pornographic for you to wear that in public. There are people in your neighborhood who would want to *kill* you for biologically being a male and walking out in public wearing a skirt like that. I am concerned for your safety, honey. And listen, when you wear that skirt to Walmart, consider the fact that children will see you. When a parent tells their child that they cannot watch R-rated movies on television, it is because there are scenes in the movie that are too sexy for children to watch, and they want to protect their child from things they shouldn't see. Roberta, that skirt is too revealing. It is not good for a child to see someone in a skirt that short. When you wear it in public, parents can't protect their children from seeing you."

I felt like a parent myself, trying to explain to a young child why Daddy said no. As Roberta listened, I felt I had gotten through to her. And when I hugged her goodbye, I really believed, deep down inside, Roberta knew that I had corrected her because I loved her.

The church had planned a picnic and swim party at a lake about an hour's drive from Sherwood. A week before the outing, Roberta called and told me she wanted to be baptized at the lake. Immediately, I had visions of what that could turn into.

"Roberta, you need to understand that the area where we are going is a gathering place for young, redneck boys. Sometimes, there are young kids up there who drink too much and are looking for ways to cause trouble. If we were to have your baptism in the lake where they are swimming, those young guys would not understand about your unique journey. They might try to hurt you, and then I would have to get involved, because I care about you. I would probably get beaten up."

"I don't want my pasta to git bea up," she responded.

"Well Roberta, that makes two of us. Let me make a suggestion. Ray Daugherty, from church, has a swimming pool in his back yard and we have baptisms there. Why don't you plan to be baptized the next time we have one of our Sunday afternoon baptism/cook-out/swim parties?" I felt relieved when Roberta seemed pleased with my suggestion.

Ray's pool was perfect for our baptisms because of the spacious deck that surrounded it. Once or twice a year, we would gather on a Sunday afternoon to baptize those who had committed their lives to follow Jesus. Then we would swim and eat burgers. When we announced our next baptism, Roberta was the first to sign up. On the Friday before the baptism at Ray's house, Roberta called and asked me what she should wear to be baptized.

"I got two bavin suits." she informed me excitedly. "One a two piece and the otha is one piece."

The picture that popped into my head was frightening. I had to come up with a diplomatic solution, so I called my Disciples of Christ pastor friend and asked to borrow a baptismal robe.

The next problem was how would we keep the wig on Roberta's head during her baptism. My minister friend suggested that I place my hand on the top of her head and have her kneel as I pushed down on her head, as opposed to lowering her back into the water in the traditional way. Thus, I could keep my hand on the wig so it would not come off in the water. I decided to go with this plan.

That Sunday afternoon, Roberta was beside herself with excitement. There was a good turn out, and Sheryl arrived with a rose to present to Roberta when she came out of the water. As we stood in the water, I asked Roberta if she wanted to say anything before I baptized her.

"I want to tank Open Doa and all of you becau I have a chuch whea I can go to lub God."

She was so childlike, and had not Jesus said, "Unless you come as little children you cannot enter the kingdom of heaven?"

As I spoke the words of baptism, I put my hand on Roberta's head, making sure I was putting pressure on the wig. As I had instructed her, she started to kneel as I pushed down. Then, when Roberta was completely under water, I expected her to start coming back up. But we had not discussed this aspect of the baptism maneuver.

I began to lift my hand, so she would know to start back up, but, as I did, I felt the wig floating off her head. I quickly pushed down again, causing Roberta to go back down even farther. Finally, I just let go and she started to rise…but so did the wig. Just before she reached the top of the water, I grabbed the wig and held it on her head. She came up sputtering, the wig a little askew, but at least it was still on her head. Mission accomplished!

Everyone applauded. Roberta exited the pool as the water-soaked saint of God she was, smiling from ear to ear. I think I heard a few wings flapping as the angels saluted. Sheryl was waiting with the rose and a hug.

I marveled at what a wonderful place Open Door was becoming. While a few people had tried to broach the subject of how uncomfortable they were with Roberta's presence at Open Door, they always got the same answer from me.

"Have you forgotten that some of us gay people make non-gay people uncomfortable in *their* churches? Have you forgotten that many of us have been ostracized from the church community because of our sexual orientation? How can we even think of doing that to Roberta?"

That usually was sufficient to silence the complaint.

Roberta was such an encourager to me. As a novice pastor, I felt insecure about my abilities when it came to writing sermons. One Sunday after the service, Roberta came up to me and said, "Good sumon today, Pasta. You like a chep at a westauwant. You pwepae a spirtal dinna fo us evewy Sunday…and hey, it always gwuat!"

Roberta liked to talk in percentages. If you saw her during the week, and asked if you were going to see her in church on Sunday, she would say, "I bout ninny eight pucent suwa I will be dere."

When someone would say to her, "Roberta, are you doing ok?" she would answer them, "Let me put it dis way, did de Titanic sink?"

Sometimes her sayings didn't exactly fit the occasion, but they were part of the whole, unusual package that was Roberta.

During the summer of 1999, I got a call from a man I had met at a Christian drama workshop in Springfield, Missouri in the early eighties. John Taylor, an instructor at the workshop, took a special interest in me, and invited me to visit him and his family in Florida, where he was director of the arts at a large church. He felt the call to be a missionary to the poverty stricken country of Honduras, where he was spending more and more of his time. I loved this dear, gentle man. He was so Christ-like in his kindness and care for others.

It was a lovely spring morning in May 1999 when I received the call from John. He said that God brought me to his mind that day, and told him to contact me and ask what I had been up to in life. Assuming that he had heard I was gay, and was concerned about my eternal soul, I launched into the whole story about struggling for years with my sexuality, finally coming to terms with it, getting fired, and starting Open Door Community Church. I finished my saga by telling John of my love story with Gary, and our wedding. There was a long pause, and then he said,

"I….I didn't know you were gay."

"Oh no!" I thought. "Here it comes! He's going to preach at me!" But I was in for a pleasant surprise.

John told me he would like to visit us, and attend our church. We decided the first of June would be a good time.

Gary and I picked John up at the airport. He was a little man in his late 50s, but from all the walking he had done in Honduras he was in great shape. The visit got off to a fine start, but I wondered how John felt about the gay issue. It had to be somewhat strange to him, yet he treated Gary and me warmly. John had a way about him that made a person feel as though he was there just for them, like they were very important to him.

On Saturday afternoon, as we sat visiting, I brought up the subject of transgender people. I asked John if he knew what that meant.

"No, I am still trying to understand the *gay* issue. I don't know if I am ready to learn something else," he replied thoughtfully.

"Well, I wouldn't bring this up, except for the fact that you will be greeted at church tomorrow by a transgender lady named Roberta."

I then told John the story of how God had brought Roberta into our lives. He listened closely to what I was saying and asked a few questions. When John met Roberta the next day, he treated her with dignity. Roberta had volunteered to read the scripture that morning. I thought to myself, no one was going to understand her with her speech impediment, and I had not even considered what scripture she would be reading until Roberta stood up and I heard her read, haltingly, these words:

Bwothas and sistas, think of what you wea when you wea called. Not many of you wea wise by human standats; not many wea infuental; not many wea of noble beath. But God chode da foolish tings ob the woold to shame de widse; God cho de weak tings of de woold to shame de stwong. He cho de lowly tings of dis woold and the depised tings and de tings that awe not to nulfy de tings that ah, so dat no one may bo…boast befoe Him. It is because ob Him dat you ah in Cwuidst Jedus, who ha becomed fo udst witdom fwom God—dat is, owea wighteouness, holiness and wedemchun. De fowa, as it is witten: "Let him who boadsts boadst in de Lowd." (I Corinthians 1:26-31 NIV)

I was humbled as I listened to Roberta, this strange-looking person reading with all the power she had within her, honored that she had found a church that would let her serve. These words of scripture, first written by the Apostle Paul 2,000 years ago, took on new life as Roberta read. They were being lived out right in front of me. God had chosen this wonderful person who, in the eyes of the world appeared foolish, to shame those of us who thought we had it all together. I thanked God for sending us this angel in disguise.

After the service at a local buffet, John made sure he sat next to Roberta. He pulled out her chair and got her a dessert. He treated her as if she were the Queen of Sheba. Roberta was giggling and acting like a child at Christmas, eating up all this attention. When it was time for John to leave, he gave me a card for Roberta on which he had written these words:

A lady deserves flowers.

It was my pleasure meeting you. Love, John

He left money in the card for me to buy roses for Roberta, which I presented to her the following Sunday. I was so moved by the Jesus I saw in John's life. I knew he still had questions about Roberta, about Gary and me, and our church, but instead of judging, he made the decision to love us. Isn't that what Jesus tried to teach us all to do?

Roberta's story has a sad, but joyous ending. Her therapist decided that his tests showed Roberta was not transgender, but a cross-dresser. Roberta started coming to church as Robert. He started working as a greeter at the local Walmart, where most people seemed to love him. Also, he took on a second job at a McDonald's restaurant, where his work schedule made it impossible for him to attend Open Door. Every time I saw Robert at Walmart, I would tell him how much we missed him.

The last time I spoke with Robert I invited him to our annual Christmas Eve service, coming up in a few weeks.

"Now, I know you will not be working on Christmas Eve, so we expect to see you at church."

"Let me put it dis way…I'm bout niney-eight pusent sewe I will not be wookin."

"So, if you are not working…. you will be at church?"

"Let me put it dis way," Robert stuttered with his usual ear-to-ear smile. "Did de titanic sink?" As he spoke these words, he patted his large belly, shaking with laughter.

A few days later, I read Robert's obituary in the paper. The funeral home gave me the name and number of a cousin of Robert's who was handling the funeral arrangements. I called, and when I told her I was Robert's pastor, she was relieved. She was not aware that Robert had been attending church, and did not know what they were going to do for a service. I offered my assistance and she was very appreciative.

Robert's cousin then filled me in on the circumstances of his death. He had gotten off work at Walmart late one evening, and not shown up for his job at McDonald's the next morning. It was not like Robert to miss work and not call in, so his supervisor went to his house. Robert's truck was in the driveway, but he did not answer the door. She called the police, who broke in and found Robert lying on the bathroom floor. He had been shaving when he had a massive heart attack. The coroner said that Robert probably died instantly.

I was sad that Robert had died alone, but I was sure that, even before his body hit the floor, his spirit was being cradled in the loving arms of Jesus.

Robert's family did not expect many to attend the funeral, so they were all surprised when the chapel at the funeral home filled to overflowing. The crowd consisted of a few family members, coworkers and customers from McDonalds and Walmart, and people from Open Door. Sheryl brought two potted poinsettias, one red for Robert and one pink for Roberta.

I spoke of my association with Robert. I did not mention Roberta, because some in his family had not met her. I told of how Robert could not do enough for the church. I also recounted his words of encouragement to me when I was struggling to find my footing as a pastor. I told about his volunteering to cut the grass at the church, and how, when the mower broke down, he took it to get fixed. But when Robert found out that fixing it would take two weeks, he bought a brand new mower in addition to getting the old one repaired. "That way the church will have a spare," he told me later.

I ended my talk by saying, "I will miss my friend, Robert. The church has grown, we have a building now, and I have a little bit of experience under my belt as a pastor, but I am 100% sure that one of my greatest teachers in life has been Robert Morris. I was his pastor, but he was my teacher and my angel. Mother Theresa said to her followers once, 'Be the living expression of God's kindness—kindness in your eyes, kindness in your smile, and kindness in your warm greeting.' That describes Robert Morris. Whether handing out bulletins at the door of Open Door Church, or greeting customers at Walmart, Robert showed us the love and compassion of his savior, Jesus. The writer of Hebrews has said, 'Do not forget to entertain strangers, for by doing so some have entertained angels without knowing it.' I believe that all of us who knew Robert were in the presence of an angel. He was our friend, sent to us from another world."

Many of Robert's co-workers and his relatives told me after the service that I had captured the essence of Robert in my tribute. I wept as I stood at his casket. On top of the casket lay the blue apron Robert had worn at Walmart. I remembered his ever present smile when greeting people. When I arrive in heaven, I am 100% sure I will be welcomed by my dear friend Robert Morris. I am sure Saint Peter has learned a thing or two from this new pearly gate ambassador.

Roberta's Baptism

Chapter 51

A Visit to Gary's Home Town

I always wanted Gary to take me to South Dakota to meet his relatives and see where he had been raised. Gary never seemed to miss his home state, or show any desire to return. But in 1999, we set out on a trip to Gary's hometown, Rapid City.

We stopped in Springfield, Missouri, where we first met at Evangel College. We took pictures in front of our old dorm and were amazed at how young the students looked. It was a special day as Gary and I remembered our first meeting. I marveled at where we were now on life's continuum.

From Springfield, we drove to South Dakota. It was a long trip, but the time we spent together in the car was good. As we got closer to his home state, I could sense Gary's stress. His mom and dad were dead, but his memories of them and his oppressed childhood were alive.

When we arrived in Rapid City, we headed for Aunt Eleanor's house. Gary was looking forward to seeing her. He had "come out" to her in a letter in 1996.

She had written back:

Gary, I know you are reading ahead, looking for my response to your letter and revelation. Somehow, I knew what you were going to tell me as I read the very first sentence, and in saying that, I'm saying I had put the pieces together thru the years and knew of your sexual preference. Guess I am saying that I am happy for you, and that I could never not love you, as I always have, and always will. I wish you and Randy great happiness and many years of love and understanding together.

Aunt Eleanor was happy to see Gary again and to meet me. She insisted that we eat with her that evening along with Gary's cousins, Kathy and Tom. They all treated me like family.

The next day, Gary showed me where he had lived as a child, and where he had attended school. He took me to see Mount Rushmore before we headed to Wyoming to visit his sister, Sherry. She was the one in Gary's immediate family with whom he had always shared a special bond.

In 1985, when I was leaving Jerry and Gary was contemplating moving to Arkansas, Sherry had written the sweetest note welcoming me to the family. At that time, she was no longer a part of the conservative church of her childhood, but a free thinker. However, Sherry had gone back to the Assembly of God church, and when Gary told her in 1992, that he was moving to Arkansas, she had not been thrilled. Later, in 1993, when he had tried through correspondence to broach the gay issue with her and offered to send her pictures of our wedding, she had written back,

> *Gary, I love you, but I can't sanction you guys as a couple. To you it's OK, and to me it's not okay. I know you would like my approval, but I just can't give it. I feel the Bible is very clear about it. This does not stop me from loving you or considering Randy as a friend. So we will never agree on it and to see the pictures would only make me sad. Gary, I'm sorry it has to be this way, but it really does make me sad. I don't know how else to say it. I don't want to hurt you, but can you try to understand my viewpoint and just love me as a sister?*

> *Geeez, I hate to end a letter on such a note. Sometimes things that need to be said are just hard to say.*

> *Take care, and say hi to Randy.*

> *Love,*

> *Sherry*

We wondered how she would respond to our visit, so when we pulled up in front of Sherry's house, we were apprehensive about the welcome we would receive.

Sherry opened the door and out ran Molly, her Pomeranian.

"Molly," Sherry yelled, "it's your Uncle Gary and Uncle Randy from Arkansas!"

Gary and I breathed a collective sigh of relief. I enjoyed meeting Sherry, who was little like Gary and cute as a button. It made my heart glad to see brother and sister getting reacquainted after seven years.

1999 ended joyously for Open Door as 48 attended our Christmas Eve service. That night my parents came to the service, along with my sister Pam and her daughter, Leandra. My mom and dad sat on the front row! I had to pinch myself to believe it was real! In our small apartment, it was breathing room only. Obviously, if we were going to grow, we had to have a larger place to worship. My personal goal for 2000 was to find our church a home.

Chapter 52

Shoe-String Faith

While 2000 started out with much promise, little did I know that I would look back on it as one of the darkest years of my life.

As I searched for a place for the church to meet, I was given a tip that there was a small church building for sale in Sherwood, not far from our duplex. I hurried to see if this could possibly be what we were looking for.

The church building itself was small, but most attractive. It was built in an L-shape design and had a steeple with a cross on top. An elderly man was working inside the church. When he found out that I was interested in buying the property, he offered a tour. The moment I walked into the building, I felt at home. Realistically, I knew that Open Door had no money to offer, yet I felt excitement building in my heart. The gentleman was one of the elders of the Baptist congregation selling the property. I asked him how much land went with the church, and he said that there were about two and a half acres.

Then I asked the real question. "How much are you asking for this?"

"Well," the man replied. "It has been appraised at $177,000.

My heart sank. He might as well have said one million dollars! Yet, after I got back in my car, I prayed.

God, for some reason, I felt at home in that building. If it is your will for us to meet here, please show me how. I know that you can work miracles and I have believed for the past four years that, when the time was right, you would work a miracle for us. So if this is the time, let me see through eyes of faith. Give me wisdom as Open Door's pastor.

The next Sunday, I preached a sermon on faith and told our congregation about the property I had found. I told them that, though we were small and had no way at this time to purchase the building, God was on the side of the underdog. Then I passed out containers with "Open Door Building Fund" on the side. I asked everyone to fill them with their spare change at home and bring them back in two months. This was the small beginning of our big commitment to step out in faith to buy a home for Open Door.

There seemed to be real excitement in the air, but almost immediately doubts began to set in. The money we needed was such a large amount for such a small group of people. I wondered if it was cruel for me to raise our congregation's hopes. But still, I kept looking for the miracle that I felt God had promised us. God was about to use a pair of shoelaces to dramatically increase my faith!

I was cleaning a house for a client when I received an urgent call from Gary. He told me that the hospital had called, and that a man I had visited was dying. His wife had asked me to come as soon as I could. I asked Gary to bring my suit to the house I was cleaning so I could change there and go with him to the hospital. Sheryl was in town having her car worked on, so I asked Gary to invite her to go with us.

When they arrived with my clothes, I tried to change quickly. As I put on my right dress shoe, the shoelace broke. Then, when I pulled on my left shoe and started to tie it, that lace broke as well. What were the chances of both shoelaces breaking at the same time? When I came out of the bathroom, I told Sheryl and Gary what had happened. Sheryl, as a kindergarten teacher, had lots of practice tying broken shoe laces, so she quickly tied mine.

At the hospital, we found that the gentleman had just passed away. We had prayer with the family, and took his widow home and arranged for food to be brought to her apartment. The next day, I took Sheryl to pick up a rental that she could drive while her car was being fixed. When I was sure she had secured the rental car, I started walking out to my car. On the way, I happened to look down, and there in front of me was a small, unopened package of some sort. I picked it up to examine it more closely. To my amazement, it was a package of brand new, black dress shoelaces. I had goose bumps. It was a *Touched by an Angel* moment. I sensed that God was saying to me, "Randy, when you are doing my work and there is a need, I will supply."

When Sheryl walked out of the rental office, I ran back to show her what I had found. Immediately, she realized the significance of my find. Both of us were awed by this modern day miracle. God was building our faith to trust Him for our new building.

Chapter 53

A Painful Phone Call

My sister Linda called one evening. My missionary friend John Taylor had asked me for her address to try to open up dialogue between the two of us.

"Randy," Linda said, "I got a letter from a man named John Taylor, and he made it sound like you think I hate you. Is that true? Do you think I hate you?"

Sensing no tenderness in her voice, my heart began to race.

"Well, Linda, I wouldn't call it hate. I think I would call your feelings for me indifference. When you come to town, you never call me. When I do see you and ask how you are, you never ask how I am."

"That is because I don't want to know about your life. Your lifestyle makes me sick! And now you pastor a church and are leading others astray by telling them that it is possible to live in open defiance to God and still call themselves Christian. I just can't stand to think about it."

My sister's words stung, but I tried not to allow my emotions to get out of control.

"Linda, can't we just love each other, the way a brother and sister should love each other, and not discuss the gay issue?"

"I can't, Randy. I have a hard time separating the two. And I know that the rest of the family thinks that I am being cruel and intolerant by believing the way I do, but the truth is, I am the one in our family who is standing up for the truth of God's word."

"Linda, I know that's what you believe, but I want us to get along. Please, Linda, I know you are going through so much with your cancer and I want to be there for you. When I try to reach out to you, you are so cold to me. How can that be pleasing to Jesus? Even if you think I am the worst sinner in the world, *how* can you treat me the way you do?

"Remember when you were in college, and you would come home on the weekends and make me French toast for breakfast because you knew how much I loved it? You would walk into my room and kiss me on the forehead and say, 'Wake up Randy. Wake up little brother, breakfast is ready.' And I would slowly open my eyes and there would be my sister. I would smile so big and jump out of bed and run into the kitchen with my mouth watering. Linda, can't you remember how close we were back then?"

"That was a long time ago," Linda responded flatly.

"That's okay, because I have a good memory, and I will always choose to remember. I love you, Linda."

"I love you too, Randy. And I will try to be more cordial to you. I really will *try*."

"Thank you, Linda. That would mean a lot to me."

"But it doesn't mean that I accept your lifestyle."

"Linda, you don't even have to say that. I know what your beliefs are. I just miss my big sister, and would like to have you back in my life."

The conversation was over. The call emotionally drained me. How could Linda attribute her cold, judgmental actions to her Christian faith? Jesus taught us to love others as we love ourselves. Then it hit me! Linda *is* loving me the way she loves herself. Her legalistic religion was so rigid, even *she* could not live up to its demands. She was disappointed in her own track record. Her rejection of me was her way of railing against her own inability to keep the law.

I wanted to scream to my sister, "There is therefore now NO condemnation to those who are in Christ Jesus!" (Romans 8:1) Instead, I thanked God for freedom from graceless religion, and for the transforming power of grace in my life.

The next day, I talked to Daddy about my conversation with Linda.

"Well Son, Linda has this strong conviction that you are wrong. I know it hurts, but I think Linda is in a lot of pain too. There is pain on both sides, Randy, and I hurt for both of you. I just hope and pray that one day our family can be together and everyone will just get along."

"Me too, Daddy, me too."

Daddy was such a sweet man who loved his family so much, yet could not see a way for all of us to get around this issue. He saw both sides, and he was not going to allow any of us to get shut out of the family. He would make sure that there was a place for each of us.

Chapter 54
My Dad, My Hero

Summer was the time for Daddy and me to take our yearly journey back to Warren, Arkansas. We loaded his truck with tomatoes, cantaloupes, cucumbers, and ears of fresh corn to bring back to family and friends. Dad was known to many as "the produce man." I looked forward to our trip because I always learned so much about Dad's history. He reminisced about his childhood and family as we visited places in his youth. Dad was 75 now, so his stories took on more meaning. I tried to memorize them so that someday, when Dad was no longer with us, I could retell them with his flair for storytelling. Even though I knew that Dad would not live forever, it still was next to impossible for me to imagine a world without him. He had always been such a large part of my life. If ever I was in trouble, I could call Daddy.

I tried to prepare myself for the time I would have to say goodbye to my parents. I would ask others who had lost a parent what the experience was like. Most would try to describe it, but then say something like, "You cannot put it into words. There's just no way to prepare yourself for it."

The older Dad got, the more I vowed to appreciate him. Recently there were new health concerns. He was having dizzy spells. Dad had always been fiercely independent. If he and I went anywhere, he insisted on driving. Now, he became frightened that he might have one of his spells, so he often asked me to drive.

On this journey to Dad's hometown, I paid extra close attention to all his stories and asked more questions than usual. As we returned to Sherwood, we started talking about the days when we lived in Walnut Ridge. I wanted him to know how much I appreciated the way he had kept my sisters and me connected to the real world.

"Dad, Mom was so involved in the church that we would have never had any culture, any literature other than the Bible, or any music other than church hymns if it hadn't been for your influence. I remember when you read to us from the classics and when you insisted on taking us to movies and plays. I am so thankful that you stood your ground and brought a television into our home. Dad, without you I would have grown up in such a vacuum."

"Well, Son, your mother thinks that I caused you kids problems growing up because of my liberal ways."

"Daddy, you know better than that. I thank God for your wisdom. You gave me the benefit of the doubt and believed in me. I will never forget the conversation we had when you told me that you loved me and nothing would ever change that. I have those words indelibly written in my heart and they will always be there until I die. You are a wonderful father. I am so proud to say that I am Randall McCain's son."

There are certain conversations you treasure, because you said what was really on your heart. This was one of them.

On Father's Day, June 18, 2000, Dad and Mom attended Open Door. At the end of the service, Gary read a tribute he had written for my father, which spoke of his love for his family and his acceptance of me. He ended it with these words:

I want to honor Randall McCain, a father with a mother's heart, a loving man unafraid to show it, with strength born of time and faith, with understanding and acceptance born of experience. Thanks Randall, for raising a great son and accepting me as well into your family.

When Gary finished, there was applause, along with lots of sniffling and blowing noses. Dad was heard to say, in his typical self-effacing way, "Y'all must be talking about somebody else."

After the tribute was read, all the fathers were asked to come forward. We snapped pictures of each of them holding the "Thanks Dad" key chains they had received from the church.

There were five fathers in attendance, and in our crowded living room, there was not much space at the front for them to stand. They formed a close line in front of the table that held lit candles in memory of the fathers who had died. Dad stood proud in his conservative suit, until suddenly he jumped forward and started beating his rear.

"My butt's on fire!" he yelled.

The candles had burned a dime-sized hole in the back of Dad's pants. Everyone giggled as he danced a jig. That Father's Day was very special. It was the last time I would purchase a Father's Day card for my sweet, dear daddy. Looking back, I am so glad we took advantage of that Father's Day to let Dad know how special he was to us.

Dad was scheduled for laser prostate surgery, supposedly a simple, outpatient procedure. My sister Linda came to help Mother during the week of Dad's operation. When I took him for his exam before surgery, the nurse asked him if he had stopped taking his blood thinner. He assured her that he had.

What I didn't know was that Dad had been warned at his previous appointment about the risk he would be taking by discontinuing this medication. A blood clot could form during the time he was off the medicine. Dad knew that he had to have the surgery, and that it could not be done without temporarily stopping the blood thinners. He faced a dilemma, yet he did not share any of this information with the rest of the family.

The night before his surgery, we ate together at my parent's house. After dinner, Dad shared with us how worried he was about the operation and asked us to pray.

"Daddy," I said, trying to comfort him. "You went through open heart surgery before, and this will be a breeze compared to that. This kind of outpatient surgery is not even invasive. You're going to come home the same day and be just fine."

Dad knew the risks he was taking. We prayed as he had asked us to, and then we went our separate ways. The next morning, I picked him up at 5:45 a.m. and drove him to the hospital. The surgery went smoothly and Dad was soon released. On the way home, we had a positive conversation. I could tell he was relieved the surgery was over.

The following day I stopped by to check on Dad. While I was there, he got up off the couch and started to stumble. I jumped up and helped him sit down.

"I had one of my spells," he said sadly. I told him he needed to rest, so I helped him to the back bedroom.

"Randy, I think I better get to the emergency room. I can't stop the dizziness and now my right arm feels weird."

Linda was getting ready to take Mom to a doctor's appointment. I told Linda what Dad had said. She walked straight into the bedroom.

"Dad," Linda spoke to him as if he were a child, "you just need to calm down. You don't need to go to the hospital. What you need is for us to pray for you. Let's all join hands."

Linda began to pray. I kept worrying that we should be getting Dad to the emergency room. I felt a little guilty for my lack of faith, but I was ready to put feet on my prayers. When Linda finished praying, she asked Dad if he felt better. He told her he did and that she should go ahead and get Mom to the doctor.

As soon as they walked out the door, Dad said to me, "Randy, you are going to have to get me to the hospital."

I could detect that he was slurring his words. I knew the signs: tingling in his right side, slurred speech. Dad was having a stroke. I had learned since Mom's stroke that if you get the person to the hospital soon enough, they can be given certain medicine that could possibly arrest the progress of the stroke.

I went into panic mode. I got Dad up and started helping him down the hallway. He had to lean on me because his right side was paralyzed. I got him down the steps and into the car.

On our way to the emergency room, Dad tried to speak, but I could not understand him. When I pulled into the emergency parking area, I jumped out and grabbed a wheelchair. I wheeled Dad into the waiting area and told the nurse what was wrong. She immediately took him back and started the preliminary work to check him in. She put Dad in a room off the nurses' station and hooked him up to an IV. The doctor came in and affirmed that Dad was in the process of having a stroke. They could not tell at this point how severe it would be, but would watch him closely.

I called Pam at the school where she was teaching. Pam cried, "Oh, no! I'll be right there."

I returned to Dad's room and he looked at me. "Randy, I think I've gotten a hold of this." He was speaking clearly again. I was both encouraged and frightened.

"Dad, that's good, but just relax. Everything will be okay. Just stay still and quiet."

I patted his hand and sat beside his bed, thinking how hard it was for me to comfort my own dad. As a pastor, I had been called in on so many serious medical situations and had always been able to keep my cool, but now I felt numb. I had to force myself even to take Dad's hand. He was frightened and needed me to comfort him, but I was so scared. The thought kept running through my mind, "This could be it! Dad could be taken from me. What would life be like without him?"

I excused myself again and went to call home. Linda and Mom had returned from the doctor. I filled Linda in on the latest, and told her I would keep them informed. Pam arrived at the hospital shortly afterwards, and the two of us talked to the doctor.

"Well, your dad has an enlarged heart," he began.

Pam looked at me and said, "We've always known that Dad had a big heart... haven't we Randy?" I knew what she meant.

"We will just have to let him ride this out. We've given him something to help him relax. Now we just have to wait and see how much damage has been done by the stroke."

This felt so wrong. Why wasn't there something else they could do? The nurse was asking what medications he was taking. Dad was trying to motion to us what he wanted to say, but at this point the stroke had completely taken his ability to speak. It was hard for me to see Dad this way. I told Pam I knew where he kept his list of medications. I would run by his house to pick it up, and then stop by home to get some things so I could spend the night with Dad.

When I got to my parent's home, Mother kept saying over and over, "This can't be happening! What would I do without Randall?"

I raced to my house, threw some stuff in an overnight bag and was walking out the door when the phone rang. It was Pam.

"Where are you?" she was screaming hysterically.

"I'm at home, getting my stuff. Pam, what is wrong?"

"It's Dad. He had another massive stroke! He stopped breathing and the nurse screamed at me...wanting to know if they should put a breathing tube down his throat. She said that I had to make the decision, but I couldn't, I just couldn't. Hurry, Randy, I need you!"

I assured Pam I was on my way, raced to the hospital and ran up to the room.

The doctor came in and broke the devastating news to us. Dad had suffered a major stroke to the brain stem. There was no hope of survival. He was not in any pain and was unaware of anything. He could die at any time.

I heard the doctor's words, but could not accept them. Dad was still breathing. I prayed for a miracle. I did not cry. I felt numb. Pam cried tears for both of us. I called Linda and broke the news. She said she would wait until morning to tell Mom.

Pam and I stayed at the hospital all night, taking turns standing by Dad's bed, holding his hand, patting him, and telling him how much we loved him. We sang songs and prayed that God was letting him hear us. Gary came to the hospital for a while, but I told him to go home and rest so he could work the next day.

The next morning, at 5:30 a.m., I called Sheryl in Hot Springs to tell her what had happened. She told me that she would call in and get a substitute for her kindergarten class and be there as soon as she could. When Sheryl walked in, I was so relieved to see her. I hugged her, and she comforted me with tears in her eyes. I could not cry. I was exhausted, having been awake more than twenty-four hours.

It was Friday, and I needed to make plans for church on Sunday morning. I asked someone to preach for me. Around noon, as I sat beside my father's bed, I started feeling very emotional. The tears that had been dammed up were getting ready to flow.

I walked down the hallway to the waiting area where I found Sheryl. I asked if she could give me a ride home. I needed to be somewhere private, because whatever was inside me was about to explode and I did not want to be in public for all to see me fall apart. I told Pam I was leaving for a short time. As we neared my duplex, I saw my dad's truck in the driveway where I had left it, having borrowed it the day before. I felt the first stream of tears, but concentrated on holding them back until we got inside.

I walked to the sofa to sit down. When I heard Sheryl shut the door, I let go. I doubled over and a screaming groan gurgled up out of my broken heart. I wailed and cried, until I thought I would lose my voice.

Sheryl asked if I wanted to be alone, and I screamed "NO!" She put her arms around me, rocked me back and forth, patted me and cried with me for at least thirty minutes.

When I was able to form words, I said to Sheryl in a little boy's voice, "I am losing my daddy. My daddy is dying. I don't want him to die, I don't want him to die! Oh, please God, don't let my daddy die!"

When I calmed down a little, Sheryl got a wet washcloth and patted my head. She called Gary and handed me the phone. When I heard his voice, I lost it again. I told him how I was feeling and that it would mean a lot to me if he would come home. Gary told me he was on his way and that he loved me.

There was no change in Dad's condition all night long. I slept very little. The next morning, the doctor told Pam and me that we should start getting his funeral plans in order. It was just a matter of hours, a day or two at the most.

That afternoon Linda brought Mom to the hospital to sit by Dad's bed for a while. She sat and held Dad's hand and spoke to him about their life together. She told him how much she loved him. "You just can't leave me, honey. Please, you can't leave."

When Linda told her they needed to go, Mom leaned over and kissed him and said, "You are my sweetheart. You always have been and you always will be. I love you honey."

They went home. I was surprised at how little time Linda seemed to want to spend with Dad, but Linda was struggling with her own mortality. Her doctor had told her that she was in stage four cancer and had only a short time to live. For her, sitting in Dad's room made death too real, too near. I felt sorry for Linda, because she was afraid and yet we could not comfort her. In Linda's twisted theology, to show fear would show a lack of faith in God.

The next morning Pam, Gary, and I went to the hospital cafeteria to eat breakfast while Sheryl and my cousin Lisa sat with Dad. The doctor told us that Dad would probably not make it through the day.

As we ate, Lisa ran in. "Hurry!" she said.

We rushed to the elevator. As soon as the door opened on Dad's floor, we raced to his room. Sheryl, holding Daddy's hand, had been afraid that we would not make it back in time, so she had started softly saying our names to Dad: "Randall, Marcelle loves you, Linda loves you, Pam loves you, Randy loves you…"

Just as we walked into the room, Dad breathed one last breath. Pam and I wept and hugged each other. We both hugged Daddy one last time. Gary had his arm around me for support. I suddenly felt a strong urge to be with Mother. I wanted to comfort her. I drove in pouring rain to Mom's house and ran in to tell her the news. I found her sitting on her bed and I put my arm around her.

"Mama, Daddy's gone, but I want you to know that we love you and we will make sure you are taken care of. Don't worry. We are here for you. I promised Daddy that we would take care of you."

She did not cry, but simply said, "He's with the Lord."

I do not remember much after that point. I was told to write an obituary. We called Brother, my Dad's uncle, and asked if he would do the funeral. While I knew it would be emotionally hard, I knew Uncle Brother would do a great job eulogizing my dad. In the obituary, I wrote that memorials could be made in lieu of flowers to the *Susan G. Komen Breast Cancer Foundation*, because both Linda and Pam battled breast cancer, or to the Open Door Community Church Building Fund. I knew how much Dad wanted us to get the church building and how he had planned to make a sizable donation. This way, all his children would benefit from his memorials. I was not aware of the hailstorm that would ensue when the family read the obituary the next day in the paper.

Linda called and told me that she was upset that I would put the church building fund in Dad's obituary.

"This is a travesty!" She spoke loudly into the phone. "I am upset and so are a lot of other people, including Mom's sister, Sue."

I tried to explain my reasons, but she would not listen.

"You have done this for selfish reasons and I am highly offended by it."

For the funeral I bought large boxes of fruit, which we had arranged on a table in the church lobby. A sign read: "Please take a piece of fruit in memory of Randall McCain, The Produce Man."

Gary and I sat with my family. I was thankful that Gary was at my side. The funeral at Mom and Dad's church in North Little Rock was followed by the graveside service in Warren, Arkansas. After the graveside service, my Uncle Brother came over and hugged me hard.

"Your dad was such an inspiration to me. He showed me how a father should love his son. I learned a lot from his example."

I knew that Uncle Brother would love to have another chance to "do it right" with his gay son, Floyd. Since Dad's death, Uncle Brother has been so good to me, giving me the acceptance he had not known how to show his own son. I know that my cousin, Floyd, is looking down from Heaven, very proud of his Baptist preacher Dad and waiting to welcome him home.

The first holiday season after you lose a close member of the family is hard. I decided I would celebrate Christmas because of the hope that Jesus brought into a dark, hopeless world. It seemed as if someone had put a dimmer switch on the Christmas lights that year. Yes, the family gathered at Mom's house, but Dad had been the glue that held the family together. When we celebrated New Year's Day 2001, I was relieved. 2000 was over and I fervently hoped that 2001 would be better.

Chapter 55

Open Door's Fifth Birthday

In 2001 Open Door would be five years old, and I decided we should celebrate that milestone in January. The only name that came to my mind for our special speaker was Peggy Campolo. We had talked many times on the phone and corresponded, yet had never met face-to-face.

I met her husband Tony when he spoke at a Baptist church in Little Rock two years before. Gary and I had attended with Bryan Canfield, our friend and faithful Open Door member. After the service, I introduced myself to Tony as Peggy's friend and told him that his wife had been such a support to me and my partner when I had been fired from my ministry position at a church. Tony immediately knew who I was.

He reached out, hugging me tight, and said, "You know I'm with you guys. If anyone in the church tries to hurt you, they are going to have to get through me *first*."

Peggy was glad to accept the invitation to speak for us. I told her that I knew it would be a blessing to the whole church, but for me, it would be a dream come true to finally meet her in person.

Peggy had begun to be more public with her advocacy work and efforts to show Evangelical churches how their exclusion of God's gay and lesbian children was unlike Jesus. Certainly, Peggy's commitment had gotten her husband in some hot water, but he was no stranger to controversy. One prominent evangelical minister suggested that Tony should not be allowed to preach the gospel because he didn't have his own spiritual house "in order," referring to Peggy's ministry.

Peggy had never thought of herself as a speaker, nor had she ever had a cause that she wanted to pour her energies into, other than being a wife and mother. But an encounter she had with Jesus Christ in 1984 opened her eyes and heart to the injustices done to her gay, lesbian, bisexual, and transgender brothers and sisters. Now she found herself pulled more and more into that arena of controversy. Everywhere she spoke, Peggy made it clear that she and her husband agreed on some issues related to the gay controversy, but disagreed on others. Both agreed that churches all over the world had mistreated gay people. They agreed that gays should have the *right* to marry in a pluralistic society. Peggy blessed such unions, but Tony, because of his interpretation of Paul's words in Romans chapter one, did not. Peggy always reminded Evangelical audiences that she and Tony were an example of how two people who differ on this issue can do Kingdom work together, love each other, and not separate.

Peggy believed that the churches in America should be a mix of gays and non-gays worshiping together, the same vision that God had given to me when we started Open Door. I could not wait to spend time with this brave woman who was willing to sacrifice her place of acceptance among evangelicals, to stand up for my rights and the rights of *all* gay, lesbian, bisexual, and transgender Christians.

The Friday finally arrived for Peggy to fly to Little Rock. I waited at the airport with bells on…not bells, but a unique lapel pin that looked very much like a spider! I had wondered if we would be able to recognize each other, but I need not have worried.

There was no mistaking this very petite, smiling, high cheekboned woman, her long hair gathered up on her head, walking confidently down the corridor of the airport terminal. When she saw me, she beamed. I could tell that she was anticipating our meeting almost as much as I was.

Her first words were, "You must be Randy, and look, you're wearing our little friend," referring to the lapel pin.

We embraced. I walked through the airport beside this woman that I had loved before I ever laid eyes on her. She was such a support to me during the past six years. She helped me believe in myself when I was being told by so many that I was flawed and unusable by God. I felt so proud walking next to her. I wanted to shout out to everyone, "This is my friend, Peggy Campolo!"

We talked non-stop on the way to the hotel where she would be staying. Later, Gary joined us for dinner. It was then I discovered the spider lapel pin was missing. I panicked! We looked everywhere and came up empty-handed. I was practically in tears! That little spider had been so much a part of our lives for the past six years. It had decorated our Christmas tree. It had been shown to many people as I shared about my good friend Peggy. Now it was lost.

When I informed Peggy, she smiled and said, "Well, our little friend was there to keep us connected until we could meet in person. Now it must be on another adventure to do some more God work."

I let my spider go and enjoyed our conversation.

The next night, we had a great turnout for Peggy's talk. As I introduced Peggy to the crowd, I told the congregation that she was the one who had planted the seed in my heart to birth Open Door. She got a standing ovation before she even said a word. Peggy told the congregation that it was a privilege to be with us and celebrate *Open Door Community Church's* fifth birthday.

"The birth and growth of this church has been part of my own journey, doing the work God called me to do. Randy and I walked together through the events of the summer of 1995 when he was fired from his ministry position, and we helped each other. I knew God was calling me to be a voice for those who had no voice, but I didn't have the courage to do it in a big way.

"God used the reality of Randy's pain and the absolute injustice of what had happened to him to strengthen me for the work I was being called to do in the church—the church that was breaking so many hearts, and surely the heart of God."

Peggy eloquently described her ministry in a poignant word picture: "I am a carrier pigeon from the misunderstood to the misinformed."

Among those challenged by Peggy's words was Micah Qualls, the young girl who sang a solo that night. She had lived through the nightmare of my firing at the church her father pastored. She was only 12 at the time and did not understand all the ramifications. She loved Gary and me and decided, as she grew older, that the church should be open to gay and lesbian people. That night, after hearing Peggy, she made a vow to God that she would become an advocate for those who did not have a place in most churches. She would stand up for her gay and lesbian brothers and sisters. Micah has kept that vow.

Peggy ended with a bang! "When asked for a definition of hope, a little boy replied, 'Hope is wishin' for what ain't gonna happen,'" she said. "That's not what I feel in this room tonight. Someday soon the light of God's justice will stream into all the closets and dark places, banishing the fear that holds so many people captive, because someday soon I believe the real church of Jesus Christ will rise up and say, 'You are wrong,' to these false prophets who tell us that *some* of God's children are not welcome in God's house!"

Our people applauded enthusiastically. We ended the service by singing "We Shall Overcome."

The next morning, Peggy got to experience the charm of a service at Open Door Community Church. Her affirming words to us would long be remembered. When it was time to take Peggy to the airport after the service, I gave her a check for her ministry, but she would not accept it.

"Randy, I want to feel that my coming here to speak was a gift to this church that I love so much. I do not say this very often, but I truly feel that, all weekend, I have felt the presence of the Holy Spirit in such a special way. I had grown weary of this work that I feel God has called me to, but this weekend has energized me to do even more Kingdom work. Thank you so much, my friend."

As we said our goodbyes, I knew that God was up to something pretty exciting in our lives and in Peggy's.

Chapter 56

Victory in Court

On March 23, 2001, we received great news. Pulaski County Circuit Court Judge David B. Bogard ruled that it was unconstitutional for Arkansas to ban consensual sex for adult, same-sex couples, therefore the Arkansas sodomy law was unconstitutional! The ruling emphasized that government oversteps when it tries to dictate highly intimate, personal decisions, and when it singles out one group of people for a rule not applied to others.

"It is consistent with this State's Constitution to hold that an adult's right to engage in consensual and noncommercial sexual activities in the privacy of that adult's home is a matter of intimate personal concern, which is at the heart of the right to privacy in Arkansas," wrote Judge Bogard in his decision.

I found out about the ruling when a reporter from the Associated Press called. Once again, I was being contacted by the local media. One question they asked was whether I thought Attorney General Mark Pryor would appeal the ruling to the State Supreme Court of Arkansas. I had spoken to Mr. Pryor. I had introduced myself and told him that I was one of the plaintiffs in the sodomy lawsuit.

"I guess we find ourselves on opposite sides in that case," he said, almost apologetically.

"Yes, we do." I replied.

"Well", the Attorney General confessed, "we both know it is an unjust law."

That convinced me that he would not appeal the lower court decision. However, Pryor was running for the United States Senate, so there would be political pressure from conservative groups in the state for him to appeal.

In a letter to the editor in the Arkansas *Democrat Gazette,* one person urged readers to call Attorney General Mark Pryor immediately, and to let him know that the "good people in Arkansas are not going to be intimidated by seven gay people." But the *Democrat Gazette,* known to be editorially conservative, actually came out favoring the ruling. In response to the question of the state's appeal, the newspaper urged Pryor to allow the ruling to stand.

Talk about exciting! To have the endorsement of the *Democrat Gazette* was a major accomplishment. Plus, after three years, we had accomplished something hardly anyone had believed possible. We had won our case against the state, and it was no longer a criminal act to be gay in Arkansas! Gary and I were no longer criminals! But our joy was dampened somewhat a few days later when it was announced that Mark Pryor *was* appealing the lower court decision to the state supreme court. Politics had obviously played a role in his decision.

Chapter 57

A Place for Open Door to Call Home

In late March 2001, I received a call from the real estate agent. He said that the Baptist church selling the property had come up with a plan that he wanted to run by me, a delayed sale contract. The realtor explained that the church would help us, since we were unable to get a loan from the bank. We would pay the sellers $20,000 down and then make payments of $1,300 a month for three years. All of this would go toward the principle, interest free. At the end of the three years, we would have a good payment history to qualify for a loan to pay off the remainder of the debt.

This sounded like a great deal, but still, we had so little money. Plus, would it be smart for us to spend all that we could scrape up to get into the building, and then be faced with making $1,300 payments each month, plus utilities, incidentals, and my small salary?

I called the treasurer and he told me that we had now collected $19,000 for the building fund. When I spoke with the others in the church, they seemed excited. Then I met with the pastor of the Baptist church. I told him that we were interested in the contract. I explained that we could probably come up with the $20,000 they were asking from us up front, but that it would take every penny we had. This would leave us with no money to finance the move into the facility.

"We were wondering if you would consider $15,000 down," I said to him.

I had met with the pastor before, and knew him to be very conservative. Yet, he never asked, and I never told, *how* open Open Door's mission statement was. As much as I had been in the news, I was surprised that someone from their church hadn't recognized me, or my name. Our meetings before had been very cordial, and we simply talked in general terms about our love for Jesus.

"Randy, we built this church ourselves. The property is zoned for commercial use, but we would like for it to remain a church and we would like for it to be a church that we feel good about. And Randy, I feel good about you and your ministry. We will take your request to the elders of the church. I am pretty sure I can convince them to change the amount."

After much prayer, long talks with many men and women whom I trusted, and a call from the real estate agent informing me that the church had consented to lower the down payment, we took the step of faith and signed the contract. When I met the agent to review the papers, I raised only one question.

"What if we sign this agreement and then, a year later, the church changes its mind and decides it does not want to sell to us. Can they annul the contract?"

"Randy," he answered, "they can get as mad as hell with you, but they will be bound to this contract. This isn't like rent-to-own. This is a title that will be signed at a title company. The only way they can get the building back is if you cannot make your payments, or cannot get financed at the end of the three years."

With this assurance, I signed the agreement. As we walked out of the building, the agent handed me the key to the church. It was a moment I will always remember. So many times, when I met the realtor at the church site and then drove out of the church parking lot, I looked in my rear view mirror and saw him locking the door to the church. I would think to myself, "One day, that key will be ours."

And now it was.

On the morning of Sunday, April 29, 2001, we gathered for worship at our home one last time. I got emotional as I watched our folks gathering in our living room. I could not help but think back to that very first Sunday when just three of us had met as Open Door. I thought about the many people who had walked in and out of our home in the past five years, seeking a safe place to worship God. Now we were closing one chapter and beginning a new one.

We had taken all the chairs over to the new building, so we stood for the short service. The only thing that remained was a tall wooden cross. Since our first church service on January 7, 1996, the cross had been on display to turn our living room into a holy place. It would be the last piece of our five-year history to make the journey to our new home.

There was such excitement in the air! Joan, a woman who attended our church, along with her 80-year-old mother, tied colorful ribbons and streamers on car antennas so that our caravan would look festive as we made our way through the Sherwood streets to 709 West Lee Avenue. As we gathered in our living room, I overheard my mom say to someone, "Isn't this exciting?"

When I walked to the front of the living room and thanked God for our courageous congregation, I thought of Paul the Apostle looking out at the faces of those who gathered in little fledgling churches he founded throughout Asia Minor. How I loved these precious people who were learning to trust God. As I addressed the congregation, my heart was filled with thanksgiving to God.

After my introductory remarks, we joined hands and sang a worship chorus.

Then, I prayed, "We thank you for this place where many have received your grace. As we travel to our new 'promised land,' to the new church building you have provided for us, we pray that your spirit will go with us and that we will have a beautiful manifestation of your grace, your mercy, and your love in the service this morning, as we worship for the first time in our new facility. We ask it in Jesus name, Amen."

As I closed in prayer, Sheryl's sons Craig and Matt picked up the cross and carried it down the street to my dad's beloved truck. The cross stood against the cab with the boys sitting on each side to steady it. Gary and I got in Dad's truck, and I got misty thinking of Dad looking down from heaven, smiling as he saw the completion of the miracle for which he had prayed. Then the caravan began.

Craig, sitting in the back of the truck, started his spiritual journey as an agnostic, but one Sunday morning, after attending Open Door for a year, he came up to me after church with tears streaming down his face.

"Randy, I know now. I know there is a God!"

"So you are not agnostic anymore?"

"No, not after this morning. I've gotten emotional before at Open Door. But today, it was not emotion; it was a force, a living force that I felt during prayer time. I know now there is a God, and that God is love."

That memory was vivid in my mind as I pulled the truck out into the street to lead the caravan to our new place of worship. Craig told me later at lunch that it was hard for him to say goodbye to our living room worship space.

"Randy," he said, tears streaming down his cheeks. "Your living room was where I first *knew* there was a God. It will always be a holy place for me."

Now God had given us a place where we could reach more people like Craig.

Our caravan consisted of about 20 cars, honking horns and shrieking excitement out of open windows as we passed down the street. We pulled into the parking lot, and the boys unloaded the cross and set it in front of the doors of the church.

I got out of the truck and stood at the front of the crowd, holding the giant ceremonial scissors that a woman in the church made for the occasion. Gary stood by my side. It was a picture perfect Arkansas spring day, with sunny skies and just a slight cool breeze. I introduced my mom to the crowd and asked her to come forward and pray the dedicatory prayer. Her beautiful white hair shimmered in the sunlight, and her stylish pink and white dress blew in the wind. She looked out at the crowd on the lawn, and before she prayed, she spoke words of greeting.

"Don't you think this is an exciting day?"

"Yes ma'am!" one of the members yelled out.

"I have been so excited this weekend, just thinking about it, that God has given us this place to meet and worship Him every Sunday. Isn't it wonderful? God is a good

God. He loves each one of us just as we are. He loves *you* that way. You're an original to God, and He loves you. So don't ever get down and think nobody cares for you, because God is there and God loves you."

After these God-inspired words, Mom prayed, "Our heavenly Father, we pray that you will bless this congregation. I pray that your work will go on and out from this church. Let this be a filling station for your people who are working for you. Keep them close to you, Lord. Let them feel your love, and God protect them from all harm. I pray that you will keep this church as a special place, so that when people come into this building, they will feel your presence.

"Oh! God! Bless the pastor. And Jesus, go with him and all who are standing behind him. Stand with them and bless them. May the news of this church spread out into this community, Lord, that people may know that there is something unusual going on at Open Door Church. It's all because of your love, Lord. Help this church to be a beacon of light to the surrounding communities, and may it be a well-known church because of the work that is being done and the blessings that are coming forth from this church. We dedicate it to you right now, Lord. You've given this church to us, and now we give it back to you. We love you, Lord, and praise you in Jesus' name. Amen."

After mother's prayer, I cut the ribbon and said, "We dedicate this building to the glory of God!"

Cheers rang out, and Craig and Matt opened the front door, carried in the cross, and placed it on the platform behind the pulpit. Forty-three attended that day, and we wondered if we would ever see that many in the church building again.

Micah Qualls joined our praise team that day to help us celebrate. She was so excited for us. It was an unforgettable Sunday, a day of miracles realized, a day of rejoicing, a day when God took a little rag-tag congregation that seemed not to have much of a chance and sided with them, enabling them to see God work miracles on their behalf. We were standing that morning smack dab in the middle of a miracle cocoon!

Randy's mom praying at the dedication of Open Door's new church building

Chapter 58

A Stormy Walk in the Rain

As 2001 drew to a close, it became apparent that Mom could no longer live alone. She fell often, and also forgot about pots on the stove that almost burned the house down. My sisters and I made the decision that it was time for Mom to move into an assisted living facility.

Mom was spending time at Linda's house in Wynne where Linda was battling for her life, taking chemo treatments that sapped her energy. Although she would have liked Mom to move in with her and her husband, this would not be a good idea because of Linda's grave situation and Mom's own poor health. Linda knew this too, but wanted Mom to spend as much time with her as possible. She felt that Pam and I were brainwashing Mother into a more lenient stance on the gay issue.

Linda knew that Mom attended our church occasionally and scolded her for it. One time, when Pam went to pick Mother up from Linda's house, Linda took her aside and accused her and me of *making* Mother go to our church with us. Pam admitted that I invited Mom, but Mother was the one who said she wanted to attend, and we *never* forced Mother to go.

Linda began to preach at Pam about how wrong it was for her to support my lifestyle in any way. She had Pam in tears, but Linda herself remained stoic.

Since Mom was preparing to move, Pam and I helped her to get ready for a yard sale in the spring of 2002. Linda and her kids came down that same weekend. While we were working the sale, Sheryl Myers stopped by for a visit.

Linda was getting ready to go on her daily walk. Sheryl saw this as an opportunity to get to know my sister better and asked Linda if she could join her. They were gone for about an hour and a half. I knew that Sheryl could hold her own with Linda in the walking department, because I had tried to keep up with her and found that she could leave me in the dust! I wondered, though, how Sheryl would fare if the conversation turned theological.

While they were gone, it started pouring rain. Pam and I rushed to move the sale items in under the carport. As we finished, I looked up to see two drenched women walking up the driveway, laughing. I grabbed my camera and said, "I need a picture of this!" Linda walked over to Sheryl and put her arm around her and said, "Aren't we a sight?!" This friendly chatter, however, was not indicative of the conversation on their walk.

Later, when Sheryl and I were alone, she gave me a blow-by-blow account. At first their conversation was just chit-chat. Then, somehow, it moved to a discussion of praise and worship music. They both commented on how much they loved the new worship chorus "Shout to the Lord," and Sheryl asked Linda a few questions about her position as music minister at her church. Sheryl then told Linda how thrilled she was with our new church building.

"Have you been in the new building?" Sheryl asked.

Linda yelled back, "NO! AND I NEVER WILL! I am praying AGAINST that church!"

"But Linda, it's a *wonderful* church."

"You are SO DECEIVED, Sheryl, and that is sad because you are such a nice person."

"Well Linda, I believe *you* are deceived, and that is so sad because *you* are such a nice person."

"Randy is deceiving so many people and that just makes me sick. I am praying that Open Door Church will fail."

"But you haven't heard Randy preach. There is something so special about his sermons and his singing."

Linda smirked and said, "Oh, there's nothing Randy likes better than to get up in front of people and put on a show! He's done it since he was a little boy!"

"You think his ministry is just a show?" Sheryl asked, surprised at Linda's anger toward me.

Linda laughed sarcastically.

Sheryl, horrified at Linda's attitude, pressed her. "Linda, do you mean to tell me you think that when Randy was just a little boy, his love for God was not sincere? It was just a show? Linda, I *know* it wasn't insincere then, or now."

Linda laughed again. "Well, you are just so deceived. You aren't even supposed to *eat* with those people."

"Well, Jesus did." Sheryl countered, righteously indignant at Linda's judgmental attitude. "Jesus didn't say anything about homosexuality, but he said a lot about loving and judging."

At this, Linda grew agitated. She screamed, "IT IS AN ABOMINATION FOR A MAN TO LIE WITH A MAN AS WITH A WOMAN!!! YOU JUST STAY OUT OF MY FAMILY'S BUSINESS!! IT'S NONE OF YOUR BUSINESS!! YOU JUST

LEAVE ME ALONE. I JUST DON'T WANT TO TALK ABOUT THIS!!"

Sheryl stayed calm. "You brought it up, Linda."

"I DID NOT!"

"Yes you did, Linda. I asked if you had been inside our new church. You said you were praying against our church, the church I love. What if I had said I was praying against *your* church because I thought *you* are a bunch of pharisaical hypocrites? Would you defend it?"

"Randy is rebelling against God!"

"Why would Randy rebel against God, Linda? He loves God. He's always loved God. Randy loves Gary the way that you love your husband and the way I love mine. Randy is the way God created him to be. Gary is a precious person, and they have such a lovely home together where they put God first and where they welcome others. What would you have Randy do?"

"I would tell him to leave Gary and get out of that sinful lifestyle and marry a woman," Linda responded, matter-of-fact.

"But he loves Gary, and Gary loves him. How sad it would be for them to separate!"

"I like Gary," Linda said, "but Randy is not obeying God."

"What would you do if it were you, Linda? What if you had been the one to discover that *you* were gay? Would you go against your natural tendencies?"

"I would obey God, no matter what. It's in the Bible!"

"Okay, but let's suppose that you are attracted to your husband, that you always have been, that you love him dearly and that he means the world to you. Now, suppose that the Bible told you that this attraction was sinful, that women are supposed to be with women. What if the Bible said that for you to be with Mike is an abomination to God? What would you do? Would you leave Mike, the man that you love, to be with a woman, because the Bible told you to? Would you leave what is natural for you, for that which is unnatural to you?"

To Sheryl's utter amazement, Linda answered, "I would."

"*What?!*" Sheryl exclaimed.

"If the Bible told me to, I would do it to obey God," Linda answered coldly.

"Well, I wouldn't, and Linda, I don't believe you would either. I love my husband and I wouldn't leave him. I couldn't be with a woman if God demanded it, because I'm just not attracted to women. I'm attracted to my husband, and you are attracted to Mike. How heartbreaking to leave your marriage for something that is unnatural for you. That's what it would be like for Randy and Gary. How could you expect that of them, and how could you think God would expect that of them? He knows their relationship is about love, and that's all that matters to God."

Linda was frustrated by Sheryl's words. It was as though she had been trapped into saying she would be a lesbian if God required it, and she didn't know how to get out of it.

At this point Linda had had a meltdown and yelled, "We are not talking about *this* anymore!!"

For the rest of the walk, they did not talk. It was a muggy morning, and Linda and Sheryl both walked at a fast clip, so both had been drenched in sweat. Then the cloud burst had caused them to walk even faster. Sheryl had learned on that walk why I had such difficulty communicating with Linda. She had encouraged me to do more to bridge the gap between Linda and myself, but now she experienced what I was up against.

It troubled me that Linda and I were not close. The estrangement became even more painful when I found out that Linda had started having episodes with blurred vision and seizures. The doctors ran tests and discovered Linda had developed a cancerous tumor on her brain. Surgery took a lot out of her.

Linda's failing health was very painful to witness. I wanted so badly to make things right between us, but how? Linda lived with a death sentence hanging over her for years. She had lived with stage four cancer much longer than anyone had expected, a miracle to many doctors, Yet the pain she endured, and the mental struggle, was relentless. When I prayed for her, I tried to imagine what Linda was going through. I tried to find greeting cards that contained encouraging words. I wrote in them that I was praying for her, and that I loved her. I never got a response from Linda. I ached inside for my big sister.

Sheryl and Linda after their walk in the rain

Chapter 59

A Surprise Visit from the Campolos

In February of 2002, Peggy Campolo called.

"Randy, I have a surprise for you," she said. "I wasn't going to tell you, but then I thought maybe I should. I am planning on coming to *Open Door* on Easter Sunday. I do not want to speak. I just want to be able to enjoy being at Open Door, the church that means so much to me."

"That's so exciting, Peggy!

"But wait," she stopped me. "There's more. I am bringing Tony with me. I want him to experience Open Door. He does not want to speak either, and I don't want you to tell anyone but Gary that he is coming. I just want Tony to be able to sit and worship with me this Easter at the church of my heart."

I almost stopped breathing from excitement! Peggy *and* Tony at Open Door! Wow! I was trying to process this as I walked around the sanctuary, talking to Peggy on my cell phone. I could not sit still, my excitement was so great. I had always admired Tony as a preacher and writer. Now he would be attending *Open Door!*

Then it hit me. I would have to preach for *Tony Campolo!* My excitement turned to fear, but I didn't let Peggy know. As soon as I hung up the phone, I called Gary.

"Guess who is coming to Open Door for Easter service?"

"Who?" he asked.

"Peggy Campolo!"

"Wonderful!"

"And she's bringing Tony with her."

"Really?"

"Yes! But here's the scary part. I'm going to have to preach for *Tony Campolo!*"

"Great! You will do just fine."

"But Gary, you know that preaching is the area in which I have always felt weak. Tony is such a skilled communicator. I'm sure there are seasoned pastors who would quake at having to preach in front of Tony, much less a novice pastor like me."

"Randy, I think it's exciting and I know you will rise to the occasion. You always do and you always underestimate your abilities. Don't worry about it. Just pray and I know God will give you the right sermon."

Peggy had informed me that she and Tony would arrive in Little Rock on Saturday afternoon and they would rent a car.

"Tony and I know how busy a pastor is on the Saturday night before Easter, but we would like to take you and Gary out to eat."

When the day arrived, we picked Tony and Peggy up at their hotel to go to dinner. I was always able to talk with Peggy. She was such a natural at conversation. I wondered how Tony would be. I also wondered if he would feel any discomfort at being with a gay couple. He and Peggy still differed on the blessing of gay marriages.

Tony treated Gary and me with the greatest of respect. He told many of his wonderful stories and we had a great time. The evening was over far too soon. I was having the time of my life.

Gary said he kept thinking, "We are sitting here with Tony and Peggy Campolo!" Both of us felt like we needed to pinch ourselves to make sure we weren't dreaming.

Some would wonder, "What's the big deal about going to dinner with Tony and Peggy Campolo?" In our minds this was monumental. As a minister, who used to have many minister friends in his life but now had very few who would even want to be seen with him, having dinner in public with Tony and Peggy was a major time of healing and affirmation. I was sitting at a table with someone who had counseled the President of the United States in the White House. Tony was someone I had admired and looked up to for years, never dreaming I would ever meet him. And now, Tony was sitting with me, acknowledging that my ministry was valid and talking with me as a fellow minister, a brother in Christ.

In my life, that night was *huge*! When we said good night to the Campolos, I rushed as fast as I could to the church to work on my sermon. I finished typing it about 3:00 a.m. and went home for a quick night's sleep.

Easter Sunday has always been my favorite day to attend church. There is such excitement in the air. God's love could not be sealed up in a tomb; He is Risen! Alleluia! As our folks started to gather, it became clear that we would have a record number of worshipers at Open Door. One hundred and forty people attended!

When it came time for me to preach, I took a deep breath and dove in. It actually wasn't that bad, considering that I had written it in the wee hours of the morning. After the service we quickly stacked the chairs, set up the tables, and put out the food for the potluck. Peggy and Tony got to experience a great meal with homemade southern cooking.

During the meal, Tony and Peggy visited with many from our congregation.

Tony later made the comment that he had never seen a congregation so excited about their church and so happy to have one to attend. Peggy was beaming. She was able that day to show Tony why she enjoyed her ministry so much.

After the meal, we awarded the Campolos with a gift basket filled with Arkansas products. As we were saying our goodbyes to them, Peggy hugged me and said, "Randy, *this* has been the most joyful and Spirit-filled Easter service I have ever attended. After being here with Tony, whom I love, and with you and Gary, whom I love, at this wonderful church I love so much, I could die tonight and be happy!"

"Oh no, Peggy," I protested. "You have far too much work left to do to die tonight. There will be many more wonderful days like this. God is using you, Peggy. We are so grateful to you for your labor of love."

"Randy, Open Door gives me the courage and the strength to continue doing what I do. I love this place more than I can tell you!"

Gary later shared that Tony had asked him, "Is Randy *always* that fired up when he preaches?" I was thrilled to get that kind of compliment from a man whose preaching ability I had always so admired.

A few days later I received an email from Peggy:

Dear Randy,

There really are no words adequate to tell you how much this past weekend meant to me… for so many reasons. First of all, it was, by any measure, the most joyful and Spirit-filled Easter service Tony and I have ever attended. But it was so much more to me, Randy. To remember where you were when the vision of Open Door was birthed is hard for me to do now. (But I know I have to remember those sad days just so I can make others believe that God can take anything and make something good out of it.) Tony was blessed beyond measure. He agreed to come because he loves me and knew it would mean so much to me, but he received far more than either of us ever dreamed. We loved the time with you and Gary, and we know very well what a sacrifice it was for you to give us time the night before Easter. And Tony now knows what a great preacher you are. Both of us were so aware of the large part Gary plays in all that happens at Open Door. Tony and I could feel how much you two love each other and how you do ministry as a team, and we were blessed to be with you.

Once again, Peggy knew just how to encourage me with her words. I could not thank God enough for bringing such a dear friend into my life.

The week after they visited Open Door, Tony and Peggy went through a life-changing event. Tony had a stroke. It was a wake-up call for him to change his diet and take better care of himself physically. I was so glad Tony was looking after his health because I felt it was vital for him to keep sharing his message of God's love and grace.

Shortly after Tony's stroke, he stayed at home with Peggy one Sunday instead of going out to preach. For their devotion time that day, they listened to a sermon I had delivered a few months before and sent to Peggy.

Tony wrote to me after hearing it.

Dear Randy:

The other morning, Peggy and I sat and listened to your message entitled, "Grace is Loose in the House." You are an outstanding preacher, and what is more important, you are faithful to the Word of God. My prayers today are that your church flourishes and that many come to know Christ through your ministry. So much depends on your success.

Yours in Christ,

Tony Campolo

Tony and Peggy Campolo Visit Open Door for Easter

Chapter 60

Victory in the State Supreme Court

On Friday, July 5, 2002, the Arkansas Supreme Court struck down the state's same-sex sodomy law. The court issued a lengthy decision that emphasized all Arkansans' expectations of privacy in their homes. It underscored that lesbians and gay men share the same constitutional protections as others. In their decision, the court proclaimed, "The General Assembly cannot act, under the cloak of police power or public morality, arbitrarily to invade personal liberties of the individual citizen.... [The sodomy law] does invade such liberties, arbitrarily condemning conduct between same-sex actors while permitting the exact same conduct among opposite-sex actors. [The State] has failed to demonstrate how such a distinction serves a legitimate public interest."

The majority opinion also stated, "We agree that the police power may not be used to enforce a majority morality on persons whose conduct does not harm others. The Arkansas equal rights amendment serves to protect minorities at the hands of majorities.

Justice Robert L. Brown wrote:

I agree completely that the State has placed the plaintiffs in a catch-22 situation. According to the State, they are dubbed criminals but have no recourse in the courts to correct this status. The idea of keeping a criminal statute on the books which no one wants to enforce is perverse in itself. This brands the plaintiffs with a scarlet letter that the State contends they should have no chance to contest in the courts of this State. The State's position comes perilously close to complete inconsistency and smacks of a no-lose proposition for the government and a no-win situation for the plaintiffs. The state's position is totally at odds with the bedrock principles of independence, freedom, happiness, and security which form the core of our individual rights under the Arkansas constitution…pronouncing moral judgments for bedroom behavior that criminalizes the conduct of this class of citizens exceeds the bounds of legislative authority and amounts to little more than a government morality fixed by a majority of the general assembly. That flies in the face of the basic constitutional rights of independence, freedom, happiness, and security.

When we started this lawsuit in early 1998, our attorneys warned that it would be an uphill battle, and would be a long, drawn-out process. They had been right, but we had won!

I was quoted on the front page of the *Arkansas Democrat Gazette*, saying, "I'm proud of the Supreme Court. I've always been proud to be an Arkansan, but I'm even more proud today."

Randy on his way to speak at a press conference after the sodomy lawsuit

Chapter 61

Saying Goodbye to a Sister

Early in 2003, my sister Pam called and told me that she had received a remarkable phone call from our sister, Linda.

"Pam," Linda had said, "I just wanted to apologize for not being a better sister to you. We were so close when we were growing up sharing a room, then being pregnant together. I know that in the past few years I have distanced myself from you, and I just haven't been a very good sister. Will you forgive me?"

"Linda, life happens, and sometimes people grow apart," Pam responded. "You moved away and we didn't see each other very often."

"I know, but when I came to town, I didn't make any effort to do things with you. I didn't even *call* you. Now, I am about to see God face-to-face, and I want to make sure that I've done everything I can to make right what I have done wrong."

"Pam," I exclaimed. "That is amazing! Maybe I'll get a call too! I hope so."

I waited, but the call never came. Linda had separated herself from Pam because Pam accepted me and Gary. As she faced death, she wanted to be sure that she didn't miss heaven because of some flaw in her character. Linda felt guilty for distancing herself from Pam, but she did not see her rejection of me as wrong. Actually, she saw her repeated rejection as a *holy* act.

This broke my heart. Still, I prayed for reconciliation before Linda left this earth.

Thursday evening, March 27, 2003, Gary and I went to meet Pam at a new little restaurant that had opened in Sherwood. Sheryl's support group for parents of gay and lesbian kids was scheduled to meet that night at the church, but for a variety of reasons most of the parents would not be able to attend. Only Dolly could come. I mentioned to Sheryl that when Dolly arrived at the church, the two of them should join us for dinner.

When Gary and I walked into the restaurant, none of the others had arrived. Then Sheryl and Dolly walked in. Dolly and I didn't get to see much of each other these days, and how I missed our fun times.

As we glanced over the menus, Pam arrived. One look at her face and I knew something was wrong. She did not have to tell me.

"It's Linda, isn't it?"

"Yes, Jana called me just a few minutes ago and told me that Linda died peacefully at home. She said that Mike was with her." Pam was teary-eyed.

"I guess we need to go tell Mom." I said. I was stoic. I asked Dolly and Sheryl to go with us to Mom's. When we broke the news to her about Linda, Mom did not cry. She started talking about Linda.

"Well, she is with Daddy now. She was such a wonderful Christian. I know she is with the Lord. She was such a good mother to her kids and she served the Lord even up to the very end."

Mom kept going on and on about what a saint Linda was, and Sheryl could see I was getting emotional. The emotion I was feeling, however, was anger—anger at Linda, who had robbed me of our relationship by clinging to her pious prejudice. As mother was sitting there eulogizing Linda with saintly superlatives, I could not listen any longer. The woman who had just died did not put me in mind of a loving Christian, but of a judgmental, uncaring, stoic, cold, unfeeling sister. I rushed from the room. I was furious!

Sheryl, Dolly, and Gary came looking for me. Sheryl thought she would find me in a puddle of tears like when dad was dying, but I had no tears. I was shocked by the amount of anger that was welling up inside of me. When Gary and I decided to go home, the others said they would join us there. As Gary drove, my anger found words.

"Linda, I am so angry with you right now! You were so *selfish*! I tried to reach out to you, to build a bridge to you, but you refused all my attempts and now it's too late! It was mean of you, Linda. *Mean!*"

Gary just let me vent.

As I tried to go to sleep that night, I kept hearing Linda's words to me, *"I don't want to know how you are doing. That is why I don't ask. Your lifestyle makes me sick!"*

I was so sad, but I also felt guilty, because I had the fleeting thought that Linda would no longer be able to constantly influence Mother to reject me. That thought really made me feel like a heel for being in any way relieved that Linda was gone.

Linda's funeral was held at the Assembly of God where she had served as music minister. Gary and I sat next to Mom and Pam in the family section. I do not remember a lot about the service. At the end of the service, helium filled balloons were brought out. We were asked to write messages to Linda on the balloons before we released them to go up into the heavens.

I took a balloon, and I wrote, "Dear Linda, you know *now* don't you? See ya in heaven. Love, your little brother, Randy." Then I watched my balloon rise higher and higher until I lost sight of it.

As we drove, I thought back over my life. The McCain family had once consisted of Mom, Dad, Linda, Pam, and me. Now we were three. Our time together in Walnut Ridge seemed like ages ago.

I thought about Pam and how thankful I was that she was still in my life. I am proud of Pam, who has weathered many storms, raised a beautiful daughter, and been a safe place for her little brother to turn to in times of crisis. Pam and I consider ourselves refugees from a war-torn life. We survived. I wish the same could be said for my sister Linda. Pam railed against the spiritual abuse while still at home. My resistance did not come until I started college. But Linda, the oldest, never fought. She surrendered! She was the one who wanted so badly to please Mom, Dad, and that loving yet demanding God to whom she had been introduced as a child.

Linda was the greatest casualty. Though Pam and I had been deeply wounded by the spiritual abuse and the mean-spirited views we were taught about God, the two of us questioned the authority of the church and rethought our views of God when challenged by life's circumstances. In that painful process, a God of unimaginable grace and compassion found us.

Linda never escaped and never imagined the grace she often sang about. Some who know our family might say that Linda was the only one of us McCain kids who lived up to her convictions and "kept the faith." I see it differently. I have reached an age that allows me to have a different perspective as I look back over our family's history. Linda never stopped pressuring herself to be perfect. She never stopped seeing herself as a disappointment to God.

I prayed for God to heal my pain and regret over never being able to reconcile with my sister, yet the sadness remained. Years later, I sat in a service at a spiritual conference where I had been asked to speak. Yolande Yaeger, a lady minister, led the worship. As I watched her, she reminded me of someone. Then it hit me: my sister Linda!

I sensed the Holy Spirit directing me to go to her after the service and tell her of my pain associated with Linda and ask her to pray for me. She listened intently as I poured out my heart to her. Then she prayed for me.

As she ended her prayer, she leaned over and whispered, "Randy, I see heaven and I see a great banquet hall. There is a beautiful table prepared with a wonderful meal. I see your sister Linda. Next to her is an empty chair. People keep trying to sit there, but each time Linda stops them and says, 'I am saving this chair for my brother.'" I broke into tears, my whole body shaking from the tremors of emotion. An inner healing was taking place in my heart. I will always be indebted to my dear friend and colleague in ministry, Yolande. From that moment in prayer, I have had nothing but warm thoughts of Linda, and I, too, am happily anticipating that moment when we will be together again. Sometimes I look up to heaven and whisper, "Linda, keep saving that chair!"

Chapter 62

Jay Bakker at Open Door

One morning while channel surfing, I ran across televangelist Jim Bakker's new religious talk show. His guest that day was his son Jamie Charles, or Jay, as he prefers to be called.

Jay was a young boy back in the days when I watched the PTL Club on television at Grandma's house. Now he was 28, with tattoos up and down his arms, and a piercing in his lip. Jay's boyish good looks and charm drew me to listen to what he had to say. I was amazed by his grasp on grace. He spoke disapprovingly of the evangelical church's legalism and political stands. He told his dad that the churches should stop being so political and negative on social issues, including homosexuality. Well, that certainly got my attention!

I sat mesmerized by this young preacher. Jay told about Revolution, the church he had started in Atlanta. Services were held in a local bar on Monday nights. He and his dad reminisced about the tragic days when PTL had fallen apart. Jay was 11 years old at the time his dad was sent to prison, while his mom, Tammy Faye, checked into the Betty Ford Clinic to fight her addiction to prescription drugs. Jay was enrolled in a Christian school, and not surprisingly, this troubled boy acted up. When the Christian school kicked him out, skateboarding street kids took Jay in and showed him love.

Jay turned to drugs and alcohol, but after a season of rebellion, he turned his life around with God's help. He moved to the town where his father was in prison, and worked tirelessly to get Jim out.

Jim wept as Jay told his story. "My son Jamie Charles taught me the meaning of grace," Jim told his television audience.

I wanted to know more about Jay and his ministry, so I searched his website and found his email address. I wrote Jay and told him how much I had always loved his family. I also shared my testimony and about the birthing of *Open Door*. I did not expect a response, but Jay wrote back thanking me for loving his family. He said that he looked forward to getting together with me and hearing more about the wonderful things God was doing at Open Door Community Church. The fact that I was a gay pastor did not seem to be a problem for him.

I extended Jay an invitation to speak at Open Door's fall conference. I was thrilled when Jay responded that he would come to speak. Days later, Jay called and we had a wonderful conversation. He told me that the gay community was so good to his family when most of the church people turned away. Jay had lots of questions about how I reconciled the scriptures and my sexual orientation.

"I want to pick your brain while I am there as to how my church in Atlanta can be more open to the gay community."

I inquired about his mother. Jay told me that Tammy Faye's cancer had worsened, and she was fighting for her life. This saddened me. I wanted so badly for God to work a miracle for this precious little lady, who had always preached and lived God's unconditional love.

From the moment Gary and I met Jay at the airport, we were aware that God was up to something special in bringing this extraordinary young man into our lives. Open Door embraced Jay with open arms. He spoke on Friday night and on Saturday morning. His messages were about grace. His delivery was conversational, not preachy.

In the last service of the weekend, Peggy Campolo spoke. Peggy thanked Jay for "teaching an old lady who prided herself in the fact that it had always been easy for her to love God's children who happened not to be straight that she still had prejudices to overcome."

She said, "In this place, this weekend, I encountered a beautiful young man with tattoos and piercings. At first he looked to me like everything I have always been afraid of. And through this man I caught a new vision of the Christ that dwells in each one of us. Thank you, Jay."

Peggy, who usually seems to be in control of her emotions when speaking, actually had trouble keeping her composure while talking about Jay. After Peggy finished, I called Jay back to the platform to greet the congregation one last time. He also was emotional.

"You guys have been awesome. I've realized how sorry I am for sometimes letting fear of what people would do to me keep me from standing up for you. It's been a struggle. When you've been kicked and beat so much you just get so tired of saying 'Could I have another please?' But my love for you is now more than my fear of them and what they'll do."

Jay was interrupted by applause from the congregation.

"Thanks for being the exclamation point on my life. I knew God was doing something in me the second I was invited here. I've always been outspoken for the gay community because of the love they showed my parents when so many in the church world rejected them. But from now on, I will strive every day to make sure that those of you who are gay have the same rights as I do, and that people know you are just as much the children of God, if not more, than we are—we being the fuddy-duddy straight folks.

"I love you guys. I've seen more of the fruit of the Spirit here than in any other church I've ever stood in. People used to go to PTL and they would say, 'Oh, it's like a little piece of heaven.' They loved that sound bite. They would use it everywhere. But it was because of all the stuff, all the *things*. I am sure people were touched by God at PTL; I know they were. But there was just so much stuff. When I come here and say I feel a little bit of heaven, it's not because of the stuff. I'm in a little purple room, but I really do feel like I've seen the kingdom of God here on earth as it is in heaven.

"Everybody here has been so loving to me. Thank you for that. Please know that you have a friend and an advocate who is standing with you. I really do believe that we at Revolution are a part of Open Door Church, and that Open Door Church is a part of Revolution. I can't wait to see what God does next. Thank you!"

Jay kept his word. He went back to Atlanta and started preaching that the church should affirm gay and lesbian people and welcome them into the life of the church. Immediately, opposition roared back. One elder resigned, saying that Jay was preaching heresy. As a result of Jay's stand, Revolution lost a $50,000 grant that had been the largest part of its financial base. This meant laying off most of his staff. But Jay stood firm!

One day, while speaking to his mom, Tammy Faye, about his experience at Open Door and the obligation he now felt to stand up for his oppressed friends in the gay community, she said to him, "Jamie Charles, you don't have to tell the whole world."

From her mother's heart, Tammy Faye said this out of concern for her son, not wanting him to face the harsh criticism she knew would come from insensitive Christians.

Jay answered her, "But Mom, I feel convicted of the Holy Spirit to speak out for those who don't have a voice in the church."

Tammy Faye reached out and grabbed her son, hugging him close. "Then you tell them! I am so proud that I have a son who will live out his convictions."

Tammy Faye was always a person who loves. She was the first televangelist to interview an AIDS patient, and she treated him with such respect. Now, she passed on that love and compassion to her amazing son.

Jay remains a great friend. He returned in June of 2006 as part of our year-long birthday celebration in commemoration of ten years of ministry. This time he was accompanied by a crew filming a reality documentary series for the Sundance Channel. *One Punk under God*, a six-week series, began airing in December 2006, spotlighting Jay's unconventional style of ministry. The crew filmed Jay speaking at Open Door.

During his message, Jay announced to the congregation that he was moving to New York City to start up a Revolution Church in Brooklyn. We took a special offering for the new work and gathered around Jay to pray that God would go with him in this new venture of ministry.

In July 2007, when Tammy Faye lost her battle with cancer, Jay asked me to officiate at her graveside service. It was an honor to eulogize this dear saint of God.

At the grave, I said,

There is nothing I can say today that will take away your grief. I wish there was. But please remember the One of whom it was said, "He was a man of sorrows and acquainted with grief." Jesus. This is what I believe Tammy Faye would want me to say to you today. Look to Jesus. Because even at her weakest, if you got very close to her and looked into her mascara-curtained eyes, you would see a reflection of Jesus, her true focus. Today she can say, "My eyes are clearly beholding my King," and Jesus Christ is wiping away every tear from the eyes of Tammy Faye.

Jay Bakker and Randy in 2005 at Jay's first visit to Open Door Community Church

Chapter 63

Becoming a Father

So many of my dreams had come true, but one dimension of my life remained unfulfilled. I still did not know what it was like to be a father. Gary and I were blissfully happy together, and God had given us a home. My mom was a part of our lives and we had our wonderful church family. I was fulfilled in the ministry to which I felt called. Yet the dream of having a son became more and more unattainable as we grew older.

Sometimes friends would ask us if we thought of adopting a child.

I would answer, "We are too old at this stage of our lives."

When I turned fifty, I contributed the little stuffed lamb I bought for my future son to a church yard sale. I consoled myself with the knowledge that, as a pastor, I had many spiritual children. But it was a deep regret to never know what a father feels in his heart for his child or his grandchildren. At times, I cried over the lost opportunity.

I think that some dreams must die so they can be resurrected in God's timing. The resurrection began when a young man named Bobby came to our church. Bobby had been raised in a strict Pentecostal home in a small town in Arkansas. This particular church was so conservative they thought most other Pentecostal churches were too liberal! They did not go to doctors when they were sick, and they did not celebrate Christmas or Easter, which they considered pagan holidays. The church had its own school so the children would not be exposed to any "outside" world view.

Bobby loved his mother very much. She became ill when Bobby was 14 and died at home, one month after giving birth to her fifth child. She was only 35. This loss was beyond devastating for Bobby. His father was left to raise four boys and one daughter. Because Bobby was the oldest, a lot of responsibility was placed on him. Bobby's dad remarried soon after his mom's death, out of necessity. Bobby loved his church and volunteered every chance he got to work for the Lord.

He knew he was different. He knew that he was attracted to boys. But he wanted to please God and the church, so shortly after high school, he married a nice young lady he met at church, thinking that this would make him "normal." They were married for six years and had two precious children.

Bobby realized that he could no longer deny who he really was deep down inside. He went through a painful crisis when the church found out about his sexual orientation. The pastor called him in and told him that he was to not only leave the church, but he was also to leave the town and never come back.

The divorce and separation from his kids devastated Bobby emotionally, spiritually, and financially. His own family rejected him. His father told him, "Why don't you just do us all a favor and go out in the street and get run over by a truck!" His siblings literally turned their backs and shunned him when they saw him in public. Bobby went through hell, and in his confusion and pain, he trampled all his convictions trying to find himself. He ended up a broken human being.

That's when he found our church. He attended regularly and volunteered long hours, helping with the upkeep and overseeing the potlucks, but he hardly ever smiled. There was such a sad aura around him. He started listening to my sermons on God's unconditional love and grace, which was so radically different from that legalistic, rules-oriented religion of his childhood and adolescence. I began to wonder if I would ever get through to him that he was adored by God. This poor young man had been so abused by religious zealots that he was having a very difficult time imagining his life as anything but hopeless.

As his pastor, I was called upon to walk with him through some difficult times. During these experiences, I felt a real desire to protect Bobby, and to let him know that he was loved and understood. I shared this with Gary, who had also become fond of Bobby. I told Gary I was beginning to develop what appeared to be paternal feelings for this young man. As we prayed, God began to show us that Bobby was kindhearted, gifted, hardworking, and talented. He just needed a family to love and believe in him. That family was Gary and me!

So, we opened our hearts and our home to Bobby, and we have been privileged to watch him blossom as he has discovered how precious he is to his Heavenly Father, and to us. My whole family adores him. I now introduce him as our son, and he tells people that we are his two dads. I now know what a dad feels in his heart toward his child. Bobby and I have had many father-son talks, and I cherish them all.

The first Christmas after Bobby moved in with us, our associate pastor, Sheryl Myers, placed a special gift under our Christmas tree: the little stuffed lamb I had sold in the church yard sale. Sheryl knew how hard it was for me to give up my cherished icon that stood for the longing to be a dad, so she purchased the lamb several years ago and took it to her kindergarten class for the children to love and play with. When God brought Bobby into our lives, she brought the lamb back home, washed it, fluffed it, and placed it under our family Christmas tree as a sign that God had not forgotten the dream He had placed in my heart.

Today, Bobby is doing well in his work and as a father to his own children.

They come and stay with us every month and on holidays. The church they belonged to forbid it's members from celebrating Christmas so it was great fun seeing their eyes as they came down that first Christmas morning and saw their stockings running over with toys and candy. I went a little overboard. I never get tired of seeing Bobby smile with a glint in his eye, and hearing his boyish laughter is music to my ears. We have legally adopted Bobby. When deciding on his new adopted name he asked if it would be wrong for him to take, as his middle name, the name I had chosen for my imaginary son; Lukas. Tears came to my eyes. I assured him it was not wrong and he had just made my heart smile. His new name is Bobby Lukas Eddy-McCain. I can remember the bruised and broken boy that God placed on our doorstep who didn't believe in himself, the young man who might have given up in hopelessness when his birth family and church family disowned him. We are finding that the Psalmist got it right when he sang, "God places the solitary in families and gives the desolate a home in which to dwell." (Psalm 68:6, Amplified Bible)

Bobby Lucas Eddy-McCain

EPILOGUE

It is now 2014 and *Open Door* just celebrated 18 years of ministry. Gary and I celebrated 20 years of marriage in October 2012 and we were legally married in New York City in August 2012. Jay Bakker officiated. We were married in Central Park and spent our honeymoon in the Waldorf Astoria. We had reserved a small room because it was all we could afford. But when the young man who was checking us in found out we had come from Arkansas to get legally married that afternoon he bumped us up to a $2,700 suite! When we returned home we hosted a wedding reception for all our friends and family who were unable to attend our ceremony. Our friends and many of our neighbors came as well as my sister Pam and her daughter Leandra, Leandra's little baby girl, the joy of our lives, Bernadette, and my mom. We now have a larger home that gives us more opportunity to minister to those God sends our way. We are harvesting the richness of relationship that comes from promises made and promises kept. The relationship Gary and I share is strong and secure. We have a son that we are proud of. My faith in God and my allegiance to Jesus Christ are stronger than ever.

My mother unexpectedly went to be with the Lord the fifth day of January 2013. Her final words to me; "I love you!"

My theology is still rooted and grounded in Jesus Christ and his death and resurrection, but it is more fulfilling and meaningful than was my old theology, which was based on legalism and judgment. I now know my place in Jesus' arms of grace, a place I always had but until now, was not sure of.

Open Door Community Church stands today as a beacon of hope to so many across the nation and around the world. We ordained Sheryl Myers to fill the position of Associate Pastor and she has been an effective dispenser of God's grace to the congregation.

We have been blessed to receive from such gifted ministers over the years: Marsha Stevens, Marvin Matthews, Southern Gospel singers, Joyce Martin, Kirk Talley, Kenny Bishop, and Lulu Roman from Hee Haw And special speakers, Peggy and Tony Campolo, Bart Campolo, John Taylor, (Missionary to Honduras), Stan Mitchell, pastor of Gracepointe Church in Nashville TN, Harold Ivan Smith, Brian McLaren, Randall Balmer, Joy Carroll Wallis, Karla Yaconelli, Mel White, Bishop Gene Robinson, Jay Bakker, Rudy and Juanita Rasmus, Pastor's of St. John's Church in Downtown Houston, TX. to name a few.

We were so honored to have Cynthia Clawson sing for us. Cynthia has been called "The most awesome voice in gospel music" by *Billboard Magazine*, and has received a Grammy and five Dove Awards for her work. When you listen to Cynthia sing and speak, you are so aware of the peace of God and the comfort of the Holy Spirit. You become mesmerized by her melodic tonal qualities, her choice of songs and her compassionate spirit.

Since her concert at Open Door, Cynthia has gotten all kinds of opposition for her willingness to sing for gay affirming churches. She answered her critics with her disarmingly loving yet passionate manner,

"I am amazed that there are those who would not want me to sing for all people, especially homosexual people. I sing for divorced people and we all know what Jesus said about divorce! No one has ever e-mailed me about that! We also know that Jesus never said anything about gay people. Not one word! How important could it have been to Him if He did not mention it?" She adds: "A person's sexual orientation is between God and them. It is none of my business. I am just a gospel singing, homosexual loving, heterosexual wife of one, mother of two who is caught up in all this violence. And, yes, I do think we are treating one another violently! This fight is not homage to our Savior who is the Prince of Peace."

Cynthia is someone I consider a friend, one of those friends that God gives you in life, that helps you believe in yourself, and in the dream God has placed in your heart. I will always be indebted to this beautiful angelic songstress who was willing to go where many angels would fear to trod, to live out her faith and also to befriend a minister hungry for fellowship with other ministers so that he could feel less excluded. God bless Cynthia Clawson and all those who came to minister to those of us considered *outcasts*. In doing so they risked losing other engagements. But they, like Jesus were willing to take the risk of loving the wrong people, as Jesus did.

In 2007, we at Open Door honored Peggy Campolo for her faithful ministry as an advocate on behalf of God's LGBT kids. Peggy, when asked about her ministry likes to reply, "I am just a carrier pigeon from the misunderstood to the misinformed. So we created the Peggy Campolo Carrier Pigeon Award to be given to those who give love support and a voice to the misunderstood children of God. Peggy would be our first recipient. President Bill Clinton sent a letter congratulating Peggy for receiving the award and for her compassionate ministry. Each year the award is given to someone in Peggy's honor. Recipients include, Peggy, Dave Ferrell, an evangelical dad who accepted his son and became a dad for many gay kids who did not have the love and acceptance of their own fathers, Jay Bakker, Cynthia Clawson, Letha Dawson Scanzoni, Co-author of *Is The Homosexual My Neighbor? A Positive Christian Response*, and *What God Has Joined Together: A Christian Case for Gay Marriage*, and Jimmy Creech, author of *Adam's Gift: A Memoir of a Pastor's Calling to Defy the Church's Persecution of Lesbians and Gays.* Also in 2013 the award was given to Roberta Showalter Kreider. Roberta is a sweet Godly Mennonite woman who became an advocate for the rights of gays and lesbians when she was in her 70's. She compiled stories of gay and lesbian people and published the books which put a face on same gender love. The 2014 recipient will be Brian McLaren.

My friend Michael Qualls is still part of my life. I am so glad I didn't hold onto the hurt and betrayal I felt towards him. He accepted an invitation to speak at our 2006 Fall Conference. He and his wife Marilyn divorced and he left Friends of His and moved to Memphis where he served as Pastor at a Cumberland Presbyterian church. He just retired from the pastorate and has taken a position at the Cumberland Presbyterian seminary in Memphis TN. I was privileged to sing at a celebration of his 35 years in ministry. He and Marilyn have both remarried and Marilyn and daughters Micah and Melanie attend our church from time to time. *Friends of His* church invited Gary and me to their homecoming this past spring. It was a moment of healing and closure. Michael had been asked to come and preach and I was asked to share in music. I spoke before singing. I told them that some of my most wonderful moments in ministry happened while serving them. But I had to be honest and say that some of my most painful moments of ministry were experienced while I was with them. Then I ended by adding,

"I hope that we all learned that the important thing is to love God and love one another."

I then sang Tori and Russ Taff's song, *We Will Stand*.

> *Sometimes it's hard for me to understand*
> *Why we pull away from each other so easily*
> *Even though we're all walking the same road*
> *Yet we build dividing walls*
> *between our brothers and sisters, and ourselves.*
> *But I don't care*
> *What label you may wear*
> *If you believe in Jesus you belong with me*
> *The bond we share is all I care to see*
> *We can change this world together*
> *If you will join with me…join and sing*
> *You're my brother you're my sister*
> *So take me by the hand*
> *Together we will work until He comes.*

There's no foe that can defeat us
If we're walking side by side
As long as there is love
We will stand.

"We Will Stand" (Victoria Taff, Russ Taff & James Hollihan)
Lyrics reprinted by permission of Tori Taff

Some of the folk from Open Door had attended the event and it was such a wonderful site to see people from both churches standing and singing along.

Gary's sister, Sherry has become an important part of our family. She came to visit us for the first time Christmas of 2009 and enjoyed her visit so much she didn't want to go back to Rapid City, South Dakota. After repeating the Christmas tradition three more times, she decided to move here to be close to her family. I asked her how she had reconciled her beliefs to include us in her life. Her answer was so profound and yet so simple.

"I was struggling with what the scriptures seem to say about homosexuality, and what Gary had told me. One day, in my devotional time, I just prayed,

'God I just don't understand.'

And God answered me and said,

'Sherry you don't have to understand. Just love your brother.'

I already loved Gary, so that was easy for me to do. I still don't understand it all, but I see how well you and Gary work together, and how happy my brother is, and I sense the presence of God in your lives, so I just do what God instructed me to do. I love you guys."

Wow! If more people could catch that message…to love their family member who is gay, the world would be a lot better off.

As I celebrate my 57th birthday, I am still unsure of many things. But, there are certain things of which I am now totally convinced:

I am convinced that gay people do not choose their sexual orientation any more than heterosexuals choose theirs.

I now know that a person's sexual orientation is a gift from God.

I know that closets are damaging to a person's soul. Masks are suffocating. Jesus said that we would know the truth and the truth would set us free.

I am glad that today, I am free to be me. I am now totally convinced that God is love, and that God's love and grace is so much more amazing and extravagant than I ever thought possible. I am 100% sure that God loves *me*, Randy McCain, a gay man.

I truly believe that it is not only possible, but preferable, for a person with a gay sexual orientation to find the person of his or her dreams, and to live out a meaningful, loving life together, till death part them. I have such a relationship with Gary Eddy. We have laughed together and cried together. We pray for and with one another. We pay our bills together, and we have a Jesus-centered home. I know by experience, that monogamy in relationship is a rich and meaningful way to live.

This past Valentine's Day, I prepared dinner for Gary and served it to him in front of our fireplace. After dinner we snuggled by the fire and he shared with me, this poem that he had written especially for me. He said he had been inspired to compose it by watching me write my life story.

> *Your quest to capture*
> *The way-back-whens,*
> *Causes me to see clearly*
> *The precious pages*
> *Of once fresh memories*
> *That fell onto shelves*
> *Of a forgetful mind.*
> *So I am re-reading those pages*
> *To take myself back*
> *To when we first were as one,*
> *The awe of forbidden love*
> *And the guiltless pleasure*
> *Of a perfect rapture.*
> *Though years have passed*
> *And books have been penned*
> *We are still writing chapters*
> *Of passion and love*
> *(With paragraphs of laundry and leaves).*
> *Chapters not to be remembered for the fireworks,*
> *But because they are Us.*
> *Books within a greater book*
> *Written on each other's pages*
> *To be read and re-read*
> *Becoming our favorite novel.*
> *I am glad our pens have mingled their ink*
> *And I pray the writing never ends.*

Judy Garland, the one for whom I naively prayed every night of my childhood, once said,

"We cast away priceless time in dreams born of imagination, fed upon illusion and put to death by reality."

I am thankful, that for me, reality did not put to death my dreams. It fulfilled them. I am still a "friend of Dorothy's" after all these years.

Once, as she was introducing a song, Judy made this observance;

"Wouldn't it be wonderful if we could all be a little gentler with each other and a little more loving, have a little more empathy and maybe we'd like each other a little bit more?"

Amen, Judy. I couldn't have said it better myself.

THE END SO FAR

Randy's Family at the reception for his legal wedding to Gary

OH! ONE MORE THING!

Last year, Gary and I joined a lawsuit again against the state of Arkansas to have our out-of-state marriage recognized by the state we love so much. The suit also called for Arkansas to allow gay marriage. Once again many did not believe we had a chance, but if life has taught me anything it's that, with God all things are possible! Just as this book was ready to go to print, on May 9, 2014, the Honorable Judge Chris Piazza ruled in our favor!

"THEREFORE, THIS COURT HEREBY FINDS the Arkansas constitutional
legislative ban on same -sex marriage through Act 144 of 1997 and
Amendment 83 is unconstitutional.

It has been over forty years since Mildred Loving was given the right to
marry the person of her choice. The hatred and fears have long since vanished and
she and her husband lived full lives together; so it will be for the same-sex couples.
It is time to let that beacon of freedom shine brighter on all our brothers and sisters.
We will be stronger for it.
IT IS SO ORDERED this 9th day of May, 2014

The attorney General immediately asked the judge for a stay so that no gay marriages would take place until the appeal process was finished. Judge Piazza refused. The following Monday morning, when the Pulaski County courthouse opened in Little Rock, gay and lesbian couples were lined up two by two to get marriage licenses. I was honored to be asked to speak at the Human Rights Campaign press conference.

Gary, Randy, and HRC President Chad Griffin at the HRC press conference in Little Rock

This is what I said:

"Gary and I were legally married in New York City. We would have preferred getting married here in Arkansas, this state that we have such a strong attachment to that we cannot imagine

living anywhere else. But we went to New York and received legal recognition of our marriage there in hopes that the fair-minded courts of this state would honor the rights given to us by the Equal Protection Clause of the Arkansas state constitution.

So we became plaintiffs.

Now I am standing here and because of Judge Piazza's right and fair ruling last Friday Mine and Gary's marriage is now legal right here in the state where I was born and raised! We are blissfully happy! I have never been prouder to be an Arkansan!

Some have said that it is impossible for two people of the same gender to happily live together. I beg to differ with those naysayers. Gary and I have been blissfully happy for twenty years and we look forward to as many more years as we both shall live. Happily Married Arkansans!"

Randy signs a marriage license at state capitol building in Little Rock

Pastor Sheryl and I entered the courthouse and began performing marriages along with other officiates. By the time Judge Piazza's ruling was stayed on the following Friday, over 500 same-sex couples had been legally married in Arkansas. Pastor Sheryl married 54 of them and I married 106!

The joy was overwhelming. Everyone in the courthouse treated everyone with the utmost respect. I could almost hear angels singing.

Arkansas was the first Bible-belt state to allow marriage equality. I believe the God Jesus taught me about was rejoicing with us. We are now waiting to hear the decision of the Arkansas State Supreme Court. WE believe it will also rule in our favor. If you want to find out what happens, we'll post the news on the website for this book: SaveJudy.com

Randy, Gary, Bobby Eddy-McCain, and the grandkids
Christmas 2012

Acknowledgements

Judy Garland … I want to especially thank Ms. Judy Garland. I sensed her near me throughout the writing process. May she never be forgotten.

Dr. Harold Ivan Smith for convincing me that my story was important and for calling to see if I had written anything that day and for adding your editing skills to this work. I appreciate your friendship.

Pastor Sheryl Myers, for your love and support and for listening to me read each day's writing over the phone and for being a constant encourager.

Peggy Campolo, for standing by me through the worst of times and for helping me see that all was not lost. For editing this work and for being my friend and connecting me to others you love.

Jay Bakker for restoring my faith in pastors and for staying true to the call you received in the little purple room. WE are so proud of you!

Neal Campbell for believing in me and my story and for making the publishing of this book a reality.

To **Dr. Richard Gilbert** for your part in the editing process and your kind words of encouragement.

My Open Door family for teaching me how to be a pastor, and for your love and support.

To Ray Daugherty for becoming family to us and for securing a future for Gary and me. You asked that I share with you each chapter as I wrote it. Here are some of your words of encouragement that motivated me to never give up:

> *Randy, I truly believe that this is a major work that will inspire many. No matter how long it may take to get the work polished for publication, the effort is worth it. This work is the life line I needed as a teenager.*
>
> *Love to you and Gary,*
>
> *Ray*

Ray, you didn't live to see the dream fulfilled but I hope God lets you know!

Also I want to say thanks to:

Our son, **Bobby Lucas Eddy-McCain** who brings so much joy into our home and lives.

My sister Pam Cate. You embrace me for who I am and never rejected me. You also shared your daughter freely with Gary and me.

My niece Leandra Cate for never turning your back on your Uncle Randy.

My great-niece Bernadette Cate; whose beautiful smile and love for life inspires me and warms my heart.

To precious friends who were willing to read my manuscript and give me feedback:

Wilda Stroman	John & Jennifer Oakley
David Kelly	Kerry Dixon
Brock Stroman	Tammy Hand Phillips
Tori Taff	Jimmy Creech
Randall Balmer	Brad Caviness
Chris Glasser	Bryan Ray

Posthumous thanks to:

Randall and Marcelle McCain (mom and dad)

Linda McCain-McGhehey (sister)

Dr. Jim Whitten

Jan Brown

Floyd White

Jayme Koch

Rev. Lehman Rorex

Rev. George Murry

Our Kickstarter Backers

We were fortunate to be starting all this around the time of the Open Door Fall Conference. Jay Bakker and Peggy Campolo were in town and we got to shoot video of them endorsing my book. We launched the Kickstarter campaign and it worked! It made publishing this book possible.

Some of you are my friends. Some of you are Neal's friends. This project was about my dream to publish my story and his dream to be a publisher, and we're grateful to all of you who helped us make it happen

All of you made it possible for us to bring *And God Save Judy Garland* to market. Some of the thanks are from me and some are from Neal.

David and Alicia Julian, thank you for being such good friends to Neal when he really needed people to believe in him again.

Greg Davis, a friend for all seasons.

David Bailey, a compassionate conservative … one of the coolest people Neal knows who lives to make the point that conservatism, when done right, never limits people's freedom.

Colin Smith

Mary Remmel Wohlleb, a believer in Randy and Gary's story.

Bob Rogers, a person who anyone on this planet would be blessed to know.

Bradley Caviness, a true geek's geek and lover of the cool stuff in life.

Andrew Cunningham, founder of the coolest, new video social network, Zarfo.com.

Debbie Taylor, Neal's favorite aunt.

Joe Johaneman, a man who gets what it means to be human. Check him out at http://www.jejohaneman.com.

Mike Murray, one of Neal's favorite friends and producer of really fun YouTube videos at TheGeekPub.com.

Alvin Herrington, a good country boy who knows the meaning of friendship.

Heidi Noel Schermaier, quite frankly, one of the coolest women on the planet.

Daneen Akers is the producer of one of THE BEST FILMS we've seen so far about what it's like to be a gay Christian who pursues faith in the face of rejection: http://www.sgamovie.com.

Terri Lindsey, Neal's MUCH appreciated and loved mom and owner of CarColorSupply.com. If you need car paint, she's your source!

Jason Dobrolecki, more proof that there are politically conservative Christians who aren't anti gay. Follow him on Twitter @jdobrolecki. He's also a good source for conversations about Pierogies.

Ken & Laura Yagelski … very good friends who also are good sources for details about Pierogies! Follow Ken on Twitter @yagelski.

Ryan Kuramitsu is a friend we met doing this project. He's a part of The Reformation Project, an organization working to fix how the church has gotten sexuality and gender identity wrong.

Susan and Nicholas Young, two of Neal's favorite people. NEXUS, the audio show Neal and Randy are producing to promote the book will be on Nicholas' network Machine.FM.

John Campbell, although not related to Neal … Neal kind of wishes he was.

Chris Pinnock is a friend that Neal met in Prague and has been an encouragement ever sense. Follow Chris on Twitter @chrispinnock.

Jeremy Cochran is a friend of Neal's who keeps inspiring Neal to keep pursuing dreams and never stop making jokes, even after tragedy.

Ned R Wilder, Jr.

Jasen and Maleea Castillo … sweetest couple on the planet.

Christine Hasan … she loves everyone and we love her!

Stephen Clarke-Willson, Ph.D. is a friend of Neal's who backed the project just because he's a good guy.

Ian McLaughlin is just AWESOME. That is all.

Viktoriia Kuznetcova

Jessica, our beloved editor. We hope this is the first of many books.

Made in the USA
San Bernardino, CA
02 September 2014